The Persuasion Industries

The Persuasion Industries

The Making of Modern Britain

Steven McKevitt

OXFORD

UNIVERSITY PRESS

OXFORD
UNIVERSITY PRESS

Great Clarendon Street, Oxford, OX2 6DP,
United Kingdom

Oxford University Press is a department of the University of Oxford.
It furthers the University's objective of excellence in research, scholarship,
and education by publishing worldwide. Oxford is a registered trade mark of
Oxford University Press in the UK and in certain other countries

First Edition published in 2018
Impression: 1

Published in the United States of America by Oxford University Press
198 Madison Avenue, New York, NY 10016, United States of America

British Library Cataloguing in Publication Data
Data available

Library of Congress Control Number: 2018935423

ISBN 978–0–19–882170–0

Printed and bound by
CPI Group (UK) Ltd, Croydon, CR0 4YY

For Adrian Bingham who showed me the way.

Preface

It is my belief that at the heart of almost all the world's problems, both great and small, there lies a communication issue. The ability to assimilate and exchange complex information is a uniquely human characteristic. However, despite tens of thousands of years of evolution, our understanding of the processes involved in human communication is extremely limited. People, it seems, are forever trying to explain what they really meant. Misunderstanding is the normal state of things.

Exactly the same can be said for brand communication. Wherever there is human communication, there is also the opportunity to persuade. For better or worse, the persuasion industries and their activities have become ingrained into modern life. Britain in the twenty-first century is a consumer society. Intoxicating and addictive commerce has occupied almost every area of modern life. Every activity, from choosing lunch to finding a life partner, now involves some form of commercial exchange. People are engaged in, immersed in, and ultimately defined by promotional culture. The things they consume rather than class, religion, geography, or occupation are often the primary form of self-identity and self-expression.

The Persuasion Industries began as an attempt to answer one important question: how did this happen? Despite their significance, very little has been written about either the persuasion industries or the impact of their activities on British society. Scholars from outside the field invariably, and incorrectly, conflate the diverse activities of the persuasion industries to 'advertising' (a point I make no apologies for repeating several times throughout this book). The term 'brand communication'—an umbrella expression for a suite of distinct corporate communications disciplines including marketing, public relations, branding, and advertising—is not widely understood and is little used outside of management science and business schools. I prefer to use the terms 'persuasion' and 'persuasion industries', which seem to offer a much more accurate description of this corporate function and its operations, goals, and objectives.

The sector's few dedicated historians also focus on advertising (there is, for example, no extant historical account of the development of public relations in Britain) and more specifically upon the business of advertising itself rather than its practice. These histories can prove somewhat disappointing for readers seeking to gain a better understanding of how the various forms of persuasion developed, how they were applied, and whether or not they actually worked.

In their modern form, Britain's persuasion industries began to emerge in the final decades of the twentieth century. Prior to that time almost all types of persuasion—from political campaigning to product advertising—were based on the theory of the rational consumer, one of the cornerstones of classical economics. It was believed that consumers were essentially logical beings whose decisions were governed by two competing forces: preferences and constraints. Consumer thought processes were believed to be linear and their behaviour essentially predictable. As such, the only way to influence their decisions was through rational appeals based on logical propositions. This thinking persisted until the 1980s, when increased academic interest in consumption outside the field of economics led to the emergence of an alternative theory of consumer behaviour. It argued, contrary to the traditional view, that people were driven not by the head but by the heart. Their conduct was complex and unpredictable, and they engaged with the world most readily at an emotional level. This idea proved to be so compelling that it completely changed society. The new economy was conceptual, epitomized not by companies trying to sell products to customers, but by brands persuading consumers to make lifestyle choices.

For many years I worked within the persuasion industries. I was fortunate enough to spend much of my career working with big brands and usually operated at a strategic level. The job was often fascinating, occasionally exciting, but almost always challenging. For many reasons, communication more often felt more like an objective than a process. In parallel to my professional life I began taking an academic interest in persuasion and the role it plays within the consumer society and have written extensively on the subject. I found that my research kept taking me back to the same question: how did we get here? Despite reading all the available literature, I was unable to find a satisfactory answer, so the logical next step seemed to be to attempt to provide one myself.

Five years later and it is fair to say that this task has proven to be more difficult than I first imagined. For all historians seeking to research the persuasion industries, there are a number of issues to overcome. First, the sector itself is essentially ahistorical. It is commercially driven and forward looking and there is little to be gained from revisiting the past. Ideas cannot usually be reheated and although successes may provide the subject matter for case studies and marketing activity, failures are wilfully forgotten by all involved. There were other issues peculiar to individual disciplines—for example, much public relations activity is conducted without a paper trail, which raised the question of an appropriate source base. Finally, given the dearth of historiography, there was also the issue of where to ground the project.

I began by looking at advertisements. Lots of advertisements. Although it did not feel like it at the time, this turned out to be a good place to start. I had wrongly believed that my professional background in this field would help me to identify trends and changes. In fact, it did not—I just felt as though I had watched a lot of advertisements. I quickly came to the realization that this was the wrong approach—and in hindsight it is easy to see how some historians are drawn into overwrought, semiotic analyses of commercials—it was what lay behind the advertisements that was really important. I think the same is true of all brand communication.

Of far more use in terms of understanding how and why marketing and public relations campaigns were put together was the archive at the History of Advertising Trust, much of which was hitherto untapped. I spent a lot of time going through the files of agencies such as Lexington, J. Walter Thompson, Collett Dickenson Pearce, and St Luke's, many of which had never been opened before or catalogued. These sources created a vivid picture of the effort involved in producing effective communication: a thirty-second commercial really does belie the complexities of its own production. It was not difficult to empathize with the frustrations of art directors and account handlers with clients who 'failed to understand' the creative direction or were directed rather than informed by the results of market research. Their sense of foreboding when a campaign had failed and the relief when it succeeded were palpable.

The primary aim of *The Persuasion Industries* is to improve our historical understanding of how persuasion developed and the role it played in the making of modern Britain, but I expect readers from many different academic fields will find it useful. Although it was written to be read from start to finish, I have structured the book in order to make it easy for readers to extract the information most relevant to their field. Whatever your background, I hope that you will find it illuminating. For my part, many of the findings were unexpected, and the project has given me a fresh perspective on the communications issues that dominate the early twenty-first century. As I write, the UK is wrestling with the implications of the vote to leave the European Union—a communication issue if ever there was one—while, in the USA, President Donald Trump's unique approach to media relations is almost without precedent. How long this strategy can shield him from the critical brickbats remains to be seen. Whether we like it or not, the persuasion industries and their activities have become integral features of advanced capitalist societies. How that plays out as social media wax and traditional media wane is a crucial question. Understanding our society's communication issues is the key to addressing many of its problems.

Steve McKevitt

January 2018

Acknowledgements

The Persuasion Industries in Britain has been the longest project of my career. It could not have been written without the help and support of my former academic supervisor, Professor Adrian Bingham, and my wife, Fiona McKevitt—neither of whom I could ever thank enough.

I would also like to thank the following people for their interest and generosity in helping to bring my initial idea to fruition: my good friend and erstwhile writing partner Professor Tony Ryan for getting the ball rolling—over a convivial liquid lunch—with the pithy observation that 'You'd probably get a Ph.D. out of that'; Professor Mike Braddock for initially agreeing to accommodate my research within the Department of History at the University of Sheffield, where I subsequently spent four very happy years; my former agent Steph Ebdon for her encouragement; Ian Daley, to whom I will forever be indebted, for teaching me how to do it properly; Professor Ralph Tench at Leeds Beckett University for his constructive criticism; my copy-editor Hilary Walford for her diligence, patience, and generosity above and beyond the call of duty; and finally Adam Swallow, my editor at Oxford University Press, for his enthusiasm and guidance.

The author and publisher would also like to acknowledge the following for their kind permission to use the tables and photographs: Haymarket Business Media, Office of National Statistics, The Audit Bureau of Circulations, WARC, Advertising Association, PRCA, The Institute for Fiscal Studies, Carlsberg UK Ltd, Volkswagen Aktiengesellschaft, Steven Kasher Gallery, Smithsonian Design Museum, McEwan's Ltd, Levi's, Bartle Bogle and Hegarty, Lucozade Ribena Suntory Ltd, Walkers Ltd, and Headland PR Consultancy LLP.

There are instances where we have been unable to trace or contact the copyright holder. If notified, the author and publisher will be pleased to rectify any errors or omissions at the earliest opportunity. All URLs cited in this book were accessed 31 December 2017.

Contents

List of Figures

List of Tables

List of Plates

Abbreviations

ABC	Audit Bureau of Circulation
ABM	Allen Brady Marsh
AIDA	awareness, incentive, desire, action
ASA	Advertising Standards Authority
ASH	Action on Smoking and Health
AVE	advertising value equivalent
BBH	Bartle Bogle and Hegarty
BMP	Boase Massami Pollitt
BRAD	*British Rates and Data Directory*
BSC	Broadcasting Standards Commission
BSP	basic selling proposition
CDP	Collet Dickenson Pearce
CIPR	Chartered Institute of Public Relations
COI	Central Office of Information
CRM	customer relationship management
DAR	day after recall
DDB	Doyle Dane Bernbach
EC	European Community
EEC	European Economic Community
EU	European Union
EMAP	East Midland Allied Press
FMCG	fast-moving consumer goods
FTSE	Financial Times Stock Exchange
GDP	Gross Domestic Product
GGT	Gold Greenless Trott
GNP	Gross National Product
HAT	History of Advertising Trust

IBA	Independent Broadcasting Authority
IPA	Institute of Practitioners in Advertising
IPC	International Publishing Corporation
IPO	initial public offering
IPPA	Independent Programme Producers Association
IPR	Institute of Public Relations
JWT	J. Walter Thompson
MMB	Milk Marketing Board
NACNE	National Advisory Committee on Nutritional Education
NBA	National Basketball Association
NME	*New Musical Express*
NPD	new product development
PPA	Professional Publishers Association
PRCA	Public Relations Consultants Association
TWBA	Tragos Wiesendanger Bonnange Ajroldi
USP	unique selling proposition
WARC	World Advertising Research Centre
WCRS	Wight Collins Rutherford Scott
WPP	Wire and Plastic Products
YOB	Youth Orientated Brand

Introduction

From White Heat to Cool Britannia

The term 'persuasion' encompasses a suite of commercial and corporate brand communication activities—notably marketing, advertising, branding, and public relations (together with public affairs)—whose object is to influence the ideas, opinions, beliefs, and/or behaviour of a target audience. Collectively, the various agencies, practitioners, consultancies, and company departments that are responsible for delivering these activities make up the 'persuasion industries'. In the UK, the various forms of brand communication all have their roots in the late nineteenth or early twentieth centuries. Advertising and public relations agencies started to adopt their modern type following the Second World War in response to a proliferation of commercial mass media, which continued to expand until the end of the century. Marketing was initially a minor internal business function carried out by the sales team and as such standalone marketing departments began to emerge only during the late 1960s, initially in response to changes in high street trading and the proliferation of the supermarkets. However, within twenty years, the department's importance, influence, and the range of activities it incorporated had vastly increased to the extent that marketing had become the driving force within many enterprises. By the late 1990s a large number of television channels, radio stations, newspapers, and magazines were vying for audience attention twenty-four hours a day, seven days a week. This expansion drove demand for a range of brand communication services both quantitatively and qualitatively by reducing the costs of engaging in persuasion for smaller companies with more limited means, but also allowing larger concerns to reach discrete audiences and run more nuanced, better-targeted campaigns. With the exception of the publicly funded BBC, brand communication, wholly or partly, financed virtually every media outlet in the UK and was also the source for much of the editorial content.

The evolution and expansion of the UK's persuasion industries during the late twentieth century have been addressed by scholars from a wide variety of academic backgrounds. Views differ in terms of whether their influence was for good or for ill, but across the spectrum the increasingly important role that persuasion industries played in the shaping of society and culture throughout this period has been consistently identified. Yet, despite brand communication's undeniable impact, there has been little sustained historical treatment of the persuasion industries' methods and practices. The focus of research to date has converged upon the business activities of a small number of high-profile practitioners and their most memorable advertising campaigns. Typically, scholars have openly ignored persuasion's methodologies, conflated its diverse operations to 'advertising', and only occasionally concerned themselves with any of its output. In those instances, academic research is primarily concentrated on the impact and effects of 'advertising' rather than its conception. The broad conclusions reached are that the UK's persuasion industries became increasingly professionalized throughout this period and, in doing so, effected a change in human behaviour that contributed directly to the emergence of the consumer society and a wider culture of promotion. Academics differ in their view of the extent to which these developments occurred and the degree to which persuasion was responsible for their causation, but little else.[1]

If we, as historians, are fully to comprehend the role played by the persuasion industries in Britain during the late twentieth century, then we must look beyond its impacts and seek to gain an understanding of how its core disciplines evolved and operated. We must also examine the manner in which persuasion's methodologies and credos were applied to meet the period's challenges of changing lifestyles, cultures, and economics to reach consumers who were benefiting from increasing levels of information, education, media, and, not least, access to finance.

Presenting a history of the UK's persuasion industries through developments in practice and application is not without its challenges. Little of the existing commentary on either the persuasion industries or the consumer society can be considered impartial. One of the most significant tests for all

---

[1] See, e.g., S. Delaney, *Mad Men & Bad Men: When British Politics Met Advertising* (London: Faber and Faber, 2016); S. Delaney, *Get Smashed: The Story of the Men who Made the Adverts that Changed our Lives* (London: Sceptre, 2007); I. Fallon, *The Brothers: The Rise & Rise of Saatchi & Saatchi* (London: Hutchinson, 1988); A. Fendley, *Commercial Break: The Inside Story of Saatchi & Saatchi* (London: Hamish Hamilton, 1995); W. Fletcher, *Powers of Persuasion: The Inside Story of British Advertising 1951–2000* (Oxford: Oxford University Press, 2008); P. Kleinman, *The Saatchi & Saatchi Story* (London: Weidenfeld and Nicolson, 1987); M. Tungate, *Adland: A Global History of Advertising* (London: Kogan Page, 2007); M. Tungate, *Branded Male: Marketing to Men* (London: Kogan Page, 2008); M. Tungate, *Luxury World: The Past, Present and Future of Luxury Brands* (London: Kogan Page, 2009); M. Tungate, *Branded Beauty: How Marketing Changed the Way we Look* (London: Kogan Page, 2011).

historians of affluence and consumption (in all forms, not just consumerism) is to engage in a serious investigation of the causes, effects, and politics of persuasion without making judgements and slipping into polemic.[2] It is not the aim of this study to draw conclusions about whether the persuasion industries were a positive or negative force within society, but rather to gain an understanding of how their applications and practices evolved and the manner and extent to which they influenced and shaped consumer behaviour. To that end, my contention is not that the persuasion industries became more professionalized during this period—and indeed there is a great deal of evidence to suggest that in many areas they did not—but rather that their activities became more pervasive and persuasive. In response to the emergence of generally better-informed consumers and rapidly changing market conditions, the persuasion industries became more socially aware, more rigorous in their methodology, and more sophisticated in their delivery. As a result, their output became generally more compelling. All of these changes extended persuasion's influence into more and more areas of everyday life.

This statement should not be misconstrued as an argument for the unfailing power of persuasion to bend all consumers to its will. On the contrary, much—possibly most—of the industries' output remained ineffective throughout the period: the majority of new product launches failed, the majority of advertising did not engage with the target audience, and the majority of public relations campaigns did not affect a change in public opinion. It is also certainly true that in the decades prior to 1969 one can find numerous examples of highly successful campaigns featuring beautifully art-directed commercials, compelling display advertisements, and effective public relations. However, before any conclusions are drawn, there are some key points to consider. First, from 1969 onwards the amount of persuasion increased significantly. By the late 1990s there was far more brand communication than ever before, and a significant proportion did succeed in its aims and objectives, much of it employing newly developed strategies and tactics that became widely adopted. Moreover, because of improvements in the quality of techniques and methodologies employed— at its best—persuasion was much more effective during this period than in previous decades and allowed brands to extend their influence much further. For the first time a coherent message could be delivered holistically across a host of channels, outlets, and media. Individually, the outputs may appear

---

[2] See P. N. Stearns, *Consumerism in World History: The Global Transformation of Desire* (New York and London: Routledge, 2006), pp. vii–x.

similar to some examples from an earlier era—a well-designed newspaper advertisement or an amusing TV commercial, for instance—but the processes underpinning their construction were much more robust (informed by academic research from the emerging fields of behavioural science and cognitive and hedonic psychology), and they were now just one component of a much greater whole. Campaigns were much more expansive, but could be delivered much more consistently, across numerous channels and media.

These changes can be crudely summarized as a shift in focus from the product to the brand—for example, during the 1960s it was perfectly possible, employing then-current methodologies of advertising, to create a compelling television commercial that highlighted a product benefit and persuaded more consumers to buy a particular brand of soap power. However, only by utilizing the strategies developed during the late twentieth century was it possible to deliver multifaceted brand positioning that could persuade consumers to buy Nike simply because it was 'Nike'. Up until the 1970s, the aim of virtually all brand communication—which almost exclusively took the form of display advertising—was to persuade the consumer into make a rational purchasing decision. A unique product benefit would be used to build a proposition—for example, consumers might be persuaded to choose a particular brand of soap powder because it 'washes whiter'. However, differentiation was difficult to achieve, as competitors could seek to challenge a proposition with one of their own—'a bluey whiteness', 'washes whiter than white', or 'not just nearly clean, but really clean'.

In contrast, by the late twentieth century brand communication was often multifaceted—incorporating public relations, corporate branding, sponsorship, and other forms of marketing as well as advertising—and delivered through many different channels. Rather than simply to promote an individual product, the overriding aim was now to occupy a market or brand position from which consumers could be invited to make lifestyle choices about a range of products or services. It is much easier to challenge a proposition than it is to dislodge a competitor from its market position. In the case of Nike, its slogan during the 1990s—'Just do it!'—sounded like an authoritative call to action. However, its actual meaning was nebulous, and it also seemed to be speaking about the consumer rather than the product. This basis of such appeals is emotional rather than rational, yet the bond they created with consumers could be robust, often deep and enduring. It was difficult for Nike's competitors directly to challenge its brand position of 'sporting excellence'; whatever consumers' personal interpretation; as long as they concluded that they themselves were a 'Just Do it!' kind of person, then Nike was probably the brand for them.

The Persuasion Industries and the Politics of Consumption

The period witnessed a number of social, political, and economic develop-ments that together provided the ideal conditions for the persuasion indus-tries' expansion. The history of the UK persuasion industries is inevitably entwined with that of the consumers they sought to influence. As such, the analysis of developments in strategy, practice, and methodology will be situ-ated in a broader discussion of the emergence of the consumer society and the significant socio-political developments of the 1980s. For the purposes of expediency, the key issues will not be demonstrated through primary-source research, but identified through an extensive historiographical review of sec-ondary literature (Chapter 1). At the broadest level, between 1969 and 1997 there was a change in the prevailing socio-political view within Britain.[3] The technological optimism of the post-war period had given weight to the notion, first espoused by Keynes in 1929, that continuing economic growth would result in a more leisured society wherein citizens would be required to work no more than a few hours each day.[4] This idea continued to gain traction, influencing thinkers in both the mainstream and counterculture, throughout the years of full employment enjoyed during the early post-war decades. During the recession of the 1970s attitudes to the leisure society hardened, and the return of economic growth during the 1980s was fuelled by policies geared instead to achieving a rise in household expenditure, under the auspices of increasing individual economic freedom.[5] Rather than a leisure society, a consumer society emerged wherein the accumulation of goods became an expression of self-identity.[6]

---

[3] For a detailed analysis of the socio-political changes that took place in Britain during this period, see J. J. Benson, *The Rise of Consumer Society in Britain, 1880–1980* (London: Longman, 1994); M. Francis, 'A Crusade to Enfranchise the Many: Thatcherism and the "Property-Owning Democracy"', *Twentieth Century British History*, 23/2 (2012), 275–97; A. Gamble, *Britain in Decline: Economic Policy, Political Strategy and the British State* (Basingstoke: Macmillan, 1994); P. Gurney, 'The Battle of the Consumer in Post-War Britain', *Journal of Modern History*, 77/4 (2005), 956–87; S. Majima, 'Affluence and the Dynamics of Spending in Britain, 1961–2004', *Contemporary British History*, 22/4 (2008), 573–97; M. J. Daunton, M. Hilton, and M. Daunton, *The Politics of Consumption: Material Culture and Ctizenship in Europe and America* (Oxford: Berg, 2001).

[4] J. M. Keynes, 'The Economic Possibilities for our Grandchildren (1929)', in J. M. Keynes, *Essays in Persuasion* (Basingstoke and New York: Palgrave Macmillan, 2010).

[5] R. Vinen, *Thatcher's Britain: The Politics and Social Upheaval of the Thatcher Era* (London: Pocket, 2010); Francis, 'A Crusade to Enfranchise the Many'; A. Gamble, *The Free Economy and the Strong State: The Politics of Thatcherism* (Basingstoke: Macmillan Education, 1988); E. H. H. Green, *Thatcher* (London: Hodder Arnold, 2006); J. Zeitlin, 'Victoria de Grazia, Irresistible Empire: America's Advance through Twentieth-Century Europe', *Journal of Cold War Studies*, 10/3 (2008), 189–91; J. Obelkevich and P. Catterall, *Understanding Post-War British Society* (London: Routledge, 1994); B. Evans, *Thatcherism and British Politics, 1975–1997* (Stroud: Sutton, 1999); E. J. Evans, *Thatcher and Thatcherism* (London and New York: Routledge, 2004); B. Jackson, R. Saunders, and B. Jackson, *Making Thatcher's Britain* (Cambridge: Cambridge University Press, 2012).

[6] J. B. Schor, *The Overworked American: The Unexpected Decline of Leisure* (New York: Basic Books, 1993); J. B. Schor, *The Overspent American: Why we Want what we Don't Need* (New York: Harper

The political and economic elevation of the needs and economic freedoms of the individual over those of society, which occurred during the 1980s in the UK and USA, also contributed to the persuasion industries' expansion. The ideology driving the Conservative and Republican governments, led by Prime Minister Margaret Thatcher and President Ronald Reagan respectively, was perfectly aligned with the aims and objectives of the persuasion industries.[7] Increasingly, global, corporate brands looked to forge strong emotional bonds with their consumers instead of simply pushing products to them. To that end, a large amount of communication output was designed to give the illusion that a personal 'one-to-one' conversation was taking place. Like many government policies at the time, this more intimate approach to persuasion also gave the impression that the individual was at the centre of society and that his or her wants and needs were of paramount importance.

During the 1980s and 1990s, the expansion of the UK's mass media gathered pace, which further increased the opportunities for persuasion. A welter of new media channels and other occasions for branding, public relations, and advertising brought down the costs of engaging in persuasion, which in turn led to more and more companies undertaking a range of promotional activities. New sectors of the market were opened up in direct response to the demands of the persuasion industries—most notably the emergence of a mass market for men's lifestyle magazines during the 1990s. However, escalating competition for consumer attention also led to communication effectively becoming an objective rather than merely a process. It became increasingly difficult to get a message to cut through and resonate with the target audience. Success relied on the development of new theories, disciplines, and skills that, over time, caused the persuasion industries to segment with entirely new corporate entities emerging in burgeoning fields. Within companies separate marketing and public relations departments were formed to deal with an increasing number of communication activities. These internal teams sought advice externally from any number of specialist firms, many newly founded, offering advertising, public relations, market research, public affairs, graphic design, product development, branding, campaign planning, and media buying—all of which were implementing strategies and tactics that purported to offer

Perennial, 1999); A. Offer, *The Challenge of Affluence: Self-Control and Well-Being in the United States and Britain since 1950* (Oxford: Oxford University Press, 2007); J. K. Galbraith, *The Affluent Society* (London: Penguin, 1999); R. J. A. Skidelsky and E. Skidelsky, *How Much Is Enough? The Love of Money, and the Case for the Good Life* (London: Penguin, 2013); F. Mort, *Cultures of Consumption: Masculinities and Social Space in Late Twentieth-Century Britain* (London: Routledge, 1996); S. Nixon, ' "Salesmen of the Will to Want" ': Advertising and its Critics in Britain 1951–1967', *Contemporary British History*, 24/2 (2010), 213–33.

[7] Gamble, *The Free Economy and the Strong State*; Francis, 'A Crusade to Enfranchise the Many'; Zeitlin, 'Victoria de Grazia, Irresistible Empire'.

deeper engagement with the consumer. In time, all these professional services became available to firms with fairly modest marketing budgets.

The net result of these contributing factors was that demand for brand communication services increased rapidly after 1980. As a consequence, the UK's persuasion industries increased not only in terms of their size, but also in their global significance—for example, spending on advertising alone increased from 0.95 per cent of GNP in 1976 to 1.53 per cent of GNP by 1990 (see also Figures 1.1 and 3.2). Spending on persuasion also increased in real terms, as GNP was also much greater by the end of the period, rising from £669,919 million in 1969 to £1,282,602 million in 1997 (chained volume measures, seasonally adjusted).[8] The persuasion industries were not only employing vastly more people than ever before but also enjoying much greater international influence. When brand communication campaigns were successful during the 1980s and 1990s—which was certainly not always—they reached far more deeply into society than those of previous decades. The inculcation of emotional appeals, based on feeling rather than on rational thinking, resulted in more areas of everyday life becoming mediated by some form of commercial exchange, as consumers themselves became embroiled in the ongoing, effervescent process of persuasion.[9]

The Historiography of the Persuasion Industries

In terms of progressing this argument, the first issue to address is the absence of any comprehensive historical account of either the persuasion industries as a whole or their salient component parts. This is evidently an important subject, and, indeed, much has been written about the persuasion industries, but very little could be considered to constitute academic history. Time and again we see analysis of the persuasion industries' output and its impact, or profiles of the businesses and the people involved in their creation, but scholars have very little to say about brand communication's methodologies. The persuasion industries themselves can be considered ahistorical to all intents and purposes—perhaps, understandably so. At a commercial level, they are exclusively concerned with the future. Former glories count for little more than a validation of capability, and, for much the same commercial

---

[8] The Office of National Statistics <https://www.ons.gov.uk/economy/grossdomesticproductgdp/timeseries/abmi/pn2> (all URLs cited in this book were accessed 31 December 2017).
[9] A. Wernick, *Promotional Culture: Advertising, Ideology and Symbolic Expression* (London: Sage, 1991); A. Davis, *Promotional Cultures: The Rise and Spread of Advertising, Public Relations, Marketing and Branding* (Cambridge: Polity, 2013); Mort, *Cultures of Consumption*; S. Nixon, *Advertising Cultures: Gender, Commerce, Creativity* (London: Sage, 2003).

reasons, failures are unlikely to be discussed at all beyond an internal post-mortem to identify key learning.

The persuasion industries' own historians are primarily concerned with the successful businesses and individuals who led them.[10] These narratives typically place Saatchi and Saatchi at the centre—together with its management and various alumni—as a representative microcosm of the industry-wide expansion that occurred and chart the agency's rise from its beginnings as a small, creative shop in 1969 to the world's biggest communication conglomerate some sixteen years later. Saatchi and Saatchi's ascent does serve as a spectacular example of both the persuasion industries' commercial expansion and persuasion's reputational migration from the shady hinterland into the spotlight. As the persuasion industries were perceived to become progressively more professionalized, revenues increased along with their social and cultural influence. Many practitioners went on to become esteemed household names—for example, Maurice Saatchi, David Puttnam, Alan Parker, Tony and Ridley Scott, Salman Rushdie, and Fay Weldon. However, while these popular histories—often relying on oral sources—are readable accounts and recount interesting events, there is a tendency within them to reduce the history of the persuasion industries to a series of turning points and key moments in the lives of great men (and a small number of women). There is a valorization of individuals such as David Ogilvy, Charles Saatchi, Tim Bell, John Hegarty, and Frank Lowe and their most popular advertising campaigns. While the contribution of these people and their work was undoubtedly significant, this approach represents a very narrow view of industries that were expanding in terms of both depth and breath, becoming embedded into the fabric of society, and playing an increasingly significant role in people's lives. Moreover, the most influential, groundbreaking work was often taking place within smaller operations rather than the big multinational concerns.

The emergence of academic literature relating to brand communication from the 1970s reflected the desire to develop a deeper understanding of the processes underpinning the various forms of persuasion.[11] The relationship between brands and consumers proved to be much more complex than anyone working in the field had previously imagined. Together with the persuasion industries' own applied research, this academic research led to the development of new strategies and tactics that were not only highly effective at building relationships with consumers over the long term, but also well placed to meet the forthcoming challenges of an increasingly globalized

---

[10] See, e.g., Fletcher, *Powers of Persuasion*; Delaney, *Get Smashed*; Tungate, *Adland*.

[11] E.g., *The Journal of Advertising* (1972), *Public Relations Review* (1975), *Journal of Consumer Research* (1975), *Journal of Business Strategy* (1981), *Marketing Intelligence & Planning* (1981), *Journal of Consumer Marketing* (1984), *International Journal of Research in Marketing* (1984).

market, a rapidly expanding mass media, and radical changes on the high street. The rise of multiple retail outlets—the so-called chain stores—provided manufacturers with convenient and consolidated access to the mass market, but these logistical benefits came at a price. The balance of power swung away from manufacturers and towards retailers. The chain stores' market dominance within their respective sectors enabled them to make high demands of their suppliers driving down costs, squeezing margins, and requiring much more in terms of marketing support for the lines they chose to stock.

In this environment, marketing came to be regarded as a much more important business function: one that could determine the success or failure of an entire operation, rather than merely provide some support to the sales prospects of a product line. Academic scrutiny of persuasion increased and so did its influence, both corporately and culturally. In a progressively crowded marketplace, the carving-out of a position became more important than the promotion of a proposition. Approaches that could facilitate the establishment of a market position were analysed, tested, and, if successful, broadly adopted. During the 1990s corporate branding became the strategy of choice for global organizations, wherein the objective was to influence how and what consumers thought about a brand rather than attempt to persuade them to purchase a particular product or service.

Over time the role of marketing expanded, touching more and more areas of the business. During the 1960s marketing had generally been regarded as a function of sales, but by the 1990s global businesses were essentially marketing-led, as its ideas provided the strategy that drove new product development, mergers and acquisitions, recruitment and corporate finance. These modern corporate brands were built from inside out rather than from the top down; consistency across all access points was the goal. No matter how you encountered brands such as Sony, Nike, Coca Cola, Apple, Levi Strauss, Audi, or Microsoft—whether through their advertising, public relations, products, customer service, retail displays, or sponsorships—they always looked and felt the same, espoused the same core values, in the same manner, and displayed the same 'personality'.

Even by the standards of the persuasion industries, in terms of its own history—and despite having a huge influence on British society from the 1980s—the discipline of public relations has certainly been poorly served. There are no general histories at all of the public relations industry in the UK during this period: an issue highlighted by one of the sector's trade bodies, the Public Relations Consultants Association (PRCA), which in 2011 commissioned its own short paper in an attempt to address this deficit.[12] Singularly

---

[12] J. Howard, *The Evolution of UK PR Consultancies 1970–2010* (London: PRCA, 2011).

Jacquie L'Etang—Professor of Public Relations and Applied Communications at Queen Margaret University, Edinburgh—has explored the professionalization of the consultancy sector in the second part of the twentieth century. However, L'Etang's research focuses on the practice of public relations in its socio-cultural, political, and economic contexts, and as such she has little to say about its methods, most notably regarding how public relations campaigns are conceived, managed, and conducted.[13] The same is also true for Miller and Dinan, whose paper covers the development of the UK public relations sector, but explicitly not its practices.[14] Yet the rise of public relations is even more profound than that of marketing. Only around one in five of the UK's FTSE 200 companies was taking public relations advice as late as 1979: in 1984 the proportion had increased to more than four in five, with the sector still several years away from reaching its peak.[15]

From White Heat to Cool Britannia, 1969–1997

The period under examination covers the major internal developments within the persuasion industries prior to the emergence of the World Wide Web (which was fundamentally to transform the environment for persuasion) and also major changes in patterns of consumption and the demands of consumers driven by a shift in socio-political thinking. The period 1969–97 is effectively bookended by the departure and arrival of two Labour prime ministers. Defeated in the general election of June 1970, the outgoing Harold Wilson had been a bold exponent of technological optimism. In 1963, Wilson, then a young and dynamic Leader of the Opposition, had promised to build a 'New Britain': a socialist society that would be 'forged in the white heat' of scientific and technological innovation.[16] These ideas were rejected in favour of the individualism of free market, stutteringly at first under Edward Heath's flip-flopping Conservative administration but with firm finality nine years later following the first of Margaret Thatcher's three election victories. Tony Blair's New Labour had very little in common with Wilson's New Britain. Under Blair, Labour's election campaign was fought on the basis that its 'third way' was the best way to run a market economy. The party's landslide victory on 1 May 1997 was secured not least because of its

[13] J. L'Etang, *Public Relations in Britain: A History of Professional Practice in the 20th Century* (Mahwah, NJ, and London: L. Erlbaum, 2004).
[14] D. Miller and W. Dinan, 'The Rise of the PR Industry in Britain, 1979–98', *European Journal of Communication*, 15/1 (2000), 5–35.
[15] D. Smith, 'Consultancy and Client: A Problem Shared Is a Problem Solved', *Public Relations Year Book 1985* (London: FT Business Information, 1984).
[16] H. Wilson, *Labour's Plan for Science* (London: Labour Party, 1963), 7.

leadership and communication team's deep understanding of persuasion and how its adroit implementation could allow their ideas to resonate with the target audience. The year 1997 not only saw the general election and the return of a Labour government, but arguably also marks a point at which promotional culture through traditional media, having become part of the mainstream, reached a peak prior to the emergence of the Internet.

For the persuasion industries themselves, 1969 was a pivotal year. Old fashioned and out of step, after twenty-five years of growth the advertising sector was at the beginning of more than half a decade of steep decline, as corporate marketing budgets were slashed. Just as they had been since before the Second World War, most leading British advertising agencies remained dominated by management and ideas imported from Madison Avenue head offices in the USA, which considered the UK to be a parochial backwater. The advertisement campaigns they produced were prepared and executed in the same manner as they had been since the 1940s. As a result, output was anachronistic. Despite the fact that more and more women were going out to work and traditional notions of family life were breaking down, the predominant target for advertisements was still the housewife, whose attention was sought through a series of tropes and scenarios that remained locked into the family life of the 1950s. Marketing was yet to exert any significant corporate influence, public relations even less so, while branding was a minor concern consisting of little more than packaging and graphic design. At the first sign of any economic downturn, marketing budgets were almost invariably cut. As such, 1969 finds the persuasion industries at a critical path. Its 'tried and tested' tropes were failing, its traditional core audience—stay-at-home wives and mothers—was disappearing, and its clients' routes to market were consolidating thanks to radical changes in retail resulting from the emergence of the supermarkets and chain stores. This in turn presented manufacturers with a new set of challenges in terms of production, distribution, and logistics. Advertising revenues began falling as manufacturers questioned its effectiveness and reduced their marketing spend accordingly.

Despite these setbacks, there were also new opportunities. The most significant occurred on 15 November 1969 with the arrival of colour broadcasting on ITV.[17] This new format offered a much more appealing platform for companies to showcase their brands and provided a stimulus to creative teams. Also of importance was the launch of *Campaign* in September 1968, the first sophisticated trade newspaper for the sector. *Campaign* was a direct replacement for the floundering misnomer *World Press Gazette*, a brand communication trade newspaper struggling to find an audience, which had been

---

[17] *Colour Television in Britain* (Bradford: National Media Museum, 2011).

purchased by publisher Haymarket earlier that year. With its clean, modern design and an uncompromising editorial style that was both deeply critical and celebratory of the sector it supported, *Campaign* proved to be an immediate success, quickly establishing itself as an authoritative, forward-looking voice within the sector. Mark Tungate, a former sector trade journalist who has written several brand communication histories, described *Campaign* as 'the bible of British adland' during this period.[18] Over the next thirty years *Campaign* was pivotal in terms of the persuasion industries' examination of itself.

Source Materials

A major archival source base for this research, the History of Advertising Trust (HAT) Archive contains a wealth of primary source material from the persuasion industries during this period. Founded in 1976, HAT focuses on all forms of brand communication, including display advertising, retail marketing, branding, direct marketing, and public relations. The archive is appropriately catalogued and preserved for the purposes of study and research. Most of the materials at HAT have been deposited by clients, but these are complemented by rescued and donated archives from manufacturers' marketing departments, advertising agencies, and public relations consultancies in the permanent collection. Therein is a welter of information in the form of internal memos, project briefs, contact reports, and production notes from the 1960s through to the end of the twentieth century. Much of the material used was not catalogued but in a raw state, stored in boxes that had not been previously examined by either archivists or researchers. In terms of identifying source materials of value within the archive, a background in the industry has proved invaluable. The histories of persuasion that dwell upon the moments of inspiration belie the huge amount of perspiration involved in the delivery of a successful campaign. Although there is a great deal of information to be gleaned from the folios of production notes, budget manifests, concept artwork, and pro-forma invoices, of much more significance for the purposes of this research—but altogether much rarer—were the proposals, contact reports, and internal memos concerning client accounts. Within these documents is revealed the real endeavour that goes into producing a marketing strategy, branding initiative, or a public relations activity: the process of approval and rejection, the challenges of selling an idea to the client, of turning creative concepts into a successful execution.

---

[18] Tungate, *Adland*, 95; Tungate, *Branded Male*.

HAT is also home to a comprehensive library of periodicals, trade media, manuals, and textbooks, and an exhaustive archive of post-war video and print advertising, catalogued by sector. During the period many agencies published their own books, primarily to generate new business as a leave-behind, work showcase for prospective clients, or a customer relationship management (CRM) initiative for existing accounts. For public relations in the 1970s, HAT's collection of publications and annual reports by the sector's two organizational bodies, the PRCA and the Chartered Institute of Public Relations (IPR),[19] provide a rare, possibly singular, source of case studies and information about developments within the sector.

For the historian, *Campaign* and the rest of the persuasion industries' trade media—notably *PR Week*, *Marketing*, *Marketing Week*, *Media Week*, *Advertising Age*, *Design Week*, and *Creative Review*—also provide a rich archive of source material. Indeed, *Campaign* provided the template for much of the subsequent trade media dedicated to the sector. Although, like *Advertising Age*, *Campaign*'s primary focus was advertising, up until the launch of *PR Week* in 1984, it was also the de facto trade publication for the UK's public relations industry. *Marketing* and *Marketing Week* covered developments that occurred 'client-side', *Media Week* (and to a lesser extent the *Press Gazette*) targeted media departments, while *Design Week* and *Creative Review* were aimed at creative teams and graphic designers. These trade media deal with a combination of news, opinion, interviews, case studies, and features, but they also present statistical analysis of economic developments, cultural trends, campaign effectiveness, and company/sectorial performance; for example, in *Campaign* news coverage of the business of advertising and public relations—relating to both clients and their agencies—was comprehensive. Output was critically reviewed on a weekly basis (usually anonymously), and there were numerous case studies of successful and not-so-successful campaigns. Feature coverage was also extensive, often containing a considerable amount of independently complied hard data, with fulsome analyses of media sectors, product categories, the evolving tastes of consumers, and further numerous case studies. Many feature topics—such as various sector reviews, education and training, consumer research and media analyses—were repeated regularly every two to three years, which makes it possible to identify trends over time.

From the outset, *Campaign* sought to catalogue the fortunes of the advertising sector and its players through the annual publication of league tables (an initiative that was also adopted by *PR Week* from 1986). These tables present a useful and illustrative guide to the development of the sector over the period. The accuracy of the figures is somewhat questionable—these were

[19] The IPR became the Chartered Institute of Public Relations (CIPR) in 2005.

unaudited surveys, relying upon turnover figures submitted by respondents themselves—but they were not published unwittingly. The newspaper itself consistently highlights the issues involved in presenting an unaudited survey and is frank about the opportunity to gerrymander the information provided. However, while it is reasonable to assume that the figures for individual agencies contain a certain amount of 'goodwill', as *Campaign* itself points out, over the course of a few years, there was very little to gain from cooking the books. The later inclusion of additional metrics, such as the number and names of clients, account wins and losses, and the number of employees, also served as a further check and balance, making suspicious anomalies much easier to identify. Furthermore, many leading agencies became publicly listed companies during the 1980s, which afforded their returns greater transparency. When taken as a whole, the league tables do provide a valid indication of sector performance and trends over the period.

It should also be remembered that trade media are written for experts and largely by experts. They contain a wealth of detailed information about the changes occurring within the persuasion industries during this period. Many of these publications can be quite arch or knowing about their subject matter, cutting through the chutzpah, hyperbole, and hoopla associated with the sector, trying to strike a balance between impartiality and celebration as their sector's most important critic and champion. This editorial stance—part faultfinder, part cheerleader—was essential. Again, *Campaign* created the template. It was provocative, and it supported quality (or in Fletcher's words 'fostered trendy agencies and trendy creative work'), but it pulled no punches and was often woundingly critical. This editorial stance—set out in a first edition editorial, which promised to be 'undeterred by bluster, unseduced by handouts'—was in stark contrast to the obsequious industry publications of the 1960s and certainly far more 'readable'.[20] *Campaign* quickly gained credibility within the industry, upon whose patronage—like the other trade media—it relied for content, subscriptions, and advertising. Readers may have recoiled at any criticism of their own operation or activities, but, despite these misgivings, may also have enjoyed a certain amount of schadenfreude when it came to the skewering of a competitor.

The trade media also help to address a perennial question that is very difficult if not impossible to quantify: 'What criteria do we use to judge a branding, advertising, or public relations campaign to be successful?' Unfortunately, there is no formula that allows for this to be determined empirically. The key issue with analysing the effectiveness of any form of persuasion is that it largely takes place not on the screen or on the page, but within the minds of

---

[20] Fletcher, *Powers of Persuasion*, 94–5; 'Statement of Editorial Policy', *Campaign,* 16 July 1968, p. 7.

its target audience. Furthermore, there is never a control group. While different treatments may be trialled or tested together, they are never rolled out in parallel; therefore it is difficult to establish the impact a campaign had in isolation. With nothing to provide a direct comparison, a question such as: 'Would a product have performed as well/better/worse in terms of sales with a different approach?' is to all intents and purposes impossible to answer definitively. Did a product launch fail because the product itself was flawed, or because the market research was misleading, when in fact the adverting and public relations campaigns were a work of genius? We cannot say.

Measurement of effectiveness is also something with which the sector as a whole, and public relations especially, has always struggled.[21] In terms of public relations activity, evaluation might be as crude as applying an advertising rate-card value to the amount of editorial coverage it generated (known as the advertising value equivalent or AVE).[22] Within the sector there was no standard evaluation system at all during the period. Attempts by the PRCA and IPR at the end of the twentieth century to introduce 'PRE-fix' as an industry standard proved to be a costly failure.[23] In the writer's own experience, whether a campaign has been a success or a failure—and to what extent—is usually, and exclusively, a matter of the client's opinion.

These difficulties have not stopped historians from seeking to establish their own success criteria—for example, Fletcher chose to focus on advertising that wins awards.[24] Notwithstanding a raft of other issues with this classification, its main shortcoming is that it is too narrow: not all effective advertising wins an award, but, equally, not all award-winning advertising is effective. Rather than attempt to square this particular circle, I have relied on the endorsement of the period's trade press as one way of identifying campaigns that were 'successful'. This is by no means a perfect measure, but it does provide a serviceable tool for the purposes of this study and offers a much broader base for analysis than Fletcher's definition. Moreover, it also offers a measure of failure, which awards do not. Awards are uncritical—not so the trade media. Media endorsement is also generally less self-serving than the allocation of effectiveness awards, and there is more of it. One must be prepared to look beyond the subjective pronouncements and to the evidence the trade media provided to support their opinion. Within the case studies and category round-ups, there is often much to be found in the form of hard data about market share, current trends, consumer spending, and comparative sector performance.

---

[21] E.g., 'Ten ways in which to overcharge PR clients', *Campaign*, 16 July 1968, p. 20.
[22] C. Wallace, 'The AVE Debate: Measuring the Value of PR', *PR Week*, 6 May 2009.
[23] D. McCormack, 'Fitzherbert to Head PRE-Fix Initiative', *PR Week*, 15 December 2000, p. 7; 'IPR Withdrawal Marks End to PRE-Fix Scheme', *PR Week*, 3 January 2003.
[24] Fletcher, *Powers of Persuasion*, 74.

There is also considerable evidence that agencies actively sought the endorsement of their trade publications—for example, Saatchi and Saatchi highly valued its close relationship with *Campaign*, which it viewed as the pillar of its corporate communication strategy.[25] The letters' pages are also testament to how seriously readers took its (often unconstructive) criticism. Moreover, one element common across the whole of the persuasion industries during this period was a magpie eye when it came to the appropriation of a successful idea, and if campaigns gained influence because they were success-ful, or at least were perceived to be successful, then imitation was the sincerest form of flattery.

The trade press provides a comprehensive source of information not only about activity within the sector, its output, and the issues affecting it but also about the effectiveness and impact of persuasion within a wider cultural context. It also highlights the political, social, and economic issues the indus-tries faced. Yet, despite the quality and quantity of material they provide, most trade media have rarely been investigated or consulted since their initial publication. A few historians, notably Winston Fletcher and Frank Mort, have made some use of the trade media archive, but otherwise these have been a largely ignored resource. One reason for this might be what some regard as a major drawback common to all these titles. While there is a great deal of discussion about the output of the industries—and to a lesser extent the corporate challenges addressed by advertising, marketing, branding, and public relations—there is very little at all about methodology. As a result, it is claimed that those looking to discover how agencies and marketing depart-ments operated, how public relations and advertising campaigns were con-ceived, or how branding projects were put together will find frustratingly little information.

There is some truth in this. Obviously, these publications were not written with the academic researcher in mind, and there is an expectation of a reasonably high level of understanding on the part of the reader. A back-ground in the sector does help with interpretation, but there is undoubtedly something of a deficiency in this respect. This shortcoming has been addressed by using the academic journals and publications of the period as source material. Periodicals such as the *Journal of Marketing* and the *European Journal of Communication* served to provide guidance and information for contemporary practitioners and as a result they contain considerable valuable information about how methodologies and strategies developed over time and the evolution of challenges that they were designed to address. The

---

[25] Fallon, *The Brothers*, 77–9; T. Bell, *Right or Wrong: The Memoirs of Lord Bell* (London: Bloomsbury, 2011), 21–2.

coverage of these journals is both impressive and comprehensive, increasingly so as the period progresses and persuasion begins to fragment into a number of discrete activities. Of the various disciplines, advertising is understandably the best served, especially during the early part of the period. The *Journal of Advertising* and *Journal of Advertising Research* deal primarily with the business of advertising and its delivery, but advertising practitioners were also sensitive to developments in behavioural psychology. Insight into the behaviour of consumers was provided by the *Journal of Advertising Psychology and Marketing*, *Journal of Consumer Psychology*, *Journal of Counseling Psychology*, *Journal of Personality*, and *International Review of Retail Distribution and Consumer Research*. As marketing developed into a strategic business function, it too was increasingly well served by academic literature such as the *Journal of Marketing*, *Journal of Market Research*, *Academy of Marketing Science Review*, and *Harvard Business Review*. An academic literature for public relations emerged later in the period but became similarly comprehensive. Of particular relevance to this study were the *Public Relations Review*, *Journal of Communication Management*, and *European Journal of Communication*. Even disciplines that developed during the period such as account planning and corporate branding were afforded academic study by the end of the period—for example, the *Journal of Brand Management and Research* commissioned and published by the Royal Society of Account Planning.

Textbooks, memoirs, and manuals from the period have also proved to be of some value. Read against the grain, these sources tend to be much more credible in their analysis of past events—in the form of case studies and hard data to provide supporting evidence—than they are in the extrapolation of future strategies, which was of course their primary objective at the time of their publication. There are several key texts that cover widespread changes in approach and strategy during the period—for example, Rosser Reeves's *Reality in Advertising* (1961), David Ogilvy's *Confessions of an Advertising Man* (1963), Al Ries and Jack Trout's *Positioning* (1972), and David Aaker's *Managing Brand Equity* (1991). Memoirs of key practitioners have proven to be of more limited usefulness, but useful nonetheless. These are a complementary source of information but have provided some valuable insights—for example, Tim Bell's *Right or Wrong* (2014), a memoir by one of the late twentieth century's leading PR specialists, offers a rare, inside view of some of the highest-profile campaigns of the period, such as the Conservative Party's 1979 General Election campaign and the privatization of various public utilities during the 1980s. John Hegarty's *Hegarty on Creativity* (2014) is concerned less with the life of its author and rather more with the challenges of running an agency during the 1980s: in essence, the difficulties involved in managing the demands and trepidations of one's clients while pushing bold, creative ideas through to delivery.

Finally, the mass media of the period are another principal source. These were the primary outlets for the output of persuasion industries, whether advertising, public relations, or corporate branding. As the media expanded, publishers and broadcast producers came to rely increasingly on the persuasion industries' output for content as well as for revenue. Indeed, by the 1990s entire sections of national newspapers and whole sectors of magazine and broadcast media were wholly reliant upon the patronage of the persuasion industries for their continued existence.

Together these materials make up the source base underpinning this investigation. Despite the scarcity of sector histories, there is in fact a wealth of material to support the historical researcher, much of which has been largely untapped.

The Author's Interpretation of the Sources

It is also relevant to outline how my own experience situates me within this project. I have been working at a senior level in the persuasion industries as both consultant and practitioner since the 1980s, occupying senior positions for much of that time. I spent the years prior to 1999 running multinational corporate communication departments within the entertainment, media, and service sectors. Since that time I have been running my own brand communication consultancies and have worked at a strategic level for a number of leading global brands. The influence of brand communication over society has also been a long-term personal interest, and over the years I have built a personal archive consisting of emails and other memoranda, proposals, case studies, campaign plans, marketing collateral, press releases, advertising materials, and magazines. I have used this information as the basis for two general, non-fiction books on the methodology of persuasion and numerous articles and papers in newspapers, journals, and magazines.[26]

This experience has proven advantageous, particularly when examining the primary source materials at the HAT Archive. The creative process is necessarily a dark art to most people: a world closed off not just to academic researchers but often also to the clients themselves—for example, much public relations activity from the period took place without any paper trail. Conversations with journalists were not recorded. Client reports typically

---

[26] E.g., S. McKevitt, *Why the World is Full of Useless Things* (London: Cyan, 2006); S. McKevitt, *City Slackers: Workers of the World...You are Wasting Your Time!* (London: Cyan, 2006); S. McKevitt, 'Busy Doing Nothing', *Guardian*, 13 May 2006; S. McKevitt, 'Why PR Really Works', *Business Insider*, 24 April 2008; S. McKevitt, *Everything Now: Communication, Persuasion and Control: How the Instant Society is Shaping What We Think.* (London: Route, 2012); S. McKevitt, 'We've Got Everything We Want—So Why Are We So Bloody Miserable?', *Huffington Post*, 29 August 2012.

contained details of the quality and quantity of press coverage with perhaps some key message analysis, but little more. Clients are commercially interested in what coverage is achieved, and, while some may have an academic interest in how that coverage was achieved, PR specialists are rarely inclined to provide enlightenment. Standard practice in the sector at the time was not even to share media contacts with the clients. The rationale for this was that such information constituted the intellectual property of the agency. Consequently, unlike advertising agencies, who could literally show prospective clients their credentials, public relations consultancies pitching for business could extol the quality of their media contacts and argue that their proposed strategic approach offered the best chances of success, but they were only ever able to offer goodwill and endeavour rather than guarantees in terms of generating appropriate coverage.

My professional background has also provided an insight into life within both corporate marketing departments and communication agencies, which again proved to be helpful where analysis of primary archive material and historic trade media was required. For example, I am familiar with the often-tedious process of developing creative ideas. I have endured countless meetings within a wide variety of corporate cultures, during which substantive proposals have been mulled over, tweaked, compromised, watered down, or rejected wholesale. I have seen perfectly well executed campaigns dismissed as failures (and vice versa) and I have wrestled with the reservations of nervous clients to ensure that the central components of the campaign are delivered effectively. The issue is that success can never be guaranteed, so stakeholders tend to look for reassurance wherever they can find it. Sometimes it pays to be bold—those occasions get written about in the histories—but sometimes it does not, which instances are readily forgotten by all concerned. Many would argue that most people's ideas do not work most of the time—a fact supported by the handful of successful examples that turn up repeatedly in the histories.

I have found evidence in many of the primary sources that similar frustrations were experienced by practitioners during the period. With every campaign there is inevitably trepidation and hope rather than expectation and certainty. However, one gets very little sense of this within the memoirs or the case studies published in *Campaign* and other trade media. These narratives tend to be self-serving to some degree, often presenting a somewhat linear path from inception to delivery. After all, practitioners are paid to get it right, so it is important for them to give the impression that they knew, or were at least highly confident, that they were going to be right, rather than saying that they settled on an idea purely because no one could think of anything better at the time, which would certainly have been the case on occasion. While it makes commercial sense in a highly competitive industry, dealing with volatility and where failure and uncertainty are commonplace, to celebrate success and position oneself as a gatekeeper, the reality is that ideas rarely emerged unchallenged or enjoyed fulsome support of all parties. The HAT Archive does provide evidence of the effort that went into successful campaigns and the often anodyne processes that ideas passed through before being tried and tested in the market—for example, in 1965 the advertising agency J. Walter Thompson (JWT) came up with the name 'Mr Kipling' in response to a brief from its client Manor Bakeries to develop a brand for a new range of cakes and sweet pies. Mr Kipling went on to become market leader in 1976 and maintained that position for over thirty years. The process by which JWT arrived at the name Mr Kipling is revealed as a lengthy, exhaustive exercise—necessarily chaotic and ad hoc at times—but one that was geared to hitting a number of clearly defined milestones and measured against pre-determined criteria.

Format and Structure

This study consists of three parts, made up of seven chapters, and a Conclusion.

The first part is a historiographical review covering the broader developments in consumer society within which the main research is situated. The subject of this research is the persuasion industries, but its object is ultimately the consumer. It is consumer wants and needs that drive the output of the persuasion industries, and gaining an understanding of the target audience's behaviour is the first step in the development of any piece of brand communication.

Chapter 1 draws out the main developments in British politics, culture, and society during this period that relate to the persuasion industries. This chapter is based mainly on academic secondary sources and examines historians' research on affluence and changes in work, leisure, gender roles, family life, political thinking, mass-media popular culture, and living standards.

Chapter 2 looks at the existing historiography regarding the persuasion industries and gives full consideration to the various academic approaches to the study of persuasion and their theoretical frameworks, to gain an understanding of how the persuasion industries both define and present themselves.

Part Two examines the main developments in the persuasion industries between 1969 and 1997. Any chronological divide is to some extent artificial, but the separations in this section (1969 to 1979 and 1980 to 1997) are based on key shifts within the sector. The decade 1969 to 1979 was one of significant change for the persuasion industries. They were forced to adapt to social and economic challenges that were rendering their tropes old fashioned and their methodologies obsolete. The period begins with six years of decline for the advertising sector that can only partially be explained by the economic recession. A landscape analysis of the persuasion industries at the beginning of the period is provided, along with a discussion of the causes and nature of this decline. A significant part of industries' response to this crisis was the development of new approaches and methodologies in marketing and advertising, which helped to produce new strategies and tactics that were generally more successful and certainly much better suited to changing market conditions and lifestyles. Public relations and branding remained small scale during this decade, as most British companies failed to comprehend how either form of brand communication could add value to their enterprise. However, new applications of persuasion were developed and refined that enabled its application to become more pervasive and provided the capability to exploit the huge cultural, political, and economic changes that would occur during the following two decades.

After 1979, changes in government in both the UK and the USA led to the emergence of a politico-economic ideology in which the needs of society were considered subordinate to the needs of the individual. Such thinking was perfectly aligned with the aims and objectives of the persuasion industries. There was also a concurrent shift in corporate strategy—driven by major changes in the market—that elevated marketing into a strategic position within businesses. A renaissance in British popular culture drove (and was in turn further fuelled by) a rapid expansion in print and broadcast media channels. Media producers also benefited from significant reductions in production costs thanks to computerization. These factors caused such an explosion in demand for brand communication services that the UK's service providers (and those in the public relations sector especially) often struggled to meet it. The increased salience of persuasion in business terms also led to more investment in applied research with a view to gaining a better understanding of consumer behaviour. This insight was used to create forms of persuasion that could facilitate much deeper relationships between brands and their customers.

Chapter 3 looks at the key methodological developments in the persuasion industries and their impact—namely the so-called creative revolution in advertising, the conception and adoption of account planning and market positioning, and the emergence of brand marketing. There is also an analysis of the mass media and their role in the delivery of persuasion and developments and challenges affecting the UK's burgeoning public relations sector.

Chapter 4 covers developments within marketing and advertising between 1980 and 1997. Consumers were becoming savvier and increasingly hardened to the tactics of the hard sell. This provided the impetus for the persuasion industries' development of new emotional models of advertising and corporate branding. There is also an exploration of persuasion's increasing specialization after 1980, which occurred in response not only to the improvements in research, methodology, and delivery, but also to the raft of opportunities presented by the rapid proliferation of media channels from the mid-1980s until the end of the period.

The expansion of public relations during the 1980s and its elevation within the hierarchy of brand communication during the 1990s is the subject of Chapter 5. This was a critical time during which the persuasion industries came to the forefront. The brands that enjoyed pre-eminence at the close of the twentieth century were those that could use all forms of brand communication to create one effective and coherent global package. To that end public relations was to prove one of the most effective vehicles for telling a brand story.

Part Three, which consists of two chapters, is an analysis of the cultivation of male consumers by the persuasion industries from 1969 to 1997. It serves as a case study of the broader developments outlined in Chapters 3, 4, and 5. Chapters 6 and 7 look at the impact of the persuasion industries on male consumption through the exploitation of opportunities presented by a series of new media. At the start of the period we find little brand communication targeting men outside the traditional categories of alcohol and tobacco ('beer and baccy'), and most advertising output was still aimed at housewives. As the period progressed there was a concerted effort on the part of brands, the persuasion industries, and the mass media to open up and explore new channels to reach male consumers. Initially tentative or faltering during the 1980s, men's lifestyle mass media emerged rapidly during the 1990s and presented a significant new market for brands to exploit with new or repositioned products and services. A key theme is the rapid expansion of popular culture, which gathered pace during the 1980s, and the assimilation of many countercultural cornerstones into the mainstream. Chapter 7 develops this theme and explores how the rise of corporate branding was to influence the expression of masculinity and notions of self-identity among young men.

A Conclusion then draws together the main findings of the study.

Part One
Out of the Shadows

The Making of Modern Britain

Chapter 1 looks at consumption, consumerism, and the emergence of the consumer society in Britain at the end of the twentieth century. It draws out the main academic debates concerning consumption and its evolving role in society and explores changes in work, leisure, gender roles, family life, and living standards in the UK in the twentieth century. There follows an examination of the impact of the New Right and its ideology in Britain in the 1980s and 1990s and also the renaissance in popular culture from the 1970s, which not only helped to drive the expansion of the mass media but was also fuelled by it. It concludes with an analysis of arguments presented by critics of affluence from the post-war period to the early twenty-first century. There is particular emphasis on the role of persuasion within market economies.

Chapter 2 begins with a detailed examination of extant historiography relating to the persuasion industries. Full consideration is given to the various academic approaches regarding the study of persuasion and their theoretical frameworks. It begins by looking at how the persuasion industries define and present themselves and at the first attempts to develop models of persuasion during the post-war period, which were based upon the notion of the rational consumer. As a consequence of the increasingly consumer-oriented nature of society, the persuasion industries expanded rapidly during the 1980s and 1990s, becoming increasingly more specialized and fragmented in the process.

1

White Heat

Consumption and the Consumer Society

Consumption and Consumerism

Among historians and social scientists there is no consensus regarding a definition of either consumption or consumerism. This is largely due to the differences in interpretation. The term 'consumption' has its origins in economics, and indeed until the second part of the twentieth century (and most profoundly during its final decades) its study was exclusively the preserve of economists.[1] As Gabriel and Lang have identified, prior to 1980 there was a general tendency on the part of scholars to see consumption as essentially ahistorical, but thereafter its social significance during the nineteenth century (and even earlier) came to be recognized.[2]

Economists traditionally took a broad and shallow view of consumption, seeing consumers within the context of the demand function as little more than the passive end of economic activity.[3] In these models consumers were typically thought of as both rational and sovereign, their informed preferences determining the production of goods and services.[4] Campbell provided a useful definition for consumption (albeit one that remained grounded in economics) as 'the selection, purchase, use and maintenance, repair and disposal of any product or service'.[5] Sociologists began to take a serious interest

---

[1] D. Miller, *Consumption and its Consequences* (Cambridge: Polity, 2012), 39–40.
[2] Y. Gabriel and T. Lang, *The Unmanageable Consumer: Contemporary Consumption and its Fragmentation* (London: Sage, 1995).
[3] F. Trentmann (ed.), *The Making of the Consumer: Knowledge, Power and Identity in the Modern World* (6th edn; Oxford: Berg, 2006).
[4] W. H. Hutt, 'The Concept of Consumers' Sovereignty', *Economic Journal*, 50/197 (1940), 66–77.
[5] C. Campbell, 'The Romantic Ethic and the Spirit of Modern Consumerism', in D. Miller (ed.), *Acknowledging Consumption: A Review of New Studies* (London: Routledge, 1995), 96–126, at 102.

in the issue of consumption during the 1980s, as they realized that people's lives were not exclusively determined by their relationship to the means of production, and further interpretations were developed.[6] Sociology had previously viewed people's relationship with work as being the fundamental determinant of their life experience, which led to the impact of consumption being ignored. Several commentators recognized this was an oversimplification and identified the active role commodities were playing in everyday life beyond their utility.[7] Lee later highlighted that in these new interpretations commodities were recognized to be performing a dual role—as both economic and cultural benchmarks—and were seemingly imbued with almost magical qualities.[8]

Although sociologists were dismissive of the shallow definitions offered by economists, their own interpretations were also criticized for tending to focus on the quest for meaning through the act of shopping, within which goods purchased became totems and symbols of self-expression.[9] While undoubtedly true to a large extent, these definitions tended to overlook the structural problems created by consumption at the heart of political and economic systems—for example, the ecological impact of consumption, the inequalities arising from increasing affluence, and the contradictions within the notion of perpetual economic growth in a world of finite resources.[10] Miles noted that discussions regarding consumption prior to the 1990s had been slow to address the complexities inherent in achieving a fulsome understanding of it social importance.[11] McCracken also recognized that culture in Western societies was becoming profoundly connected with consumption: 'Without consumer goods, certain acts of self-definition and collective definition in this culture would be impossible.'[12]

Miller argued that these changes in the utility of commodities had resulted in a consumer society: one in which 'commodities are increasingly used to express the core values of that society, but also become the principal form through which people come to see, recognise and understand those values'.[13] Wernick identified that a feature of the consumer society was a culture of

---

[6] B. Fine, 'Addressing the Consumer', in Trentmann (ed.), *The Making of the Consumer*, 291.

[7] Gabriel and Lang, *The Unmanageable Consumer*.

[8] M. J. Lee, *Consumer Culture Reborn: The Cultural Politics of Consumption* (London: Routledge, 1993).

[9] T. Princen, M. Maniates, and K. Conca, *Confronting Consumption* (Cambridge, MA, and London: MIT Press, 2002), 1–20.

[10] Ibid.; A. Offer, *The Challenge of Affluence: Self-Control and Wellbeing in the United States and Britain since 1950* (Oxford: Oxford University Press, 2007); S. McKevitt, *Everything Now: Communication, Persuasion and Control: How the Instant Society is Shaping What We Think* (London: Route, 2012).

[11] S. Miles, *Consumerism: As a Way of Life* (1998; London and Thousand Oaks, CA: Sage, 2006), 3.

[12] G. D. McCracken, *Culture and Consumption: New Approaches to the Symbolic Character of Consumer Goods and Activities* (Bloomington IN: Indiana University Press, 1988), p. xi.

[13] Miller, *Consumption and its Consequences*, 40.

promotion. He argued that cultural products were full of complex signifiers that communicated promotional messages and, moreover, that these messages were coincident with our manufactured symbolic world.[14] McCracken also argued that the manner in which commodities were created and used was central to any discussion of consumption, thereby extending the view beyond an end product of the demand function to include the influences, experiences, and motivations of the consumer both prior to and after making a purchase.[15]

Although definitions of consumption and consumerism have tended to become increasingly inclusive and expansive, the terms continue to mean different things to different commentators. American writers and historians of advertising have tended to associate consumerism with the development of a movement to protect consumer rights.[16] However, it is a much more useful term in its sociological context, where consumerism is differentiated from consumption by including the psychosocial aspects surrounding the act of consumption. To that end Miles offers a key distinction. He argues that consumerism is a broad concept dealing with the complexities surrounding consumption: 'Consumption is an act, consumerism a way of life.'[17] Although Miller draws a similar conclusion, he does not feel the need to make such a distinction, arguing instead that consumption itself is a much more active process than the economic act of buying things, because it also involves the manner in which goods and their symbolic meaning are transformed by consumers.[18] Carrier goes even further by also noting the role of persuasion and argues that consumers' understanding of consumables they confront is moulded by external factors.[19]

The pursuit of an all-encompassing, exhaustive theory of consumerism is beyond the purview of this study. Consumption was clearly important above its economic level by the 1980s, and, despite the fact that its many conceptions have become overly theoretical, it is an activity grounded in reality rather than social and economic theory. Consumerism not only structured lives at the end of the twentieth century but it also gave consumers the impression that they enjoyed a high degree of economic freedom, although in essence this freedom was limited and manifestly artificial. Both Benson and Lansley have discussed these historical changes at length, with the latter placing particular emphasis on the rise of the New Right at the end of the

---

[14] A. Wernick, *Promotional Culture: Advertising, Ideology and Symbolic Expression* (London: Sage Publications, 1991), 182.

[15] McCracken, *Culture and Consumption*, 104–18.

[16] See, e.g., W. Fletcher, *Powers of Persuasion: The Inside Story of British Advertising 1951–2000* (Oxford: Oxford University Press, 2008), 76–7, 78–9, 175.

[17] Miles, *Consumerism: As a Way of Life*, 4.   [18] Miller, *Consumption and its Consequences*, 64.

[19] J. G. Carrier, 'The Limits of Culture: Political Economy and Anthropology of Consumption', in Trentmann (ed.), *The Making of the Consumer*, 271–88.

1970s, whose policies in both the UK and the USA were responsible for the valorization of many aspects of consumerism.[20] Other commentators have argued instead that consumption has always been a factor in modern life-styles. Indeed, Veblen identified the status conferring qualities of consumer goods in 1899. However, there is a compelling argument that the influence, importance, and practice of consumerism had increased markedly by the end of the twentieth century (so too, it should be said, had the relevance of the ideas posited by Veblen).[21] Although Marx's understanding of commodities was entirely within in the context of the production process, he did identify progressive 'commodification' through which all aspects of social life would become increasingly subjected to market forces and predicted that even relationships and other more personal aspects of life would thus be commercialized.[22] Throughout the 1980s and 1990s, consumerism did indeed become ingrained into many areas of everyday life in the UK in this manner. Significant aspects of society previously excluded from the demands of the market—such as education, politics, and religion—were having to adapt to a new hegemony within which the needs and wants of the consumer were paramount. Consumption had always been a feature of consumer capitalism, but its form and manner were now markedly different: ubiquitous and pervasive but also ephemeral, constantly shifting, and always looking for new areas and means through which it could assert its influence. In the words of Miles, British homes became 'temples to the religion of consumerism'.[23]

The Consumer Society

There is some debate among historians about when the original consumer revolution took place.[24] Many view consumerism as largely a feature of

[20] J. J. Benson, *The Rise of Consumer Society in Britain, 1880–1980* (London: Longman, 1994); J. J. Benson, *Affluence and Authority: A Social History of Twentieth-Century Britain* (London: Hodder Arnold, 2005); J. J. Benson and L. Ugolini, *A Nation of Shopkeepers: Five Centuries of British Retailing* (London: I. B. Tauris, 2003); S. Lansley, *After the Gold Rush: The Trouble with Affluence: 'Consumer Capitalism' and the Way Forward* (London: Century, 1994).

[21] N. McKendrick, J. Brewer, and J. H. Plumb, *The Birth of a Consumer Society: The Commercialization of Eighteenth-Century England* (1982; London: Hutchinson, 1983); C. Williams, *Consumer Behavior: Fundamental and Strategies* (New York: West Publishing, 1982); T. Veblen, *The Theory of the Leisure Class* (1899; Fairfield, NJ: A. M. Kelley, 1991); D. Miller, *Theory and Issues in the Study of Consumption* (London: Routledge, 2001).

[22] K. Marx and F. Engels, *Capital* (1867; Chicago and London: Encyclopaedia Britannica, 1990).

[23] Miles, *Consumerism: As a Way of Life*; McKendrick, Brewer, and Plumb, *The Birth of a Consumer Society*.

[24] See, e.g., P. N. Stearns, *Consumerism in World History: The Global Transformation of Desire* (New York and London: Routledge, 2006); L. B. Glickman, *Consumer Society in American History: A Reader* (Ithaca, NY, and London: Cornell University Press, 1999); F. Trentmann, *Empire of Things: How We Became a World of Consumers, from the Fifteenth Century to the Twenty-First* (London: Penguin, 2016).

industrialization that emerged from around 1850 onwards, while others argue that the revolution occurred much earlier, in the cities of France and the Low Countries during the seventeenth century.[25] In this latter model consumerism was triggered by the widespread realization among shop-keepers and manufacturers that consumer wants and needs were infinitely stretchable, and not limited by the conventions of a subsistence lifestyle.[26] Clearly there is going to be evidence of consumer behaviour in human history for as long as there has been commerce, but for our purposes, as McKendrick et al. argue, the consumer revolution that occurred during the second half of the nineteenth century is arguably the first, but certainly the most important.[27] Here it is possible for the first time to identify a society within which material possessions were becoming valued for their fashion-ability as much as their durability. The retail landscape changed, symbolized by establishment of department stores in towns and cities offering an expanded range of products including the first 'consumer durables'—house-hold goods, appliances, and other products that do not have to be purchased frequently because they are built to last for an extended period of time (usually more than three years).[28] As a result, advertising became wordier and increasingly manipulative in style.[29] Leisure also emerged as a consumer activity for the first time in any real sense. The travel agent Thomas Cook was founded in 1840 in response to the opportunities for day trips and holidays presented by the establishment of mass public transportation systems.[30] Guidebooks became popular.[31] There was also a huge growth in sporting activity, which began to professionalize in the 1850s and rapidly expanded in popularity among both participants and spectators, with the establishment of various governing bodies. Musical hall theatre, a form of entertainment that paved the way for the emergence of cinema after 1900, was also enormously popular—particularly with the working classes.[32]

Benson considers that many of the key developments to increase consumer capacity that emerged during this period and into the twentieth century were the result of industrialization and a rapidly expanding population. For example, Henry Ford endorsed the notion of a homogeneous market in

---

[25] Stearns, *Consumerism in World History*, 17–19, 25–7; Glickman, *Consumer Society in American History*, 5–7.

[26] Stearns, *Consumerism in World History*, 18–19.

[27] McKendrick, Brewer, and Plumb, *The Birth of a Consumer Society*.

[28] Trentmann (ed.), *The Making of the Consumer*, 7–14; Stearns, *Consumerism in World History*, 47–55.

[29] Ibid. 47.

[30] J. Hamilton, *Thomas Cook: The Holiday Maker* (Stroud: The History Press, 2005).

[31] T. Parsons, *Worth the Detour* (Stroud: The History Press, 2008).

[32] G. Cross, *Time and Money: The Making of Consumer Culture* (London: Routledge, 1993); R. Koshar, *Histories of Leisure: Leisure, Consumption, and Culture* (Oxford: Berg, 2002); Stearns, *Consumerism in World History*, 53–62.

which factory workers would consume the products they manufactured.[33] In order to achieve that position, wages had to be maintained above subsistence levels to ensure a surplus and the price of manufactured goods kept low enough to ensure affordability. 'Fordism' also allowed producers of manufactured goods to reduce their overheads. These savings could be passed on to the consumer, but they also protected margins and allowed new lines to be introduced into the market very cheaply.[34] Goods that were initially considered a luxury became everyday items, and markets for a range of products— from clothing and furniture to processed food and cars—enjoyed a radical transformation.[35] This trend picked up pace as post-war workers enjoyed greater access to finance.[36] This was achieved not only through increases in the average wage but also as a result of legislation affecting consumer credit. For example, a relaxation in the hire purchase regulations in 1954 made electrical appliances more affordable to ordinary people (if, at the same time, actually more expensive).[37]

Bocock argued that after 1950 consumption sectors become more specific and focused.[38] From this point it came to play an increasingly important role in people's lives. With surpluses increasing consumers' spending power, manufacturers and retailers were able to address wants rather than needs. They were able to convert the former into the latter through a process of symbolic endowment—for example, the need for a functional jacket is converted into the need for a fashionable, functional jacket, because 'jacket' has become a vehicle through which wearers can express their self-identity.[39] Some commentators such as Bell viewed this development as a form of liberation for the working classes because it allowed them access to an aspect of society that was previously exclusive to the upper and middle classes, while others argued—like Murray—that it was actually eroding their individuality. However, as Schor identified, the crucial issue was that this was a new form of self-expression for many people and one that was expensive to maintain.[40] Regardless of its effects, consumerism was to become ubiquitous and consolidated its position as a global way of life during the 1980s.[41]

---

[33] Benson, *The Rise of Consumer Society in Britain*.
[34] M. C. Heil, 'Professional Service Firm Marketing—the Next Generation: Quality Oriented Service, Results Driven Strategy', *Journal of Professional Services Marketing*, 10/2 (1994), 5–18.
[35] Miles, *Consumerism: As a Way of Life*, 7; Stearns, *Consumerism in World History*, 139–42.
[36] R. Bocock, *Consumption* (London and New York: Routledge, 1993).
[37] N. Whiteley, *Design for Society* (London: Reaktion, 1993); S. McKevitt and A. Ryan, *The Solar Revolution: One Planet, One Solution: How to Fuel and Feed 10 Billion People* (London: Icon, 2014), 174–5.
[38] Bocock, *Consumption*.   [39] Miles, *Consumerism: As a Way of Life*, 7.
[40] D. Bell, *The Cultural Contradictions of Capitalism* (New York: Basic Books, 1996); Cross, *Time and Money*; R. Murray, 'Fordism and Post-Fordism', in M. Jacques and S. Hall (eds), *New Times: The Changing Face of Politics in the 1990s* (1989; London: Lawrence & Wishart, 1990); J. B. Schor, *The Overworked American: The Unexpected Decline of Leisure* (New York: Basic Books, 1993).
[41] Miles, *Consumerism: As a Way of Life*, 7–8.

Consumption and Persuasion

The emergence of persuasion runs parallel to the emergence of this consumer society. During the seventeenth century commercials began to proliferate in the weekly newspapers available in towns and cities and ever since that time consumption has not only been accompanied by advertising but also actively promoted through it.[42] Baudrillard described advertising as the means through which the capitalist system appropriates social goals for its own aims and imposes its own objectives.[43] Galbraith regarded advertising as a system that promotes artificial rather than authentic gratification.[44]

The emergence of broadcast mass media in the post-war period and a series of technical innovations in print considerably increased the reach of advertisers, allowing them to foster encouragement for consumption among new groups of people who were able to exploit opportunities to consume, owing to an increase in their spending power—for example, children and teenagers.[45] By 1980, a consumer culture was becoming established within which—as Lunt and Livingstone identified—involvement with material culture was so profound that 'mass consumption infiltrates everyday life, not only at levels of economic processes, social activities and household structures, but also at the level of meaningful psychological experience affecting the construction of identities, the formation of relationships and the framing of events'.[46]

Lee examined the burgeoning consumer society during the 1980s and concluded that the aesthetics and manner of consumption had become increasingly diverse as producers gained a greater understanding about the behaviour of consumers; markets segmented and vast numbers of niches were opened up that could be exploited through a variety of new channels.[47] Hall and Jacques identified that these trends enjoyed the full support of the prevailing political ideology throughout the 1980s.[48] Miles went even further, arguing that the British government was proactive in ensuring that consumerism became the primary focus of its citizens' lives. This objective was supported by large sections of the working-class electorate who were 'keen to take advantage of the opportunity to buy their own Council House and take their annual holidays abroad'.[49] Consumerism eventually came to be seen as a democratic proposition in Britain, and both leading political parties promoted

---

[42] Stearns, *Consumerism in World History*, 19.
[43] J. Baudrillard, *Selected Writings*, ed. M. Poster (Cambridge: Polity, 2001).
[44] Glickman, *Consumer Society in American History*, 42.
[45] Stearns, *Consumerism in World History*, 140.
[46] P. K. Lunt and S. M. Livingstone, *Mass Consumption and Personal Identity: Everyday Economic Experience* (Buckingham: Open University Press, 1992), 24.
[47] Lee, *Consumer Culture Reborn*.   [48] Jacques and Hall (eds), *New Times*.
[49] Miles, *Consumerism: As a Way of Life*, 10.

it to the electorate as a fundamental political freedom.[50] The 1997 Labour Party Manifesto enshrined many consumerist policies that had previously been the preserve of the Conservative Party, such as promoting personal prosperity for all, the acceptance of the global economy as a reality, and a commitment not to increase either the basic or the top rates of income tax.[51] Consumption was now common currency for politicians on either side of the political divide, and, as Ewen noted, its value structure could be exploited from both sides of the political spectrum.[52]

It is difficult to determine whether the final decades of the twentieth century witnessed a completely new form of consumerism or merely the intensification of some longstanding aspects. However, it can be argued with some confidence that society in Britain during the 1990s was characterized not by subsistence, as it had been previously, but by exchange. As Wernick noted and Marx had predicted, many areas of modern life were indeed now occupied by commerce for the first time.[53] Miles argued that by this point consumerism was significant not merely at an economic and social level but at the level of cultural change.[54] Whether globalization—a process that placed the consumer at the heart of the business and persuasion at its head—contributed to cultural standardization or diversity is also a moot point, but what can be said is that through the activities of global businesses—such as Nike, McDonalds, Apple, Microsoft, BMW, and Coca Cola—consumerism exerted a significant cultural influence, for good or ill, that was greater than ever before.[55] Deregulation of television advertising and the establishment of satellite and cable services in the UK at the start of the 1990s both had a huge impact on the penetration of global organizations into everyday life. They were now able to achieve ubiquity through advertising and other forms of persuasion—most notably public relations and corporate branding—via a myriad of channels. As Stearns noted, the emergence of new types of marketing and brand communication at the end of the twentieth century is an important part of modern economic history.[56]

Galbraith recognized that to succeed with successive product launches producers must ensure that consumers are never wholly satisfied by what they consume and that any satisfaction offered by commodities is fleeting and ephemeral. The reason that consumers continue to consume despite this

---

[50] R. Keat, N. Abercrombie, and N. Whiteley, *The Authority of the Consumer* (London: Routledge, 1994).

[51] 'New Labour: Because Britain Deserves Better', in *The 1997 Labour Party Manifesto* <http://www.politicsresources.net/area/uk/man/lab97.htm>.

[52] S. Ewen, *Captains of Consciousness: Advertising and the Social Roots of the Consumer Culture* (1976; London: Basic Books, 2001).

[53] Marx and Engels, *Capital*; Wernick, *Promotional Culture*.

[54] Miles, *Consumerism: As a Way of Life*, 11–12.

[55] Stearns, *Consumerism in World History*, 137–8.   [56] Ibid. 153.

dissatisfaction is because they accept and pursue the false promises of consumer capitalism made to them through advertising. Consumers do have freedom—but it is only the freedom to consume more goods and services that will return them to the status quo; in the long run they will be materially better off, but not happier, at which point they will simply consume more commodities.[57] Miles suggested that one of consumerism's greatest ideological strengths is that, regardless of their level of awareness, consumers are willing to forgo any deep analysis of its shortcomings because it offers them a compelling framework for the construction of a self-identity.[58] Jameson argued that, because consumerism is characterized by contradictions such as this, within market societies both affluence and misery tend to increase.[59]

Consumption, Individuality, and Self-Identity

While there is strong evidence that consumption did indeed extend its reach into more areas of social life than ever before at the end of the twentieth century, there is also a considerable risk, which many sociologists fail to avoid, that in accepting this point consumerism is thereby reduced to a personal search for meaning through the process of shopping. As Miller identified, this assumption falsely elevates shopping into 'a devotional ritual that both affirms and constitutes some transcendent force'.[60] He argued that simplification occurs because sociologists tend to concern themselves with the question of *how* we shop rather than *why* we shop.[61]

Miller demonstrated that shopping is more often than not a chore wherein, rather than spending money, the objective becomes saving money. In this model shoppers are able to draw on a wide range of tactics to legitimize their purchases—for example, they can claim they saved money because they got two items for the price of one (ignoring the fact that they have still spent money), or can persuade people that an item was cheap because they bought it in a sale or on Amazon.[62] People are motivated by thrift. For example, nobody ever claims they 'got a really bad deal' when they buy a new car; on the contrary, the deal is always deemed to be a good one, despite the fact this is a big-ticket item that almost without exception will be worth less than whatever they paid for it the moment the transaction is completed. Miller argued that, particularly where shopping for groceries and household is concerned,

---

[57] J. K. Galbraith, *The Affluent Society* (London: Penguin, 1999).

[58] I. Miles, 'Time, Goods and Wellbeing', in F. T. Juster and F. P. Stafford (eds), *Time, Goods and Wellbeing* (Ann Arbor: University of Michigan Press, 1985), 119–22.

[59] Jameson, quoted in J. Ash and E. Wilson, *Chic Thrills* (London: Pandora, 1992), 4.

[60] Miller, *Consumption and its Consequences*, 78.   [61] Ibid. 67.   [62] Ibid. 80.

thrift ensures that the household retains as many of its resources as possible when engaged in consumption.

Household shopping usually involves making purchases for other people. Miller recognized that women usually carried out this activity, and that their relationship with commodities was considerably more complex than existing sociological and economic models implied.[63] This is because of a binary aspect regarding their relationships with other family members. First, there is normative aspect—an implied moral adjudication about the way a husband, daughter, brother, or mother ought to be—and then there is the actual aspect—which is everything they know about their husband, their daughter, or their son. As such, there is a difference between—say—how a husband thinks a wife or child should behave and their actual behaviour. Miller argued that purchases are often designed to diminish the discrepancy between the normative and the actual aspects. By way of illustration, he presents his 'peanut butter theory'. Peanut butter is reasonably healthy when compared to a lot of junk food on offer, yet at the same time it is something that most children enjoy eating; it represents a compromise between what they ideally should eat (normative) and what they will eat (actual).[64] There are times where only the normative aspect is considered. On these occasions purchases can result in failure. Miller offered the example of men who buy sexy lingerie for their wives at Christmas only to see it returned to the shop on Boxing Day, 'as the actual partner refutes the projected norm of what men think women should be like and should want'.[65]

Feminist commentators also shared Miller's more nuanced interpretation of domestic consumption. Delpy, taking a Marxian view, contended that relationships in families are fundamentally exploitative and based on economic power. For her, domestic consumption was neither unitary nor undifferentiated.[66] Whitehead also emphasized men's power over the distribution of resources within the family unit, which could put significant pressure on the weekly shop, and Pahl further highlighted the fact that, regardless of the system of control and financial management adopted, men tended to enjoy greater personal spending power and freedom in the context of domestic spending.[67] Within poorer households, this inequality in spousal spending

---

[63] Ibid. 64–89.   [64] Ibid. 70.   [65] Ibid. 71–2.

[66] C. Delphy and D. Leonard, *Close to Home: A Materialist Analysis of Women's Oppression* (London: Hutchinson, in association with the Explorations in Feminism Collective, 1984).

[67] A. Cornwall, E. Harrison, and A. Whitehead, *Gender Myths and Feminist Fables: The Struggle for Interpretive Power in Gender and Development* (Oxford: Blackwell, 2008); S. Jackson and S. Moores, *The Politics of Domestic Consumption: Critical Readings* (London: Prentice Hall, 1995), 53–66; J. Pahl, 'Household Spending, Personal Spending and the Control of Money in Marriage', *Sociology*, 24/1 (1990), 119–38.

could cause extreme hardship.[68] A woman's responsibility to provide was often disproportionate to her control over the resources made available to her; hungry children were her concern; the money to feed them, her husband's. As Deem observed, this disparity in spending power and the gendered division of labour also meant that in terms of leisure the home could have markedly different meanings for men and women.[69]

Consumerism in the consumer society of late-twentieth-century Britain is a complex issue. While it is evident that commodities were ascribed a symbolic meaning by consumers, the processes by which they were ascribed and what meaning they were given are far from straightforward. These decisions were affected not only by a range of economic and social factors but also by context and circumstances. Yet, it should be remembered that—however imaginatively consumers were ascribing their meanings, whether they were shopping expressively for themselves or sacrificially for other members of their household, and whatever their economic circumstances, gender, or demographic group—the choices they made are always within limits prescribed to them by consumer capitalism and, as such, subject to manipulation.

It is persuasion that gives consumerism its shape and provides consumers with a set of rules. These functions have too often been overlooked. At the extremis, Loziak argued that a preoccupation with social change led theorists to neglect the ways in which the capitalist system was itself monitoring such changes to facilitate its own reproduction: 'At the same time, and consistent with this, it has been busy in commodifying experiences and human relations, and in formally regulating spheres of life that were once open to informal or democratic control, or left to the individuals to sort out for themselves.'[70] As Miles claims, Loziak's conclusion that consumerism has had an entirely reductive impact on people's lives and culture, rendering them meaningless, is certainly going too far. However, the argument that the commodification of culture came to play an increasingly prominent role in everyday life is compelling. By the late twentieth century consumerism had been accepted as a natural way to live in Britain. As Keat highlighted, despite the inequalities it produced, the notion that consumer sovereignty—however artificial—was highly seductive.[71] Fiske also pointed out that capitalism is lived through, validated, and invigorated by its commodities and their consumption.[72]

---

[68] G. Wilson, *Money in the Family: Financial Organisation and Women's Responsibility* (Aldershot: Avebury, 1987).

[69] R. Deem, *All Work and No Play? A Study of Women and Leisure* (Milton Keynes: Open University Press, 1986).

[70] C. Lodziak, *Manipulating Needs: Capitalism and Culture* (London: Pluto Press, 1995), 22.

[71] Keat, Abercrombie, and Whiteley, *The Authority of the Consumer*.

[72] J. Fiske, 'The Cultural Economy of Fandom', in L. A. Lewis (ed.), *The Adoring Audience: Fan Culture and Popular Media* (London: Routledge, 1992).

The individuality demanded by consumerism is arguably its key strength. Consumers are not victims. Although the sovereignty they are offered gives them personal freedom only within the bounds determined by the market, the opportunity to maximize their personal freedom and the meaning it gives to their lives is deemed to be ample compensation. This contradiction has vexed critics who can pinpoint consumerism's numerous shortcomings and construct compelling economic, social, and psychological arguments for reining in consumption, yet find these ideas very difficult to sell out in the real world. From the mid-twentieth century the relatively small number of critics of affluence have been remarkably consistent in their analysis and conclusions, yet they remain at the margins in the sense that their ideas have never been wholeheartedly adopted—publicly at least—by a mainstream political party.

The expanding literature of consumption has developed our understanding of the central role material culture played in British lifestyles at the end of the twentieth century and also contributed to our knowledge of its impact on social relationships, self-identity, and self-expression. Yet these scholars have had surprisingly little to say about the means by which market capitalism presents and promotes these ideas. For example, Miller discusses the importance of the idealized 'normative aspect' in our understanding of household consumption, but says nothing about how these idealized versions of wife, father, or son are constructed.[73] Miles concludes that 'the dreams of consumerism give meaning to people's lives' but engages in no analysis about how these dreams are shaped and manipulated beyond simply recognizing that they are.[74] Trentmann acknowledges that there has been little research in terms of consumerism's evolution into 'a master category of collective and individual identity', but he does not consider what impact persuasion may have had in the shaping of those identities.[75]

British society underwent huge social and economic changes during the 1980s, arguably more so than any other post-war decade. Consumption was not only at the heart of this change but also a key characteristic of the consumer society that emerged. While historians of the left and right differ in their interpretation of these changes—and most notably in whether they were for better or for worse—almost without exception they are united by the fact that they identify the Conservative government, led by Prime Minister Margaret Thatcher—which was very much the vanguard of the so-called 'New Right' in terms of its ideology—as a driving force.[76]

---

[73] Miller, *Consumption and its Consequences*, 69–83.
[74] Miles, *Consumerism: As a Way of Life.*
[75] Trentmann (ed.), *The Making of the Consumer*, 1–30.
[76] There are numerous examples. For a selection, see Eyal Zamir and Doron Teichman (eds), *The Oxford Handbook of Behavioral Economics and the Law* (Oxford: Oxford University Press, 2014);

The New Right in Britain

At the time of Margaret Thatcher's initial election victory in May 1979, the UK economy was weak. Unemployment was running at a post-war high of 700,000 and productivity levels were among the lowest in Europe.[77] The underlying causes of this malaise were identified, to varying degrees, as an overreliance upon manufacturing (much of it publicly owned, typified by outdated business practices and antiquated plant and machinery), a failure to invest in research and development, and the poor state of industrial relations. Yet by 1990 the major concerns of Britain's citizens seemed to have changed completely. Depending on one's political viewpoint, either an economic miracle or a catastrophe had taken place. One indisputable change was that within the new privately owned and rapidly growing service economy the City rather than the trade union movement was front of mind. Vast swathes of the electorate had become property owners and, albeit fleetingly in many cases, share owners. Home ownership increased from 50 per cent of households in 1971 to 68 per cent in 1991, by which time close to eleven million people owned shares directly.[78] Citizens had become consumers: materialistic, aspirational, and enjoying the benefits of their newfound financial liquidity owing to rising property prices and much broader access to personal credit.[79] Many of the Keynesian principles that drove Britain up

Benson, *The Rise of Consumer Society in Britain*; B. Evans, *Thatcherism and British Politics, 1975–1997* (Stroud: Sutton, 1999); E. J. Evans, *Thatcher and Thatcherism* (London and New York: Routledge, 2004); M. Francis, 'A Crusade to Enfranchise the Many: Thatcherism and the "Property-Owning Democracy"', *Twentieth Century British History*, 23/2 (2012), 275–97; A. Gamble, 'The Thatcher Myth', *British Politics*, 10/1 (2015), 3–15; A. Gamble, *The Free Economy and the Strong State: The Politics of Thatcherism* (Basingstoke: Macmillan Education, 1988); E. H. H. Green, *Thatcher* (London: Hodder Arnold, 2006); P. Gurney, *Co-Operative Culture and the Politics of Consumption in England, 1870–1930* (Manchester: Manchester University Press, 1996); M. Hilton, 'The Fable of the Sheep, or, Private Virtues, Public Vices: The Consumer Revolution of The Twentieth Century', *Past & Present*, 176/1 (2002), 222–56; M. Hilton, *Consumerism in Twentieth-Century Britain: The Search for a Historical Movement* (Cambridge: Cambridge University Press, 2003); B. Jackson, R. Saunders, and B. Jackson, *Making Thatcher's Britain* (Cambridge: Cambridge University Press, 2012); S. Majima, 'Affluence and the Dynamics of Spending in Britain, 1961–2004', *Contemporary British History*, 22/4 (2008), 573–97; J. Obelkevich and P. Catterall, *Understanding Post-War British Society* (London: Routledge, 1994); Trentmann, *Empire of Things*; R. Vinen, *Thatcher's Britain: The Politics and Social Upheaval of the Thatcher Era* (London: Pocket, 2010); J. Zeitlin, 'Irresistible Empire: America's Advance through Twentieth-Century Europe', *Journal of Cold War Studies*, 10/3 (2008), 189–91.

[77] J. Denman and P. McDonald, *Unemployment Statistics from 1881 to the Present Day* (London: Office of National Statistics, 1996).

[78] *A Century of Home Ownership and Renting in England and Wales* (London: Office of National Statistics, 2013), <http://webarchive.nationalarchives.gov.uk/20160105160709/http://www.ons.gov.uk/ons/rel/census/2011-census-analysis/a-century-of-home-ownership-and-renting-in-england-and-wales/short-story-on-housing.html>; J. Moore, 'British Privatization: Taking Capitalism to the People', *Harvard Business Review*, 70/1 (1992), 115–24.

[79] E. Fernandez-Corugedo and J. Muellbauer, *Consumer Credit Conditions in the United Kingdom* (London: Bank of England, 2006), 4.

until the late 1970s (and into the ground, some argued) were regarded as old fashioned, hidebound, or stymying.

In reality, this version of events is somewhat simplistic. As Vinen and Mort argued, this '1980s society' comprised of credit-rich, home-owning share-holders did not really get underway until Thatcher secured a second term of office in 1983.[80] Moreover, the Thatcher government's most radical budget of spring 1988, which slashed taxes and openly encouraged consumer spending (later described by then chancellor Nigel Lawson as a 'provocative budget' designed to accelerate social and cultural change in Britain; by Mort as his 'most spectacular and controversial'; and by Vinen as one that was received initially as a triumph but retrospectively condemned), did not occur until almost a year after her third general election victory.[81] Indeed, Thatcher's first term in office did very little to prove that it would be anything other than yet another misguided attempt to rejuvenate Britain's failing economy. Beckett provides evidence that, hampered by the fact that control of the money supply proved far more difficult in practice than it had in principle, the initial experiments with monetarism were as big a disappointment to those within the government as those outside it.[82] As Thatcher's monetarist mentor Milton Friedman rather damagingly pointed out in an interview with *Time* in 1981: 'Unfortunately, actual practice has not conformed to policy.'[83] The high interest rates that monetarism demanded and the relative strength of the pound (by the late 1970s sterling had become an important petro-currency, thanks to the initial production of oil from the North Sea) resulted in a large foreign exchange appreciation. The value of the pound rose from approximately \$1.50 to \$2.50 in 1980 alone.[84] This dramatic rise adversely affected Britain's exports and manufacturing sector, making UK goods prohibitively expensive overseas. The UK's weak manufacturing sector bore the brunt, as the economy plunged into recession. Unemployment rose to three million people, while inflation remained in double figures.[85]

---

[80] Vinen, *Thatcher's Britain*, 178–209; F. Mort, *Cultures of Consumption: Masculinities and Social Space in Late Twentieth-Century Britain* (London: Routledge, 1996), 1–18.

[81] Vinen, *Thatcher's Britain*, 200–9; Mort, *Cultures of Consumption*, 1; Nigel Lawson quotation taken from the title of chapter 46 in N. Lawson, *Memoirs of a Tory Radical* (London: Biteback, 2010).

[82] A. Beckett, *Promised you a Miracle: UK80–82* (London: Allen Lane, 2015), 41–58; T. Casey, *The Social Context of Economic Change in Britain: Between Policy and Performance* (Manchester: Manchester University Press, 2008), 44–83.

[83] M. Johnson, 'Britain: Embattled but Unbowed: As Britain Reels from Recession and Political Turmoil, Thatcher Soldiers on', *Time*, 16 February 1981, <http://content.time.com/time/magazine/article/0,9171,954658,00.html>.

[84] *Historical Exchange Rates*, <http://www.ukforex.co.uk/forex-tools/historical-rate-tools/historical-exchange-rates>.

[85] See also T. Bell, *Right or Wrong: The Memoirs of Lord Bell* (London: Bloomsbury, 2014), 61–8; Vinen, *Thatcher's Britain*, 101–34.

The view that Thatcher was somewhat fortunate to secure a second term is probably correct.[86] Her success is often attributed to the surge in popularity following Britain's victory in the Falklands War, but in truth it owed almost as much to the fact that its first-past-the-post electoral system did not reward aggregate popularity. The emergence of the SDP, which in alliance with the Liberals performed well at the ballot box, split the opposition vote, which meant that, despite securing more than 625,000 fewer votes than in 1979, the Conservatives were returned with an increased majority of 166—a lead that meant the party could be confident about the possibility of two further terms in office.[87]

The growth experienced by the advertising sector during Thatcher's first term was modest. Spend on advertising rose by just 0.05 per cent of GNP between 1979 and 1983. However, during this period several key developments occurred that were to make a significant contribution to the imminent expansion of persuasion industries. These can be categorized as either systemic—such as the proliferation of nuanced media channels and the fragmentation of the target audience, which created countless opportunities for content production—or political and economic. Examples of the latter include a reduction in the cost of living and the impact of legislation such as the Housing Act 1980 (Right to Buy), the Enterprise Allowance Scheme 1981, and the Telecommunications Act 1984 (the first in several privatizations of publicly owned utilities).[88] Together these developments contributed to a further major, society-wide social change, at the heart of which was a general softening in attitude towards the cornerstones of market capitalism: personal (leveraged) debt, consumption, share and property ownership, commerce, and entrepreneurism.[89]

The economic changes wrought by Margaret Thatcher's increasingly confident Conservative administrations during the 1980s had wide-reaching, often unintended, cultural and social implications. The Housing Act (1980) and Telecommunications Act (1984) led respectively to the widening of home and share ownership in the UK.[90] Council tenants who exercised the right

---

[86] Ibid. 134–54.

[87] R. Kimber, *British Governments and Elections since 1945*, http://www.politicsresources.net/area/uk/uktable.htm>.

[88] *Housing Act 1980*, <http://www.legislation.gov.uk/ukpga/1980/51/contents> (25 July 2016); *Employment and Training Act 1981*, <http://www.legislation.gov.uk/ukpga/1981/57/contents>; *Telecommunications Act* <http://www.legislation.gov.uk/ukpga/1984/12/contents>.

[89] *Conservative Manifesto 1979*, <http://www.politicsresources.net/area/uk/man.htm>; P. N. Balchin and M. Rhoden, *Housing Policy: An Introduction* (London: Routledge, 2002), 188; J. Foreman-Peck and R. Millward, *Public and Private Ownership of British Industry 1820–1990* (Oxford: Clarendon Press, 1994), 1.

[90] 'The Top 150 UK PR Consultancies 1998: Overview: Growing up: Public Affairs and Investor Relations Proved Lucrative for Most Top 10 Agencies', *PR Week*, 24 April 1998; *Housing Act 1980*; *Telecommunications Act*.

to buy their home at a vastly discounted price were part of a national property boom that witnessed nationwide house prices soar by 16 per cent in 1987 and 35 per cent in 1988. Although there was a crash at the end of the decade, the long-term trend continued upwards. In January 1983, when Halifax Building Society started tracking historical house prices in the UK, the average British home cost £29,696 (£99,873 at 2018 values); at the end of 1997 the same homes had risen to £70,296 (£125,586 at 2018 values).[91] The Telecommunications Act included provisions for the privatization of British Telecom. While this was not the first publicly owned asset to be sold—in 1972, the state-owned travel agency Thomas Cook was bought for £22.5 million by a consortium of private businesses made up of Trust House Forte, Midland Bank, and the Automobile Association—it was the first privatization on such a major scale.[92] The transformation in 1984 of British Telecommunications (the statutory organization) into British Telecommunications plc (the privately owned, stock-market listed business) was at the time the largest initial public offering (IPO) in world history.[93] In relation to the persuasion industries, the most notable aspect of both this flotation and others that followed over subsequent years was the initiative to target individual investors rather than financial institutions. Initially this was a pragmatic decision. Now in power, the Conservatives were unable to convince the City financiers that the publicly owned corporations constituted a worthwhile investment, which is unsurprising, given that they had spent several years in opposition highlighting how poorly managed, unprofitable, and inefficient they were. However, targeting ordinary citizens was not an insignificant challenge in itself. Few people owned share portfolios, and ordinary members of the public had little or no knowledge about how shares could be bought and sold. They needed to be educated. This kind of challenge—where a complicated message needs to be explained via the media—was perfect suited for a public relations campaign, which in this instance would be supported by advertising rather than led by it. As a result, the privatizations were to prove the catalyst for the rapid, massive expansion of the UK public relations sector by 1990.[94]

It is difficult to regard the policy of privatization of public utilities as an unqualified success, and historians disagree about whether they were sold too cheaply or, indeed, whether they should have been sold at all. However, a fifth of adults in the UK did buy into at least one initial public offering (encouraged

[91] *A Century of Home Ownership and Renting in England and Wales*.
[92] *Thomas Cook Packaged and Sold*, <http://news.bbc.co.uk/onthisday/hi/dates/stories/may/26/newsid_3003000/3003665.stm>.
[93] L. Wakeham, N. Monck, D. Clemeti, B. Carsberg, G. Grimstone, and A. Gamble, 'The Privatisation of British Telecom (1984)', in *The 'S' Factors—Lessons from IFG's Policy Success Reunions* (London: Institute for Government UK, 2012), 45–59.
[94] Francis, 'A Crusade to Enfranchise the Many'.

by the fact that the share price tended to be below market value, thereby providing them with the opportunity to make a swift profit).[95] Margaret Thatcher's own political aim was rather more than 'merely increasing economic rationality'; her desire was to achieve a paradigm shift in industrial policy and instil British citizens with 'vigorous virtues' and family values.[96] Ultimately this change was to prove notional rather than actual. Despite the deregulation of financial markets, which after the so-called Big Bang on 27 October 1986 made it far simpler to trade shares on the London Stock Exchange, figures from the Office for National Statistics show that, in terms of value, the percentage of the UK stock market owned by UK individuals was higher in the 1960s and 1970s in than the 1980s. In 1981, UK individuals owned 28 per cent of available shares. However, this figure had fallen to just 20 per cent by the end of Thatcher's time in office in 1990.[97] Much of the financial deregulation was technical in nature—for example, the abolition of fixed commission charges and the distinction between stockjobbers and stockbrokers on the London Stock Exchange—but its cumulative impact was profound. The Big Bang effectively marked the end of the historic system of open-outcry and its replacement with computerized, screen-based trading on 27 October 1986.[98]

British citizens also benefited from a sustained reduction in the cost of living, which increased their sense of well-being by providing them with more disposable income. The impact of the so-called green revolution in global agriculture, which began in the 1980s and continued for another three decades, resulted in much lower food prices across the board. Food accounted for a third of household income during the 1950s in comparison with just 17 per cent by the end of the century.[99] The effects of this reduction in living costs were both qualitative and quantitative. From 1980 onwards, much more meat was consumed per capita, while offal—a staple of the school canteen and many home cooked meals up to the late 1970s—practically vanished from the dinner table altogether. The consumption of bread, potatoes, and green vegetables declined, to be replaced by rice, pasta, and, most notably, cheap processed food, which had previously been prohibitively expensive. The variety of food on offer also grew significantly. By the end of the twentieth century a medium-sized supermarket was stocking approximately 45,000 products.[100] Eating out also became more affordable, and food

---

[95] A. W. Turner, *Rejoice! Rejoice!: Britain in the 1980s* (London: Aurum Press, 2013), 228.

[96] Vinen, *Thatcher's Britain*, 283.

[97] *Share Ownership—Register Survey Report—2012* (London: UK Office of National Statistics, 2013), http://www.ons.gov.uk/ons/dcp19975_314425.xml.

[98] *Financial Services Act 1986*, <http://www.legislation.gov.uk/ukpga/1986/60/contents>.

[99] *National Food Survey 1940–2000* (London: Office for National Statistics, 2004), <https://data.gov.uk/dataset/family_food_open_data>.

[100] Ibid.

outlets proliferated throughout town and city centres. By 2000 restaurant dining had become the most popular recreation activity in the UK and the USA, ahead of both watching and participating in sport, going to the movies, and shopping (which took second place).[101]

The impact of these changes can be seen clearly in the figures for gross domestic product (GDP) and real household disposable income per head. From 1969 to 1997 in the UK, GDP and real household disposable income per head grew on average by 1.9 and 2.4 per cent per year respectively. During the 1970s real household disposable income per head tended to increase more than GDP per head in times of economic growth and decrease more than GDP per head in times of recession. This correlation changes in the 1980s, with real household disposable income per head continuing to rise during the recession of the early 1990s, although more slowly than in the preceding few years (see Figure 1.1).[102]

Collectively these systemic, economic, and political developments contributed to the major social and attitudinal changes that occurred during the decade. It was not just that Britain was a market economy as it entered the 1990s; it was an advanced consumer society.

Popular Culture and the Expansion of Mass Media

British popular culture was also buoyant after the 1970s. TV, film, popular music, comedy, literature, and theatre all experienced an export boom that contrasted starkly with Britain's economic decline. For example, the 1980 film *Chariots of Fire*—a quintessentially British success story of stiff upper lip, Corinthian spirit, and Olympian sporting excellence—was a surprising commercial and critical success in the USA.[103] It was produced and directed by former stalwarts of the advertising industry David Puttnam and Hugh Hudson. Where they led, others would follow.[104] Bill Forsyth's movie *Gregory's Girl*, a low-budget, offbeat comedy set in the Scottish new town of Cumbernauld and reportedly produced for just £200,000, grossed over £25 million following its international release in 1981.[105] In popular music, British

---

[101] *Leisure outside the Home: Market Review* (Hampton: Key Note, 2010), <www.researchandmarkets.com/.../leisure_outside_the_home_market_review_2010.pdf> (16 August 2017).

[102] D. Bovill, *Patterns of Pay: Estimates from the Annual Survey of Hours and Earnings, UK, 1997 to 2013* (London: Office of National Statistics, 2014); S. Carrera and J. Beaumont, *Income and Wealth* (London: Office of National Statistics, 2010), 3.

[103] See T. Cateforis, *'Are we not New Wave?': Modern Pop at the Turn of the 1980s* (Ann Arbor: University of Michigan Press, 2011); *Chariots of Fire* <http://www.imdb.com/title/tt0082158/>.

[104] For full filmographies, see <www.imdb.com>. See also D. Rees and L. Crampton, *Q Rock Stars Encyclopedia* (London: Dorling Kindersley, 1999).

[105] Ibid.

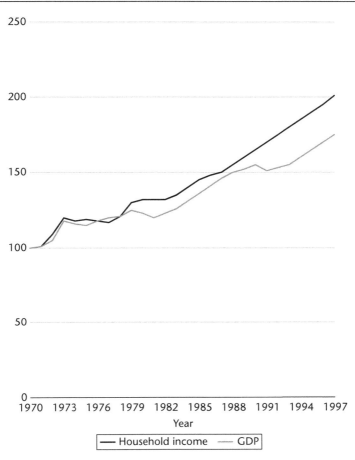

Figure 1.1. Real household disposable income per head and gross GDP per head UK, 1970–1997.

Note: Household income adjusted to real terms using the expenditure deflator for the household sector; GDP adjusted to real terms using the GDP inflator. Index numbers: 1970 = 100.

Source: Carrera and Beaumont, *Income and Wealth* (London: Office for National Statistics, 2010), 3.

acts such as Led Zeppelin, Pink Floyd, Black Sabbath, Fleetwood Mac, and the Rolling Stones were among the biggest selling artists in the world during the 1970s, while New Wave (essentially a loose collection of UK musicians playing more melodic, accessible derivatives of punk rock) provided a staple for global audiences tuning into MTV after its foundation in 1981.[106] By the mid-1980s British popular music had reached a commercial peak. In April 1984, forty of the US Top 100 singles were by acts of British origin. Just over a year later on

---

[106] Cateforis, *Are we not New Wave?*

25 May 1985, no fewer than eight of the US Top 10 singles were by UK artists.[107] Although its popularity would ebb and flow, British music remained the biggest overseas influence on the US charts right through to the end of the century.

Britain's creative industries flourished as a result of the progressively less paternal and homogenous attitudes towards content, but they were also given fresh impetus by the proliferation of media channels. From the introduction of the X certificate by the British Board of Film Censors in 1951, there was a steadily increasing acceptance on the part of government, broadcast, and print media authorities that audiences for entertainment in all forms were fragmented and that censorship should take the target consumer into consideration.[108] Prior to the 1960s, films were routinely censored as a means of social control—for example, scenes were removed from the 1955 movie *Rebel without a Cause* to 'reduce the possibility of teenage rebellion'.[109] Throughout the 1960s and 1970s a process of liberalization took place, which, on the one hand, allowed content to be produced for adult consumption that was increasingly more graphic in its depictions of sex and violence, but also allowed entertainment across the board to become more nuanced.[110] There was a rapid fragmentation in the types of film, music, TV, and literature produced to the extent that the scope of entertainment available during the 1980s was much wider than ever before. People were no longer merely 'fans of popular music'; they were 'fans of popular culture' instead. As such, subcultures and their associated media proliferated. These varied hugely in size, popularity, and wider cultural significance, but all were shaping individual tastes to some extent. Increasingly, content producers from both within and outside the mainstream targeted children, teenagers, and young adults. For example, during the 1980s, the world 'alternative' became a loaded expression for all kinds of music, comedy, and television that had little in common other that the fact it was not considered part of the mainstream. Yet devotees—usually young people—knew how to find their preferred forms of alternative culture: tucked away late at night on national radio and TV schedules or inside a raft of specialist newspapers and magazines such as *NME*, *Melody Maker*, *Crash*, *Zapp!*, *ZigZag*, *Smash Hits*, *The Face*, and *Blitz*.

Testament to this cultural fragmentation was the arrival in 1982 of Channel 4. The long-awaited fourth channel was a public/private hybrid: commercially funded but ultimately state-owned and operated. ITV had

---

[107] *Billboard Hot 100 25 May 1985* <http://www.billboard.com/charts/hot-100/1985-05-25>.

[108] *The X Certificate* <www.screenonline.org.uk/film/id/591679/index.html>; J. Hill, *'What shall we Do with them when they're not Working?': Leisure and Historians in Britain* (Manchester: Manchester University Press, 2012); A. Bingham, *Family Newspapers? Sex, Private Life, and the British Popular Press 1918–1978* (Oxford: Oxford University Press, 2009).

[109] *Rebel without a Cause* <http://www.imdb.com/title/tt0048545/alternateversions>.

[110] *The 1970s*, <http://www.bbfc.co.uk/education-resources/student-guide/bbfc-history/1970s>.

long opposed any challenge to its own advertising revenue, and reassurance was provided by Channel 4's remit, set out in the 1977 Annan Report, which required the provision of programming for minority groups. Founder CEO Jeremy Isaacs went even further, supporting the idea that 'broadcasters should no longer seek to serve a mass audience . . . the days of an entire family sitting in a row watching television were behind us. Millions of people were now living on their own.'[111] At its launch Isaacs committed Channel 4 to providing an alternative to the existing channels: 'Society is not a slab of solid feeling . . . We catered for the interests of individuals who could make viewing choices on their own, and for themselves.'[112] Channel 4's early schedules were loaded with alternative comedy (*The Comic Strip*), alternative music (*The Tube*), alternative soap operas (*Brookside*), and even alternative news (*The Friday Alternative*). Much of this content was provided largely by the burgeoning independent production sector. In May 1982 Isaacs wrote to the Independent Programme Producers Association (IPPA) council to report that Channel 4 had issued over 400 commissions since its inception.[113]

New channels were also emerging in printed media. The developments of digital printing (the adoption of which was hard fought, perhaps brutally so, by Rupert Murdoch at News International) and desktop publishing (which allowed editors to finetune layout and experiment with design before going to print) also vastly reduced production costs and steadily improved output quality. Several new newspapers were launched during the 1980s—including *Today, Mail on Sunday, Independent, Independent on Sunday*, and *Sunday Correspondent*—with varying degrees of success. From 1989, there was a trend among existing publications to extend pagination and introduce new sections and supplements. For example, the *Sunday Times* added the annual *Sunday Times Rich List* and the *Funday Times* in 1989; *Style & Travel, News Review*, and *Arts* in 1990, *Culture* in 1992, and separate *Style* and *Travel* sections in 1994.[114] The 1980s and 1990s were also the golden age of magazine publishing, with new, mass-market categories emerging in both women's and men's sectors, and the arrival of a new variety of specialist consumer magazine—in essence buyers' guides—in film, home entertainment, video games, travel, weddings, interior design, gardening, home computing, music, fashion, motoring, and home improvement.

Britain's Advanced Consumer Society

During the late 1980s and 1990s many people in Britain certainly felt wealthier than ever before. The economic growth and falling unemployment of the

---

[111] Beckett, *Promised you a Miracle*, 330.   [112] Ibid.   [113] Ibid. 94–5.
[114] A. Neil, *Full Disclosure* (London: Macmillan, 1996).

mid-1980s continued, albeit fitfully, until the end of the century. This increased sense of employment security combined with the liberalization of financial markets and rising house prices to make people feel that they were better off. Nigel Lawson's 'provocative budget' of 1988 introduced a wide range of tax reforms—including a major reduction in both the top rate and basic rate of income tax—with the aim of accelerating the cultural changes taking place within British society by delivering 'prosperity to the many'.[115] Lawson's budget drew unilateral support from the right and widespread opposition from the left, but, as Mort identified, commentators on both sides all shared the same 'expansive view of consumer society' in which 'consumption featured as a whole way of life'.[116] Unfortunately this boom in consumer spending was financed not, as Lawson had hoped, by the fruits of increased productivity but rather by an increase in personal debt. Across UK society attitudes to indebtedness, risk, commerce, enterprise, and consumption were altering fundamentally. As Marron noted, these were the early stages of a long-term process through which consumer credit—as provided by high-street banks, credit-card companies, and other major financial institutions—lost much of the moral and cultural stigma associated historically with personal debt. Consumer credit became normalized: it was presented as just one financial tool among a wider set that allowed consumers to maintain, promote, and enhance their own well-being.[117]

Commentators and critics of affluence have concluded that the salient effect of making personal credit more readily available among the mass of the population was the impact it had on consumption. Offer noted that the decline in household savings rates to almost nothing was partly compensated by the rise of the stock market and increasing house values.[118] A whole range of material goods and services designed to offer hedonistic lifestyles in this new form of leisure have attracted the attention of scholars. Benson highlighted the increasing importance of shopping as a leisure activity, and shopping venues in particular became the subject of academic study.[119] Schor's two books on work, leisure, and spending in the USA—essentially meta-analyses of a larger number of studies and surveys—highlighted a steady increase in working hours from the mid-1970s, a process she described as

---

[115] Lawson, *Memoirs of a Tory Radical*, 66, 818.   [116] Mort, *Cultures of Consumption*, 2, 3.

[117] D. Marron, 'Producing Overindebtedness: Risk, Prudence and Consumer Vulnerability', *Journal of Cultural Economy*, 5/4 (2012), 407–21.

[118] Offer, *The Challenge of Affluence*, 66.

[119] Hill, '*What Shall we Do with them when they're not Working?*' See also Benson, *The Rise of Consumer Society in Britain*; S. Benson, 'The Department Store: A Social History', *Journal of American History*, 84 (1997), 674–5; J. De Groot, *Consuming History: Historians and Heritage in Contemporary Popular Culture* (London: Routledge, 2009); R. Hewison, *The Heritage Industry: Britain in a Climate of Decline* (London: Methuen, 1987).

'the unexpected decline of leisure'.[120] Following Becker and Linder, Schor asserted that people had become victims of their own rising aspirations.[121] Becker and Linder argued themselves that as people got richer and consumed more and more consumer goods, they would have less and less time to spend with each item. Linder predicted that leisure time would eventually become hectic as people tried to keep up with the usage of a steadily accumulating mountain of possessions:

> Economic growth entails a general increase in the scarcity of time…As the volume of consumption goods increases, requirements for the care and maintenance of those goods also tends to increase: we get bigger houses to clean, a car to wash, boats to pop for the winter, the television sets repair, and have to make more decisions on spending.[122]

Swenson introduced the concept of time famine to describe the new high-consumption lifestyle. Consumption was highly addictive,but relatively unsatisfying, because earning the money to pay for it—or to service the debt it created—took up more and more time, and social relationships suffered as a consequence. Swenson argued that countries with the most prosperity had the most time famine and, as a result, citizens who experienced the most stress.[123]

Offer supported these views but also highlighted the human impact of this increasing level of consumption. He argued that there is an initial feel-good factor that comes with the sense of being better off or more affluent that is initially profound, particularly at lower income levels, but becomes increasingly difficult to sustain over time. This is due to the fact that increases in wealth provide more rewarding status—typically achieved through the acquisition of goods, services, or home improvements—at the bottom of the income scale. Unlike income, status cannot increase significantly for everyone over long periods of time; eventually it takes enormous increments of income to move very small distances upwards in terms of status. Offer argued that increased market competition promoted hedonism over other forms of satisfaction, since hedonic reward is easy to identify, package, and sell. As such, the 'invisible hand assumption'—a core doctrine of free-market economics, which assumes that the unfettered choice of individuals maximizes the welfare of society—is undermined by the pervasiveness of inconsistent consumer

---

[120] Schor, *The Overworked American*, 23; J. B. Schor, *The Overspent American: Why We Want What We Don't Need* (New York: Harper Perennial, 1999).

[121] G. Becker, 'A Theory of the Allocation of Time', *Economic Journal*, 75/299 (1965), 493–517; S. B. Linder, *The Harried Leisure Class* (New York: Columbia University Press, 1970).

[122] Ibid. 4, 33.

[123] R. A. Swenson, *Margin: Restoring Emotional, Physical, Financial, and Time Reserves to Overloaded Lives* (Colorado Springs, CO: NavPress, 2004).

preferences. The fact that investment in advertising alone amounted to more than 1.5 per cent of GNP at times is indicative of a high level of consumer response to external suggestions not all of which could be considered 'information'. Indeed, the range of choices increases the cognitive burden of buying decisions, because it places stress on individuals, especially where it is difficult for them rationally to differentiate between competing products or services.[124]

Just as the changes in economic policy that occurred in the UK during the 1980s were undoubtedly auspicious for budding entrepreneurs, so too were they for the persuasion industries. Mort noted the sea change that took place in retailing at this time. Shops were no longer warehouses of goods but rather the symbolic representation of those goods themselves. They had become an integral part of the marketing process. These sentiments were exemplified at the time by comments made by Sir Terence Conran, then chairman of the Store House Group. Conrad argued that the most important component of any company was the point of sale (brand) rather than the manufacture of commodities (products). One direct consequence of this shift was the enhanced prestige of 'those professionals who dealt in the symbolic representation of goods and services'.[125]

Keynes and the Critics of Affluence

Across all relevant fields historians concur almost without exception that the persuasion industries played a significant role in the emergence of a modern consumer society in Britain at the end of the twentieth century. However, beyond identifying the persuasion industries' importance, commentators have very little if anything to say about its methods and practices.[126]

Since the mid-twentieth century, critics of affluence, from J. K. Galbraith and Juliet Schor to Avner Offer and Robert and Edward Skidelsky, have contended that, while the persuasion industries (again, invariably conflated to just 'advertising') are an important driving force of growth in capitalist societies, they are also part of a cyclical process that succeeds by creating a form of dissatisfaction among consumers. This can be fleetingly assuaged by increased consumption, but that only leads to further dissatisfaction and in turn fuels yet more consumption. In advanced consumer societies, this cycle is maintained because the goods purchased go beyond the fulfilment of a basic

---

[124] Offer, *The Challenge of Affluence*, 67–9, 244, 273, 274–5.
[125] Mort, *Cultures of Consumption*, 6.
[126] Galbraith, *The Affluent Society*; Schor, *The Overworked American*; Offer, *The Challenge of Affluence*; R. J. A. Skidelsky and E. Skidelsky, *How Much Is Enough? The Love of Money, and the Case for the Good Life* (London: Penguin, 2013).

economic need. Their benefits are often almost entirely conceptual and sub-jective, providing a sense of status, self-identity, and self-worth.

Thorstein Veblen, the Norwegian–American economist, first identified 'conspicuous consumption'—the notion that consumer spending becomes the market through which people can reveal their income to the outside world—in the late nineteenth century.[127] This argument was later articulated with clarity by the American liberal economist John Kenneth Galbraith in *The Affluent Society*. Galbraith became concerned at the manner in which American post-war society was becoming wealthier during the late 1950s. Following Veblen, he argued that increasing material production of con-sumer goods that addressed wants rather than needs and the encouragement of their consumption through marketing, public relations, and advertising did not necessarily lead to increased societal well-being. Demand for goods was not organic, rather it was stimulated by outside forces—most notably the advertisers—rather than from within the consumers themselves. Once the basic needs of most citizens had been met (for food, clothing, and shelter), companies were forced to generate an artificial demand for their products and established the 'machinery for consumer-demand creation' that would allow them to do this.[128] Galbraith called this 'the dependence effect', wherein new wants were increasingly created as part of the same process by which they were satisfied.[129] As such, it was a form of market capitalism that increased rather than decreased inequality. Instead of improving well-being, the whole economy became geared towards maximizing consumer spending and the stockpiling of products instead.[130] Many contemporary commenta-tors expressed similar concerns—for example, Lewis Mumford, Daniel Bell, Christopher Lasch, and Rachel Carson were all critical of consumer culture. However, perhaps the most notable was Vance Packard, a social critic whose popular book *The Hidden Persuaders* explored, somewhat sensationally, the use of motivational consumer research and behavioural psychology by advertisers.[131]

Although widely read and well regarded, *The Affluent Society* was paid little heed by the political and economic majority in either the USA or the UK. Raising levels of affluence remained a policy objective for mainstream political parties on both the left and right throughout the century, and governments did very little to prevent the underlying processes of consumer

---

[127] T. Veblen, *What Veblen Taught: Selected Writings of Thorsten Veblen* (New York: Augustus M. Kelley, 1964); Veblen, *The Theory of the Leisure Class*.
[128] J. Newsom, *Four Years Old in an Urban Community* (London: Penguin, 1970), 158.
[129] Ibid. 170.   [130] Ibid.
[131] D. Horowitz, *The Anxieties of Affluence: Critiques of American Consumer Culture, 1939–1979* (Amherst, MA: University of Massachusetts Press, 2005); V. Packard, *The Hidden Persuaders* (New York: David McKay, 1957).

capitalism from grinding on. In Britain, a succession of administrations remained committed to full employment and wage increases. The quality of life for most UK citizens was improving, and the expectation was that it would continue to do so. Increases in the standard of living came to be seen as the norm rather than the exception.

Compelling though his argument was, Galbraith promoted views that were at odds with the prevailing theory of the time: that increasing affluence would lead not to a consumer society, but rather to a leisure society. In Britain, the post-war economic boom of the 1950s and 1960s fuelled political and economic speculation that the final decades of the twentieth century would be a period of substantive change. Across many fields—notably transportation, medicine, media, telecommunications, computing, and space exploration— these changes were driven by high-profile, scientific, and technological innovations. Technology was also having a material impact on the lives of ordinary people both at work and at home.[132] The denouement of this process, widely anticipated by mainstream politicians and countercultural commentators alike, was the leisure society—an economic future first predicted by economist John Maynard Keynes.[133] Keynes's vision was inspired by technological optimism. Following the crash of 1929, he noted that innovative technologies, which had raised living standards with startling regularity over the previous two centuries, had become stymied by the depression. He believed that this slowdown would in fact prove to be little more than a blip and that 'the standard of life in progressive countries one hundred years hence will be between four and eight times as high as it is today'.[134]

In that regard Keynes proved correct. In real terms GDP in the UK more than doubled between 1930 and 1969 and increased almost fivefold by 1997.[135] However, he also predicted that as a result of this growth humanity would be close to solving the fundamental economic problem of scarcity, allowing the vast majority of people's economic needs to be assuaged without their labour. In Keynes's estimation, the average citizen living at the end of the twentieth century would be required to work no more than three hours per day. Although he did concede that it would be theoretically possible to persuade individuals to work longer hours by giving them the opportunity to consume more goods in return, he dismissed this notion almost out of hand. He argued that, if they were given a clear choice between consuming more goods and

[132] For an economic overview of this period, see R. Floud and P. Johnson, *The Cambridge Economic History of Modern Britain* iii. *Structural Change and Growth, 1939–2000* (Cambridge: Cambridge University Press, 2003).
[133] J. M. Keynes, *Essays in Persuasion* (Basingstoke and New York: Palgrave Macmillan, 2010).
[134] Ibid. 325–6.
[135] Ibid. 329; H. L. Officer and S. H. Williamson, *What was the UK GDP then?*, <http://www.measuringworth.com/ukgdp/>.

enjoying more leisure time, people would willingly choose to escape the drudgery of work. Indeed, his primary concern was not whether the leisure society would occur but what preparations governments should be making for its inevitable arrival. People would need something to occupy their newfound leisure time that could direct their energies fruitfully, so replacing work with some form of 'productive leisure' would be the main challenge for society in the future, providing leaderships with a new priority.

The expansion of the economy in the decades following the Second World War gave weight to Keynes's predictions. The trend throughout the century had been for a dramatic reduction in working hours. Prior to the First World War, employees in manufacturing and industry laboured for an average of nine or ten hours per day, six days per week, but by the 1960s the typical working week had declined to forty hours. The number of working days also fell, initially with the introduction of a week's annual leave in 1938, which rose to two weeks following the Second World War.[136] The fall in working hours was inversely proportional to earnings. Between 1950 and 1968 there was almost a tripling in both the average male earnings and hourly earnings. Even allowing for inflation, average weekly earnings for men rose by 56 per cent in the UK from £7.30 in 1950 to £22.53 in 1968 (at 2018 values, the equivalent of an increase from £246 per week to £390 per week).[137]

The lives of ordinary citizens improved steadily throughout the 1950s and 1960s as wages increased, while the establishment of a national electricity grid and increased access to consumer credit brought exciting new technology into the home.[138] The domestic electricity supply allowed houses to become filled with time-saving white goods acquired through hire-purchase agreements.[139] Together with the reduction in working hours, the introduction of labour-saving technology into the home led to increasing amounts of free time— more in fact than ever before in the modern era. The consumption of brown goods also increased. Invariably bought on the 'never-never', TVs, radios, and record players provided a raft of home entertainment possibilities. In turn, this expansion stimulated demand for content in the form of records, magazines, books, and other print and broadcast media.[140]

Although the introduction of this technology into the home undoubtedly improved the quality of life for most owners, it also led to the recurrence of a perennial historic dilemma. First posed by economist David Ricardo in 1817,

---

[136] *Holidays with Pay Act 1938*, <http://www.legislation.gov.uk/ukpga/Geo6/1-2/70/enacted>; Floud and Johnson, *The Cambridge Economic History of Modern Britain*, iii. 110.
[137] *Historical Mean Gross Weekly Earnings* (UK: Office of National Statistics, 2016), <www.ons.gov.uk/ons/about...i.../historical-mean-gross-weekly-earnings.xls>.
[138] Stearns, *Consumerism in World History*, 139–42.
[139] G. Hornsby, *The Secret Life of the National Grid* (London: BBC, 2010).   [140] Ibid.

it concerned 'the influence of machinery on the different classes of society' and most notably the 'opinion entertained by the labouring classes, that the employment of machinery is frequently detrimental to their interest'.[141] Despite all the domestic benefits, there were widespread panics during the 1960s about 'technological unemployment' as firms first began introducing computers and robots into the workplace. Many feared that jobs for skilled workers would soon disappear owing to widespread automation.[142]

Together with the scientific breakthroughs in industry, the emergence of consumer technology provided a platform for Leader of the Opposition Harold Wilson to map out a compelling, hi-tech future for the nation at the Labour Party's annual conference in 1963.[143] The speech, which was arguably the most memorable Wilson ever made, contributed to a long-running discussion about the role of science in public life. C. P. Snow had used his 1959 Rede Lecture to rail against technophobia, accusing the political class of being 'natural Luddites' ignorant of science and engineering and unfit to govern in a changing world.[144] Wilson espoused the same technological optimism as Keynes to align himself and his party with the scientists and cemented his reputation as a technocrat. Focusing on the implications of these scientific and technological changes for society as whole, Wilson discussed 'the Britain that is going to be forged in the white heat of this revolution'.[145]

Many future members of Wilson's cabinet shared their leader's view. One of them was Tony Benn, the Minister of Technology between 1966 and 1970. At this time Benn was particularly enamoured by the possibilities of nuclear energy and was a strong advocate for its benign use in the UK. In 1966, Benn was handed responsibility for the development of a civil nuclear programme. Although he later changed his mind, Benn initially felt that electricity produced by nuclear power was a clear case of 'beating swords into ploughshares'.[146] As a junior MP, he had completely bought into the 'atoms for peace' sentiment espoused by President Eisenhower in 1953 and the promises for the imminent emergence of nuclear fusion made by US Atomic Energy Commissioner Lewis L. Strauss. In a notable 1954 speech, Strauss had predicted boldly that

> our children will enjoy in their homes electrical energy too cheap to meter ... It is not too much to expect that our children will know of great periodic regional famines in the world only as matters of history, will travel effortlessly over the seas

---

[141] 'From not Working to Neural Networking', *The Economist Special Report on Artificial Intelligence*, 25 June 2016, pp. 4–7; D. Ricardo, *On the Principles of Political Economy and Taxation* (1817; London: Dover, 2004), 72.

[142] 'The Return of the Machinery Question', *The Economist*, 25 June 2016, p. 12.

[143] H. Wilson, *Labour's Plan for Science* (London: Labour Party, 1963).

[144] C. P. Snow, *The Two Cultures and the Scientific Revolution* (Cambridge: Cambridge University Press, 1960).

[145] Wilson, *Labour's Plan for Science*, 7.

[146] J. Adams, *Tony Benn* (London: Macmillan, 1992), 440–3.

and under them and through the air with a minimum of danger and at great speeds, and will experience a lifespan far longer than ours, as disease yields and man comes to understand what causes him to age.[147]

In this climate of rapid technological change, even the most remarkable achievements could be taken for granted. On 24 July 1969, an estimated global TV audience of 500 million people watched live pictures of Neil Armstrong as he became the first man to walk on the Moon.[148] In its July 1969 edition, *New Scientist* declared that, in view of what was shortly to come, the Apollo 11 Mission was itself merely a trifle, 'a matter of no greater moment than just peering into the high recesses of a trapeze act in the Big Top at a circus'.[149]

The same technological optimism could also be found within popular culture; for example, the 1968 MGM feature film *2001: A Space Odyssey* was a serious attempt to depict a plausible future on the big screen.[150] *2001* was the result of collaboration between author Arthur C. Clarke and film director Stanley Kubrick, and the most notable example of an emerging genre known as hard science fiction, which was characterized by an emphasis on scientific accuracy and technological detail. This was the first big-budget, science-fiction movie for several decades, and, with technical advice provided by Frederick Ordway III, an engineer at the Marshall Spaceflight Center, it was grounded in real science.[151] MGM's promotional literature made much of this, declaring confidently at the time that 'everything in *2001: A Space Odyssey* can happen within the next three decades, and ... most of the picture will happen by the beginning of the next millennium'.[152] Beyond all the hoopla, the film was to have a huge and enduring influence on depictions of interstellar life in popular culture.

These developments and the possibilities they suggested also inspired the counterculture. In 1970, Richard Neville (a co-editor of *Oz* magazine and one of the movement's leading figures in the UK) published *Play Power*, a collection of largely self-contained writings about the European underground scene in the late 1960s.[153] In the final section of the book entitled 'The Politics of Play' Neville maps out his own vision for a leisure society along with the opportunities for and barriers to its achievement. In many respects 'The Politics of Play' can be read as a response to some of the questions posed by

---

[147] D. Bodansky, *Nuclear Energy: Principles, Practices, and Prospects* (New York and London: Springer, 2004), 32.

[148] S. W. Carmichael, *Moon Men Return: USS Hornet and the Recovery of the Apollo 11 Astronauts* (Annapolis, MD: Naval Institute Press, 2010), 236.

[149] 'Journey to the Moon', *New Scientist*, 17 July 1969.

[150] S. Kubrick, *2001: A Space Odyssey* (Los Angeles: MGM, 1968).

[151] A. Johnson, *2001: The Lost Science* (London: Apogee, 2012).

[152] A. Castle, J. Harlan, and C. Kubrick, *The Stanley Kubrick Archives* (Cologne and London: Taschen, 2005).

[153] R. Neville, *Play Power* (London: Paladin, 1971).

Keynes and Galbraith. While Neville fully embraced both Keynes's technological optimism and belief that the leisure society was imminent, he totally
rejected his economic commitment to the provision of full employment.
Neville argued that full employment would become impossible to maintain,
as rapid growth, due to 'highly efficient' technological innovation, would lead
to a huge, irreversible increase in the number of unemployed. Instead, he
predicted with some certainty that by the end of the century work would
become completely automated: 'Most jobs can be eliminated. Who will build
the hospitals? Mr Digital Computer and his jolly gang of electric circuits and
cybernetic steam shovels.'[154]

Although Neville's situation analysis is similar to that of many on the left—
including several in the then incumbent Labour government—he drew
markedly different conclusions. To highlight these, he made an insightful
distinction between his own alternative left of the counterculture and the
new left of the mainstream. For Neville, the new left was about the right to
work and improving pay and conditions; in contrast, the alternative left
was driven by the right not to work at all. He argued that people needed
money rather than employment and that the state could and should provide everyone with a stipend so that work itself would become optional and
voluntary. In this workless society, people's new incentives would be pleasure, pride, and social responsibility rather than financial compensation.
Neville believed that, rather than leading to a shortfall in the number of
key support professionals—doctors, lawyers, teachers, et al.—their ranks
would actually be swelled by 'those released from uninspiring drudgery'.
Furthermore, although future technology would address all basic needs,
there would still be room for anyone who wanted to launch a 'custom-
built business' oriented towards a specialized market: 'But unless you want
to build a better mousetrap, it will be your duty to live off National
Assistance.'[155]

Despite the auspices, 1969 was arguably the year that this wave of technological optimism reached its peak. Britain at the end of the century was
undoubtedly a more affluent nation, but it was not a leisure society in the
shape that either Keynes or Neville had predicted. The decline in normal
working hours continued until 1980 but then levelled out, with overtime
rising throughout the 1980s and 1990s to an average of between three and
four hours a week. Wages increased significantly, and so did consumer spending. Ultimately Galbraith, who regarded projections of increased leisure
time as little more than a 'conventional conversation piece', proved closer to
the mark.[156] In their book *How Much Is Enough?* British economic historian

---

[154] Ibid. 221.   [155] Ibid. 207–11, 218–21.   [156] Ibid., p. 221.

Robert Skidelsky and philosopher Edward Skidelsky defined seven basic, universal goods that are fundamental to what they term 'the good life': health, security, respect, personality, harmony with nature, friendship, and leisure.[157] Following Galbraith, they concluded that, despite decades of increasing wages, people possessed no more of the basic goods at the end of the century than they had in the 1970s, and in some respects far fewer. Leisure—which they defined as not 'simply time off work, but free, non-purposeful activity'—experienced a change in nature.[158] Time away from work did not increase after 1990, and leisure became increasingly more passive; for example, participation in sport fell from 48 per cent to 43 per cent during the 1990s. Their conclusion was that 'Keynes's vision of middle-class culture spreading to the masses with the increase of leisure has not been realised'.[159] Although Skidelsky and Skidelsky's brief theoretical discussion of persuasion (conflated once more to 'advertising') engaged in no analysis of its methods and practices, they did recognize that it had a powerful effect on consumers ('inflam[ing] our tendency to insatiability') and also argued that there was a strong case for its restriction.[160]

Also following Galbraith, British economic historian Avner Offer put forward a comprehensive case for the need to manage the problems created by the affluent societies in *The Challenge of Affluence*.[161] Offer began with an iconoclastic dismantling of one of the sacred cows of free market economics—the notion that that freedom of choice, competition, and wealth creation are essential to increasing societal well-being. Offer contended that the opposite is true; that, in fact, 'affluence breeds impatience and impatience undermines well-being'.[162] Significantly, he also challenged the theory of the rational consumer.[163] This is one of the key assumptions underlying classical economics—namely, that individuals know what they want and seek to make the most of the available opportunities given the scarcity constraints they face. Drawing on research in the field of behavioural economics, Offer argued this ideal of how individual choice works was founded on 'contestable premises'.[164] Market order can be efficient and fair only if buyers and sellers reliably and consistently know what they want. However, in reality, people do not possess a set of unique, well-ordered preferences based on a full understanding of all available options. Nor do they have a thorough knowledge of themselves, their goals, and the strategies to achieve them. Not only does this mean that they do not behave as economists assume, but it also leaves them wide open to the influence of persuasion.[165]

Juliet Schor, a professor of sociology at Boston College, also recognized this condition and believed it had allowed consumers to become 'victims of [their]

[157] Skidelsky and Skidelsky, *How Much Is Enough?*, 146–67.   [158] Ibid. 174.   [159] Ibid. 179.
[160] Ibid. 208–11, 210.   [161] Offer, *The Challenge of Affluence*, 179.   [162] Ibid. 1, 15–38.
[163] Ibid. 69–70.   [164] Ibid. 270.   [165] Ibid. 103–38.

aspirations' and more demanding in terms of goals, rewards, experiences, and achievements.[166] Following Veblen, Becker, and Linder, Schor argued that in affluent societies spending becomes the vehicle through which people establish social position.[167] This conspicuous display of wealth and leisure is the market that reveals an individual's income to the outside world. Put simply, affluent people spend visibly to show everyone else how wealthy they are. At the end of the century this led to the work/life dilemma, as the workers who toiled longer hours than ever were also the consumers with an ever-lengthening list of things to buy. Galbraith had earlier proposed a complementary argument to this on the utility of labour.[168] He noted the increase in working hours but identified a paradox in which the word 'work' had come to describe an activity that was exhausting, dispiriting, and dull for some people but a source of prestige, pleasure, and enjoyment for others: 'But this is not all. Those who most enjoy work are all but universally the best paid. This is accepted. Low wages are for those in repetitive, tedious, painful toil. Those who least need compensation for their effort and could best survive without it are paid the most.'[169]

While the critics of affluence all agree that persuasion (all forms are conflated to 'advertising') is a major influence on aspirations, desires, and lifestyle choices, they too have very little to say about its practices. Interestingly, Offer concurred with Schor, Skidelsky and Skidelsky, and Galbraith that advertising is a major influence on aspirations, desires, and lifestyle choices but noted that, 'for all the resources at its command, advertising has little awareness of its own methods'.[170] He also quoted an unnamed speaker at a JWT seminar who said that 'communication is not an exact science and advertising is simply communication between people. Mass communication to be sure, but just people talking to people.'[171] Offer argued that, because people do not make rational choices, the legal attitude to advertising is misconceived owing to the fact that it applies a 'test of reason to claims that are designed to bypass the filter of reason'.[172] Galbraith and Skidelsky and Skidelsky went even further. They all identified the same problem—namely, why do people who seem to have everything always want even more? For Galbraith the answer is that 'advertising, and related activities, creates the wants it seeks to satisfy'.[173] Skidelsky and Skidelsky's more nuanced view of persuasion's function is slightly more specific: 'Advertising may not create

---

[166] Schor, *The Overworked American*, 23; Schor, *The Overspent American*.
[167] Veblen, *What Veblen Taught: Selected Writings of Thorsten Veblen*; Becker, 'A Theory of the Allocation of Time'; Linder, *The Harried Leisure Class*.
[168] J. K. Galbraith, *The Economics of Innocent Fraud: Truth for our Time* (Boston: Houghton Mifflin, 2004).
[169] Ibid. 18.   [170] Offer, *The Challenge of Affluence*, 115.   [171] Ibid.   [172] Ibid.
[173] Galbraith, *The Affluent Society*, 128.

insatiability, but it exploits it without scruple, whispering in our ear that our lives are drab and second-rate unless we consume "more".'[174] Both Galbraith and Skidelsky and Skidelsky called for curbs on advertising to rein in consumers, but they are woolly on what that means in practice and entirely unconvincing as to how such a policy might be effected.

These critics of affluence are from different academic backgrounds, writing at different times and in different tones, yet they share much in terms of issue identification, analysis, and conclusions. Their arguments, particularly in Offer's case, are comprehensive and compelling. Yet, despite the importance of the issues they raise, the historical literature on affluence forms a comparatively small body of information. To some extent the pre-eminence of free market economic theory explains the paucity of commentators in this field. The notion that raising levels of affluence was to the benefit of citizens enjoyed support across the political spectrum. It became the salient economic objective of successive governments throughout the post-war period and right up until the end of the century. Likewise, economic growth—another widely held political goal—was also perceived almost universally as a positive force and one that would increase the wealth of all people. However, as the critics of affluence point out, although successive governments had seen affluence as a mechanism for increasing well-being—both privately through increased consumption and publicly as a result of increased taxation revenues—they are neither the same thing, nor necessarily mutually compatible.

[174] Skidelsky and Skidelsky, *How Much Is Enough?*, 40.

2

Rational Appeal

Perspectives on Persuasion

How the Persuasion Industries Define and Present Themselves

The broad range of corporate communication disciplines delivered by the persuasion industries—marketing, advertising, branding, and public relations—are united by a single, common purpose: influencing the opinions and/or the behaviour of their target audience. For both practitioners and sector historians, the history of the persuasion industries in the period 1969–97 is one of rapid expansion and increasing professionalization. Unlike the historians of affluence, scholars in this field do segment the various practices that emerge (although timelines vary). In summary, the typical arc runs from ad hoc and often shadowy practices with nineteenth- or even eighteenth-century roots into fully formed, professional occupations by the late twentieth century.[1] During

---

[1] See, e.g., S. Anthony, *Public Relations and the Making of Modern Britain: Stephen Tallents and the Birth of a Progressive Media Profession* (Manchester: Manchester University Press, 2012); S. Delaney, *Get Smashed: The Story of the Men who Made the Adverts that Changed our Lives* (London: Sceptre, 2007); A. Fendley, *Commercial Break: The Inside Story of Saatchi & Saatchi* (London: Hamish Hamilton, 1995); W. Fletcher, *Powers of Persuasion: The Inside Story of British Advertising 1951–2000* (Oxford: Oxford University Press, 2008); J. E. Grunig, 'Public Relations Research: A Legacy of Scott Cutlip', *Public Relations Review*, 17/4 (1991), 357–76; P. Gurney, 'The Battle of the Consumer in Post-War Britain', *Journal of Modern History*, 77/4 (2005), 956–87; S. Hatfield, 'Hall of Fame: A (Very) Brief History of Advertising', *Campaign*, 20 December 1999; M. Hilton, *Consumerism in Twentieth-Century Britain: The Search for a Historical Movement* (Cambridge: Cambridge University Press, 2003); S. Majima, 'Affluence and the Dynamics of Spending in Britain, 1961–2004', *Contemporary British History*, 22/4 (2008), 573–97; R. Marchand, *Advertising the American Dream: Making Way for Modernity, 1920–1940* (Berkeley and Los Angeles: University of California Press, 2003); B. Martin, *Difficult Men: Behind the Scenes of a Creative Revolution: From the Sopranos and the Wire to Mad Men and Breaking Bad* (London: Penguin, 2013); M. P. McAllister and E. West, *The Routledge Companion to Advertising and Promotional Culture* (London: Routledge, 2014); M. Tungate, *Adland: A Global History of Advertising* (London: Kogan Page, 2007); R. Williams, 'Advertising: The Magic System', *Advertising & Society Review*, 1/1 (2000); R. Winer and S. Neslin (eds), *The History of Marketing Science* (Singapore: World Scientific NOW, 2014).

the post-war period each discipline was transformed, developing its own proto-cols and methodologies. Professional membership bodies were established that laid down working frameworks and codes of ethics in an attempt to standardize best practice. From the late 1960s, educational programmes and professional qualifications were introduced, and industry magazines, awards, and trade journals further legitimized the different occupations. Service provision frag-mented. During the final decades of the century, highly specialized agencies and consultancies emerged and were handling promotional activities on behalf of their clients on a global basis. Many of these agencies became international concerns themselves.

This narrative fits advertising and arguably branding much better than it does marketing and public relations. Marketing and public relations are harder to define. In the case of the former this is because there is overlap with other areas, most notably product development and economics as well as other forms of persuasion. For public relations the issue is a lack of transparency; public relations output is at best discreet but more often than not invisible. Despite the fact that public relations became one of the most influential and widely employed forms of persuasion in British society at the end of the twentieth century, there have been very few studies conducted on either its development or its impact. As Francis Ingham, CEO of industry body Public Relations Consultants Association (PRCA), said in 2011: 'For an industry which prides itself on its writing skills, it is obviously ironic that no readable history of the modern public relations consultancy exists.'[2]

Winston Fletcher was the most important UK sector historian. Fletcher was a practitioner himself, serving as president of the Institute of Practi-tioners in Advertising (IPA) and also as chairman of the Advertising Associ-ation. He wrote fourteen books on marketing and advertising including *Powers of Persuasion*. Published in 2008, it remains the most complete history of the British advertising industry. Fletcher's tone is occasionally irreverent but certainly more scholarly than the other extant histories or memoirs by former sector practitioners. These titles tend to be readable and racy but somewhat lacking in academic rigour. For example, Fallon, Delaney, Bell, and even Fletcher himself all present the history of British advertising as a series of turning points and landmark campaigns, performed mostly by great men.[3] Much supporting evidence is provided by anecdote. Although they are often entertaining, many of these tales are uncorroborated and fail to withstand cursory academic scrutiny. Yet—and perhaps this is a mark of the

---

[2] Jane Howard, *Evolution of UK PR Consultancies* (London: PRCA, 2010).
[3] I. Fallon, *The Brothers: The Rise and Rise of Saatchi & Saatchi* (London: Hutchinson, 1988); Fletcher, *Powers of Persuasion*; Delaney, *Get Smashed*; T. Bell, *Right or Wrong: The Memoirs of Lord Bell* (London: Bloomsbury, 2014).

sector—one can often find a dubious claim made in one text repeated as fact elsewhere.[4] Partly for that reason, as Nixon identifies, media historians and sociologists are usually broadly critical and suspicious of the sector's own literature, which can in turn lead them to be dismissive when it comes to considering persuasion's significance and effectiveness.[5] For example, Goldman and Papson argue that advertising presents consumers with an artificial image of themselves and their social relations and imbues the products with false meaning through the creation of promotional signs and symbols.[6] Their view is supported by Noam Chomsky, one of the persuasion industries' most ardent critics:

> Take a course in economics, they tell you a market is based on informed consumers making rational choices. Anyone who's ever looked at a TV ad knows that's not true . . . The goal [of advertising] is to undermine markets by creating uninformed consumers who will make irrational choices and the business world spends huge efforts on that.[7]

However, despite their criticism, media scholars—like the critics of affluence—say very little about the practices of the persuasion industries itself. In 1991, the sociologist Andrew Wernick coined the term 'promotional culture'.[8] In a detailed meta-analysis of advertising and marketing output (promotional texts), Wernick's *Promotional Culture* showed how persuasion, by spreading into more and more facets of everyday life, was having a fundamental impact on cultural formation, social interaction, and self-identity through the provision of social currency. Following Wernick, Aeron Davis offered one of the deepest historical analyses of the UK persuasion industries in *Promotional Cultures*, yet conceded that he could offer readers 'only brief introductions to the actual practices of these professions'.[9] Although this seems somewhat akin to writing a history of the motorcar with 'only brief introductions' to what is going on under the bonnet, Davis argued that the impact of the persuasion industries was considerable and recognized that the pervasive, promotional

---

[4] For one example, see the various discussions of Saatchi and Saatchi's 'Labour isn't working', a poster produced for the Conservative Party in 1978, in Fallon, *The Brothers*, 148–51; Fletcher, *Powers of Persuasion*, 158–63; Delaney, *Get Smashed*, 171–4; Bell, *Right or Wrong*, 52–61.

[5] S. Nixon, ' "Salesmen of the Will to Want": Advertising and its Critics in Britain 1951–1967', *Contemporary British History*, 24/2 (2010), 213–33.

[6] R. Goldman and S. Papson, *Nike Culture: The Sign of the Swoosh* (London: Sage, 1998); R. Goldman and S. Papson, 'Advertising in the Age of Hypersignification', *Theory, Culture and Society*, 11/3 (1994), 23–54; R. L. Goldman, *Reading Ads Socially* (London: Routledge, 1992).

[7] N. Chomsky, *Necessary Illusions: Thought Control in Democratic Societies* (London: Pluto, 1989); N. Chomsky, *The State–Corporate Complex: A Threat to Freedom and Survival* (Toronto: University of Toronto Press, 2011)—transcript of a speech given at the University of Toronto, 7 April 2011.

[8] A. Wernick, *Promotional Cultures: Advertising, Ideology and Symbolic Expression* (London: Sage, 1991); A. Davis, *Promotional Cultures: The Rise and Spread of Advertising, Public Relations, Marketing and Branding* (Cambridge: Polity, 2013), 1.

[9] Ibid., p. x.

culture found at the end of the twentieth century went far beyond their activities. A raft of other professions had adopted promotional practices—for example, lawyers, journalists, scientists, campaigners, company executives, and politicians.[10] Persuasion's influence had extended well beyond simply encouraging people to buy goods or services that they otherwise would not; it had become fundamental to shaping their world view of what was attractive or unattractive, good or bad, acceptable or unacceptable. In essence, it had changed human interaction itself.

Although Davis's presentation of promotional culture and its influence is compelling, his understanding of the persuasion industries themselves is rooted in the textbook rather than the field. His descriptions of how advertising and public relations work are anachronistic and misleading—for example, he makes the assertion that all successful advertising campaigns require a message, when in fact they do not.[11] There is also a common misunderstanding, not peculiar to Davis but throughout the literature, that the persuasion industries act in concert, share common interests, or are somehow working towards a common goal. I argue that not only is persuasion rarely ideological, but those within the persuasion industries are rarely working with each other and usually are working against each other. This goes beyond agencies promoting rival products or brands. The most successful campaigns are by their nature disruptive. Even within teams responsible for promoting the same product or brand, conflict is the normal state of affairs. This can lead to unexpected consequences.

Advertising Appeals and the Rational Consumer

The rational consumer is one of the key underpinning principles of neoclassical economics.[12] It is a model of decision-making, which states that individual consumers know what they want and make the most of the available options given the constraints of scarcity. The main assumption behind the rational consumer principle is that individuals have both preferences and constraints. The former define what they want to consume and the latter what

---

[10] Ibid. 3–5.   [11] Ibid. 38–9.

[12] Jan Callebaut, Hendrix Hendrickx, and Madeleine Janssens, *The Naked Consumer Today: Or an Overview of why Consumers Really buy Things, and what this Means for Marketing* (Antwerp: Censydiam, 2002), 66–8; D. J. Goodman and M. Cohen, *Consumer Culture: A Reference Handbook* (Santa Barbara, CA, and Oxford: ABC-CLIO, 2004), 30–1; R. E. Hall, *The Rational Consumer: Theory and Evidence* (Cambridge, MA: MIT Press, 1990), 30–1; C. V. Jansson-Boyd, *Consumer Psychology* (Maidenhead: Open University Press, 2010), 69; A. Offer, *The Challenge of Affluence: Self-Control and Wellbeing in the United States and Britain since 1950* (Oxford: Oxford University Press, 2007), 252–4; E. Silberberg and W. C. Suen, *The Structure of Economics: A Mathematical Analysis* (Boston: Irwin/McGraw-Hill, 2000), 252–4; Eyal Zamir and Doron Teichman (eds), *The Oxford Handbook of Behavioral Economics and the Law* (Oxford: Oxford University Press, 2014), 471–5.

they can actually consume—for example, a female consumer might want to purchase a brand new, two-seater, prestige sports car, but her choice is mitigated because she needs a vehicle capable of transporting her family and can afford to spend only £15,000. In this instance, she will choose a car that goes furthest to meeting her preference within those constraints. Economists also use the term 'utility' to describe the level of satisfaction that consumers will derive from the goods or services they procure. Rational consumers will, therefore, choose between different goods and services so as to optimize the amount of satisfaction or 'total utility'.[13]

The notion of a rational consumer is simplistic but useful. Its effects seem to be reflected in reality, and it also appeals to common sense: presented with a suite of options, who would not choose the best for themselves given their own preferences and constraints? The theory was refined throughout the twentieth century, and the rationality implied was eventually narrowed down to just the authorization behind the consistent ranking of choices on offer.[14] For most of the twentieth century the marketing activity of companies seeking to increase the consumption of their products or services was based on appeals to rational consumers. Brand communication, usually through advertising, involved associating a product with particular qualities in the minds of the target audience, which would persuade them to choose it ahead of its competitors.

The major economists of the nineteenth century paid little heed to advertising, but neither did most large commercial concerns.[15] It was the technological innovations associated with mass production and distribution at the turn of the twentieth century that created an environment for large-scale marketing activities to flourish. Advertising agencies grew quickly to exploit this opportunity.[16] J. Walter Thompson (JWT) became the first international advertising agency with the opening of its London office in 1899. From this point advertising continued to expand rapidly in terms of scale and influence, which finally made it the object of academic interest following the Second World War. Economic analysis then proceeded at a furious pace, producing a substantial literature.[17] Scholars were able to draw on an increasingly broad range of economic, sociological,

---

[13] W. J. Baumol, A. S. Blinder, and C. Swan, *Economics Principles and Policy* (New York: Harcourt Brace Jovanovich, 1979), 98.

[14] T. Grüne-Yanoff, 'Paradoxes of Rational Choice Theory', in S. Roeser, R. Hillerbrand, P. Sandin, and M. Peterson (eds) *Handbook of Risk Theory: Epistemology, Decision Theory, Ethics, and Social Implications of Risk* (Dordrecht and London: Springer, 2012), 499–516.

[15] K. Bagwell, 'The Economic Analysis of Advertising', Discussion Paper No. 0506–01, Department of Economics, Columbia University, New York, 2005.

[16] History of Advertising Trust (HAT), J. Walter Thompson (JWT), London, Advertising Agency, Account Files and Other Office Papers, 1983.

[17] Bagwell, 'The Economic Analysis of Advertising'.

and psychological research, and by the early 1960s the relatively straightforward processes of persuasion had become more formally articulated as advertising theory.[18] Two schools of thought emerged. The dominant view, at least among its critics, was that advertising was persuasive, altering consumers' tastes and stimulating demand for products through differentiation (which may or may not be spurious) with the aim of creating brand loyalty, rather than in ways grounded on the product or service itself. This approach implied, as Galbraith pointed out, that advertising had no real value to consumers and was focused on the assuagement of wants that were themselves artificial. In this context, advertising could also be regarded as anti-competitive; because it was concentrated on markets characterized by high profits and prices, it provided an effective, expensive barrier to entry into those markets.[19]

The second view emerged under the auspices of the so-called Chicago School during the 1960s.[20] It argued that many markets suffered from imperfect consumer information, which makes the process of investigation onerous and deterred consumers from learning of a product's existence let alone its price or quality. Advertising provided consumers with low-cost information about these products and markets. It was imperfections within markets themselves that lead to inefficiencies, not the advertising itself: if consumers did not know about better products, how could they buy them? Advertisers were deemed to be providing a service by letting consumers know about their products, thereby minimizing their research costs. Here the inference runs counter to the persuasion school: advertising not only promoted competition among established products and services; it also facilitated market entry for new lines.[21]

During the 1970s, a final view surfaced that was also associated with the Chicago School. It held that advertising was complementary to a product or service and need not provide any information at all.[22] For example, advertising a brand of coffee might help it appeal to consumers who value social prestige by associating the brand with an aspirational, affluent lifestyle. There

---

[18] McGuire, 'An Information Processing Model of Advertising Effectiveness', in H. L. Davis and A. J. Silk (eds), *Behavioral and Management Science in Marketing* (New York and Chichester: Wiley, 1978), 156–80.

[19] See N. Kaldor, 'The Economic Aspects of Advertising', *Review of Economic Studies*, 18/1 (1950), 1–27; and also E. H. Chamberlin, *The Theory of Monopolistic Competition: A Re-Orientation of the Theory of Value* (Cambridge, MA: Harvard University Press, 1962); A. Marshall and C. W. Guillebaud, *Principles of Economics* (9th Variorum Edition; London: Macmillan for the Royal Economic Society, 1961).

[20] See, e.g., T. W. Adorno and M. Horkheimer, *Dialectic of Enlightenment* (1997; London: Verso, 1999).

[21] G. J. Stigler, *The Theory of Price* (New York: Macmillan, 1977).

[22] G. J. Stigler and G. S. Becker, 'De Gustibus Non Est Disputandum', *American Economic Review*, 67/2 (1977), 76–90.

would be no need to provide any actual information about what the coffee tastes like or why they might prefer it to a different brand in order to achieve this.[23]

Economists continue to debate which of these views is correct, but this study does not seek to contribute directly to that discussion. It is not my intention to imply that one of these analyses is necessarily more valid that any of the others. For the purposes of this investigation it is simply important to note that all advertising will fall into one or more of these three categories (which of the three is dependent upon the product or service being advertised, the target audience, and the medium or channel being used for communication).

It must also be remembered that marketing activity is often created and executed by a raft of third providers—such as advertising agencies, PR specialists, graphic designers, media buyers—rather than by companies themselves. Brand communication activity is created in response to a brief from the client and is never executed by any of these service providers without the client's consent and approval. Whether the process of client approval is a conduit or barrier to success is a moot point. It is probably one or the other on occasion—for every brilliant idea that has been watered down by the client there is another hare-brained idea that failed to pass muster. However, it is a system that does not necessarily promote risk-taking or even success in itself. The primary concern of the third-party agency may also vary from time to time—for example, if fearful of losing an account, it may seek to second-guess the desires of the clients rather than search for an optimum solution by taking them outside their comfort zone or by radically challenging the brief. These issues are key considerations that drove the development of the persuasion industries throughout the period. Charles Saatchi was the founder of Saatchi & Saatchi, which became the biggest advertising agency in the world during the 1980s. He began his career as a copywriter at Collett Dickenson Pearce (CDP) but left, along with business partner Ross Cramer, in 1967 to establish their own creative ideas consultancy, CramerSaatchi. Following the departure of Cramer in 1970, he founded Saatchi & Saatchi, a full-service advertising agency, with his younger brother Maurice. The pair remained two of the sector's leading figures into the twenty-first century. Saatchi identified client satisfaction as the primary corporate objective, not just for his own firm but for all successful advertising agencies: 'We were maniacally driven to impress our clientele, and if all other businesses cared as much about providing

---

[23] R. Vaughn, 'How Advertising Works: A Planning Model', *Journal of Advertising Research*, 20/5 (1980), 27–33.

satisfaction as ad agencies, we would have no need for automated customer service helplines everywhere.'[24]

Within the sector literature ideological discussions rarely if ever take place. Critics of persuasion such as Chomsky, Williams, and Herman see it as inherently ideological: a bulwark of capitalism and neo-liberalism.[25] However, while there is much to support their arguments, they do presume a false homogeneity and give the impression of a sectorial coherence that is not present in reality. They also vastly underestimate the pragmatism within the industry itself. At a macro-economic level the persuasion industries are undoubtedly in favour of capitalism and a market economy, but at a micro-level many of the people and companies carrying out brand communication are often not ideologically driven at all. By way of illustration, Tim Bell notes that he was the only Conservative Party supporter employed at Saatchi & Saatchi when the company began work on its account in 1978.[26] The apparent world view of those working within the sector is typically pragmatic, some might say cynical, and often incumbent entirely on the entity being promoted—for example, during the 1970s Saatchi & Saatchi produced a series of award-winning, anti-smoking advertisements for the Health Education Council despite several members of the account team being heavy smokers themselves. Upon losing the account in 1983, the agency began almost immediately working for Silk Cut, its first cigarette client and for whom it also produced a series of award-winning advertisements.[27] The commitment, especially within the creative teams, was often to the process alone and nothing else.[28]

This does not mean that its practitioners were ungoverned by principles, rules, or processes in the choices they made about what to promote, the development of methodology, or the execution of their ideas. By the early 1960s two ostensibly competing approaches had emerged, both of which purported to guarantee the production of effective advertising campaigns. Sometimes rather grandly referred to as theories or even philosophies, both approaches were simply a distillation of features found to be common to successful campaigns of the past, but together they provided the template for the majority of advertisements produced over the following decade and into the late 1970s. Both approaches viewed brand communication as a

---

[24] G. Monkman, *Life Lessons from Charles Saatchi* (2013), <http://www.adnews.com.au/news/life-lessons-from-charles-saatchi>.

[25] Chomsky, *Necessary Illusions*; Williams, 'Advertising: The magic system'; E. S. Herman, *Manufacturing Consent: The Political Economy of the Mass Media* (London: Bodley Head, 2008).

[26] Bell, *Right or Wrong*, 41–3.   [27] Fallon, *The Brothers*, 84–5.

[28] See D. Ogilvy, *Confessions of an Advertising Man* (London: Southbank, 2004), and also R. Reeves, *Reality in Advertising* (London: Macgibbon & Kee, 1961); R. Reeves, *Reality in Advertising* (London: Macgibbon & Kee, 1961). Both Reeves and Ogilvy are extremely critical of creatives who think only about 'their art' rather than 'the art of selling'.

simple and entirely linear process that could be adequately explained by the acronym AIDA. It was believed that marketing activity succeeded by creating Awareness, provoking Interest, and in turn awakening Desire, which ultimately resulted in an Action.[29] In the behavioural approach—the more important of the two, sometimes referred to as 'the hard sell'—the development of advertising was rooted in the ideas of behavioural psychology.[30] It held that properly executed campaigns could produce a conditioned response—namely, a change in attitude or purchasing behaviour. The consumer was seen as rational but passive, so a great deal of repetition was required for the advertising message—or selling proposition—to achieve the desired effect. The behavioural approach was most notably adopted by the Ted Bates agency. In 1961 Rosser Reeves, who was a senior executive at the company, wrote *Reality in Advertising*. This was the clearest distillation of Bates's pioneering take on the behavioural approach developed during the 1940s and 1950s, at the heart of which was the unique selling proposition (USP). Reeves's conviction was that the purpose of advertising was to sell products: nothing more nor less. Advertisements were not a showcase for the cleverness of the copywriter or the aesthetics of the art department. The USP was the key to producing effective advertising. The process began with an 'interrogation of the product' to discover any attributes that could be claimed as unique. These could be genuine differences between the product and its competitors or even shared characteristics that could be claimed because no one else was promoting them. One of these identified attributes would be chosen to give the product 'pulling power' and turned into a proposition unique to the product. For example, a brand of soap powder might contain a unique enzyme that is particularly effective at removing stains from white clothing and bedding. Its unique proposition could be that it 'washes whiter' than other soap powders. This winning USP would be turned into a message that could be used in all advertising and hammered home to consumers through a process of repetition.[31]

The USP proved a successful long-term strategy for many products—for example, Persil's 'Persil washes whiter'; Anadin/Anacin's 'Relieves pain fast'; M&Ms 'Melt in the mouth not in the hand'; and Colgate's 'Cleans your breath while it cleans your teeth'.[32] It was adopted wholesale by many leading agencies and upon its publication *Reality in Advertising* won plaudits from

---

[29] See, e.g., Fletcher, *Powers of Persuasion*, 57–61, and W. Fletcher, 'Those Wonderful Folks Revisited', *Campaign*, 13 December 1974, pp. 24–6.
[30] Reeves, *Reality in Advertising*.   [31] Ibid.
[32] *Superbrands Case Studies: Anadin/Anacin*, <http://www.campaignlive.co.uk/article/776370/superbrands-case-studies-anadin?src_site=brandrepublic>; *The Story of M&M's Brand*, <http://us.mms.com/us/about/history/story/>; *Colgate: Our Company History*, <http://www.colgate.com/app/Colgate/US/Corp/History/1806.cvsp>.

several leading industry figures.[33] Yet, despite its widespread use, the USP had some notable shortcomings, not least that it was very much a hard sell. Consumers often complained that adverts based on a USP were annoying, boring, or irritating (although that did not necessarily stop them from buying the products). It was also, as Fletcher points out, reliant on the (frequent) articulation of the USP, and some propositions may not be easily put into words. The USP worked best of all for the sorts of fast-moving consumer goods (FMCG) that were consistent or changed little over a long period of time. For categories where turnover of products was much higher—for example, electrical goods, cars, and apparel—the USP worked less well, because it was the changes in these products that needed to be advertised.[34] However, none of these drawbacks prevented many advertising agencies from searching for a USP in inappropriate product categories during the 1960s. There were also issues with Reeves's process for identifying a USP, which, despite his own claims to the contrary, was not particularly empirical. The concept of the USP was easily misunderstood and often inexpertly applied, producing advertisements that were ineffective. However, despite these shortcomings, it remained the leading advertising strategy well into the 1970s. Reeve's protestations that *Reality in Advertising* was not 'a theory derived in terms of itself', but rather a pattern 'sifted out from thousands of campaigns and from accumulated masses of data', served only to highlight not just his own book's major shortcoming but one common to almost all advertising manuals.[35] At their best, advertising manuals can be very good in their analysis of existing campaigns, using hindsight to identify successful trends, elements, and features. However, they are generally far less convincing when it comes to extrapolating what will work in the future.

The second approach to advertising was a rather loose set of ideas derived from the psychodynamic school that became characterized as 'the soft sell'. It was developed by David Ogilvy, who, like Reeves, was also an advertising executive.[36] Ogilvy was the founder of the Ogilvy & Mather agency, and like Reeves (who was in fact at one time his brother-in-law) he believed that the function of advertising was to sell. Where Ogilvy differed was in his view that information about the consumer (rather than about the product) was of

---

[33] For example, the following are some of the reviews of the 1961 edition printed inside the jacket: 'By far the best book on advertising I have ever read. Like radar, Rosser Reeves penetrates the advertising fog' (Gerard Lambert Warner-Lambert Pharmaceutical); 'It was inevitable that someone, some day, would write the definitive book on advertising. Rosser Reeves has done it' (Alfred Politz, Alfred Politz Research Inc.); 'Rosser Reeves has broken new ground in advertising theory. This book will change advertising' (Oscar Lublow, President, Daniel Starch & Staff, Inc.); 'A great polemic—of equal importance to Claude Hopkins's historic book. I shall order 400 copies—one for every officer and employee and one for each of our clients' (David Ogilvy, President, Ogilvy, Benson and Mather).

[34] Fletcher, *Powers of Persuasion*, 68–9.   [35] Reeves, *Reality in Advertising*, 44, 45.

[36] Ogilvy, *Confessions of an Advertising Man*.

paramount importance. He also felt that consumers should be credited with some intelligence and would respond much more favourably to 'brand stories' rather than hectoring propositions repeated ad infinitum. Instead of a proposition, Ogilvy argued that building a story behind the brand could help it appeal to consumers. In comparison to that of Reeves, Ogilvy's output was subtle and appeared more sophisticated. It was focused on the creation of an appealing image rather than simply pushing a message. His notable successes included long-running campaigns for Rolls Royce: 'At 60 miles an hour the loudest noise in this new Rolls Royce comes from the electric clock'; Dove: 'Creams your skin while you wash'; and Schweppes: 'The man from Schweppes is here.'[37]

Ogilvy and Reeves are typically presented as fierce rivals: the figureheads of two competing strategies, creativity versus effectiveness.[38] Yet much of this supposed rivalry was self-serving, generating column inches and profile for both executives and their agencies. There is evidence that, if the men were not exactly lifelong friends, relations between them were rarely less than cordial, and the mutual admiration was genuine. For all the bluster, there is actually very little difference between the two strategies and certainly much less than has been previously argued.[39] Haygood's analysis of the men's private archives revealed that Ogilvy and Reeves both felt they shared similar guiding principles.[40] He highlighted that both men were influenced by advertising pioneer Claude Hopkins and media researcher Alfred Politz. They also exchanged ideas. In 1949 Ogilvy sent a personal memo to Reeves in which he referred to a BSP or 'basic selling proposition', which he felt should be 'the heart and guts of every ad'.[41] Indeed, Ogilvy's own soft sell can be viewed as nothing more than a plea for the subtle execution of the USP. Is 'Creams your skin while you wash' really so very different from 'Cleans your breathe while it cleans your teeth'? As Haygood concluded: 'The hard sell and soft sell dynamic was, in large part, a media construction.'[42] Behind the rivalry played out for the benefit of the media there is very little to support the view that these were competing philosophies. It is more useful to think as Ogilvy and Reeves with their hard and soft sells as two sides of the same coin; at most they were different styles underpinned by the same rationale.

Even as late as the mid-1970s, the influence of both Reeves and Ogilvy remained considerable. The hard and soft sells appealed strongly to an industry that was quasi-scientific, producing advertising that was narrow in both scope and target audience. They were also easy for the client to understand.

---

[37] Ibid. 112, 123.   [38] See, e.g., Fletcher, *Powers of Persuasion*, 64–74.   [39] Ibid.
[40] D. M. Haygood, '"Hard Sell or Soft Sell?" The Advertising Philosophies and Professional Relationship of Rosser Reeves and David Ogilvy', *American Journalism*, 33/2 (2016), 169–88.
[41] Ibid. 186.   [42] Ibid. 188.

At this time the public face of advertising agencies was maintained by suited account executives, responsible for managing relationships with clients who were businessmen first and foremost. Client–agency relationships were usually chummy and long term, with meetings typically conducted informally on the golf course or over dinner. The key internal roles within the agency were the researchers and strategists, who could be called upon occasionally to meet the client if it was deemed appropriate. The creative department—consisting of the writers and artists who actually put together the advertisements—was kept largely out of sight. Agencies would rely on research to 'prove' to clients that a particular creative execution provided the optimum solution and wherever possible would demonstrate a strong statistical link between marketing expenditure and sales. The clients themselves were happy to be reassured by 'scientific proof' that their spending—on what many still regarded as a rather vulgar requirement of enterprise—was delivering a return. Advertising was ultimately all about increasing sales, with very little attention paid to objectives such as changing consumer perceptions or building a brand. Clients and agencies were in it together for the long term and accounts rarely changed hands. This inertia was reflected in the first league table of agencies, published by *Campaign* in 1969, which was dominated by the long-established, satellite offices of huge American firms (see Table 2.1). Advertising itself was overwhelmingly targeted at housewives, as clients on the whole looked to their agencies to

Table 2.1. Top 19 UK advertising agencies, 1968

Rank	Agency	Billings (£m)	Billings (£m, 2018 values)
1	J. Walter Thompson	20.19	331.69
2	Marius Wynne-Williams	18.97	318.42
3	Ogilvy and Mather	12.51	209.98
4	Young and Rubicam	10.41	174.73
5	SH Benson	9.80	164.49
6	Hobson Bates	9.00	151.07
7	London Press Exchange	8.97	150.56
8	Lintas	8.71	146.21
9	Dorland	7.10	119.18
10	Erwin Wasey	6.53	109.61
11	Collett Dickenson Pearce	5.90	99.03
12	Pritchard Wood	5.69	95.51
13	Foot Cone and Belding	5.50	92.32
14	McCann-Erickson	5.50	92.32
15	Horniblow Cox-Freeman	4.10	68.82
16	Garland-Compton	4.00	67.14
17	Benton and Bowles	3.50	58.74
18	Lonsdale Crowther	3.30	55.39
19	Colman Prentis and Varley	3.10	52.04

Sources: Figures for agencies one to ten from Legion Publishing (*Campaign*, 14 February 1969); Pritchard Wood figure from Haymarket Publishing (*Campaign*, 15 September 1989); remaining figures from MEAL (*Campaign*, 6 February 1970).

help sell packaged food, toiletries, cosmetics, beverages, and other household goods (see Tables 2.1–2.3).[43]

Together this combination of narrow objectives, cod philosophy, and cosy relationships resulted in advertising that changed very little throughout the 1950s or 1960s. USPs were driven home with slogans, characters, and jingles. The social and cultural changes in Britain during the late-1960s were to upset this equilibrium. Harold Wilson, with his northern accent, pipe, and Gannex raincoat, cut a far more personable, down-to-earth figure than either the departing Alec Douglas-Home or his more imposing predecessor Harold

Table 2.2. Top 20 UK advertisers, 1968

Rank	Company	Ad spend (£m)	Ad spend (£m,2018 values)
1	Lever Brothers	5.87	101.52
2	Proctor and Gamble	5.40	93.39
3	Mars	3.96	68.49
4	Cadbury Bros	3.86	66.76
5	Pet foods	3.84	66.41
6	Gallagher	3.76	65.03
7	Van den Berghs	3.45	59.67
8	WD and HO Willios	3.27	56.55
9	Rowntree	2.94	50.85
10	Kellogg Co. of Great Britain	2.62	45.31
11	H. J. Heinz	2.59	44.79
12	John Player and Sons	2.14	37.01
13	Colgate Palmolive	2.02	34.93
14	Beecham Proprietary Medicines	2.006	34.69
15	Shell Mex and BP	2.005	34.68
16	IPC Magazines	1.96	33.90
17	Birds Eye Foods	1.94	33.55
18	British Leyland	1.69	29.23
19	National Dairy Council	1.68	29.05
20	John Mackintosh	1.66	28.71

Source: *Campaign*, 15 September 1989.

Table 2.3. UK television advertising by product sector, 1970

Rank	Product sector	% of total
1	Food	38.5
2	Household products	14.7
3	Beverages	9.1
4	Toiletries and cosmetics	7.4
5	Household appliances	3.4
6	Publishing	3.3
Total		76.4

Source: World Advertising Research Centre (WARC).

[43] Delaney, *Get Smashed*, 18–21; W. Fletcher, 'Those Wonderful Folks Revisited', *Campaign*, 13 December 1974; Fletcher, *Powers of Persuasion*, 54–7.

Macmillan. In a more egalitarian climate, young people had more disposable income and were spending more money than ever before. For the first time mass-market, popular culture—music, art, fashion, film, and theatre—was being produced by the working classes, for the working classes, creating new kinds of consumers and a new kind of consumption.[44]

Expansion and Specialization

Scholars generally concur that the spectacular growth of both the persuasion industries and the retail sector during the 1980s and 1990s was a consequence of the increasingly consumer-oriented nature of society. However, as an explanation of persuasion's success, this analysis only goes so far. Clearly there was an increased opportunity for persuasion during this period, and consumer confidence and optimism remained high. However, it is difficult to imagine that the simplistic techniques and strategies of brand communication in the early 1970s would have been capable of delivering the promotional culture identified by Wernick—namely, culture that is 'saturated in the medium of promotion'.[45]

Following Wernick, Davis argued that throughout this period the influence of persuasion extended more and more deeply into society to such an extent that by the mid-1990s 'no object could be separated from the promotion of itself and all of the objects linked to it through communications ... connected by an endless chain of mutual reference and implication'.[46] Individual consumers became absorbed into this promotional culture. Bourdieu first used the term 'cultural intermediaries', which Davies adapted to 'promotional intermediaries' to describe people employed in occupations involving presentation and representation, and 'in all the institutions providing symbolic goods and services ... and in cultural production and organisation'.[47] Through this process, wide sections of society became engaged in, immersed in, and ultimately defined by promotional culture.

Davis built a convincing case (as did Wernick before him). However, what is lacking not just from Davis but from all the histories is a satisfactory explanation to the question—how did this happen? How did public relations, a cottage industry—barely an afterthought in marketing campaigns prior to 1980—become such a driving social force during the 1990s? How did it come to shape tastes and form and harden opinions to such an

---

[44] See T. Fisher, 'The Sixties: A Cultural Revolution in Britain', *Contemporary Record*, 3 (1989), 22–3; A. Marwick, *The Sixties: Cultural Revolution in Britain, France, Italy, and the United States, c.1958–c.1974* (London: Bloomsbury, 2012).

[45] Wernick, *Promotional Culture*, 2.   [46] Davis, *Promotional Cultures*, 2.

[47] P. Bourdieu, *Distinction: A Social Critique of the Judgement of Taste* (Cambridge, MA: Harvard University Press, 1984), 359.

extent that it was steering and guiding political leaders? How did branding—little more than a byword for packaging during the 1970s—become a suite of empathetic, nebulous, yet hugely persuasive and pervasive lifestyle choices? And how did advertising—the sometimes humorous vignettes pushing FMCG products that appeared between articles and TV programmes and on billboards during the early 1970s—establish itself in the vanguard of British society by the mid-1980s to such an extent that it was actually dictating popular culture rather than simply reflecting it?

Both Fletcher and Delaney identify the 1980s and 1990s as two periods of rapid growth for the advertising industry, punctuated by a recession at the turn of the decade. At a corporate level this expansion resulted in an overarching consolidation, with companies achieving scale through the acquisition of their competitors. Beneath this conglomeration, and particularly within small and medium-sized enterprises, increasing specialization was taking place. For both historians, the issue is primarily whether or not this consolidation was a benefit to the industry and its practitioners.[48] Growth during this period for the public relations sector was even more explosive. Neither Miller and Dinan nor L'Etang are concerned with general questions of the public relations' commercial success. Nor do they discuss the development of its methodologies, strategies, and tactics. L'Etang's primary interest is in how public relations' rapid expansion contributed to its failure to professionalize. Miller and Dinan seek to quantify the determinate political and historical reasons rather than functional developments or the pervasive commercial rationale behind public relations' rise.[49]

Across the board, expenditure on persuasion increased dramatically throughout the period (see Tables 2.4–2.9). At 2018 values, there was a twenty-three-fold increase in advertising expenditure between 1969 and 1997, with the biggest rises occurring either side of the 1990–3 recession (although, as a percentage of GNP, advertising peaked in 1989, the UK economy grew much more rapidly during the 1980s and 1990s than it had done in the previous decade). The proliferation of media channels lowered entry costs and encouraged large numbers of new advertisers into the market. As a consequence, the shape of British advertising changed. One result of this propagation of consumer culture from 1990 onwards was that the companies now spending the most on advertising were no longer FMCG brands but retailers. In 1968 not one of the Top 20 advertisers was a retailer. However, by 1990 the sector represented seven of the Top 10 spending brands (see Tables 2.4 and 2.5).

---

[48] Fletcher, *Powers of Persuasion*, 245–54; Delaney, *Get Smashed*, 203–12.
[49] J. L'Etang, *Public Relations in Britain: A History of Professional Practice in the 20th Century* (Mahwah, NJ, and London: L. Erlbaum, 2004), 228–9; D. Miller and W. Dinan, 'The Rise of the PR Industry in Britain, 1979–98', *European Journal of Communication*, 15/1 (2000), 27–8.

The burgeoning demand for marketing services and low start-up costs created a steady stream of new agencies. This led to the specialization identified by both Fletcher and Delaney. Creative production became separated from media buying. Boutique shops began to open specializing in a single service, either outsourcing the other or leaving clients to make their own arrangements. Throughout the late 1980s and 1990s further specializations occurred with the establishment of a large number of agencies focusing on a single discipline, such as graphic design, branding, internal communication, trade marketing, in-store marketing, direct marketing, and planning. Clients were in theory able to cherry pick the most capable providers in each discipline.

The expansion in demand for public relations was no less profound. Although the headline spend on public relations consultancies is lower than

Table 2.4. Total UK advertising expenditure as a percentage of GDP, 1989–1997

Year	Expenditure (£m, at 2018 values)	Percentage of GDP (at market values)
1976	1,590	0.95
1978	2,468	1.10
1980	3,438	1.12
1982	4,239	1.15
1984	5,530	1.29
1986	7,035	1.38
1988	9,367	1.50
1989	10,407	1.53
1990	10,490	1.44
1991	10,082	1.33
1993	10,868	1.30
1995	12,999	1.41
1997	15,440	1.44

Source: WARC.

Table 2.5. Top 10 UK advertisers, 1990

Rank	Company	Advertising spend (£m)	Advertising spend (£m, 2018 values)
1	Tesco	26.31	62.32
2	McDonald's	16.93	40.10
3	Woolworths	16.33	38.68
4	ASDA	14.57	34.51
5	Benson & Hedges	14.32	33.92
6	B&Q	14.01	33.19
7	British Satellite Broadcasting	13.78	32.64
8	Whiskas	12.77	30.25
9	MFI Stores	12.75	30.20
10	Texas Home Care	12.53	29.68

Source: WARC.

Table 2.6. Top 20 UK public relations consultancies, 1989

Rank	Company	Billings (£)	Billings (£m, 2018 values)
1	Shandwick	21,687,000	55.4
2	Corporate Communications	11,334,041	28.9
3	Burson-Marsteller	9,306,000	23.7
4	Dewe Rogerson	8,664,100	22.1
5	The Grayling Group	8,501,300	21.7
6	Hill and Knowlton	7,746,000	19.8
7	Valin Pollen	7,068,000	18.0
8	Paragon Communications	6,291,000	16.1
9	Countrywide Communications	5,760,600	14.7
10	Granard Rowland Comm	4,703,719	12.0
11	Broad Street Group	4,568,133	11.6
12	Burston-Marsteller	4,507,601	11.5
13	Daniel J Edelman	4,497,400	11.5
14	Biss Lancaster	4,345,657	11.1
15	Counsel Group	4,090,000	10.4
16	CGI Sterling	2,978,367	7.6
17	Citigate Comms Group	2,714,862	6.9
18	PRP	2,608,546	6.6
19	Infopress	2,383,552	6.1
20	Hall Harrison Cowley	2,348,000	6.0

Source: 'Special Report', *PR Week*, 24 May 1990.

Table 2.7. Top 20 UK public relations consultancies, 1997

Rank	Company	Billings (£)	Billings (£m, 2018 values)
1	Shandwick UK	25,384,000	45.3
2	Bell Pottinger Communications	23,639,000	42.2
3	Hill and Knowlton	18,753,000	33.5
4	Countrywide Porter Novelli	17,039,032	30.4
5	Dewe Rogerson	13,062,365	23.3
6	Incepta Group (Citigate)	11,433,494	20.4
7	Weber PR Worldwide	10,417,177	18.6
8	Euro RSCG International Comms	8,146,841	14.6
9	Edelman PR Worldwide	7,127,300	12.7
10	The Grayling Group	6,940,700	12.4
11	Charles Barker BMSG	6,840,850	12.2
12	Medical Action Communications	6,530,000	11.7
13	Text 100	6,182,486	11.0
14	Scope Ketchum Communications	5,673,476	10.2
15	Freud Communications	5,504,383	9.8
16	GCI Communications	5,109,100	9.1
17	College Hill Associates	4,647,827	8.3
18	Fishburn Hedges	4,542,006	8.1
19	Harvard PR	4,314,000	7.7
20	Key Communications	4,263,100	7.6

Source: 'Special Report', *PR Week*, 24 April 1998.

Table 2.8. Top 20 UK advertising agencies, 1980

Rank	Company	Billings (£m)	Billings (£m, 2018 values)
1	Saatchi and Saatchi	83.00	400.3
1	J. Walter Thompson	83.00	400.3
3	D'Arcy-MacManus and Masius	75.00	361.7
3	McCann-Erickson	75.00	361.7
5	Ogilvy Benson and Mather	61.20	295.1
6	Collett Dickenson Pearce	60.89	293.7
7	Young and Rubicam	46.41	223.8
8	Foote Cone and Belding	45.22	218.1
9	Ted Bates	39.64	191.2
10	Allen Brady and Marsh	39.12	188.7
11	Dorland Advertising	38.00	183.3
12	Leo Burnett	37.50	180.9
13	Wasey Campbell-Ewald	35.20	169.8
14	Boase Massimi Pollitt	32.20	155.3
14	Lintas	32.20	155.3
16	Benton and Bowles	28.23	136.2
17	Davidson Pearce	28.00	135.0
18	Doyle Dane Bernbach	27.05	130.5
19	Geers Gross	24.00	115.8
20	Grey Advertising	22.10	106.6

Source: *Campaign*, 2 January 1981.

Table 2.9. Top 20 UK advertising agencies, 1987

Rank	Company	Billings (£m)	Billings (£m, 2018 values)
1	Abbot Mead Vicars	355.86	937
1	Ogilvy & Mather	271.08	757
3	Saatchi and Saatchi	260.26	726
4	J. Walter Thompson	252.64	705
5	BBP DDB	246.55	688
6	Grey Advertising	214.86	600
7	Bates Dorland	203.93	569
8	M & C Saatchi	194.73	544
9	Publicis	192.23	537
10	McCann Erickson	182.81	510
11	D'Arcy Masius Benton & Bowles	177.45	495
12	Lowe Howard-Spink	171.25	478
13	Ammirati Puris Lintas	150.32	420
14	Euro RSCG WNEK Gosper	134.14	374
15	TBWA Simons Palmer	133.69	373
16	Leo Burnett	131.91	368
17	GGT (merger of BST-BDDP and GGT)	118.96	332
18	Bartle Bogle & Hegarty	113.85	318
19	WCRS	109.30	305
20	Young and Rubicam	105.03	293

Source: *Campaign*, 6 March 1998.

that on advertising agencies, this is in part due to the fact that, unlike advertising, there are relatively few production costs associated with the delivery of public relations. Moreover, media achieved via public relations is essentially free, so clients are often paying only for their consultants' time and sundry expenses. A closer analysis reveals a rate of growth in the demand for public relations services that is comparatively greater than the increased demand for advertising services. In 1979, 78 per cent of Fortune Top 500 US companies took external public relations advice compared with just 21 per cent of the Top 500 listed British companies. In the UK there was a significant increase over the next three years to 36 per cent in 1982 (in comparison with 82 per cent in the USA). However, by 1984, the figure had almost doubled, with 69 per cent of UK companies now using external public relations consultancy, versus 84 per cent in the USA (see Figure 2.1).[50] Following the recession at the turn of the decade, this rapid expansion continued throughout the 1990s. By 1997 the Top 150 public relations agencies were collectively billing £350.3 million (£626 million at 2018 values).[51] The biggest consultancies had become international organizations, yet the vast majority on the list had been incorporated after 1980, including several in the Top 20—namely, Text 100 (1981), Bell Pottinger (1987), Citigate (1987), Weber (1987), Freud Communications (1990), and Key Communications (1993).[52]

A small number of British advertising agencies grew to become genuine global corporations, but scale was invariably achieved through acquisition rather than organic growth. For its fulfilment this strategy primarily demanded financial and business acumen rather than creative brilliance. The rise (and subsequent fall) of Saatchi & Saatchi, which features heavily in many of the histories, is a case in point. The brothers' fleeting realization of their dream to become the biggest advertising agency in the world belied the fact that, behind a small number of headline-grabbing campaigns for the likes of the Conservative Party or British Airways, there was a huge amount of straightforward and unremarkable (albeit effective) FMCG work for high-spending clients such as Sainsbury Pet Foods, Proctor & Gamble, Gillette Right Guard, and Ross Foods.[53] Commercial expertise rather than creative flair invariably drove the biggest operations. In 1985 Saatchi's finance director Martin Sorrell—a Harvard Business School-educated, MBA graduate—left the firm to become CEO of a supermarket

---

[50] D. Smith, 'Consultancy and Client: A Problem Shared Is a Problem Solved', *Public Relations Year Book 1985* (London: FT Business Information, 1984), 9.
[51] 'The Top 150 UK PR Consultancies 1998: Overview: Growing up: Public Affairs and Investor Relations Proved Lucrative for Most Top 10 Agencies, but the Levels of Growth in Last Year's Top 150 Survey have Steadied', *PR Week*, 24 April 1998.
[52] Company incorporation dates from Companies House.
[53] C. Oxley, *The Real Saatchis: Masters of Illusion* (London: Channel 4, 1999).

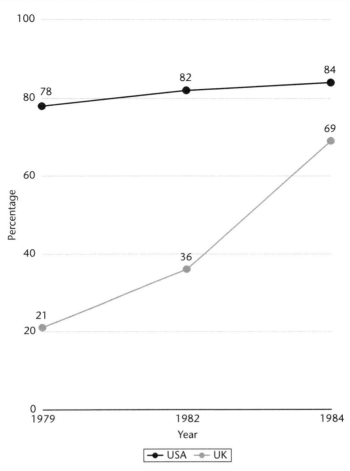

Figure 2.1. Percentage of Top 500 UK and USA companies taking advice from public relations specialists, 1979–1984.
Source: PCRA.

trolley manufacturer, Wire and Plastic Products plc. Through a process of acquisition Sorrell quickly transformed the business into WPP, the world's largest marketing services business. In 1987 he acquired his former employer's biggest competitor, J. Walter Thompson (including JWT's public relations agency Hill & Knowlton and the MRB Group), for $566 million.[54] WPP's success was entirely due to Sorrell's understanding of the sector from a business perspective and his expertise in raising corporate finance,

[54] A. Rawsthorn, 'Split Personality which Made JWT Vulnerable: How did this Prestigious Worldwide Agency Fall Victim to WPP's Audacious Bid?', *Campaign*, 3 July 1987.

not the quality of his company's creative work—decent though it was—or the number of award-winning campaigns it had produced.[55]

By 1997 many of the most successful independents in public relations, advertising, market research, media buying, planning, and graphic design that incorporated during the 1980s and early 1990s had been acquired by one of the 'big five' global conglomerates: WPP, Omnicom, Interpublic, Dentsu, and Publicis. However, many of these businesses still retained their own corporate identities and were often run as separate cost centres, competing directly with other companies within the same group. For example, by the end of the century WPP had added several leading public relations firms to its portfolio: Cohn & Wolf, Hill & Knowlton, Burston-Marsteller, and Ogilvy Public Relations, all of which continued to operate independently. Likewise, Omnicom wholly owned both Ketchum Communications and Freud Communications, but both companies remained as separate, standalone operations.[56]

The process of acquisition is one explanation for the volatility that was a feature of the league tables published annually in *Campaign* and *PR Week*. League tables for advertising agencies were printed annually in *Campaign* from 1968 and for public relations consultancies in *PR Week* from 1986. The turnover in firms from one year to the next is striking, particularly lower down the chart, where many flourished for little more than a couple of years. Higher up the list others burned brightly, but their success usually led to acquisition or merger with one or more of their competitors. These were interesting times for the persuasion industries, and the rise and fall of its various players during this period form a major part of several memoirs and histories. They are also well documented in the contemporary trade and national press.[57]

While there is much evidence to support the notion that a distinct promotional culture emerged in the UK, as described by Wernick and Davis, once again there is little if any satisfactory examination of how it operated. Discussion of persuasion's methodology is entirely absent in Wernick, Davis, and

[55] C. Marshall, 'The King of Farm Street: Martin Sorrell—Is WPP about to Go Shopping? And is Y&R Next on its Shopping List', *Campaign*, 5 October 2000.

[56] *An Abbreviated History of WPP*, <http://www.wpp.com/wpp/about/whoweare/history/> (acccessed 25 July 2016); 'The Omnicom Shopping Spree: How Wren and Co. Picked their Targets', *Adweek Eastern Edition*, 14 October 1996; L. Rich, 'Omnicom Grows Organically', *Adweek, Eastern Edition*, 10 February 1997.

[57] E.g. Bell, *Right or Wrong*; P. Kleinman, *The Saatchi & Saatchi Story* (London: Weidenfeld & Nicolson, 1987); Fallon, *The Brothers*; Oxley, *The Real Saatchis*; J. Hegarty, *Hegarty on Advertising: Turning Intelligence into Magic* (London: Thames & Hudson, 2011); S. Kessler, *Chiatt/Day: The First Twenty Years* (New York: Rizzoli International, 1990); J. Salmon and J. Ritchie, *Inside Collett Dickenson Pearce* (London: Batsford, 2000); A. Law, *Creative Company: How St Luke's Became 'The Ad Agency to End All Ad Agencies'* (New York: Wiley, 1999); Tungate, *Adland*; Fletcher, *Powers of Persuasion*; Delaney, *Get Smashed*; T. Mason, 'Where Can Saatchis Go Now it's Hit its Ultimate Goal?', *Campaign*, 23 May 1986; L. O'Kelly, 'BBH—A Flair Hard to Beat', *Campaign*, 9 January 1987; Rich, 'Omnicom Grows Organically'; Rawsthorn, 'Split Personality which made JWT vulnerable'.

L'Etang. Frank Mort's rigorous, semiotic analysis of the sector's output is helpful in the context of his own account of changes in patterns of male consumption but cannot be interpreted as an investigation of the persuasion industry's methodology. Both Delaney and Fletcher rely on the identification of individual campaigns as key turning points to build their argument. Delaney focuses on moments of inspiration by a few highly creative individuals, which gives the impression that all great advertising is down to these 'eureka moments'. This view is supported by the creative directors he interviews. However, this implies far too crude a modus operandi for a multi-billion-dollar sector. Most campaigns were undoubtedly functional rather than inspirational but achieved their commercial objectives nonetheless. More often perspiration rather than inspiration was required. By way of illustration, an internal JWT memo from Jean Currie reveals the origins of the brand name Mr Kipling.[58]

Launched in 1967, Mr Kipling was one of the most successful brands in its category until the end of the century, and its 'exceedingly good' strapline became part of the cultural fabric—the punchline of numerous jokes and comedy sketches.[59] However, rather than a moment of inspiration, the brand name was arrived at (rather than conceived) after a lengthy process and for 'a series of perfectly comprehensible tactical and marketing reasons'.[60] A broad number of routes were initially considered and discounted. A specialist brand name was perceived as too close to the competition—namely, McVities, Lyons, and Cadburys—while a specialist company was dismissed as 'too monolithic'.[61] A third approach considered was the creation of an individual. The possibility of creating a female character was immediately discarded, as it would set the brand in competition for the harried, former cake-baking housewives who comprised the launch's target audience. Finally, the team settled on a male—'A master baker or cake maker' whose personality would be sympathetic, an elderly man who had been making cakes all his life.[62] Only now could the search for a name begin. A long list was compiled—'from Buttercup Cakes to Master Baker Cakes—before the group focused on those with an alliterative quality such as 'Carry Cakes'.[63] 'In this group, having exhausted the hard C sounds were names beginning with K—and among them was Kipling.' However, although 'Kipling Cakes

[58] J. Currie, 'Mr Kipling: Memo from Jean Currie to Michael O'Grady', HAT, Advertising Agency, Account Files, 1967.

[59] E.g. 'Asking a Trotter if he knows anything about chandeliers is like asking Mr Kipling if he knows anything about cakes', from the BBC TV series *Only Fools and Horses*, reported in ' "I used to miss my dad until I learned to punch straight": 30 of the Best *Only Fools And Horses* One-Liners', *Daily Mirror*, 5 December 2012.

[60] J. Currie, 'Mr Kipling: Memo from Jean Currie to Michael O'Grady', HAT, Advertising Agency, Account Files, 1967.

[61] Ibid.   [62] Ibid.   [63] Ibid.

[was a name which] sounded nice, it didn't seem to have much of the personality of the master baker that we had created—until Llwellyn suddenly said Mr Kipling and all at once the man came to life'.[64]

This straightforward creative process is far more typical of ideas generation in practice than the moments of brilliance highlighted by Delaney. Fletcher offered by far the more rigorous analysis of the two, but in his search for turning points he placed a great deal of emphasis on advertising effectiveness awards and put forward the following rationale:

> From a historical perspective I believe it to be justifiable to concentrate—but not exclusively—on the minute number of award-winning, high-profile campaigns. It is justifiable because they occupy a greater share of the public interest than their commercial importance dictates, because they influence future creative trends, because they are more stimulating, more engaging, more fascinating, than the prosaic stuff.[65]

This argument is unconvincing and Fletcher's emphasis on awards is dubious. The criteria for judging awards are a moving feast, and the process of selection is opaque and often politically motivated. The attitude towards entering awards also varied from agency to agency and from client to client. Indeed, a very strong case could be made in support of the view that awards are given to agencies who are best at entering awards (or who bother to enter awards) rather than the best agencies or the best advertising per se. However, Fletcher's contention that public mindshare was dominated by a small number of campaigns, which in turn shaped the future of industry thinking, is probably correct. The sector's thirst for ideas was such that there was little concern for where successful ones originated. Creative teams often 'borrowed' shamelessly from other popular cultural sources in the search for inspiration. For example, in 1989 CDP produced a television advertisement for Hamlet cigars called 'Photo Booth'. In the advert the actor Gregor Fisher plays a bald man trying frantically to cover his head with a few wisps of straggly hair while awaiting the photo booth's flash, with predictably comic results. Fletcher describes this advert with characteristic hyperbole: 'For most people the funniest by far ... Fisher's performance is worthy of an Oscar, but he—and the commercial—had to make do with a galaxy of awards.' However, despite all the plaudits, the advert itself is nothing more than the refilmed version of an old sketch originally written by Philip Differ and performed by Fisher on an obscure BBC2 comedy show called *Naked Video*, which first aired on 12 May 1986.[66] The only creative contribution CDP could possibly claim is that in their version the character smokes a consolatory cigar at the end of his

---

[64] Ibid.   [65] Fletcher, *Powers of Persuasion*, 74.
[66] B. Johnson, *Naked Video* (London: BBC Two, 1986).

tribulations. Regardless of how many awards it garnered, originality was not something CDP could claim for 'Photo Booth'.

In their enthusiasm for moments of genius both Fletcher and Delaney overlook the pragmatism at the heart of the creative process. They are correct in the sense that the idea is hugely important, but where the idea comes from is not. Execution rather than originality is the key. In 1983 Gold Greenless Trott produced a successful, long-running, and award-winning TV campaign for Holsten Pils. The adverts featured comedian Griff Rhys Jones, whose performance was superimposed into a series of classic film noir movie clips featuring Marilyn Monroe, John Wayne, George Raft, and Humphrey Bogart (see Figure 2.2). The idea was lifted wholesale from the 1982 film *Dead Men Don't Wear Plaid*. Directed by Carl Reiner, the movie starred comedian Steve Martin, whose performance is intercut into scenes of classic film noir in an identical manner to that of Rhys Jones.[67] GGT's successful application of this idea to the business of selling lager is undoubtedly inspired, arguably just as important as the idea itself in this context, but by no means can it be considered original.

Throughout the period, and increasingly so during the 1980s and 1990s, ideas from popular culture and the counterculture were appropriated by

Figure 2.2. *John Wayne*: still from TV advertisement, featuring actor Gryff Rhys Jones and archive footage of John Wayne, for Holsten Pils, produced by Gold Greenness Trott, 1983. (Courtesy of Carlsberg UK Ltd.) See also plates section.

[67] C. Reiner, *Dead Men Don't Wear Plaid* (New York: Universal Pictures, 1982).

brands and used in their advertising. However, as Frank identified, rather than being co-opted by consumer culture, the counterculture of the 1960s was intrinsically linked to it from the outset.[68] Advertising culture in the 1980s and 1990s espoused many of the values championed by the counterculture throughout the preceding decades, which integrated perfectly with the notion of liberation through personal choice rather than mass action. Frank commented that, by 1997, the 'fantasies of rebellion, liberation, and outright "revolution" against the stultifying demands of mass society are commonplace' within the mass cultural products of the United States, as indeed they were within the UK.[69] This attitude is apparent in the interviews, articles, and memoirs of advertising executives, who strove (from the late 1950s in the USA and the late 1960s in the UK) to be the 'hippest thinkers' around; challenging prevailing management theories that encouraged conformity for the simple reason that conformity didn't sell.[70] However, this was not one-way traffic. Persuasion was also returning the gift and inculcating itself into popular culture.

---

[68] T. Frank, *The Conquest of Cool: Business Culture, Counterculture, and the Rise of Hip Consumerism* (Chicago: University of Chicago Press, 1997).
[69] Ibid. 4.   [70] Ibid. 224–37.

Part Two
Into the Vanguard

The Persuasion Industries in Britain, 1969–1997

The chapters in this section deal directly with the persuasion industries, concentrating on developments in the production of advertisements, brands, marketing strategies, and public relations campaigns in Britain.

While there was, as industry historians claim, an evolution in the nature of persuasion during this period, this transformation went much further than the practitioners themselves (or the services they provided) simply becoming 'more professionalized'. As persuasion became more pervasive, it also became more specialized, but more importantly it also changed in nature. A new emotional model of brand communication emerged, which provided companies with the means to develop deeper, wider-reaching relationships with their consumers. This statement comes with a strong caveat. While these new methods could be undoubtedly more effective when executed well, they did not constitute a foolproof system that guaranteed success. Much of the industry's output remained ineffective throughout the period: the majority of new product launches failed, the majority of advertisements did not engage with the target audience, and the majority of public relations campaigns did not affect a change in public opinion. Yet, when they did succeed, these new strategies were hugely successful. They were also ultimately responsible for creating a new kind of corporate entity, one that was built from the inside out rather than from the top down, and global rather than national in both aspect and ambition: the modern corporate brand. These corporate brands were positioned to exploit the most significant cultural, political, and economic change during the period: the emphasis on the individual rather than society. Epitomized by young companies such as Nike, Virgin, Apple, and Microsoft, and revitalized veterans such as Levi Strauss, Vauxhall, Coca Cola, and McDonalds, corporate brands pioneered the use of persuasion in a variety of forms that were conceptual and emotional in nature.

If the 1970s could be described as a period of rapid evolution for the persuasion industries, then the following two decades witnessed nothing less than a revolution. Persuasion entered the vanguard of British society. The core argument presented is that not only did the new forms of persuasion play a key role in bringing about a major societal change, but that without them, this would have been very difficult, arguably impossible, to achieve. During the 1980s and 1990s, the persuasion industries became progressively more fragmented. Diverse specialisms developed into standalone service providers—for example, public relations, branding, design, media buying, planning, retail marketing, and direct marketing. In contrast, this was also a period of corporate consolidation during which four global conglomerates emerged to swallow up most of these new players. Divergence allowed persuasion to become more nuanced and more effective, while sectoral convergence provide a holistic framework through which its innovative applications could become much more embedded into everyday life.

The growth of the persuasion industries was also reliant on external factors. The economic and political climate of the times enshrined the same values, aims, and objectives as the persuasion industries themselves—namely, aspiration, commerce, accruing material goods, property ownership, and economic growth. As a consequence, the persuasion industries were able to undertake a huge expansion, and the totems of promotional culture grew significantly in importance.

From the 1970s, consumers were becoming increasingly desensitized to the established tactics and tropes of the hard sell. The need for continued, effective audience engagement led to the emergence of a new methodology—born out of the growing body of sector-related academic research and based on emotional rather than rational appeals—that allowed the persuasion industry to respond to this challenge.

As a result, all forms of persuasion became increasingly sophisticated throughout the 1980s and 1990s. However, consumers, benefiting from improved levels of education and information, also became less biddable.

The specialization within the persuasion industry also helped to improve the quality and effectiveness of output, which enabled the successful exploitation of a raft of new opportunities in fields such as sponsorship, public relations, and brand extension. The rapid proliferation of media channels through to the end of the century (as a result of technological innovation) also extended persuasion's breadth and penetration. This combination of new delivery methods, more compelling output, and extended reach made it possible for the first time to run campaigns targeting new and discrete audiences. Most notable in this regard was a significant increase in activity targeting males and particularly young men aged 16–30. Conversely, as a result of the same media fragmentation, reaching the kind of mass audiences achievable from the 1950s to the 1970s became much more difficult.

3

Planning for Success

Persuasion in the 1970s

Advertising in Decline, 1968–1976

The decline in advertising that occurred in Britain between 1968 and 1976 has been ignored or overlooked by several commentators, while others have simply attributed it to a general slowdown in the British economy following two decades of expansion.[1] However, as Fletcher recognized, this tells only part of the story.[2] Optimism about the future among businesses and consumers remained high into the early 1970s; wages also continued to increase, while consumer expenditure grew year on year until 1973 before declining slowly (see Figure 3.1). Indeed, the figures were even worse for the sector than they first appear. Not only were they masked by an increase in classified advertising during the period, but this was also a time during which an entirely new medium came into its own.[3] The arrival of colour television broadcasting in Britain should have given the industry an obvious fillip, providing clients with the best possible platform for their products. Moreover, the decision of the Independent Broadcasting Authority (IBA) not to charge a

---

[1] S. Delaney, *Get Smashed: The Story of the Men who Made the Adverts that Changed our Lives* (London: Sceptre, 2007); J. L.'Etang, *Public Relations in Britain: A History of Professional Practice in the 20th Century* (Mahwah, NJ, and London: L. Erlbaum, 2004); M. Tungate, *Adland: A Global History of Advertising* (London: Kogan Page, 2007), 73–88; S. King, 'Has Marketing Failed or was it Never Really Tried?', *Journal of Marketing Management*, 1/2 (1985), 1–19.

[2] W. Fletcher, *Powers of Persuasion: The Inside Story of British Advertising 1951–2000* (Oxford: Oxford University Press, 2008), 84–9.

[3] The form of advertising that brands and agencies produce is called display advertising. Display advertising can be carried in a variety of media and is designed to attract attention. It is by nature intrusive. Classified advertising is very different. It is typically discreet—a form that consumers proactively look for, usually in the form of listings or in small ads sections within newspapers and magazines. The ads are usually categorized (classified) by type—e.g,. cars, property, second-hand items, clothing, dating, etc. As such, classified advertising has relatively little to do with the persuasion industries.

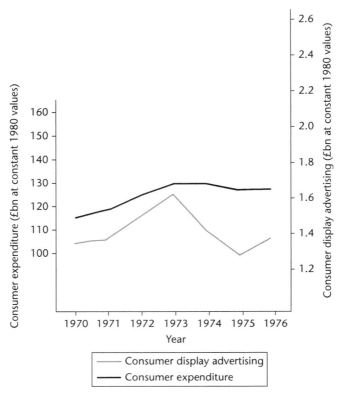

Figure 3.1. Total consumer expenditure at constant (1980) values and consumer display advertising as a percentage of it, 1970–1976.
Source: WARC and Office of National Statistics.

premium for showing ads in colour (unlike their counterparts in printed media a few years earlier) removed a prohibitive barrier to entry. In fact, colour TV probably did much to mitigate the fall in advertising expenditure at a time that should have been one of significant growth for the industry.[4]

A much more likely explanation is that the inability of the sector as a whole to respond to the creative challenges presented by big changes in both the market and society led to a loss of confidence on the part of clients. In larger agencies any possible response to a demand for better creative output was stymied by hidebound business practices and an inability to attract fresh talent. In the late 1960s, advertising was still controlled predominantly by large, US-based corporations with little scope or interest in developing new talent or their ideas.[5]

---

[4] Fletcher, *Powers of Persuasion*, 85.   [5] Delaney, *Get Smashed*, 95.

By 1970, advertising was still aimed largely at housewives, locked into cosy depictions of traditional family life and looking increasingly out of step with the times as a consequence. In trying to make sense of the cultural changes taking place in society, many clients came to the conclusion that their long-standing partners at the advertising agency were neither the men nor the means to help them reach out to this new market. Again, an illustration is provided by the launch of Mr Kipling by Manor Bakeries in 1967. Manor Bakeries initially briefed its advertising agency JWT in 1965, tasking it with the launch of a new range of packaged cakes in response to similar lines by competitors such as McVities, Cadbury, and Lyons. JWT's approach to this task was typical. First of all the product was 'interrogated' to identify a unique selling point. Extensive market research was then commissioned to establish whether there was any demand for packaged cakes and if so what kind of cakes housewives (the target audience) would prefer. A proposition was developed based on 'the exceedingly good' quality of the cakes. Yet, despite a seemingly obvious opportunity, three years of research findings, and the creation of a name conceived specifically so that the brand would not compete with Mum's home cooking, a tepid launch was followed by extremely disappointing sales.[6]

What is absent from the research and client correspondence in the run-up to the product's launch is any acknowledgement of the fact that the lives of women were changing at the time. Therein lay the opportunity. Historically cakes were either bought fresh from local bakeries or cooked at home. By 1968, women were far more likely than ever before in the post-war period to be going out to work and consequently had far less time on their hands to produce home-cooked cakes or shop at several specialist retail outlets. The supermarkets, which were growing their market share within the grocery sector and specializing in processed food, offered them a solution to that problem. Quite simply, Mr Kipling was not being sold in the right outlets, and as result Manor Bakeries were not selling enough cakes.[7] On 17 May 1968, JWT held a review board meeting to discuss 'the dire position of Mr Kipling and the fact that if Manor Bakeries does not act upon all of both our recommendations, the operation is doomed to financial failure. The attendant implications for JWT, as a heavy partner in the entire venture, were sufficiently obvious.'[8] In a plainly exasperated internal memo, written by account executive William J. Kenney on 27 July 1968, the source of the brand's problems is 'very quickly and correctly identified as the Manor Bakeries

---

[6] HAT, JWT (1967), 1966, 1967, 1968, 1969, HAT 50/1/21/2.
[7] Ibid., internal memo, M. O'Grady, 20 March 1968.
[8] Ibid., internal memo, John Davis, 17 May 1968.

management', and their failure to make 'the proper decisions' and ensure the product was available on supermarket shelves.[9]

This kind of blame and back-covering within the correspondence is fairly typical when a project involving two parties appears to go awry and one of those parties—in this case the agency—is effectively subordinate to the other. The unease evident within this client–agency relationship was by no means unique to JWT and Manor Bakeries. *Campaign*'s creative review of 1969 pulled no punches in highlighting an industry-wide malaise.[10] Provocatively entitled 'Oh, what a dull uninspiring year! Here's proof', the feature singled out campaigns by several top agencies including: JWT's NatWest Bank launch ('stuffy pretentious, pompous...bland'); Ford's Capri coupé launch ('The next big non-event'); Garland Compton's campaign for BOAC ('a parade of puns'); Bensons' Austin Maxi launch for British Leyland ('pointless and shabby'); Pritchard Wood, also for British Leyland ('a bore'); Ogilvy for British Steel ('a boring recitation'); and Leo Burnett for the launch of Giro Bank ('Insulting is what it really is').[11] Long-term relationships notwithstanding, many businesses decided that their incumbent ad agency was simply not up to the task. *Campaign*'s first editorial of 1970 explained: 'Accounts changed hands rapidly: clients whose accounts had appeared permanent fixtures in some agencies suddenly decided 1969 was the year to make a move.'[12] For example, Guinness shifted its business for the first time in over four decades from Bensons to JWT, while Hovis moved its account to CDP after seventy years with John Haddon.[13]

In response to this unwelcome client volatility, the agencies themselves took a closer look at their own creative work, with many concluding that a change of creative director was required. Between May and December 1969, changes in creative director or creative department restructures occurred at the following Top 20 advertising agencies: Horniblow Cox-Freeman, Foote Cone and Belding, Vernons, Coleman Prentis and Varley, London Progressive Advertising, McCann Erickson, Benton & Bowles, Crawfords and Greys, and Lintas.[14] Yet, despite the increase in demand, creative talent was relatively thin on the ground. Stuffy, old-fashioned, and boring, advertising did not seem like a desirable destination for Britain's burgeoning art and design school graduates.[15] As a result of these factors (and in contrast to GDP) by 1970 the advertising sector was in the midst of a steep and protracted decline (see Table 3.1).

For some, however, the advertising sector's moribund state, in stark contrast with the vibrant, cultural changes taking place across British society in the

---

[9] Ibid., internal memo, William J Kenney, 26 August 1968.
[10] 'Oh, what a Dull Uninspiring Year! Here's Proof', *Campaign*, 2 January 1970, pp. 26–7.
[11] Ibid.   [12] '1969: The Big Year of Change', *Campaign*, 2 January 1970, pp. 17–18.
[13] Ibid.   [14] Ibid.   [15] Delaney, *Get Smashed*, 20–1.

Table 3.1. Total UK advertising expenditure as a percentage of GDP, 1964–1976

Year	Expenditure (£m, at 2018 values)	Percentage of GDP (at market values)
1964	549	1.23
1966	590	1.15
1968	664	1.14
1970	731	1.06
1972	943	1.09
1974	1,198	1.06
1976	1,591	0.95

Source: World Advertising Research Centre (WARC).

1960s, presented an opportunity. Throughout that decade one US advertising agency had been consistently producing successful advertising campaigns that conformed to neither Reeves's nor Ogilvy's versions of the traditional model. Doyle Dane Bernbach (DDB) was a Manhattan agency founded in 1949 by Ned Doyle, Bill Bernbach, and Mac Dane, initially producing adverts for Ohrbach's department store. Quirky and Jewish, DDB was considered out of step with the rest of the hard-selling WASPs of Madison Avenue in terms of both its ethnicity and its philosophy. In 1959, DDB's pioneering work for Volkswagen brought the agency to worldwide attention. *Think Small*, a campaign created by art director Helmut Krone and copywriter Julian Koenig to launch the Beetle in the USA, was the epitome of Bernbach's view that 'Good taste, good art, and good writing can be good selling'.[16] These advertisements could not have been further from Reeves's hard sell: largely just white space with a tiny image of the Beetle itself to highlight its simplicity and minimalism and copy that extolled the advantages of owning a small car (see Figure 3.2). Their focus was on the characteristics of the consumer rather than the product; instead of claiming 'This is a great car because of the following reasons . . .', it simply says 'If you're a person like this, then this is a car for you'. The advertisement was subtle and unassuming, but it proved to be highly effective. The campaign ran for many years and was voted the all-time, number one in *Advertising Age*'s 'The Century of Advertising'.[17] In 1960, DDB applied a similar approach to its new client Avis, the automotive rental company. Avis was then the number two brand in the US market, but rather than shy away from that fact DDB chose to make a virtue of it with a self-effacing campaign that argued 'At Avis, we try harder because we're number two'. It proved another enduring success and remained part of the company's slogan into the twenty-first century.[18]

---

[16] A. Hiott, *Thinking Small: The Long, Strange Trip of the Volkswagen Beetle* (London: Random House, 2012), 3–7, 253–331; Bernbach, quoted in B. Garfield, 'Top 100 Advertising Campaigns of the Century', *Advertising Age*, 29 March 1999.

[17] Ibid.   [18] Tungate, *Adland*, 49.

Figure 3.2. *Think Small*: display advertisement by Doyle Dane Bernbach for the Volkswagen Beetle, 1959. (Courtesy of Steven Kasher Gallery, New York.) See also plates section.

In the UK, admiration for the work of DDB united many of the young creatives and executives struggling with the working practices and output of British advertising agencies. Among them were David Puttnam, Alan Parker, Ridley Scott, Tim Bell, Frank Lowe, and John Hegarty. John Hegarty has described the state of the industry he joined as 'complete crap' and dysfunctional with very little idea about how to product effective advertising.[19] Several of the sector's other new entrants, including Charles Saatchi, Frank Lowe, Dave Trott, and Peter Mayle, had spent time working in New York. Here they witnessed the impact DDB's campaigns were having on the industry at first hand and returned to Britain brimming with new ideas and working methods. They were generally disappointed by what they found when they returned to UK agencies, which were parochial, weak minded, and backward looking in comparison, producing advertising that was unimaginative and insipid.

The Creative Revolution

One UK agency in particular was inspired by the work of DDB to push its own creativity in a similar direction. Collett Dickenson Pearce (CDP) was founded in London in 1960 by John Pearce and Ronnie Dickenson. It was allegedly an early acquisition target for DDB, which briefly considered turning CDP into its UK office.[20] John Pearce initially targeted niche clients with modest budgets for whom his agency could provide effective advertising. His view was that, although based on sound strategy, most advertising was ineffective because it was so interminably dull. Pearce's aim—to produce advertising that was 'inspirational, enterprising, and most of all noticeable'—might appear somewhat obvious today, but at the time it was at odds with the prevailing view among UK advertising agencies almost to the point of uniqueness.[21]

Throughout the 1960s CDP produced inspirational and noticeable advertising for a raft of middle-market, middlebrow brands such as Benson & Hedges, Aer Lingus, Whitbread, Hamlet, Chemsstrad and Harvey's Bristol Cream. Rather than ape the approach of DDB, CDP produced sophisticated advertisements with a British sensibility and abandoned the tropes and clichés predominant in the advertising of the time. For example, Alan Parker's colloquial copy for Harvey's Bristol Cream was one of the first instances of informal English being

---

[19] 'Sir John Hegarty on how the Industry has Lost its Courage', *AdAge*, 16 September 2014; J. Hegarty, *Hegarty on Advertising: Turning Intelligence into Magic* (London: Thames & Hudson, 2011), 57–68.
[20] This anecdote, told by Mary Pearce, wife of John Pearce, appears in several histories—e.g. Delaney, *Get Smashed*, 56–9.
[21] J. Salmon and J. Ritchie, *Inside Collett Dickenson Pearce* (London: Batsford, 2000), 8–16.

used in advertising. Parker claimed in 2012 that even CDP's senior managers were surprised by the approach: 'I remember the first ad that I did for CDP (for Harvey's Bristol Cream)—John Pearce, the boss, read it and he said that they'd spent years trying to put Harvey's Bristol Cream on a pedestal and along comes Alan Parker and he starts selling it off of a barrow.'[22] Visually, photographers David Bailey, Terence Donovan, and Helmut Newton provided print ads with a look and feel that were perfect for the new colour supplements at the *Sunday Times* and the *Observer*. Meanwhile CDP's TV commercials pioneered the use of celebrities appearing in character rather than simply as hectoring endorsees. The work itself was CDP's shop window. By 1970, the agency was hovering outside the Top 10 and one of the few to win praise from *Campaign* in its end of year review.[23]

Over the next twenty years the diaspora of CDP alumni—along with the agency itself under the tutelage of managing director Frank Lowe and creative director Colin Millward—would play a leading role in the growth of the UK advertising industry and exert a global influence over the production and delivery of brand communication. The creative staff at CDP, the majority of whom trained under Millward, included many future leading lights of British advertising: Tony Brignull, Rooney Caruthers, Ross Cramer, Graham Fink, Richard Foster, Malcolm Gluck, Neil Godfrey, John Hegarty, Dave Horry, John Horton, Gray Joliffe, Tony Kaye, Terry Lovelock, Frank Lowe, Alfredo Marcantonio, Barbara Nokes, John O'Driscoll, Alan Parker, David Puttnam, Charles Saatchi, John Salmon, Geoff Seymour, Alan Waldie, Tim Warriner, Paul Weiland, and Robin Wright. Freelance workers included Ridley Scott, Tony Scott, Adrian Lynne, and Hugh Hudson.[24] The companies founded by several of these erstwhile employees—including Saatchi & Saatchi, Bartle Bogle and Hegarty, Lowe Howard-Spink, Boase Massami Pollitt, Abbot Mead Vicars—had different corporate objectives, cultures, and practices but shared an understanding that the most successful advertising was reliant on the quality of the idea and the manner of its expression. Creativity, previously locked away out of sight by advertising agencies that viewed it as little more than a necessary evil, was now at the heart of the business.

Neither Reeves nor Ogilvy had much time for creativity. Reeves viewed it with disdain: 'Do you want fine writing? Do you want masterpieces? Or do

[22] 'Our Mad Men', *Campaign*, 22 March 2012.
[23] See 'Oh, what a Dull Uninspiring Year! Here's proof *Campaign*, 2 January 1970, pp. 26–7. The following CDP campaigns are described: Ford Capri ('cracking good ads...'), Nibble Snacks ('masterpieces of casting and direction...'), and Viyella shirts ('photographs you could almost eat...').
[24] See T. Bell, *Right or Wrong: The Memoirs of Lord Bell* (London: Bloomsbury, 2014), 21; Delaney, *Get Smashed*, 56–72, 88–102; I. Fallon, *The Brothers: The Rise & Rise of Saatchi & Saatchi* (London: Hutchinson, 1988), 19–24; Fletcher, *Powers of Persuasion*, 70–3, 92–4, 144–5; Hegarty, *Hegarty on Advertising*, 57–9, 92; M. Tungate, *Adland: A Global History of Advertising*, pp. 74–81.

you want to see the goddamned sales curve start moving up?' Ogilvy was also suspicious: 'I occasionally use the hideous word "creative" myself for lack of a better.' He described the role of the agency as 'Sell—or else!'[25] However, the elevation of creativity was not merely an intellectual or procedural change; in practice it meant completely altering the working environment. Teams were no longer organized in vertical lines of account management/research/art direction/copywriting/media buying and housed in separate offices. Workplaces became open plan with teams mixed down project lines rather than separated by job function. Agencies began organizing themselves in matrices rather than hierarchies, and, as a result, projects became more collaborative and job roles much more fluid. For example, Alan Parker was originally hired as a copywriter at CDP but showed a flair for art direction and soon found himself working as an in-house director; David Puttnam joined CDP aged 21 and acquired a reputation as a top account executive and salesman before demonstrating a real aptitude for film production and project management; like Parker, Charles Saatchi began life as a copywriter but became one of the most celebrated creative directors of the 1970s and, together with his brother Maurice, the industry's most successful corporate executive in the 1980s.[26]

CDP workers were encouraged to develop their own work patterns to achieve high standards. The emphasis was on productivity and quality of output rather than timekeeping. These relaxed working conditions became the norm across the sector, as new agencies in particular attempted to establish the best working practices to promote creativity. Rather than the last redoubt, advertising began to look like a career of choice for graduates—a fun way to earn a decent living—and so it began to attract the best creative talent. For art school leavers in film, photography, and graphic design, or for those interested in a literary career, advertising presented an opportunity for regular, playful work in an agreeable environment that was challenging and well remunerated.[27] Much of this new intake had been inspired by the counterculture, and they were now taking some of those ideas with them into the corporate world. There are numerous examples of this. After beginning their creative careers in advertising, Lindsay Anderson, Stephen Frears, Hugh Hudson, Richard Lester, Adrian Lyne, Alan Parker, David Puttnam, Karl Reisz, Salman Rushdie, Ken Russell, John Schlesinger, Ridley Scott, and Tony Scott (to name but a few of the most well known) all progressed into the fields

---

[25] R. B. Evans, *Production and Creativity in Advertising* (London: Pitman, 1988), 10; M. Tungate, *Adland: A global history of advertising*, pp. 35–41; M. Tungate, *Adland: A global history of advertising*, pp. 35–41; D.M. Haygood, ' "Hard sell or soft sell?" The advertising philosophies and professional relationship of Rosser Reeves and David Ogilvy', pp. 169–88.

[26] See Salmon and Ritchie, *Inside Collett Dickenson Pearce*. For further examples, see Bell, *Right or Wrong*; Delaney, *Get Smashed*; Fallon, *The Brothers*; Fletcher, *Powers of Persuasion*; Tungate, *Adland*.

[27] Delaney, *Get Smashed*, 70–7; Fletcher, *Powers of Persuasion*, 70–3, 92–4; Tungate, *Adland*, 74–81; Hegarty, *Hegarty on Advertising*, 57–68.

of film, literature, or broadcast media. These individuals were all heavily influenced by the counterculture and in many cases, part of it themselves.

An immediate result of these changes was that the quality of advertising in the 1970s improved markedly. The approach that CDP had successfully pioneered in the 1960s for largely mid-market, middle-class products was applied by others to more mainstream markets—for example, Saatchi & Saatchi built its early reputation on the back of hard-hitting campaigns for the Health Education Council (an account carried over from Cramer-Saatchi) such as 'The Pregnant Man'. In truth this was a client that offered the perfect showcase for a new agency's creative credentials. With no product to sell as such, merely ideas to promote (and smaller budgets), charities were far more likely to take a creative risk than an established FMCG brand.

For those mass-market consumer brands considering a more creative approach, CDP's work for clients such as Hovis provided evidence of the effectiveness of creativity. Since the mid-1960s, healthy eating had been one important component of the counterculture, and by end of the decade these ideas were gaining widespread acceptance across British society.[28] Along with many other processed foods, white bread began to receive criticism for its low nutritional value.[29] Mindful of this growing concern, CDP ditched the brand's long-standing slogan 'Don't ask for brown bread, ask for Hovis' and practically ignored the product altogether. Beginning in 1973, with *Boy on a Bike*, written by Geoff Seymour and directed by Ridley Scott, the campaign CDP produced consisted of a set of nostalgic childhood reminiscences narrated by an unseen grandfather figure (the on-screen, child character in later life). The advertisements proved not only popular but also extremely durable. A series of formulaic stories following the same template as the original were shown over the next thirty years, lodging the brand in public consciousness. Hovis 'the brand' became synonymous with beautifully shot, 'wholesome' depictions of yesteryear, voiceovers in strong regional accents, and the strains of Dvořák's 'New World' Symphony. By saying little if anything about the product itself (and certainly nothing as straightforward as 'Don't ask for brown bread', which invited a direct comparison with 'inferior' competitors), the campaign promoted brand values over product qualities. Through this juxtaposition, Hovis 'the bread' came to be seen as a 'wholesome' alternative to white loaves.[30] Hovis was by no means an isolated success. When, in December 1999, *Campaign* selected the '100 Best British Ads of

---

[28] W. J. Blasco, *Appetite for Change: How the Counterculture Took on the Food Industry* (New York: Cornell University Press, 2007); A. B. Bobrow-Strain, *White Bread: A Social History of the Store-Bought Loaf* (Boston: Beacon Press, 2012), 88–90.

[29] Ibid. 165, 178–9.

[30] Salmon and Ritchie, *Inside Collett Dickenson Pearce*, 71–5, 116; Delaney, *Get Smashed*, 88–103; Fletcher, *Powers of Persuasion*, 206; Hegarty, *Hegarty on Advertising*, 58.

the 20th Century', more than 20 per cent came from the 1970s—a greater proportion than any other decade.[31]

CDP's high regard for creativity was shared by another independent agency. Founded in 1968, Boase Massami Pollitt (BMP) shared the same philosophy as CDP, but its output was stylistically and tonally very different. CDP built its reputation on the back of work for brands such as Hamlet, Heineken, Hovis, and Benson & Hedges, for whom it produced humorous, beautifully shot, and handsomely art-directed real-life commercials. In contrast, BMP became associated with the creation of memorable and enduring but brash and larger-than-life characters, such as the Cresta Bear, the Smash Martians, and the Sugar Puffs Honey Monster. Between them, these two agencies produced some of the most popular and effective campaigns of the 1970s. For example, from CDP, Hamlet *Happiness Is A Cigar* (1967); Heineken *Refreshes the Parts* (1973); Hovis *Boy on a Bike* (1973); Cockburns Port *Shipwreaked* (1974); Birds Eye Foods *Return of Captain Birdseye* (1974); Olympus Cameras *Who Do You Think You Are—David Bailey?* (1976); Parker Pens *Finishing School* (1976); Fiat Strada *Hand Built by Robots* (1977); and Benson & Hedges *Surrealism* (1977). BMP was responsible for Cresta *It's Frothy Man* (1973); Smash *Martians* (1973); St Ivel *Prize Guys* (1975); Hoffmeister Lager *Follow the Bear* (1976); Sugar Puffs *Honey Monster* (1976); Pepsi Cola *Lipsmackinthistquenchin* (1978); and Courage Best *Gercha* (1979). The two agencies were not alone. Others also went on to build strong reputations for their creative output during the 1970s—for example, the UK offices of Doyle Dane & Bernbach (founded in 1965), TWBA (1973), and Saatchi & Saatchi (1970).[32]

The elevation of creativity should be seen neither as a replacement for Reeves's hard sell nor as a simple development of Ogilvy's soft sell. It was a separate approach that was at heart conceptual rather than factual. It brought the non-message elements of advertisements into play by persuading consumers to engage with an idea rather than a tangible product benefit. Callaghan conducted the seminal study into the emotional power of advertising in 1974, which indicated that a liking or preference towards an advertisement could lead to the development of a positive attitude towards a brand and ultimately to higher purchase intention.[33] These emotional connections could be quite nebulous. In the case of Hovis, 'wholesomeness' is a fairly vague concept (and indeed Hovis itself was nothing more than white bread with some added wheatgerm), but, unlike, say, 'healthy' or 'tasty', it is also a

---

[31] 'The 100 Best British Ads of the 20th Century', *Campaign*, 22 December 1999.

[32] *Doyle Dane Bernbach*, <http://www.historygraphicdesign.com/the-age-of-information/the-new-york-school/483-doyle-dane-bernbach>; Hegarty, *Hegarty on Advertising*, 139; 'Agency will Give Clients Money Saving Guarantee', *Campaign*, 11 September 1971, pp. 1, 5.

[33] F. Callahan, 'Advertising Influences on Consumers', *Journal of Advertising Reserach*, 14/3 (1974), 45.

difficult concept to challenge. In effect, the claim for wholesomeness simply made consumers feel there was 'something good' about the bread and that this quality could somehow be transferred to their own family life.[34]

In a similar manner, the campaign created by John Webster at BMP for Cresta, a fizzy drink aimed at children, also connected consumers with an idea. In these commercials a sunglasses-wearing polar bear takes a sip of Cresta and is immediately compelled into a crazy dance that ends with him exclaiming, 'It's frothy man!' On the face of it there seemed to be nothing new about a cartoon character shouting a slogan—both were tropes of the hard sell—but here the hook was not the catchphrase or even the product itself; it was the bear's reaction, which was to be repeated in playgrounds up and down the country. The idea that consumers willingly engaged with was not one that invited rational analysis; it was the not the product they were after but that feeling.[35]

The strength of the emotional connections created through the non-message parts of the advertisements meant that creativity was particularly effective in categories where there was very little difference (or, arguably in many cases, no difference at all) between competing products—for example, beverages, toiletries, and tobacco. The challenge of trying to promote a product that is no different from any of its competitors is brought into sharp focus by a round-up of sun-cream advertising featured in *Campaign* in July 1970. Nine adverts are featured in all, each one promising a longer golden tan. Individually, they generally illustrate the generic benefits of a sun cream quite well, but as a whole they are almost entirely interchangeable; why any consumer should plump for Coppatan over Coppertone or any of others remained a mystery.[36]

Creativity did not replace either of the traditional approaches; rather it was incorporated into them. Much of the advertising produced was still a vehicle for a rational 'message-into-action' proposition. For example, played out by its popular Martians, Smash's proposition was that it was quicker and easier to prepare than traditional, old-fashioned mashed potatoes, so 'For mash get Smash'. However, the impact of creativity went much further than improving the quality of the output. Initially the large agencies responded to their clients' own demands for better creativity by buying it in. This not only boosted salaries for creatives but also improved their status internally within the agencies and raised their profiles externally among existing and prospective clients. Fitting maverick talent into the more rigid corporate structures of

[34] M. Threadgould, *Bread: A Loaf Affair* (London: BBC, 2010).
[35] Delaney, *Get Smashed*, 73–7; N. Werber, T. Baker, D. Carr, and M. Millers, *John Webster: The Human Ad Man* (London: London School of Communication Arts, 2013).
[36] 'The Sunshine People Who Keep Us in the Dark', *Campaign*, 24 July 1970, pp. 12–13.

traditional agencies did not always prove easy and was often superficial. In 1970, John Webster, later the creator of the Cresta Bear at BMP and one of the outstanding creative directors of the period, was initially recruited as a creative director by Hobson Bates, a large but somewhat old-fashioned agency. Webster soon discovered his appointment was not the embracement of creativity he was led to believe, but in fact a tactic for maintaining the status quo. Although his ideas were presented to clients, he felt that there was never any intention of using them; their purpose was to provide some context before the agency persuaded the client to choose a more conservative idea.[37]

Planning and Positioning

Despite initially only paying it lip service, all the big British agencies eventually embraced creativity. The catalyst for this change of heart was the structural and strategic development of two established practices: account planning and market positioning. Account planning was a discipline initially born in the UK out of market research that emerged in parallel within the agencies JWT and BMP.[38] Likewise, market positioning was less a revolutionary new approach (as it has been described elsewhere) and more the successful evolution of a number of extant, closely related concepts into a new convergent and competitor-oriented form.[39]

Account planning is an inaccurate and misleading name for what was in fact a new system of campaign development. During the 1950s most marketing activities (and marketing plans in particular) were executed by the advertising agency. Agencies traditionally undertook market research on behalf of their clients prior to creating campaigns. The research team's findings would be presented to the client by the account management team to provide reassurance or justification for the campaign strategy and proposed execution, after which point they would no longer be involved in the project. From 1960 onwards, corporate marketing departments became increasingly sophisticated and engaged in more of this market research work themselves. Marketing teams were understandably uncomfortable with the notion that their advertising agencies were responsible for measuring their own performance and began developing in-house evaluation systems.[40] Although the research tools available at the time were simplistic, they soon became broadly adopted. Most

[37] S. Carter, *John Webster: The Earth Person's Adman* (London: adam&eveDDB, 2014).

[38] S. Pollitt, 'How I Started Account Planning in Agencies', *Campaign*, 20 April 1979, pp. 29–30.

[39] R. Demaris, 'Positioning: The Battle for your Mind (Book Review)', *Journal of Marketing*, 56/1 (1992), 122.

[40] M. Baskin and D. Pickton, 'Account Panning: From Genesis to Revelation', *Marketing Intelligence & Planning*, 21/7 (2003), 416–24.

notable among them was a system called 'Day After Recall' (DAR) developed by the marketing team at Proctor and Gamble.[41] DAR involved interviewing a target audience sample the day after an advertisement had first been broadcast and recording the percentage of people who remembered it. By repeating this process over time, it was possible to compare each new advertisement with the brand's historic performance. If the recall figures were comparatively low, the advert could be revised or even dropped. The drawback with DAR and similar evaluation systems was that they could be employed only after the advertisement had been produced and broadcast; therefore mistakes could be identified only after a huge amount of expenditure.[42]

Around 1965, Stanley Pollitt, then working as an account executive at Pritchard Wood, recognized that a trained researcher could make a greater contribution to the campaign process. While account teams were inclined to pander to the clients and creative departments tended to be guided by no one but themselves, these research specialists—the account planning department—would represent the consumer throughout the various stages of campaign development.[43] When BMP opened in 1968, Pollitt immediately put this idea into practice and assigned a planner to work alongside the account manager for every client. It was a more robust and rigorous way to create campaigns. The planner's role was to analyse the product's values and position in the market and develop a set of objectives for the campaign. At each stage the creative work was tested with either focus groups or depth interviews with target audience members to gain insights into the consumer's responses, wants, and desires. This information was in turn used to revise and refine the creative.[44]

In principle, advertisements that emerge through account planning should be a lot more effective, but planning also provided clients with the reassurance that thorough research and scientific testing underpinned their campaigns. At the same time as Pollitt was introducing planning at BMP, Stephen King, then working at JWT, proposed an almost identical system that would provide clients with empirical evidence to support the proposed campaign's effectiveness rather than rely on their gut feeling. King's process involved integrating researchers in much the same way as Pollitt's, to synthesize an advertising message from business and product objectives and market conditions. In 1968, JWT established a new department called 'account planning'.[45] Creative

[41] 'Testing Methods', *Advertising Age*, 15 September 2003.
[42] S. Pollitt, 'How I Started Account Planning in Agencies', *Campaign*, 29–30.
[43] Ibid. 29–30.
[44] S. Pollitt and P. Feldwick, *Pollitt on Planning: Three Papers on Account Planning* (Henley-on-Thames: Admap, 2000).
[45] H. K. Anheier, M. Kaldor, and M. Glasius, *Global Civil Society 2004/5* (Oxford: Oxford University Press, 2004); S. King, J. Lannon, and M. Baskin, *A Master Class in Brand Planning: The Timeless Works of Stephen King* (Hoboken, NJ: Wiley, 2007); S. King, *What is a Brand?: The Definitive*

departments almost universally disliked account planning, regarding it as a trumped-up way of simply asking consumers what they thought. However, in reality, this was not yet another pedantic procedure to hamstring their ideas— it was the opposite. Under account planning, the best creative idea was still selected on judgement alone. The difference was that it was now subjected to testing and scrutiny much earlier in the process, after which it could be ditched or refined and retested again. This cycle could be repeated as many times as it was felt necessary.

D'Souza identified four discrete stages of the function of account planning. An initial *strategy development stage* involved a situation analysis of the client brief and existing data and the commissioning of further research to aid the development of an insight into the consumer relationship with the brand and its advertising. The strategy was then defined and agreed with the client. This led to the *creative development stage*. A creative brief was prepared incorporating the brand positioning and proposition. This was given to the creative team, who developed ideas, which were further evaluated, researched, and finessed until a definitive route was identified. This route was then submitted for client go-ahead in the *approval stage* before execution. Finally, performance was tracked and evaluated in the *post-campaign stage*.[46]

Account planning was an expensive process, but it encouraged clients to take risks. Without planning, challenging and innovative ideas were easy to write off, and their uptake was often reliant entirely on the persuasiveness of the account manager or the boldness of the client.[47] By incorporating the consumer's views and responses into the development process, planning made it much easier to get these ideas signed off. The function was eventually adopted by agencies worldwide, but it remained a discipline unique to Britain until the mid-1980s. By providing a sound base for creativity to flourish, planning was a key factor in the global success enjoyed by the UK's advertising sector over the following decades, giving them a significant edge over the competition.[48]

Al Ries and Jack Trout introduced the concept of market positioning through a series of articles in *Advertising Age* in 1972.[49] They defined position-ing itself and also highlighted the need for its introduction by arguing: 'To succeed in an over-communicated society, a company must create a position

---

Essay on Brand Building (London: JWT, 2008); S. King, *The JWT Planning Guide (1974)* (London: Royal Society of Account Planning, 2009).

[46] S. D'Souza, *What is Account Planning?* (London: Royal Society of Account Planning, 1986).

[47] H. Habberstad, *Anatomy of Account Planning* (London: Royal Society of Account Planning, 2000), 4–9.

[48] Ibid. 32–42; Baskin and Pickton, 'Account Planning', 416–24.

[49] A. Ries and J. Trout, *The Positioning Era Commeth: Reprint of a Three-Part Series in* Advertising Age (Chicago: Crain Publications, 1972); A. Ries, 'Position Properly, Broaden Base, don't Extend Line', *Marketing News*, 15 November 1974.

in the prospect's mind, a position that takes into consideration not only a company's own strengths and weaknesses, but those of its competitors as well.'[50] The issue of whether positioning was something entirely new and different or just some reheated ideas that were smartly presented has been a matter of some debate.[51] However, regardless of its originality, positioning was to prove a hugely influential and effective strategy over the coming decades.

According to positioning theory, the consumer's mind can be viewed as a set of compartments—or 'positions'—that a company can attempt to fill. This is comparatively easy to achieve if the desired position is empty or uncontested but very difficult if a competitor already occupies it.[52] At heart, positioning was an update of the concept of product differentiation. However, like planning, the real innovation by Ries andTrout was to make it external in nature: to consider the consumer and not just the product. Positioning took place not in the store or on the shelf but 'in the mind of the consumer'. A further concept called 'master plan positioning' purported to show how a company's product strategy could be designed to exploit this situation by differentiating brands for different market segments, thereby occupying a number of positions in the mind of the consumer.[53]

The rationale for positioning was straightforward and compelling. First, it acknowledged that different consumers bought the same products for different reasons and, secondly, that their decision to purchase *Brand X* over *Brand Y* was based on what they thought was different about it. The implication for marketers was that lots of slightly differentiated brands, each serving a different need, would be much more successful than one single product serving them all. For example, a toothpaste manufacturer that expanded its range to focus separately on cavity protection, white teeth, fresh breath, and healthy gums would collectively sell far more units than one single brand purporting to do all those things at the same time.

The cognitive models of the time (which underpinned the approaches of Ogilvy and Reeves) and the coevolving marketing function presumed that consumer behaviour was linear—that people generally made rational purchasing decisions based on evaluating the attributes of competing products. Most organizations firmly believed that effective brand communication should consist of appeals to rational consumers that addressed their needs and wants. This customer-oriented/company-oriented view contrasted with the competitor-oriented view offered by Ries and Trout. They argued that many

[50] A. Ries and J. Trout, *Positioning: The Battle for your Mind* (New York and London: McGraw-Hill, 2001), 24.

[51] J. P. Maggard, 'Positioning Revisited', *Journal of Marketing*, 40/1 (1976), 63–6.

[52] A. Ries and J. Trout, *Marketing Warfare* (New York and London: McGraw-Hill, 1986), 1.

[53] Ries and Trout, *Positioning: The Battle for your Mind*, 3–4.

consumer decisions, particularly those for low transactional products, were much simpler than had been previously believed and often relatively thought-less. Over the following decades further research in the field of behavioural economics bore out many of their findings, but for many years critics continued to argue that, for high-ticket items such as cars or computers, rational consumers tended to make rational decisions. However, even in these categories, increasing evidence emerged over time that demonstrated that emotional appeals could work just as well, if not better.[54]

Like planning, positioning became widely adopted. For companies, the resulting increase in the number of product lines raised costs, as it was much more expensive to package and market seven or eight separately positioned brands rather than one, yet in many cases the advantages of positioning justified this investment. By making it easier to target segments of the market, positioning allowed companies to grow faster, but, furthermore, it forced corporate minds to think more proactively about their brand image. Customers were also more likely to buy a new product if it came with some endorsement—for example, they would be more likely to buy the extension of a familiar brand that focused on a single benefit than a completely new brand that did the same, say, *Crest for Fresher Breath* rather than *Fresho Breath*. It is the consumers' understanding of the familiar, parent brand (in this example, 'Crest') that influences their purchasing decision. Thus, several new products could be rolled out by this process of brand extension, which as well as being more effective was considerably cheaper than launching a raft of new products. Branding—which had hitherto meant little more than developing a product name, logo, and packaging—started to incorporate more conceptual elements, such as company image positioning, which could be used to influence the consumer's perception of a whole range of products.[55]

Businesses began thinking in terms of their brand rather than their products. For example, in 1934, sportswear manufacturer Lacoste had been the first company to put a logo on the front of a garment—then known as a tennis shirt.[56] In 1972, Ralph Lauren was looking for a way to make his identically styled shirts more 'clubbable' and to that end displayed a polo player logo prominently on the breast of his new Polo range.[57] This was no mere copycat initiative. Unlike Lacoste's shirts, which targeted tennis players exclusively,

[54] Demaris, 'Positioning'; Ries and Trout, *Positioning: The Battle for Your Mind*, 122–5.

[55] Maggard, 'Positioning Revisited', 63–6; G. Davies, 'Positioning, Image and the Marketing of Multiple Retailers', *International Review of Retail, Distribution and Consumer Research*, 2/1 (1992), 13–34; M. S. Byron, 'The Marketing Value of Brand Extension', *Marketing Intelligence & Planning*, 9/7 (1991), 9–13; H. Jowitt and G. Lury, 'Is it Time to Reposition Positioning?', *Journal of Brand Management*, 20/2 (2012), 96–103.

[56] 'Rene Lacoste Obituary', *The Times*, 14 October 1996, p. 25.

[57] L. Rothman, 'How Ralph Lauren Came up with his Iconic Polo Brand', *Time*, 20 September 2015, <http://time.com/4055543/ralph-lauren-polo-shirt/>.

Lauren's clothing was not aimed at polo players at all but at the high end of the mass market. Lauren's strategy was to leverage the concept of polo— 'English', 'exclusive', 'elitist', 'tailored', 'upper class', 'sport of kings', and so on—in order to occupy a premium position in the mind of consumers.[58] Testament to his success is the fact that a majority of the English-speaking world began to refer to these garments generically as polo shirts rather than tennis shirts. Logos notwithstanding, the items were essentially identical, yet the conceptual, aspirational Ralph Lauren brand undoubtedly connected with consumers at that time in a very different way from the practical, functional Lacoste product.

A pioneer of this brand-first approach was the US-based footwear manufacturer Nike. The simple swoosh logo had been synonymous with the sportswear brand's name since 1971, but it was only in 1976 that Nike hired its first advertising agency.[59] Seattle-based John Brown & Partners created the first 'brand advertisement' for their new client the following year.[60] *There Is No Finish Line* was the first in a long line of campaigns within which no product was shown at all (see Figure 3.3). Judged by the standards of 1960s, advertising this conceptual approach made little sense: no product is shown, there is no

Figure 3.3. *There Is No Finish Line*: designed by John Brown & Partners, USA, 1977. (Gift of Various Donors; 1981-29-205, Courtesy of Cooper Howett Collection, Smithsonian Design Museum, NY.) See also plates section.

---

[58] Ibid.   [59] 'Champions of Design', *Campaign*, 1 December 2013, p. 42.
[60] R. Goldman and S. Papson, *Nike Culture: The Sign of the Swoosh* (London: Sage, 1998).

message, no proposition, and no call to action—just an ambiguous statement, a nicely art-directed photograph, and a logo. However, because the advertisement is knowingly empty, it invites interpretation and seems to be saying something much bigger than 'quality sports footwear'. The conclusion might be drawn that training is not simply a means to an end but a never-ending process of self-improvement. This is one of the earliest examples of an emotion-into-action appeal. Unlike a proposition-based rational message-into-action appeal—in which consumers are persuaded to make a product choice—the emotional appeal encourages them to make a brand or lifestyle choice instead. In this example, if consumers are simply looking for new running shoes, they might choose a pair of Adidas, Reebok, New Balance, or any number of qualitatively similar products that will all do the job equally well. However, if they buy into the idea that exercising is somehow helping to make them a better person, then they will probably choose Nike. And the evidence is that overwhelmingly people did choose Nike. In the year following the campaign's launch the company's revenues doubled to $28 million. By 1979, Nike was selling half of all running shoes bought in the USA and in addition to its footwear business was also making and marketing its own range of sports clothing.[61]

Goldman and Papson described 'the genesis of "new" advertising in the 1980s', which replaced the 'formulaic and over-determined frameworks' of the 1960s and 1970s. In their view, the changes were not so much advantageous as necessary if advertising was to avoid a crisis brought about by consumers' acclimatization to its 'routinized messages and reading rules'.[62] There is much to support the idea that consumers had become inured to advertising that is dull or boring; indeed, one could argue that advertising would have evolved to reflect the tastes of consumers regardless of the changes in methodology. However, positioning and planning can be seen as a direct response both to the emergence of the 'savvy, media literate viewers' that Goldman and Papson identify and also to the consumer impatience and dissatisfaction identified by Offer.[63] Both processes credited the consumer with much more sophistication than had either Ogilvy or Reeves, and in many cases (but by no means all) the 'new' advertising campaigns produced were more engaging and affecting than ever before. This was despite the much greater challenge

---

[61] 'Nike: The Internationalization Strategy of Adidas', in D. Holtbrügge and H. Haussmann (eds), *The Internationalization of Firms: Case Studies from the Nürnberg Metropolitan Region* (Augsburg: Rainer Hampp Verlag, 2017), 21.

[62] R. Goldman and S. Papson, 'Advertising in the Age of Hypersignification', *Theory, Culture and Society*, 11/3 (1994), 23–54; 'EEC Council Television without Frontiers Directive, Article 15', *Official Journal of the European Communities*, 298/23 (1989), 15.

[63] Goldman and Papson, 'Advertising in the Age of Hypersignification', 24; A. Offer, *The Challenge of Affluence: Self-Control and Wellbeing in the United States and Britain since 1950* (Oxford: Oxford Univeristy Press, 2007), 1.

Table 3.2. Total UK advertising expenditure as a percentage of GDP, 1978–1988

Year	Expenditure (£m, at 2018 values)	Percentage of GDP (at market values)
1978	2,468	1.10
1980	3,438	1.12
1982	4,239	1.15
1984	5,530	1.29
1986	7,035	1.38
1988	9,367	1.50

Source: WARC.

of achieving communication through a fragmented media and a hyperactive audience.[64]

For the advertising agencies in the UK, positioning and planning also meant more work, more fees, and greater profits. Towards the end of the 1970s, advertising expenditure was rising both in real terms and as a percentage of GNP. It would continue to do so for the next decade (see Table 3.2). However, in the long term, arguably the biggest benefactor of positioning and planning was neither advertising nor marketing but public relations, thus far poorly understood in the UK and as a consequence largely overlooked, often mocked, and considerably undervalued.[65]

Public Relations: The New Persuaders

Marketing and public relations are the major external functions of a firm. Public relations is a distinct communications discipline that should not be conflated with other forms of marketing. Grunig and Hunt provide a typical example of the standard definition: 'Public relations activities are part of the management of communication between an organisation and its publics.'[66] There is some debate as to whether this is an accurate description; for example, Boltan and Hazleton argue that definitions such as this tend to present public relations as a neutral communication channel, underplaying its actual practice as a means of persuasion. In that regard, Lippman offered a more critical but arguably more accurate assessment of public relations as 'the manufacture

---

[64] Goldman and Papson, 'Advertising in the Age of Hypersignification', 49.

[65] See C. Spencer, 'Applying Account Planning to Public Relations', *Journal of Communication Management*, 4/1 (1999), 95–105.

[66] J. E. Grunig and T. Hunt, *Managing Public Relations* (New York and London: Holt, Rinehart and Winston, 1984).

of consent'.[67] However, despite this debate, almost all definitions of public relations concur that it can be considered as the practice of presenting the public face of an individual or organization and the articulation of its aims, objectives, opinions, beliefs, and views.[68] Public relations is used to encourage target audiences to engage sympathetically with these values at both an emotional and a rational level. It is also worth noting that an organization's public relations aims and objectives can often be completely different from those of its other marketing and brand communication activities.

The majority of public relations is carried out through the media. Occasionally, communication is directly with the target audience, through a speech or stakeholder event, for example; but more usually it takes place through a third-party conduit or media channel. At a practical level, much of the PR specialist's job involves the production of materials that are useful to the press, broadcasters, and other media. However, building effective relationships with journalists who work therein is of paramount importance. The goal of this activity is to push relevant messages out through media channels to target audiences or 'publics'. The results of public relations activity are dependent upon the quality of the material, the strength of the media relationships, and the impact of the message, but it should achieve coverage that is broadly or wholly supportive of those aims and objectives.[69]

Although it is usually delivered via the same or similar media, public relations has two major advantages over advertising. First, it is usually invisible, utterly indistinguishable from other forms of editorial, and therefore hugely more persuasive than advertising.[70] Consumers react very differently to advertising and editorial. As Goldman and Papson identify, when individuals are viewing advertisements, there is an understanding that the content is trying to persuade them to take a view; consequently, advertising messages are met with a degree of scepticism, as people choose either to accept or to disbelieve the information presented.[71] However, communication about the same product or service through a seemingly impartial third party—for example, a newspaper review, magazine feature, or TV programme—is much more

---

[67] C. H. Botan and V. Hazleton, *Public Relations Theory II* (Mahwah, NJ, and London: L. Erlbaum, 2006), 23; W. Lippmann, *Public Opinion* (New York and London: Free Press, 1997).

[68] For definitions of public relations and its role in organizations, see G. M. Broom and D. M. Dozier, 'Advancement for Public Relations Role Models', *Public Relations Review*, 12/1 (1986), 37–56; S. M. Cutlip, A. H. Center, and G. M. Broom, *Effective Public Relations* (London: Prentice Hall, 2006), 5–7; Grunig and Hunt, *Managing Public Relations*, 7–8, 22; D. W. Stacks, *Primer of Public Relations Research* (New York: Guildford Press, 2011), 21–2; R. Tench and L. Yeomans, *Exploring Public Relations* (Harlow: Pearson, 2013), 4–7.

[69] For an overview of the public relations function, see Tench and Yeomans, *Exploring Public Relations*, 21–33, 83–120, 235–50, 300–13.

[70] T. Cheng, H. Brisson, and M. Hay, *The Role of Content in the Consumer Decision Making Process* (New York: Neilsen, 2014).

[71] Goldman and Papson, 'Advertising in the Age of Hypersignification', 23–54.

compelling. It is treated as informative rather than persuasive and deemed worthy of attention.[72] Public relations coverage does not directly encourage consumers to make a purchase, but it can achieve that end by creating a positive image—or position—about the product, service, or brand in the minds of consumers.[73] Secondly, public relations is comparatively inexpensive when compared to advertising, because the editorial coverage secured is 'free'. For these reasons, there are few things more effective at galvanizing opinion than a well-executed public relations campaign.

Despite these benefits, public relations is not without its shortcomings. There are three notable disadvantages, the most important of which is that public relations is very difficult to control and results can never be guaranteed. Marketers dislike this unpredictability—with advertising there is at least a sense that you get what you pay for. Secondly, a public relations story is generally run only once in each publication, whereas an advertisement can be run again and again. Finally, unlike advertising, public relations rarely contains a call to action. Public relations is good at building awareness, at pushing a message, or at promoting an idea, but it is much less effective at directly increasing the sales of a product or adoption of a service. As such, its role in the marketing mix is often unclear, and its relationship with marketing itself can easily become competitive rather than collaborative.[74]

In 1978, Kotler and Mindak highlighted the historic issue of relations between the two disciplines within US organizations in order to address the new challenges emerging from the market.[75] They identified four classes of enterprise with respect to their use of marketing and public relations. Class One comprised organizations that barely used either function—for example, small service businesses or non-profit organizations. Class Two organizations were those with well-developed public relations functions but no marketing function—for example, hospitals or educational establishments. Class Three represented those businesses with a strong marketing function but running very little in the way of public relations. Class Four enterprises were those operating strong public relations and marketing functions—typically (in the USA) those listed in the Fortune 500 companies. Within Class Four companies, public relations and marketing were in most cases run as separate departments.[76]

---

[72] Cheng, Brisson, and Hay, *The Role of Content in the Consumer Decision Making Process*, 11.

[73] C. Black, *The PR Professional's Handbook* (London: Kogan, 2014), 94–102; Tench and Yeomans, *Exploring Public Relations*, 235–51, 395–409.

[74] P. J. Kitchen, *Public Relations: Principles and Practice* (London: Thomson, 1997), 6–21, 223–38.

[75] P. Kotler and W. Mindak, 'Marketing and Public Relations: Should They Be Partners?', *Journal of Marketing*, 42/4 (1978), 13–20.

[76] Ibid.

In the UK, the salient issue was not so much the nature of the relationship between public relations and marketing but rather the fact that there was typically no relationship at all. In 1968, the UK public relations sector was tiny, employing less than 10,000 people with a reported combined turnover of £80 million. The public sector accounted for much of this annual spend and also a large proportion of professional PR specialists. Until the 1970s, public relations in the UK took place predominantly within the public sector and most conspicuously through campaigns run by the Ministry of Information (later called the Central Office of Information (COI)), which was the British government's in-house marketing and communications agency.[77] The few private companies that did engage meaningfully in public relations activity spent an average of £2,000–3,000 per year (£34,000–£51,000 in 2018 values).[78] By way of comparison, at the same time in the USA businesses were spending around £1,050 million on public relations, and the sector employed around 150,000 professionals.[79] Growth remained slow in the UK throughout the 1970s, as did the disparity with the USA. Ten years after its 1969 foundation, the UK public relations industry's corporate trade body—the Public Relations Consultants Association (PRCA)—had only eighty-four members.[80] In 1979, 78 per cent of the Fortune Top 500 companies were taking public relations consultancy advice, compared with just 21 per cent of the top 500 UK businesses.[81]

Perhaps this lack of corporate interest in public relations prior to the 1980s goes some way to explaining the dearth of academic literature noted by L'Etang and Pieczka.[82] If histories of British advertising are thin on the ground, then those of public relations are practically non-existent. There are only two key histories of British public relations, by Anthony and by L'Etang.[83] Only L'Etang offers an analysis of the period 1969–97. Her conclusions are compelling. Despite the tremendous growth experienced by the sector during the 1980s and 1990s, L'Etang regarded the dominant theme in the history of the public relations industry as that of a failure to

---

[77] S. Anthony, *Public Relations and the Making of Modern Britain: Stephen Tallents and the Birth of a Progressive Media Profession* (Manchester: Manchester University Press, 2012); 'Ten Ways in which to Overcharge PR Clients', *Campaign*, 16 July 1968, p. 20.
[78] Ibid.   [79] Ibid.
[80] 'A Decade of Growth', in *The Public Relations Yearbook 1990* (London: PRCA, 1989), 44–9.
[81] D. Smith, 'Consultancy and Client: A Problem Shared is a Problem Solved', *Public Relations Year Book 1985* (London: FT Business Information, 1984). Note that figures reported are from a series of independent surveys into public relations use in the USA and UK carried out by Carl Byoir & Associates between 1979 and 1984.
[82] M. Pieczka, 'The Disappearing Act: Public Relations Consultancy in Theory and Research', unpublished paper, ICA Annual Conference Montreal, Canada, 2008; L'Etang, *Public Relations in Britain*.
[83] Anthony, *Public Relations and the Making of Modern Britain*; L'Etang, *Public Relations in Britain*.

professionalize.[84] The explanation provided for this paradox was that the sector's two professional bodies—the Institute of Public Relations (IPR) founded in 1953 to represent individuals and the PRCA founded in 1969 to represent consultancies—were established too late to exercise control or influence over their practitioners. Indeed, few practitioners bothered to join either organization. By the end of the twentieth century, the IPR had only 3,900 members out of Britain's estimated 45,000–60,000 practitioners.[85] As a consequence, there was a reluctance—arguably an inability—on behalf of these trade bodies to impose regulatory standards or codes of practice. Very few members were ever expelled for breaches of the code of conduct.[86]

Throughout the 1960s and 1970s, public relations remained small scale in comparison with advertising and few would have countenanced that a spectacular rise to prominence was imminent. Most public relations activity took place not in consultancies but in public-sector press offices, as British businesses, unlike their American counterparts, remained largely blind to the appeal of public relations campaigns. In 1970, a *Campaign* report highlighted the yawning chasm between UK and US public relations firms. J. R. O'Dwyer, the largest US agency, enjoyed billings of $8.37 million and employed 348 people. The second largest, Ruder & Finn, with $6.00 million in billings, employed 328. As the paper said: 'No British PR company has a total fee income remotely approaching these figures and few have an international operation comparable with the top US firms'[87] (see Table 3.3). For business leaders during the 1960s and 1970s—a time of economic underperformance and the diminishing international status for the nation as a whole—communication was seldom a salient issue. When businesses were forced, often reluctantly, to deal with the media, the managing directors expected respectful questions by deferential journalists that they might or might not deign to answer.[88]

The fact that public relations had such a long way to go before it was seen as a vital marketing function was indeed, as L'Etang identified, due to the structural problems within the sector and its governance.[89] Prior to 1980s, there was almost no academic literature produced on the subject of communications, and even for practitioners themselves there were few guides or publications beyond those published by the IPR. Consequently, there was almost no awareness of the value of public relations as a business tool among those

---

[84] Ibid. 1–19, 220–9.
[85] Ibid. 221; see also N. Tobin, 'Can the Pofessionalisation of the UK Public Relations Industry Make it More Trustworthy?', *Journal of Communication Management*, 9/1 (2005), 56–64.
[86] J. L'Etang, 'The Myth of the "Ethical Guardian": An Examination of its Origins, Potency and Illusions', *Journal of Communication Management*, 8/1 (2003), 53–67.
[87] 'H&K Tops PR List', *Campaign*, 27 February 1970, p. 19.
[88] J. Howard, *The Evolution of UK PR Consultancies 1970–2010* (London: PRCA, 2011), 6, 8, 12–14.
[89] L'Etang, *Public Relations in Britain*, 103, 123.

Table 3.3. Top 20 UK public relations consultancies, 1968

Rank	Company	Billings (£)	Billings (£m, 2018 values)
1	Lexington	227,750	3.94 million
2	Planned PR	200,000	3.46
3	Forman House	174,744	3.02
4	Bensons PR	153,810	2.66
5	Michael Rice	153,302	2.65
6	Voice and Visions	146,462	2.53
7	Infoplan	142,013	2.45
8	Harris and Hunter	125,100	2.16
9	Parker PR	120,255	2.08
10	Lonsdale Information	97,280	1.68
11	Link	97,269	1.68
12	Burston-Marsteller	91,995	1.59
13	F. J. Lyons	86,903	1.50
14	Astral	80,021	1.38
15	Interlink	76,644	1.32
16	PR Counsel	75,948	1.31
17	Macleish	57,898	1.00
18	PRP	48,937	0.86
19	Hadley Byrne	48,842	0.85
20	Interflow	46,567	0.80

Source: *Campaign*, 1 July 1970, p. 18.

outside the sector.[90] Yet, in part, the fault also lay with many of the practitioners themselves. The development of planning and positioning led advertising agencies to recruit staff with marketing, sales, or research backgrounds who could analyse the market position of their client and identify the campaign requirement. As client marketing departments became more sophisticated, so the agencies moved their own people with a marketing background into account planning positions. The overall quality of output improved dramatically as a result.[91]

The public relations sector underwent no similar sector-wide evolution. Almost all its practitioners remained, at best, bit players engaged in a fringe activity—typically ex-journalists or personable young women who 'got stuff into the press' in support of the main advertising campaign—but more often than not they were omitted altogether. The results of public relations, often random and ineffectual in the marketing terms of the period, were reported to marketing directors who knew a great deal about advertising but very little about what public relations, when executed effectively, was capable of doing for them. Evidence for the lowly status of public relations in the UK can be found within the pages of *Campaign*. With one or two pages dedicated to the sector each week along with the occasional feature—and the lack of any other

---

[90] Howard, *The Evolution of UK PR Consultancies*, 12; Pieczka, 'The Disappearing Act'.
[91] B. Garfield, 'Top 100 Advertising Campaigns of the Century', *Advertising Age*, 29 March 1999.

media—*Campaign* was effectively the sector's trade paper until the launch of *PR Week* in 1984. However, within its editorial it often seemed to spend as much time mocking public relations as it did promoting the discipline. The tone was set in its launch issue with a lead feature in its 'Close Up/PR' section entitled 'Ten ways in which to overcharge PR clients'. The paper suggested, somewhat unnecessarily, that this article would 'make provocative reading for the PR man'.[92] Another typically provocative example is provided by a 1970 editorial, which opined: 'Journalists are always complaining that public relations men are useless... but the business often gives the impression of trying to prove the journalists right.' The piece went on to attack practitioners for being blind to both their clients' objectives and the elements that go into making a good story and accused them of bombarding the media with old and useless information as a consequence.[93]

Variations on this theme continued to appear regularly throughout the decade—for example, articles entitled 'Many Firms Unhappy with PR' in 1970, 'Why Press Officers are Walking a Tightrope' and 'Putting Paper Qualifications into PR', both from 1974; and 'Don't Sleep in the Subway: An "Idiot's Guide" to PR' from 1975.[94] In January 1975, *Campaign* ran a feature about the communications of the Community Relations Commission (CRC) entitled 'Can Public Relations Solve the Colour Problem?', drawing the conclusion that it almost certainly could not. Noting that public relations was used largely by government and large corporations like energy companies, but very little by consumer brands, *Campaign* argued that the work was carried out by non-specialists incapable of developing effective communications strategies: 'A two-day PR workshop is viewed as preparation enough for community relations officers.'[95] In November 1980, the paper was still flagging up ineffective practices regarded as endemic in the public relations industry. A business media study into the feelings of 154 journalists towards public relations consultancies and industrial and corporate public relations departments revealed that 'more than half the 440 press releases sent out each month by public relations firms are never used. Only 44.6% were considered well written.'[96] A raft of protest from infuriated PR specialists invariably followed each negative story, filling the letters page over the following weeks with demands that the discipline should be taken more seriously. They were routinely ignored. The stereotypical PR specialist was usually

[92] 'Ten Ways in which to Overcharge PR Clients', *Campaign*, 16 July 1968, p. 20.
[93] 'Leader', *Campaign*, 9 October 1970, p. 13.
[94] 'Many Firms Unhappy with PR', *Campaign*, 13 July 1970, p. 2; 'Why Press Officers are Walking a Tightrope', *Campaign*, 28 June 1974, p. 21; 'Putting Paper Qualifications into PR', *Campaign*, 27 September 1974, p. 41; 'Don't Sleep in the Subway: An "Idiots" Guide to PR', *Campaign*, 17 January 1975, p. 44; 'Are PR Shops More Objective?', *Campaign*, 5 December 1980, p. 13.
[95] 'Can Public Relations Solve the Colour Problem?', *Campaign*, 31 January 1975, p. 21.
[96] 'Media Blasts Poor PR Standards', *Campaign*, 21 November 1980, p. 4.

junior, attractive, female, and without any executive authority. A PR specialist's work, it was assumed, consisted largely of typing press releases—or 'handouts'—mailing them out to journalists, and then ringing them up a couple of days later to see whether or not they were interested in running the story.[97]

How much of this criticism was justified? To understand that we would really need to look at the quality of the advice that PR specialists were giving to their clients at the time. Unlike advertising, little public relations output from the period exists beyond press releases, which provide little indication of strategy or methodology. The HAT archive does, however, contain a small number of public relations proposals from the period produced by Lexington, the leading UK public relations agency of the time, a position it maintained until the late 1970s. Lexington was an affiliate of JWT, and it is reasonable to assume that its proposals were more professional than most or, at worst, fairly typical of the sector. One rare example from 1970 is a detailed status report and proposal for a major, national public relations programme on behalf of Kraft, which was looking to leverage its £25,000 sponsorship of the 1972 Great Britain Olympic team. Public relations campaigns on this scale were unusual in 1970, and the document provides an illuminating insight into the capabilities of top-level UK public relations consultancies at this time.[98]

The proposal begins by listing a set of aims. However, these are more the kind of things the client would like to include in the plan rather than a definitive list of deliverable objectives.[99] For example, 'to secure an exclusive British Olympic/Kraft in-store promotion' is in fact not an objective at all, but a method. Other stated objectives are either so vague or all-encompassing that they could not possibly be achieved in any measurable way—for example, 'to promote the corporate strength of the Kraft Company' or 'for Kraft to be seen to be giving consumers the opportunity to support the British Athletic team'. There is no mention of any target audience beyond a rather hazily realized 'Supporters of the British Olympic team.' A clearly defined target audience is important in public relations terms. It is used to help identify and develop key messages and appropriate media outlets, but also to measure campaign effectiveness. Yet this is such a broad, unsegmented category one could plausibly argue that includes almost everyone in Great Britain. It is hard to conceive of JWT, or any other leading advertising agency for that matter, getting away with such a similarly broad definition of the target audience, one that pays such little heed to demographics. Given that the media for both advertising and public relations campaigns are the same in this instance, Lexington would surely not have found this information difficult to come by.[100]

[97] J. Howard, *The Evolution of UK PR Consultancies*.
[98] HAT, JWT (1970), Kraft Olympic 1972 proposal, Lexington PR. [99] Ibid. 1.
[100] Ibid.

The proposal then explores 'The Theme', which appears to be a colloquial term for 'strategy'. However, there is little strategy in evidence, rather a collection of random ideas and concepts under the headline 'Kraft would like to present consumers with the opportunity to contribute towards providing facilities for training the British Olympic Team', which once again bears little relationship to the real, attainable marketing and sales objectives of Kraft. Given the absence of a strategy, it is hard to describe these ideas as 'tactics'. In their defence, they do seem to have been designed to stimulate journalists, but some look destined not to come off ('Kraft Cheese Stakes. A fun race, time and place to be agreed. Possibly Loughborough'), while others seem somewhat at odds with the elite athletes' drive for a gold medal ('Relay Team with the total collection of Cheese they will consume during training period for Helsinki'). A few ideas seem to pander directly to the client's ego rather than to any identifiable need or demand from the media ('A bank of photographs of leading athletes will be established specifically for the Trade Press to accompany stories on the developments in the Kraft Olympic promotion').[101]

Charging for this kind of work presents its own problems. At the outset, the clients are not quite sure what they are getting beyond a lot of enthusiasm. During the campaign, there is the feeling that they are not quite in control of what is going on or why it is going on, but that issue is almost impossible to surface. At the end of the proposal is a list of public relations coverage achieved to date—a mix of local, trade, and national press—leading to the inevitable conclusion that quantity is the only measurement criteria.[102] The proposal comes across as energetic and well intentioned, but fails to answer three key corporate communication questions—namely: Why are we doing this? To whom are we speaking? What will it achieve in terms of actual sales?

It is not unreasonable to draw broader conclusions about how typical an example this document is of public relations in the UK at the time. Indeed, a vagueness of purpose and execution continued to hamper the development of public relations throughout the 1970s. Before it could be treated as a marketing discipline, and be paid for as an effective and important corporate service, public relations agencies needed to rid themselves of the flippancy with which they handled their accounts. That required specialists with marketing and sales experience as well as press and public relations experience who could speak the same language as their clients, produce planned campaigns, and relate their activities to tangible—occasionally even measurable—achievements relevant to agreed marketing, sales, and business objectives.

Given the lowly status of public relations in the UK during the late1970s, it is remarkable that this moribund sector would go on to exert such a profound

---

[101] Ibid. 2–6.   [102] Ibid. 6.

influence over British society during the 1980s and 1990s, becoming arguably the most significant of all the persuasion industries. The key question is how did public relations make this transformation from afterthought to thought leader? There is an argument that the introduction of positioning provided public relations with a strategic framework. Positioning involved manipulating what consumers were already thinking (as Ries and Trout put it, to 'retie connections that already exist') rather than creating something new and different.[103] One of public relations' strongest and most defining characteristics is its influence over the exchange of information, stories, beliefs, and demands between an organization and its publics. In short, owing to its covert nature, public relations could impact upon positioning in ways that advertising could not. Positioning allowed public relations agencies to relate their actions directly to selling 'something', whether that was a service, a product, a capability, a success, or an idea. However, as Miller and Dinen identified, there was no single innovation in theory or practice to account for the sector's rapid expansion. Positioning was a tool for directing public relations activity more effectively, but it was definitely not a new method of carrying out public relations nor was it a catalyst for growth.[104]

A more significant development was the shift in ideological emphasis from society to the individual, which followed the election victory of Margaret Thatcher's Conservative Party in 1979. The aims and objectives of the persuasion industries were perfectly aligned with this new political thinking, which allowed their activities to occupy the centre stage. In this regard, the subsequent expansion of the City (Britain's finance sector) and the reform of the UK stock market in the mid-1980s were to prove particularly pivotal for public relations, providing a high-profile showcase for what PR-led campaigns could achieve in their own right.[105]

While this political development was crucial, there is also some evidence that, during the late 1970s, at least a handful of practitioners were beginning to think differently about the discipline. There was a growing awareness about the strengths of public relations and how they might best be applied to establish a market position rather than merely pushing a message in support

---

[103] Ries and Trout, *Positioning: The Battle for your Mind*, 5.

[104] D. Miller and W. Dinan, 'The Rise of the PR Industry in Britain, 1979–98', *European Journal of Communication*, 15/1 (2000), 5–35.

[105] For an overview, see B. Evans, *Thatcherism and British Politics, 1975–1997* (Stroud: Sutton, 1999); E. J. Evans, *Thatcher and Thatcherism* (London and New York: Routledge, 2004); M. Francis, 'A Crusade to Enfranchise the Many: Thatcherism and the "Property-Owning Democracy"', *Twentieth Century British History*, 23/2 (2012), 275–97; A. Gamble, *Britain in Decline: Economic Policy, Political Strategy and the British State* (Basingstoke: Macmillan, 1994); A. Gamble, *The Free Economy and the Strong State: The Politics of Thatcherism* (Basingstoke: Macmillan, 1994); E. H. H. Green, *Thatcher* (London: Hodder Arnold, 2006); B. Jackson, R. Saunders, and B. Jackson, *Making Thatcher's Britain* (Cambridge: Cambridge University Press, 2012); R. Vinen, *Thatcher's Britain: The Politics and Social Upheaval of the Thatcher Era* (London: Pocket, 2010).

of advertising. This new thinking, coupled with the low quality of the existing sector, provided an opportunity for these more capable operators. In 1974, Peter Gummer, a Cambridge graduate, former trade journalist and younger brother of the future Conservative Party chairman John Selwyn Gummer, founded Shandwick. In just seven years Gummer's company had surpassed the established US firms of Charles Barker, Hill & Knowlton, Edelman, and Burston-Marsteller to become the largest public relations consultancy in the UK.[106] As public relations spending in the late 1970s was still dominated by the public sector, it is perhaps no surprise that several pioneers emerged from politics rather than commerce. From its inception in 1985, the business run by Tim Bell under a variety of names (before settling on Bell Pottinger) was Shandwick's biggest UK competitor. During the 1970s, Bell was the managing director of advertising agency Saatchi & Saatchi, for whom he also ran the Conservative Party account in the run-up to the 1979 general election. Gordon Reece, the Conservative Party director of publicity, appointed Saatchi & Saatchi because he wanted an agency that understood television. Bell claims he was handed the account—against his better judgement—because he was the only Conservative voter in the business.[107] Reece was heavily influenced by the spin doctors then working for the Republican Party in the USA, the campaigns run by both sides during the 1976 US presidential election, and also the victorious campaign of the Australian Liberal Party in 1977. Realizing that the forthcoming British election would be a televisual contest, Reece took the radical decision to switch the emphasis away from heavyweight political programmes and secured appearances for his prospective prime minister on populist shows, which would provide less opportunity for confrontational interviewing. Margaret Thatcher even appeared as a guest on the children's TV show *Jim'll Fix It*, which provided a huge family audience (in Bell's words, long before 'people knew the grim reality' about presenter Jimmy Savile).[108] Bell and Reece developed a communication strategy that aimed to make voters increasingly exasperated with the incumbent Labour government. Rational debates about perceived Labour strengths such as health, education, and social services were to be avoided. Instead, only emotive discussion was encouraged within the media. Labour leader Jim Callaghan would be portrayed as old, boring, out of touch, and patronizing wherever possible in contrast to 'ordinary grocer's daughter' Margaret Thatcher, whose modest background, dredged up at every opportunity, gave her a natural rapport with the concerns of 'ordinary voters'.[109]

---

[106] 'Once is not Enough for Chadlington', *Daily Telegraph*, 12 September 2004, <http://www.telegraph.co.uk/finance/2894726/Once-is-not-enough-for-Chadlington.html>; *Huntsworth: Group Board* <https://web.archive.org/web/20090426121238/http://www.huntsworth.com:80/people/>; The Peerage, *Richard Gardiner Case, Baron Casey* <http://www.thepeerage.com/p19112.htm>.
[107] Bell, *Right or Wrong*, 42.   [108] Ibid. 41–2.   [109] Ibid. 52–60.

The target audience identified for this public relations activity was broad. It included so-called C1 and C2 manual workers fed up with industrial stagnation, young and first-time voters without deep party affiliations, and disaffected female Labour voters. The media channels required to reach this audience would take the Conservative Party out of its traditional broadsheet-and-*Daily-Mail* comfort zone, and the support of a red top tabloid was identified as vital to the campaign's success. To that end, Bell arranged a series of one-on-one briefings between Margaret Thatcher and the *Sun*'s editor Larry Lamb and also the newspaper's owner, Rupert Murdoch. The purpose was to persuade the pair that their readers' dissatisfaction with the state of the country could be resolved by voting Conservative. In return for their support, the *Sun* and other media outlets would be drip fed exclusive gossip and insights. The extent to which Bell and Reece were able to extend their influence into the press was considerable.[110] The *Daily Mail* ran articles Bell had specially written for them, including, during election week itself, the notorious front-page story 'Labour's Dirty Dozen: 12 Big Lies they Hope will Save them'.[111]

This campaign was an early example of corporate branding whereby an identity is achieved through a positioning strategy. Like much of marketing, brand identity is a nebulous concept but undeniably important. There exists no agreed, singular definition of the term, but for the purposes of this discussion the following, originally suggested by Farquhar, is sufficient.[112] He argues that, in marketing terms brand identity is what gives a product added value: it is a central idea, notion, or concept, successfully delivered consistently across all channels and access points to a very broad audience. As a result, brand identity is what makes Coca Cola worth more than cola, Shell worth more than gasoline, and Nike worth more than trainers. The key to identity is consistency. Just as people expect the identity of family or friends to remain the same, so they don't expect surprises when they buy Coke, Shell, or Nike. In contrast to Callaghan's government, wherever and however you viewed Margaret Thatcher's Conservative Party in the run-up to the election, it always looked exactly the same. Bell recalls a researcher telling Thatcher that he had discovered 'the dynamite revelation that Callaghan owned three houses', to which she replied, consistently on message: 'Yes, it is wonderful, because we would like it if everybody owned three houses.'[113] Bell and Reece's version of positioning achieved through audience out-take was a distant remove from

---

[110] Ibid. 46–51.

[111] 'Labour's Dirty Dozen: 12 Big Lies They Hope Will Save Them', *Daily Mail*, 25 April 1979, p. 1.

[112] R. A. Bailey, 'An Exploration of the Meanings of Hotel Brand Equity', *Service Industries Journal*, 26/1 (2006), 15–38; P. H. Farquhar 'Managing brand equity', *Journal of Advertising Research*, vol.30.4 (1989), pp. 7–12.

[113] Bell, *Right or Wrong*, 59.

the output-based process of writing press releases and following them up with a nuisance phone call: a sniper's rifle rather than a scatter gun. The effectiveness of this approach was evident, and further potential applications did not go unnoticed.

Persuasion on the up

The persuasion industries in Britain underwent significant changes during the 1970s that would allow them to play a more central role in society over the next two decades. Advertising arrested a systemic decline through the promotion of creativity and introduction of planning. The quasi-scientific approaches typified by Ogilvy and Rees that proliferated during the 1960s remained initially popular but were to decline steadily in influence. The quality and effectiveness of advertising also increased at a time when new channels were emerging—for example, colour magazines and television, independent radio stations, and children's TV programmes. This resulted in lower entry costs for advertisers, allowing more firms to engage in some form of persuasion. New consumer audiences also emerged following the breakdown of the nuclear family (a staple of post-war advertising), with working women, teenagers, and children all contributing to new patterns of consumption. As the decade progressed, positioning provided a strategic framework for anyone wishing to reach out to a broad audience in a more intelligent and effective manner. It was an approach quickly adopted by new brands such as Nike, Apple, and Virgin, but also by established operators such as Coca Cola and the UK Conservative Party.

Together these theoretical and practical changes resulted in advertising output that was generally much more effective and engaging and also created an environment for specialist disciplines—such as branding, public relations, and design—to emerge. Yet, above all, it was the political change in the UK and USA that allowed persuasion to take its place in the forefront during the 1980s and 1990s. Margaret Thatcher and her government seemed to be completely aligned with the aims and objectives of the sector. For the first time, ideas such as personal wealth, aspiration, ambition, and the accumulation of property and goods would be found equally in political rhetoric and advertising copy.

Although not quite the finished article, the UK persuasion industries entered the 1980s in far better shape than they had been in the early 1970s and were well positioned to take advantages of the imminent changes within the global economy. The brands and agencies that emerged to dominate the consumer society over the latter part of the twentieth century were those that could turn all these advances into an effective and coherent global package. In November 1980, British advertising agencies won a record nine top prizes in the tenth annual US Television Festival in Chicago USA.[114] In 1986, Saatchi & Saatchi became the biggest agency in the world, following the purchase of Ted Bates. The acquisition was funded by a £406 million rights issue—the second largest that the London stock exchange had ever seen.[115] Both creatively and commercially, Britain's recently failing persuasion industries were—somewhat surprisingly—leading the world.

[114] 'UK Agencies Scoop Top US Ad Awards', *Campaign*, 5 December 1980, p. 2.
[115] Fletcher, *Powers of Persuasion*, 205–6.

4

Hearts and Minds

Marketing and Advertising, 1980–1997

An Emotional Model of Brand Communication

Across the board, historians of brand communication, promotional culture, and affluence identify an increase in the influence of persuasion from 1980 onwards. For those outside the industry—namely, the commentators and historians of consumption, affluence, and promotional culture—the key drivers of this change were external, quantitative, and opportunistic.[1] In short, a number of factors combined to create the perfect conditions for persuasion and promotional culture to flourish: the political and economic zeitgeist, a proliferation in the number of media channels, an increase in disposable household income, and a reduction in the price of consumer goods relative to income. In general, the industry histories share this analysis but also look more closely at the internal changes that affected the sector. However, despite being more introspective, their focus is almost exclusively on the corporate story. In this version of events, rapid market growth during the early 1980s leads to the emergence of an aggressive takeover culture, culminating in a global consolidation during the late 1990s (this narrative is

[1] See, e.g., N. Chomsky, D. Barsamian, and A. Naiman, *How the World Works* (London: Hamish Hamilton, 2012); A. Davis, *Promotional Cultures: The Rise and Spread of Advertising, Public Relations, Marketing and Branding* (Cambridge: Polity, 2013); J. L'Etang, *Public Relations in Britain: A History of Professional Practice in the 20th Century* (Mahwah, NJ, and London: L. Erlbaum, 2004); D. Miller and W. Dinan, 'The Rise of the PR Industry in Britain, 1979–98', *European Journal of Communication*, 15/1 (2000), 5–35; S. Nixon, *Hard Sell: Advertising, Affluence and Transatlantic Relations, c.1951–69* (Manchester: Manchester University Press, 2013); A. Offer, *The Challenge of Affluence: Self-Control and Wellbeing in the United States and Britain since 1950* (Oxford: Oxford University Press, 2007); J. B. Schor, *The Overspent American: Why We Want What We Don't Need* (New York: Harper Perennial, 1999); R. Skidelsky and E. Skidelsky, *How Much Is Enough? The Love of Money, and the Case for the Good Life* (London: Penguin, 2013); A. Wernick, *Promotional Culture: Advertising, Ideology and Symbolic Expression* (London: Sage, 1991).

often epitomized in microcosm by the overreaching expansion of Saatchi & Saatchi).[2] There is occasionally some discussion of the specialization that took place within advertising (for example, the establishment of standalone creative and media shops from the mid-1980s is covered by Fletcher in some detail), and there is an acknowledgement that account planning had become widely adopted across the USA and Europe by 1990 (it had become a function of all major British agencies a decade earlier).[3] With the notable exception of L'Etang, who argues to the contrary—and compellingly—where public relations is concerned, there is also widespread support for the view that the sector became progressively more professional. While these sector interpretations are reasonable in principle, none of them offers more than a cursory analysis. Yet, there is evidence to suggest that the persuasion industries became increasingly effective from 1980 onwards. This was not a time of consolidation rather than innovation, as Fletcher argued, but one of influence and profound, long-lasting change.[4]

It is important to remember that the issue with analysing any form of persuasion is that it largely takes place within the heads of consumers. Early attempts to develop a methodology by Reeves and Ogilvy floundered partly because they focused on the output rather that the outtake—that is to say, on the advertisements themselves rather than the effect they were having on consumers. For both men, the most effective adverts were utilitarian—those that conveyed the product benefit to the consumer in the best way possible—and emotion was a distractor that simply interrupted the consumer's processing of the advert's message.[5] Even the most creative adverts of the 1970s did little more than communicate product benefits in a highly effective way. For example, *For Mash Get Smash!* presents the case for choosing instant mashed potato, *It's Frothy Man!* highlights the product difference between Cresta and other soft drinks, and *Boy on a Bike* draws attention to Hovis's heritage and establishes the brand as a wholesome, healthy alternative to white sliced bread.[6] In terms of creative quality, these advertisements were generally

---

[2] See, e.g., S. Delaney, *Get Smashed: The Story of the Men who Made the Adverts that Changed our Lives* (London: Sceptre, 2007); A. Fendley, *Commercial Break: The Inside Story of Saatchi & Saatchi* (London: Hamish Hamilton, 1995); I. Fallon, *The Brothers: The Rise & Rise of Saatchi & Saatchi* (London: Hutchinson, 1988); P. Kleinman, *The Saatchi & Saatchi Story* (London: Weidenfeld & Nicolson, 1987); W. Fletcher, *Advertising: A Very Short Introduction* (Oxford: Oxford University Press, 2010); A. Law, *Creative Company: How St Luke's Became 'The Ad Agency to End All Ad Agencies* (New York: Wiley, 1999); D. Rogers, *Campaigns that Shook the World: The Evolution of Public Relations* (London: Kogan, 2015); D. Trott, *Predatory Thinking* (London: Pan, 2014); M. Tungate, *Adland: A Global History of Advertising* (London: Kogan Page, 2007).

[3] Fletcher, *Advertising: A Very Short Introduction*, 70.   [4] Ibid. 168–212.

[5] P. Stout and J. Leckenby, 'Measuring Emotional Response to Advertising', *Journal of Advertising*, 15/4 (1986), 35–42.

[6] R. Scott, *Boy on a Bike* (London: Collett Dickenson Pearce, 1973); J. Webster, *For Mash get Smash!* (London: Boase Massimi Pollit, 1974); J. Webster, *It's Frothy Man!* (London: Boase Massimi Pollitt, 1974).

much better than any produced before, but their methodology and objectives remained the same: to persuade consumers to make rational choices about products.

In 1974, Callaghan conducted the seminal study into the emotional power of advertising which indicated that a liking or preference towards an advertisement could lead to the development of a positive attitude towards a brand, resulting ultimately in a higher purchase intention.[7] It was an intriguing conclusion that encouraged further researchers to look more deeply into emotional appeals over the next few years. Their findings were consistent with Callaghan's analysis—emotional appeals appeared to be a much more effective means of communication than conventional, rational appeals, producing higher levels of recall and more positive reactions. By the early 1980s, a body of academic research, drawing heavily from the emerging fields of cognitive and hedonic psychology and behavioural economics, was suggesting that consumers' outtake from advertisements was far more sophisticated than anyone had previously imagined.[8]

It became increasingly apparent that across many categories rational appeals based on product benefits were, if not redundant, then certainly less effective than emotional appeals based on brand values. This proved to be particularly apposite when emotional appeals connected with consumers at the so-called experiential level. Based on earlier work by Barret-Lennerd and Elliot et al., Stout and Leckenby described three levels of emotional response called descriptive, empathetic, and experiential.[9] At the initial descriptive level, respondents display the ability to recognize emotions expressed by others. Here the subject recognizes and understands the thoughts and feelings of the characters in an advertisement but does not necessarily experience any emotions him or herself. Those feelings occur at the second empathetic level of response, which is defined as the subject experiencing the same emotion as a character depicted on the page or screen. However, at this level the subject's response is dependent upon the stimulus and how well he or she relates to it

[7] F. Callahan, 'Advertising Influences on Consumers', *Journal of Advertising Research*, 14/3 (1974), 45.

[8] It is worth considering that account planning is commercial research rather than academic research. The purpose of planning is to find out whether or not an advertisement works, not how it works, or why it does not work. These questions were arguably of professional interest to the individual researchers, but there was neither the funding nor the business need to produce answers.

[9] Stout and Leckenby, 'Measuring Emotional Response to Advertising', 35–42; G. T. Barrett-Lennard, 'The Empathy Cycle: Refinement of a Nuclear Concept', *Journal of Counseling Psychology*, 28/2 (1981), 91–100; R. Elliott, H. Filipovich, L. Harrigan, J. Gaynor, C. Reimschuessel, and J. K. Zapadka, 'Measuring Response Empathy: The Development of a Multicomponent Rating Scale', *Journal of Counseling Psychology*, 29/4 (1982), 379–87; M. H. Davis, 'The Effects of Dispositional Empathy on Emotional Reactions and Helping: A Multidimensional Approach', *Journal of Personality*, 51/2 (1983), 167–84.

personally. The most intense emotional response occurs at the third level, the experiential. This is a true emotional response, wherein the subject exhibits valenced feelings occurring as reactions to events that are relevant to him or her. Valence is a term used in psychology when discussing emotions; it refers to the intrinsic attractiveness (positive valence) or averseness (negative valence) of an event, object, or situation. Depending on the viewer's interpretation, outlook, and personal goals, these events can be real or imagined, historical or anticipated. As such, while an experiential emotional response may be caused by the action, characters, or a scene in the commercial, it is self-relevant and may not necessarily be identified with any or all of those elements.

To illustrate the differences between the three response levels let us imagine a TV commercial for a breakfast cereal set in a kitchen-diner where a family is enjoying a humorous but hectic start to the day. At a descriptive level, the viewer might recognize that the family is happy and that they are all enjoying spending time together but may experience no other feelings at all. At an empathetic level, the viewer might be able to feel the love the mother feels for her family, having got them up in time for work and school and making sure they leave for the day well fed. However, at an experiential level, the same viewer might realize that his or her own family never spends breakfast time together and is not as close as the one depicted in the commercial so may actually experience sadness.[10] It was found that viewers would respond to any emotional content, regardless of whether or not it carried a message. By implication this meant that commercials could influence consumers in entirely unintentional and unexpected ways. In support of this proposition, Stout and Leckenby found that by far the most effective commercials were those that engaged viewers experientially. Experiential emotional responses were positively related to a more positive attitude to the advertisement and the brand but also to greater brand and advertisement content recall. Numerous subsequent studies into emotional appeals continued to support their effectiveness. If they did not actively dismiss rational appeals outright, collectively they presented emotional appeals as a compelling alternative. For example, Mitchell and Olsen, and Gorn, looked specifically at the effectiveness of non-product elements of advertisements; Choi and Thorson discovered that 'emotional' print ads resulted in higher recall of product name, brand category, and ad content; and Pelsmacker and Geuens argued that experiential appeals could help to mitigate the abstract nature of service offerings. Others looked at the impact of emotion appeals on messaging (Liu and Stout) and product type (Shavitt, Golden and Johnson, Holbrook and Shaughnessy, and

---

[10] Stout and Leckenby, 'Measuring Emotional Response to Advertising'.

Johar and Sirgy).[11] Ultimately, advertising based on emotional appeals was shown to affect customers' reactions to advertisements, to enhance their attention, and to affect brand attitudes.

This body of research eventually led to the development of an alternative emotional model of advertising that attempted to provide an explanation for how it worked and suggest how its effectiveness should be measured.[12] In 1981, Kahneman, regarded by many as one of the founders of behavioural economics, first used the terms System One (fast) and System Two (slow) thinking to describe the different mental processes used to make decisions. System One thinking is fast, instinctive, and emotional, associative and effortless. In contrast, System Two thinking is deliberative and logical, analytical and rule-governed—consequently far more effortful but flexible enough to assimilate and process new information. For example, if one is asked what $2 + 2 =$, then the answer is provided effortlessly via System One experience. However, working out the answer to $97 \times 37 =$ would take some time to

[11] A. Mitchell and J. Olson, 'Are Product Attribute Beliefs the Only Mediator of Advertising Effects on Brand Attitude?', *Journal of Marketing Research*, 18/3 (1981), 318; G. Gorn, 'The Effects of Music in Advertising on Choice Behavior: A Classical Conditioning Approach', *Journal of Marketing*, 46/1 (1982), 94–101; Y. Choi and E. Thorson, *Memory for Factual, Emotional, and Balanced Ads Under Two Instructional Sets: Proceedings of the American Academy of Advertising Annual Conference 1983* (New York: American Academy of Advertising, 1983), 160–4; P. De Pelsmacker and Maggie Geunes, 'The Communication Effects of Warmth, Eroticism and Humour in Alcohol Advertisements', *Journal of Marketing* Communications, 2/4 (December 1996), 247–62, at 16; S. Shavvitt, 'The Role of Attitude Objects in Attitudinal Functions', *Journal of Experimental Social Psychology*, 26 (1990), 124–68; S. Shavvitt, 'Value Expressive versus Utilitarian Advertising Appeals: When and why to Use which Appeal', *Journal of Advertising*, 20/3 (1992), 23–33. L. Golden and K. A. Johnson, 'The Impact of Sensory Preferences and Thinking versus Feelings Appeals on Advertising Effectiveness', in R. P. Bagozzi and A. M. Tybout (eds), *Advances in Consumer Research* (Ann Abbor: Association of Consumer Research, 1983), 203–8; M. B. Holbrook and J. O'Shaughnessy, 'The Role of Emotion', *Advertising Psychology and Marketing*, 2 (1989), 45–54; J. S. Johar and M. Joseph Sirgy, 'Value-Expressive versus Utilitarian Advertising Appeals: When and Why to Use Which Appeal', *Journal of Advertising*, 20/3 (1991).

[12] See A. Tversky and D. Kahneman, 'The Framing of Decisions and the Psychology of Choice', *Science*, 211/4481 (1981), 453–8; D. Kahneman and D. T. Miller, 'Norm Theory: Comparing Reality to its Alternatives', *Psychological Review*, 93/2 (1986), 136–53; D. Kahneman, 'Maps of Bounded Rationality: Psychology for Behavioral Economics', *American Economic Review*, 93/5 (2003), 1449–75. See also A. R. Damasio, *Descartes' Error: Emotion, Reason, and the Human Brain* (New York: G. P. Putnam, 1994); R. I. Haley and A. L. Baldinger, 'The ARF Copy Research Validity Project', *Journal of Advertising Research*, 40/6 (2000), 114–35; R. Heath, 'How the Best Advertisements Work', *AdMap*, 27 (2002); R. Heath, D. Brandt, and A. Nairn, 'Brand Relationships: Strengthened by Emotion, Weakened by Attention', *Journal of Advertising Research*, 46/4 (2006), 410–19; R. G. Heath, A. C. Nairn, and P. A. Bottomley, 'How Effective Is Creativity? Emotive Content in TV Advertising does not Increase Attention', *Journal of Advertising Research*, 49/4 (2009), 450–63; R. Heath, 'Emotional Engagement: How Television Builds Big Brands at Low Attention', *Journal of Advertising Research*, 49/1 (2009), 62–73; R. Heath, 'Creativity in Television Advertisements does not Increase Attention', *AdMap*, 512 (January 2010), 26–8; O. Wood, 'Using an Emotional Model to Improve the Measurement of Advertising Effectiveness', unpublished paper, Market Research Society Annual Conference, London, 2010; O. Wood, 'How Emotional Tugs Trump Rational Pushes: The Time has Come to Abandon a 100-Year-Old Advertising Model', *Journal of Advertising Research*, 52/1 (2012), 31–9.

calculate using rule-governed, System Two processing. As such, we have a limited capacity for System Two thinking, because it involves quite a lot of hard work. While in principle many people have the capability, know-how and skills to work out the answer to $97 \times 37 =$, few can be bothered to do so in practice.[13]

The traditional models of brand communication based on rational appeals to rational consumers implied that people made purchasing decisions about an advertised product only after a series of cognitive, System Two decisions that moved them from unawareness through awareness, understanding, and persuasion to purchase. In contrast, emotional appeals relied on effortless System 1 thinking and not only influenced what consumers paid attention to but also channelled their thoughts and encouraged associations, which in turn guided judgements and simplified decision-making. Offer, following Thaler and Kahneman, noted that in many situations consumers act in a manner that is inconsistent with economic theory, and on such occasions economic theory makes systematic errors in predicting behaviour.[14] Wood later argued that understanding this behaviour was the key to producing more effective advertising. His research revealed that 'emotion-into-action' appeals strongly outperformed all traditional forms of rational appeal such as brand linkage, cut-through measures, and even message delivery.[15] Wood concluded: 'Emotional advertising is more effective than message-based advertising, and focusing on communicating a message might actually inhibit success and lead to less efficient advertising.'[16]

For creative teams, producing brand communication based on emotional appeals was an entirely different challenge. Rational brand communication was product focused and communicated the benefits of unique features and differences to the consumer. Emotional brand communication operated in reverse, beginning with an understanding of the consumer rather than the product. In most cases the creative execution requires a narrative element to engage the audience rather than a proposition. The work of many researchers in consumer behaviour and related fields of social science shared the view first expressed by Weick that people think narratively rather than argumentatively or paradigmatically—for example, Adaval and Wyer, Arnould and Wallendorf, Bruner, Hirschman, Holt and Thompson, Padgett, Schank, and Zukier.[17] If

[13] D. Kahneman, *Thinking, Fast and Slow* (New York: Farrar, Straus and Giroux, 2011).

[14] Offer, *The Challenge of Affluence*; R. Thaler, 'Toward a Positive Theory of Consumer Choice', *Journal of Economic Behavior and Organization*, 1/1 (1980), 39–60; Kahneman, *Thinking, Fast and Slow*.

[15] Wood, 'How Emotional Tugs Trump Rational Pushes', 31–9.   [16] Ibid. 38.

[17] R. Adaval and R. S. Wyer, 'The Role of Narratives in Consumer Information Processing', *Journal of Consumer Psychology*, 7/3 (1998), 207–45; E. Arnould and M. Wallendorf, 'Market-Orientated Ethnography: Interpretation Building and Marketing Strategy Formulation', *Journal of Market Research*, 31 (1994), 484–504; J. S. Bruner, *Acts of Meaning* (Cambridge, MA, and London: Harvard University Press, 1990); E. Hirschman, 'Humanistic Inquiry in Marketing Research:

rational advertising can be regarded as a lecture, then emotional advertising tells a story. Stories and storytelling are central to achieving a deep understanding of consumer psychology.[18] Learning via storytelling is more memorable and retrievable than lecture-based learning.[19] Lecture-based forms of brand communication tend to elicit challenging or argumentative thinking; conversely, brand communication with a narrative element tends to encourage vicarious participation on the part of the audience.[20] Moreover, narrative brand communication encourages conversations between consumers, which persuades them to view 'brands' as anthropomorphic entities whose products or services are props to express their own self-identity.[21]

Within advertising, this storytelling element can be explicit, but an inferred narrative can be just as effective. Apophenia is a weakness of human cognition defined as 'unmotivated seeing of connections [accompanied by] a specific feeling of abnormal meaningfulness'.[22] It is a consequence of the ability to recognize causes and effects, identify patterns, and make logical deductions without first-hand experience that is unique to humans. For example, imagine going for a walk in the forest the day after a heavy thunderstorm and coming across a badly scorched oak tree riven in two and perhaps still smouldering slightly. The conclusion likely to be drawn is that it had probably been hit by lightning the previous day. These complex, causal links are beyond the cognitive capabilities of all other animals, even our closest relatives chimpanzees and bonobos. However, the downside of this ability is that we can often imagine causal patterns where none exists. Cases of apophenia are numerous, from simple associations, such as the man in the moon and cheese toasties with the face of Christ on them, to more complex examples, such as astrology or the so-called gambler's fallacy (the notion that, if something happens more

---

Philosophy, Method, and Criteria', *Journal of Marketing Research*, 23/3 (1986), 237; D. Holt and C. J. Thompson, 'Man-of-Action-Heroes: The Pursuit of Heroic Masculinity in Everyday Consumption', *Journal of Consumer Research*, 31/2 (2004), 425–40; D. Padgett and D. Allen, 'Communicating Experiences: A Narrative Approach to Creating Service Brand Image', *Journal of Advertising*, 26/4 (1997), 49–62; R. C. Schank, *Scripts, Plans, Goals and Understanding: An Inquiry into Human Knowledge Structures* (Hillsdale, NJ: Erlbaum, 1977); H. Zukier, 'The Paradigmatic and Narrative Modes in Goal-Guided Inference', in R. M. Sorrentino and E. T. Higgins (eds), *Handbook of Motivation and Cognition* (New York: Guildford Press, 1986).

[18] Jennifer E. Escalas and B. Stern, 'Sympathy and Empathy: Emotional Responses to Advertising Dramas', *Journal of Consumer Research*, 29/4 (2003), 566–78; D. B. Holt, *How Brands Become Icons: The Principles of Cultural Branding* (Boston: Harvard Business School Press, 2004).

[19] Schank, *Scripts, Plans, Goals and Understanding*; Bruner, *Acts of Meaning*.

[20] B. O. Boller, 'Viewer Empathy in Response to Drama Ads: Development of the VEDA Scale', unpublished working paper number 402–489, Fogleman College of Business and Economics, Memphis State University, Memphis, TN, 1989; 'EEC Council Television without Frontiers Directive', *Official Journal of the European Communities*, 298/23 (1989).

[21] See K. Wertime, *Building Brands & Believers: How to Connect with Consumers* (Singapore: Wiley, 2002); Holt and Thompson, 'Man-of-Action-Heroes'.

[22] S. Fyfe, C. Williams, O. J. Mason, and G. J. Pickup, 'Apophenia, Theory of Mind and Schizotypy: Perceiving Meaning and Intentionality in Randomness', *Cortex*, 44/10 (2008), 1316–25.

frequently than normal during a certain period, it will happen less frequently in the future, even though the odds remain the same each time, like the throw of a dice or the numbers on a roulette wheel). We are constantly searching for meaning and linking events with possible outcomes. In its more benign state, apophenia is nothing more than the mild side effect of our powerful capacity to make sense of the world around us. It allows us to interpret information, make plans, and extrapolate outcomes. To a great extent, art, film, music, and literary appreciation can all be seen as forms of apophenia—especially at the most self-indulgent level where subjects are drowned in meaning and suffocated by overanalysis.[23]

In summary, brand communication based on emotional appeals can be more persuasive, memorable, and enduring than that based on rational appeals. Emotional appeals themselves are most effective when they connect with the respondent at an intimate, experiential level, because this gives the impression that the communication is intimate or personal in nature. These connections are best achieved by using a strong narrative element, although the narrative itself need not be explicit, and in many cases it is better if can be inferred by the viewer.

The rise of Margaret Thatcher and the emergence of a consumer-focused, market economy provided the persuasion industries with an opportunity, and the creative revolution of the 1970s, which was ultimately a product of the counterculture, and subsequent industry specializations provided the capability, but it was ultimately the successful application of this new emotional model that allowed persuasion to drive into new areas and gave marketers the opportunity to build much deeper connections with their consumers.

Storytelling: A Narrative Approach to Persuasion

Mass advertising based on emotional appeals began to emerge in two of the most heavily regulated sectors: cigarettes and alcohol. The first call to restrict tobacco advertising in the UK came from the Royal College of Physicians in 1962.[24] This ultimately led to a ban on all TV advertising for cigarettes in 1965 under powers granted by the 1964 Television Act (although commercials for cigars and rolling tobacco were allowed up until 1991).[25] Printed media campaigns were still permitted but came under increasingly strict guidelines. By 1986, depicting any person smoking in advertising for cigarettes was completely prohibited, regardless of the medium. Although, in comparison,

---

[23] Ibid.   [24] *Smoking and Health* (London: The Royal College of Physicians, 1962).
[25] *Television Act* <http://www.screenonline.org.uk/tv/id/1107497/>.

alcoholic drinks advertising was subjected to fewer controls, it too became increasingly regulated. In 1970, the Advertising Codes of Practice initially tightened alcohol advertising, and commercials were no longer allowed to encourage drinking in general; they could only promote specific brands. Further restrictions added in 1976 banned advertising that depicted a drink being enjoyed on social occasions, that encouraged overindulgence, or that gave the impression that drinking was necessary for social success or acceptance.[26] From 1989, UK television advertising as a whole was subject to new cross-border regulation from Europe. Article 15 of the EEC's *Television without Frontiers Directive* set out a series of restrictions specifically for alcoholic drinks' advertising, including a ban on appeals to improve physical, social, or sexual performance and any content that was aimed at or depicted children.[27]

Beyond the limitations on their promotion, the two categories had one other thing in common: although both sectors were dominated by strong brands, there was often very little difference between the competing products themselves. Rational appeals to consumers of lager or cigarettes were difficult enough to construct in normal circumstances. Like many FMCG categories, competing products were essentially chemically identical, making any proposition based on superior taste or flavour entirely subjective. There was a further risk in that such claims actively invited a challenge or even outright rebuttal, but in any event the progressively restrictive legislation systematically ruled out such traditional approaches. Until the late 1960s, cigarette advertising was similar to most FMCG advertising. Rational appeals were based on propositions concerning flavour or dubious benefits such as improved sexual attractiveness, concentration, or even sporting prowess. For example, Consulate 'Cool and fresh as a mountain stream', Marlboro 'The filter cigarette with the unfiltered taste', Tipplalet 'Blow smoke in her face and she'll follow you anywhere', and Silk Cut 'It takes two weeks to turn on to the mild taste of Silk Cut'.[28]

Commercials for beer in the 1960s likewise focused on taste (often underpinned by some form of brand heritage) but also on alcoholic strength, similarly questionable claims for improved sexual attraction, and, as they typically targeted men, the more abstract concept of 'manliness'. There is also an association with refreshment and revitalization as a reward after a hard day's work or an essential part of a relaxing evening—for example, Bass 'Reserved for beer drinkers', Heineken 'Why Holland limits Heineken to its

---

[26] *ASH: Key Dates in the History of Anti-Tobacco Campaigning* (2015), <http://www.ash.org.uk/files/documents/ASH_741.pdf>.
[27] 'EEC Council Television without Frontiers Directive'.
[28] *History of Advertising Trust* www.hatads.org.uk.

closest allies', Skol 'Steel yourself for Skol special strength', and Double Diamond 'Double Diamond works wonders'.[29]

Although the execution varies, whether for alcoholic drinks or cigarettes, the strategy in all these advertising campaigns is the same. A distinctive product feature is identified, and a benefit is attached to it in order to create a proposition; this then forms the heart of the message that is communicated to the consumer via a creative execution. These feature–benefit propositions were not simply pulled out of the air but supported by consumer insights emerging from market research. A typical example is the 1964 relaunch of Bacardi white rum in the UK, which was handled by the advertising agency JWT.[30] In the year prior to launch, JWT conducted extensive market research, for which it charged the client £3,000 (£61,000 at 2018 values). A qualitative study was commissioned to identify the scale of opportunity among those who, 'at present, are not rum drinkers', and a test market operation was carried out in Ipswich, Suffolk. The result of all this research was a campaign that focused on the brand's return to the UK market after a twenty-five-year absence. It positioned the spirit as a 'fun alternative' to whatever members of the target audience were drinking at the moment. This rather thin proposition was supported by hard facts about the product's provenance and serving suggestions. The campaign was a classic execution of rational appeal advertising.[31]

The restrictions regarding the promotion of cigarettes precluded advertisers from developing a traditional product-based proposition and forced their advertising agencies to take a different approach. Tasked with leading an overhaul of the Benson & Hedges brand for a relaunch in 1977, Frank Lowe highlighted the narrow creative parameter. Not only were images of people smoking forbidden, but neither could they use images of people looking happy or enjoying themselves, or in fact, any pleasant images—such as pastoral landscapes or blues skies—that might imply there was anything positive about cigarettes.[32] Denied the opportunity to develop a rational appeal, advertisers resorted to making nebulous emotional appeals instead. The goal remained the same—to communicate in a memorable way something distinctive and relevant about the product—but the strategy and style of execution were completely different.

Between 1975 and 1978, Rothmans International plc ran a campaign called *Man in Control* to promote its premium cigarette brand Rothmans King Size. The campaign was conceived and produced by advertising agency McCann-Erickson, which was appointed to handle the brand's advertising in 1974.[33]

---

[29] Ibid.
[30] HAT, JWT (1966), Briefing for Charrington Vintners Ltd and Bacardi International Ltd.
[31] Ibid.
[32] F. Lowe, *Dear Lord Leverhulme, I Think we may have Solved your Problem* (Oxted: Hurtwood, 2002).
[33] 'Agency Review', *Campaign*, 20 December 1974, p. 21.

Beneath the slogan 'When you know what you want', each advert featured a man's hand and wrist holding a cigarette in a series of racy locations: the wheel of a sports car, the helm of a speed boat, or the joystick of a passenger jet. An expensive watch was partially concealed by the cuffs of a crisp shirt and tailored suit (perhaps featuring a pilot's brocade). Together the images and tagline invited a narrative interpretation. They seemed to be telling a story, but it was left to the viewer to infer what that story might be (although they were clearly being pointed in the direction of 'international playboy in the James Bond mould'). The advertisements said nothing at all about Rothmans cigarettes, but a great deal about the aspirations of the men who might smoke them: 'You are probably not an international playboy, but we bet you'd like to be. You might not have the blonde girlfriend, the sports car or the exciting job as the pilot, but for just 46p a pack you can have yourself a tiny slice of that lifestyle.' These adverts are relevant and memorable. However, they are based not on a rational appeal that highlights some distinctive feature of the product, but on an emotional appeal that resonates with the consumer's fantasies and desire to lead a glamorous lifestyle (see Figure 4.1).

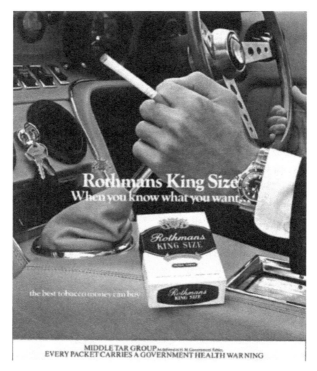

Figure 4.1. *Man in Control*: display advertisement from the *Sunday Times Magazine*, produced by McCann-Ericsson for Rothmans King Size, 1976. See also plates section.

The commercials produced by Collett Dickenson Pearce (CDP) for Gallagher's cigarette brand Benson & Hedges went even further, doing away with a suggestive narrative altogether. Reflecting later on the hugely successful campaign, Frank Lowe provided a typically arch explanation for the strategy: 'I went to Alan Waldie (the project's lead creative) and said, "We've got to do something that nobody will understand. Because if they can't understand it they can't ban it."'[34] In fact, Waldie spent several months struggling fruitlessly with the brief before presenting his only idea: a series of arresting, surrealist-inspired but copy-free posters featuring the distinctive Benson & Hedges gold box in a series of bizarre locations such as a mouse hole, a birdcage, and a sardine tin. Fletcher makes the bold assertion that 'the commitment of the agency to the campaign . . . was total'. However, Delaney reveals that not only was this idea unpopular among senior creatives within the agency, but that Lowe himself sought reassurance from chairman Colin Millward before he was willing to present it to the client, 'with an unusual amount of trepidation' and without any supporting market research.[35] That the campaign won approval at all was due in large part to CDP's reputation for groundbreaking creative work and the strength of their relationship with the client, but also to the quality of the images themselves. It was a unique approach, and, as *Campaign* described it: 'A great example of the advertising industry turning to creativity in the face of adversity' (see Figure 4.2).[36]

The campaign was undeniably successful and ran for more than a decade—to the equally enduring bafflement of some. Fletcher asked: 'How could mouse holes, chameleons, ants, bees and ghastly plaster ducks enhance the image of an expensive, fashionable brand? Why would anyone be tempted to smoke cigarettes resembling an oily tin of sardines, or an electric plug?', before concluding: 'The truth is, nobody knows.'[37] While Fletcher is rightly sceptical of what he describes as the ad industry's 'accepted dogma'—that people enjoyed the mystery of the advertisements and attempting to solve them made them feel sophisticated—there is in fact a straightforward explanation for the campaign's popularity. Both the Benson & Hedges and Rothmans campaigns functioned in a similar manner, with one subtle difference. The images in the Rothmans campaign

---

[34] 'An Iconic Agency at the Height of its Power', *Campaign*, 31 August 2007.
[35] W. Fletcher, *Powers of Persuasion: The Inside Story of British Advertising 1951–2000* (Oxford: Oxford University Press, 2008), 144, 143–7; Delaney, *Get Smashed*, 150–5.
[36] S. Hatfield, 'Hall of Fame: A (Very) Brief History of Advertising', *Campaign*, 20 December 1999.
[37] Fletcher, *Powers of Persuasion*, 146. See also Delaney, *Get Smashed*, 153.

Figure 4.2. *Bird Cage*: display advertisement produced by Collet Dickenson Pearce for Benson & Hedges King Size, 1983. See also plates section.

invited the viewer to *make* a connection; the Benson & Hedges adverts invited the viewer to *make up* a connection.

The Rorschach psychological test, in which a respondent's perceptions of random, symmetrical inkblots are recorded and then analysed, works in much the same manner.[38] The interpretation of the Rorschach test is not based primarily on what the individual sees in the inkblot (the content), because respondents tend to see broadly the same thing. For example, Card IV is usually perceived by respondents as a large, occasionally threatening figure that they typically describe as an animal skin, hide, or rug (see Figure 4.3). This perception is compounded by the common impression of inferiority (respondents describe 'looking up' at the image), which serves to elicit a sense of authority. The human or animal content seen in the card is almost invariably classified as male rather than female.[39] Despite the stereotypical nature of these responses, the image is genuinely nothing more than an inkblot. People do not always pick out patterns. Random images—such as a Jackson Pollock painting or a TV screen filled with white noise—are usually seen for what they are: not every slice of toast contains the head of Christ. It is only when that randomness is given an impression of order that conforms to one of the templates in our mind that we see a pattern. It is the same ability that allows us to recognize children's drawings of Mummy and Daddy or

---

[38] I. B. Weiner, *Principles of Rorschach Interpretation* (2nd edn; Mahwah, NJ, and London: L. Erlbaum, 2003).
[39] Ibid.

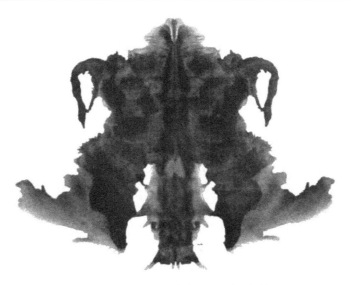

Figure 4.3. Card IV of the Rorschach Test.

recognize cartoon cats and mice for what they represent, even though they look nothing like their real-life incarnations. In the Rorschach image, the illusion of order is provided by the symmetry (achieved by folding the paper to produce a mirror image). In the Benson and Hedges advertisements, it is the form that provides the illusion of order—these are recognizably cigarette advertisements, they appear in the same places as other cigarette advertisements, and they even carry a government health warning. We also know from experience that all advertisements carry a message; ergo these advertisements must be carrying a message.

Each Benson & Hedges commercial was beautifully shot and art directed. Production budgets were lavish. Produced by the Alan Parker Film Company, the 1978 TV advertisement *Swimming Pool*—directed by Hugh Hudson and art directed by Alan Waldie—was cited at the time as the most expensive commercial ever made.[40] The campaign won numerous advertising awards and even earned plaudits from art critics.[41] The individual adverts are mysterious, regularly described as surreal or unfathomable, each one appearing to present a single clue to an inscrutable puzzle or conundrum—a complex code that needs to be cracked before its secrets are revealed.[42] If they are viewed as a

---

[40] HAT, CDP, HAT 59/3/3/1.

[41] Ibid.; E. Lucie-Smith, 'Posters: Short-Lived Emblems of a Changing Era/The Link between Art and Advertising', *Campaign*, 26 September 1986.

[42] *Top 10 Surreal TV Adverts* <http://www.campaignlive.co.uk/article/top-10-surreal-tv-ads/909509#>.

whole, there appears to be a theme. With their opulent cinematography and arresting juxtaposition of images, the advertisements look as though they are trying to tell us something important—possibly about Benson & Hedges cigarettes. Yet, just like the Rorschach blots, the campaign is devoid of meaning; there is no puzzle to solve, no big idea to understand—it really is nothing more than a collection of pretty pictures. However, the reaction of consumers to the Benson & Hedges commercials is stereotypically similar to that of respondents to the Rorschach cards. Viewers project their own narrative interpretation onto the adverts, and, while this is typically vague, they draw a broadly similar conclusion that they are seeing 'something good', 'something interesting', 'something clever', and most importantly 'something I like'. For non-smokers engagement stops there, but, as Stout and Leckenby identified, among those positively disposed towards smoking (that is, a smoker or someone thinking about starting smoking), this is likely to elicit an experiential response resulting in a more positive attitude to the brand.[43]

Perhaps his self-professed inability to comprehend also explains Fletcher's assertion that the Benson & Hedges campaign 'failed to have much creative influence', which contrasts starkly with Delaney's claim that it 'ushered in an era of grandiose, opulently styled commercials'.[44] Fletcher's statement flies in the face of the fact that this opaque, essentially messageless form of advertising became almost standard for the cigarette industry. By the mid-1980s, a similar aesthetic was being adopted by several premium brands, notably Silk Cut (another CDP client), John Player, Superkings, and Rothmans.[45]

In one respect at least Fletcher is correct—the Benson & Hedges commercials did not result in a deluge of surrealist-inspired, meaningless advertising. However, they did highlight the extent to which advertising could move away from explicit rational appeals. If consumers were given something to think about by advertising that demanded attention and consideration, and also given the freedom to question and explain it for themselves, then most of them would end up drawing positive conclusions about the brand, which could be converted into sales.

For many years the Hamlet account at CDP was essentially a production line of visual comic sketches wherein the subject, after failing to overcome an adversity of some description, settled for a consolatory puff on a mild cigar instead, thereby realizing that *Happiness Is a Cigar Called Hamlet*. In the body of client–agency correspondence for this account at the History of Advertising Trust Archive, discussion is focused on the quality of the jokes and whether or not they support the central value of 'happiness'. At no time are the actual

---

[43] Stout and Leckenby, 'Measuring Emotional Response to Advertising', 35–42.
[44] Fletcher, *Powers of Persuasion*, 147; Delaney, *Get Smashed*, 156.
[45] HAT, CDP, HAT 38/1–10.

product, its benefits, or its unique selling points mentioned in any meaningful way. For example, there is a folder of client–agency correspondence from 1995 concerning the production of a sixty-second TV commercial based on a game of Hangman. The concept is pitched, approved, and finally produced. The client correspondence reveals that several detailed discussions took place about this creative concept. There is a clear sense that all parties feel the idea should be working and are frustrated that it is not. There are client directives about the point at which the cigar smoke should rise and even the distance between the letters that appear on screen. The creative process is less than smooth running, and the client clearly takes some convincing to sign the project off, which causes further frustration within the agency: 'Just to let you know what is (or rather isn't) happening on Hamlet . . . [They] are very keen to get this commercial in the cinemas for Christmas (maybe they should pull their fingers out?).'[46] However, the issues discussed are purely creative and relate to the consumer perception of the brand; again, there is no evidence of any discussion taking place about the product at all, and it is certainly never mentioned. The fact that these adverts are promoting cigars seems incidental; they could be promoting almost anything—pens, chocolate, coffee, lager. Moreover, there is no concern as to how the creative concept might support and promote the product, only over the tone and whether or not it can be made funny enough without causing offence.[47] The resulting advertisement is not one of the long-running campaign's finest. It is an example of an idea that sounds great in the pitch but is actually very difficult to deliver on the page: the concept is more compelling than the execution. This is not an uncommon occurrence.

In advertising of this kind, a discussion about the product is usually unnecessary because there is no quantifiable advantage or proposition to communicate. Instead, the goal is to persuade consumers that they will experience an emotional benefit if they use the brand. They empathize with the situation rather than with the product. In the case of Hamlet, the intangible benefit is in the 'sense of happiness' felt when smoking this particular brand of mild cigars—even following the most exasperating of experiences—rather than, say, the taste or the provenance of the tobacco contained in any actual mild cigar itself.

Successful emotional propositions did not need to be based on well-defined product benefits; they could be built instead upon more nebulous values and feelings or even lifestyle choices instead. Within advertising for alcoholic beverages there was a similar switch in focus from the product to the

---

[46] HAT, CDP, HAT 38/2/4, letter from Alex Horner to Angela Gordon and Philip Libou, 10 November 1995.
[47] Ibid.

consumer. Narrative content often focused on lifestyle moments, seeking to describe the consumer and the usage occasion rather than the product and its benefits. Throughout the 1980s and 1990s CDP produced a series of emotional-appeal, TV commercials for several beer brands on behalf of its client Scottish and Newcastle Breweries, including Tartan Special, McEwan's Export, Kestrel Lager, and Younger's Scotch Bitter.[48] The execution varied, and each brand had its own overarching creative themes and narrative style, but there was a single, unifying concept. While the adverts were witty, irreverent, and engaging, saying a great deal about the brand's consumers, they had almost nothing to say about the products themselves. For the viewer, the outtake is invariably: 'Here is the kind of person who enjoys this particular brand of beer.'[49] For example, *Escher*, a 1986 commercial for McEwan's Export, used high production values and an M. C. Escher theme to convey the drudgery of work and escape from it (see Figures 4.4 and 4.5).[50] People toiling endlessly in the factory were juxtaposed with a group of friends enjoying a night out in a glitzy bar. Similarly *Let off Steam*, a commercial for the same brand from 1989, juxtaposed a young male factory worker enjoying a Friday night drink with breathtaking location shots of Iceland—exploding geysers, hot springs, and crashing waterfalls—to a foreign language, world music soundtrack (see Figures 4.6 and 4.7).[51] As in the Hamlet campaign, the value expressed in all these cases is simple—'escape'—yet this style of advertising invites viewers to make their own further connections between the brand and the images on screen and to draw positive conclusions about the lifestyles of the kind of people who drink McEwan's Export.

During the 1980s, emotional propositions were introduced to underpin new and established brands—for example, *Coke Is It!* Coca Cola (1982), *Vorsprung durch Technik*, Audi UK (1983), *Think Different*, Apple (1986), and *Just Do It*, Nike (1988).[52] One advantage enjoyed by emotional appeals over rational appeals is that they do not alienate any viewers—owing to the fact they are vague and unspecific, they look and sound inclusive. Furthermore, rational propositions such as *For Mash Get Smash!* or *It's Frothy Man!* lose meaning as soon as they are applied outside their product category. Emotional

---

[48] HAT, CDP, HAT 38/2/3.

[49] HAT, CDP. The archive contains many other examples. See HAT 38/3/19: *Caber* (1982), *Inspector* (1982), *Miss Highland Queen* (1984), and *Caddy* (1984) for Tartan Special; HAT 38/3/18: *Dream Job* (1983) and *Happy Birthday* (983) for Kestrel; HAT 38/3/20: Octopus (1984) and Rocket (1985) for Youngers Scotch Bitter; HAT 38/1/3: *Shores* (1985), *Escher* (1986) and *Steam* (1989) for McEwan's Export.

[50] HAT, CDP, HAT 59/11/10/91.   [51] HAT, CDP, HAT 59/15/10/123.

[52] 'The Birth of "Just Do It" and Other Magic Words', *New York Times*, 21 June 2013, p. 3.; S. Kessler, *Chiatt/Day: The First Twenty Years* (New York: Rizzoli International, 1990).

Figure 4.4. and 4.5. *Escher*: stills from TV and cinema advertisement produced by Collet Dickenson Pearce for McEwan's Lager, 1986. (Courtesy of McEwan's Ltd.) See also plates section.

Figure 4.6 and 4.7. *Let off Steam*: stills from TV and cinema advertisement produced by Collet Dickenson Pearce for McEwan's Lager, 1991. (Courtesy of McEwan's Ltd.) See also plates section.

propositions are typically much more flexible. What does the simple and memorable tagline 'Just do it!' or the even more deliberately opaque 'Vorsprung durch Technik' actually mean? The answer is whatever the consumer *thinks* they mean—and they can be guided to the right conclusion by the accompanying imagery, whether, in the case of *Just Do It*, that is a moody picture of basketball legend Michael Jordan, an indistinct silhouette jogging through a lakeside forest, a hip-hop artist photographed in Queens NYC, or a shot of a running shoe.

This strategy could also be applied to reposition a struggling brand. In 1982, Bartle Bogle & Hegarty (BBH)—the agency behind Audi's *Vorsprung durch Technik*—was awarded the Levi Strauss UK advertising account following a competitive pitch.[53] The win was significant for BBH, a start-up agency looking to make a name for itself and headed by John Hegarty, erstwhile creative director at Saatchi & Saatchi and TWBA. However, there was an element of risk for both the agency and the client. Levi Strauss was an iconic American brand with over a century of heritage, but in the UK it was in trouble. The company had been initially concerned at the results of a 1981 survey, which revealed that its advertising was trailing to that of its main competitor, Wrangler, in terms of consumer awareness, and, indeed, Levi's share of the UK's £600 million jean market fell from 18 per cent to 14 per cent between 1981 and 1984.[54] The key issue was the brand values that Levi's found itself associated with: cowboys, the open road, and rock and roll. Within the world of contemporary 1980s fashion, homegrown British culture was being celebrated, and as such Levi's touchstones of traditional Americana were found somewhat lacking in terms of relevance. Following the punk rock explosion of the mid 1970s, British music was flourishing both at home and overseas. In the UK, pop music exerted a big influence over youth culture, which had fragmented and become tribal in nature. At the same time the retail boom meant that inexpensive, fashionable clothing was much more widely available than ever before. New high-street fashion outlets such as Next (a rebrand of the Hepworth's stores) and Concept Man, both launched in 1982, together with Principles, which was founded two years later, were giving young people the affordable opportunity to dress up in the style of the bands they followed.[55] An influential style press emerged to support these largely urban,

[53] J. Hegarty, *Hegarty on Advertising: Turning Intelligence into Magic* (London: Thames & Hudson, 2011), 161.
[54] P. Jobling, *Advertising Menswear: Masculinity and Fashion in the British Media since 1945* (London: A & C Black, 2014), 158; T. Mason, 'The Dangers of Standing Still in the Volatile UK Jeans Race', *Campaign*, 5 May 1987.
[55] *Next: Company History* <http://www.nextplc.co.uk/about-next/our-history>; J. Hall, 'From Chelsea Girl to Concept Man: History of River Island', *Daily Telegraph*, 20 March 2011, <http://www.telegraph.co.uk/finance/newsbysector/retailandconsumer/8392059/From-Chelsea-Girl-to-Concept-Man-history-of-River-Island.html>; A. Jamieson, 'Fashion Chain Principles to Close

image-conscious subcultures led by magazines such as the *Face*, *Blitz*, and *I-D* (not to be confused with the established fashion press that featured women's apparel).[56] The pop stars these titles featured—from groups such as Culture Club, Duran Duran, The Human League, ABC, Scritti Politti, and Spandau Ballet—did not wear jeans.

Lacking relevance among its core 16–24-year-old audience and faced with declining sales, Levi's was open to fresh ideas. Hegarty claimed that BBH considered a number of radical routes for its new client—for example, recommending that Levi's cease the production of denim jeans altogether and become a casual clothes manufacturer instead—before deciding to reconstruct the brand on the 'enduring values of toughness, integrity, and simplicity'.[57] BBH's answer was to suggest not that jeans were fashionable but rather that they were stylish: an item of clothing capable of transcending fashion. The first product of this new strategic vision was a poster campaign for black denim jeans. The adverts showed a flock of white sheep going in one direction, with a single black sheep travelling in the other. The strapline read 'When the world zigs, zag'.[58] No product was shown. The advert's focus was the consumer, and it projected an image of the kind of person who would wear black denim, which was a fairly new material at the time (see Figure 4.8).[59]

Despite declining sales, the first few years of BBH's appointment were judged to be a success, and in 1985 Levi's charged the agency with the European relaunch of its flagship product, the 501 jean. The objective was to turn the product, a revamp of the classic Levi Strauss jean with a button-down fly, into an essential fashion item. The physical launch of the product was beleaguered with issues. Notwithstanding the market perception of jeans per se, a recommended retail price of £20.00 meant that 501s were considerably more expensive than all competing brands. Furthermore, the garment performed very poorly in market research with the target audience, which perceived the styling—and the button-down fly in particular—to be old-fashioned. Initial distribution proved difficult, with Selfridges, a key retail outlet, declining to stock the product at all, reasoning that its customers would baulk at the price point. The pan-European nature of the brief also

66 Stores and Axe Majority of Staff ', *Daily Telegraph*, 7 March 2009 <http://www.telegraph.co.uk/finance/recession/4953599/Fashion-chain-Principles-to-close-66-stores-and-axe-majority-of-staff.html>; R. Unworth, 'Hepworth Buys CES Offshoot', *The Times*, 12 May 1981, p. 19.

[56] R. Unworth, 'Hepworth Buys CES Offshoot', *The Times*, 12 May 1981, p. 18; F. Mort, *Cultures of Consumption: Masculinities and Social Space in Late Twentieth-Century Britain* (London: Routledge, 1996), 24, 44, 79, 86.

[57] Hegarty, *Hegarty on advertising*, 163.   [58] HAT 62/5/1101; HAT 62/5/1101.

[59] Hegarty, *Hegarty on Advertising*, 164–89; Delaney, *Get Smashed*, 184–202; L. O'Kelly, 'Levi Sales Soar as BBH Unveils New Ads', *Campaign*, 7 November 1986; C. Wilkins, 'Why we Keep Looking back to a Golden Past/Nostalgia Is Big Business in Advertising', *Campaign*, 27 February 1987.

Plate 1. *John Wayne*: still from TV advertisement, featuring actor Gryff Rhys Jones and archive footage of John Wayne, for Holsten Pils, produced by Gold Greenness Trott, 1983. (Courtesy of Carlsberg UK Ltd.)

Plate 2. *Think Small*: display advertisement by Doyle Dane Bernbach for the Volkswagen Beetle, 1959. (Courtesy of Steven Kasher Gallery, New York.)

Plate 3. *There Is No Finish Line*: Nike brand advertisement, designed by John Brown & Partners, USA, 1977. (Gift of Various Donors; 1981-29-205, Courtesy of Cooper Howett Collection, Smithsonian Design Museum, NY.)

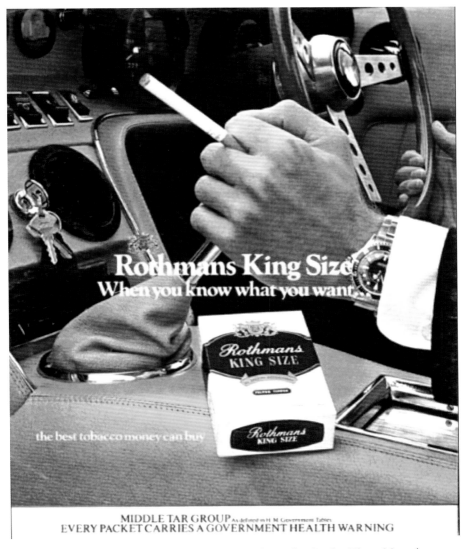

Plate 4. *Man in Control*: display advertisement from the *Sunday Times Magazine*, produced by McCann-Ericsson for Rothmans King Size, 1976.

Plate 5. *Bird Cage*: display advertisement produced by Collet Dickenson Pearce for Benson & Hedges King Size, 1983.

BLACK LEVI'S.
LEVI'S
WHEN THE WORLD ZIGS, ZAG.

Plate 6. *When the world zigs, zag*: display advertisement produced by Bartle Bogle and Hegarty for Levi Strauss Black Levi's, 1982. (Courtesy of Bartle Bogle and Hegarty Ltd and Levi's®.)

Plates 7 and 8. *Escher*: stills from TV and cinema advertisement produced by Collet Dickenson Pearce for McEwan's Lager, 1986. (Courtesy of McEwan's Ltd.)

Plates 9 and 10. *Let off Steam*: stills from TV and cinema advertisement produced by Collet Dickenson Pearce for McEwan's Lager, 1991. (Courtesy of McEwan's Ltd.)

Plates 11 and 12. *Laundrette*: stills from TV and cinema advertisement produced by Bartle Bogle and Hegarty for Levi Strauss 501s, 1986. (Courtesy of Bartle Bogle and Hegarty Ltd and Levi's®.)

Plate 13. *Daley Thompson breaks training for refreshment*: stills from TV and cinema advertisement produced by Leo Burnett for Lucozade, 1983. (Courtesy of Lucozade Ribena Suntory Ltd.)

Plate 14. *Gets to your thirst fast*: stills from TV and cinema advertisement produced by Leo Burnett for Lucozade Sport, 1990. (Courtesy of Lucozade Ribena Suntory Ltd.)

Figure 4.8. *When the world zigs, zag*: display advertisement produced by Bartle Bogle and Hegarty for Levi Strauss Black Levi's, 1982. (Courtesy of Bartle Bogle and Hegarty Ltd and Levi's®.) See also plates section.

presented a significant creative challenge, as the central idea would need to transcend linguistic and cultural boundaries.[60]

In Hegarty's own words, BBH's response was to 'put the brand at the centre... [and make] the product the hero... but wrapped it in emotional power'.[61] The centrepiece of the campaign was a TV ad called *Laundrette*. Set in a nostalgic version of 1950s America—because it was felt that the European audience would 'totally reject Reagan's America'—it featured a young man in a crowded laundrette nonchalantly stripping off to his boxer shorts in order to stone wash his 501s.[62] There was no voiceover, no jingle, and no text other than the 501s logo, which appeared discretely at the bottom of the screen just before the end of the commercial. Audio was provided by Marvin Gaye's 1968 hit 'I heard it through the grapevine'. Together the story, setting, and sound-track conveyed a mood of confidence, style, and irreverence that combined to make 501s seem cool (see Figures 4.9 and 4.10).

Measured purely in commercial terms, the campaign, which included other executions in the same style, was an unqualified success. In the first quarter of 1986, sales in Europe across Levi's entire range rose by 20 per cent, in comparison with a worldwide increase of just 10 per cent, and year-on-year sales of

---

[60] Hegarty, *Hegarty on Advertising: Turning intelligence into magic*, 64–89; Delaney, *Get Smashed*, 184–202; I. Anscombe, 'The Marketing of a Lifestyle', *The Times*, 15 July 1985, p. 7; I. Anscombe, 'Goodbye to Bond and Bangles', *The Times*, 17 July 1985, p. 11; G. Kemp, 'The Levi Story: Mistakes that Failed to Kill a Classic Product/Advertising US Denim Clothes', *Campaign*, 23 May 1986.

[61] Hegarty, *Hegarty on Advertising*, 175.

[62] *BBH* director Tim Lindsay, quoted in G. Kemp, 'The Levi Story: Mistakes that Failed to Kill a Classic Product/Advertising US Denim Clothes', *Campaign*, 23 May 1986.

Figure 4.9 and 4.10. *Laundrette*: stills from TV and cinema advertisement produced by Bartle Bogle and Hegarty for Levi Strauss 501s, 1986. (Courtesy of Bartle Bogle and Hegarty Ltd and Levi's®.) See also plates section.

501s increased by some 800 per cent.[63] However, the campaign was to have an even bigger cultural and creative impact on the world at large. Over the next two years 'I heard it through the grapevine' was rereleased as a single across Europe (on a special Levi's record label) and became a hit again in the UK, France, Ireland, Netherlands, Germany, Italy, Spain, and Belgium.[64] Further adverts in the series yielded further chart hits for Ben E. King and Sam Cooke, while even the star of *Laundrette*, Nick Kamen, had his own, fleetingly successful, music career. The original creative treatment for *Laundrette* had the actor dress down to a pair of Y-fronts. However, the UK censors deemed this to be too revealing and suggested a pair of boxer shorts might be a more acceptable replacement. As a direct consequence, sales of boxer shorts rocketed, with the formerly ubiquitous Y-fronts becoming almost immediately regarded as old-fashioned.[65] In 1986, the Wight Collins Rutherford Scott (WCRS) agency produced an advert for Carling Black Label that was, right up until the final five-second punch line, an almost identical, shot-for-shot pastiche of *Laundrette*, even using several of the same actors.[66] Not that WCRS was the only agency considering a parody. A creative team at Lowe Howard-Spink Marschalk was developing a similar idea for its client Heineken, but abandoned it once it became apparent WCRS had beaten them to it.[67]

Thinking Global

The Levi's 501 campaign's biggest impact of all was arguably upon the persuasion industries themselves. It was a vivid demonstration that on an international scale advertising could actual shape popular culture rather than simply follow it. The press and public relations it generated internationally and its global influence upon popular fashion and music tastes (as much as the increased sales) provided the inspiration for numerous copyists. Consumers all over the world had willingly bought into the whole idea of 501s as a symbol of self-expression rather than merely a pair of jeans. The campaign reshaped Levi Strauss in a manner that was credible and distinctive by using emotional appeals that could unite people around the brand rather than separate them from it. Levitt termed this form of consistent, mass-marketing 'the globalization of markets'.[68] For the advertisers, marketers, and PR specialists working for and on behalf of consumer brands, it was auspicious. Businesses began

[63] Ibid.
[64] Chart positions available at <www.infodisc.fr; wwwultratop. be>; <www.irishcharts.ie>; <www.officialcharts.de>; <www.officialcharts.com>.
[65] Hegarty, *Hegarty on advertising*, 176–8; N. Corey-Wright, *I Love 1986* (London: BBC, 2006).
[66] HAT 59/11/10/762.   [67] 'Carling Ads Get The Levis Look', *Campaign*, 19 December 1986.
[68] T. Levitt, 'The Globalization of Markets', *Harvard Business Review*, 61/3 (1983), 92–102.

to place much greater importance on their persuasion experts. As Mort said, these disciplines became 'the leading edge of economic processes' that were now taking place not in factories and manufacturing sites but on the high street.[69]

The success of brand communication based on emotional appeals was also representative of the wider changes occurring in the cultural landscape of Great Britain. Preoccupations with aspiration, wealth, and self-image were coming to the fore. Schor argued that this led to previously invisible brands becoming much more visible—for example, there was an increased desire to wear clothing emblazoned with a manufacturer's logo or to drink branded bottled water. Symbols indicating hidden features within a product also began to emerge such as 'Pentium Inside' on a personal computer to show the power of the microprocessor or a 'Quattro' badge to indicate that this particular Audi was the more expensive, four-wheel-drive version. By the early 1990s, the visible logo had become ubiquitous, an essential component in the marketing of almost every product. As fashion designer Tommy Hilfiger said: 'I can't sell a shirt without a logo. If I put a shirt without a logo on my selling floor next to a shirt with a logo—same shirt, same colour, and same price—the one with the logo will blow it out. It will sell ten times over the one without the logo. It's a status thing as well. It really is.'[70]

The UK's emergent consumer economy came at a cost: for anyone wishing to reap its benefits, it was expensive. While in continental Europe workers continue to take progressively more of their rewards in the form of leisure during the 1980s and 1990s, in the UK (and the USA) the shift towards shorter working began to reverse. Britain continued to allow longer working hours than the forty-eight-hour-week limitation permissible under the 1993 EC 'Directive on working time' by successfully lobbying for a voluntary opt-out by employees. In contrast, France restricted working hours to just thirty-five hours per week.[71] The rationale supporting this decision was, as Offer identified, a preference for economic growth over leisure in the balance of well-being.[72] Furthermore, the expansion of the service sector and the introduction of technology across the board led to work in many fields becoming more interesting or more intellectually rewarding. The persuasion industries themselves become more playful places to work than they had been during the 1960s and early 1970s. As people aspired to 'an interesting job' rather than

---

[69] Mort, *Cultures of Consumption*, 3. See also C. Gardner and J. Sheppard, *Consuming Passion: The Rise of Retail Culture* (London: Routledge, 1989); W. Kay, *Battle for the High Street* (London: Corgi, 1989).
[70] Schor, *The Overspent American*, 46.
[71] 'EC Directive on Working Time (93/104/EC) <http://eur-lex.europa.eu/legal-content/EN/TXT/?uri=CELEX%3A31993L0104>.
[72] Offer, *The Challenge of Affluence*, 327.

'a steady job', employment in the marketing service sector became an end in itself rather than simply a means to an end. The creative industries—which incorporated music, film, TV, video games, publishing, media, advertising, marketing, public relations, and the creative arts—became one of the most popular career destinations among undergraduates and grew to represent 7 per cent of the UK economy by 1997.[73] Davis, following Wernick, identified these trends as the emergence of a promotional culture that extended beyond the persuasion industry's attempts to encourage consumers to buy things. Businesses and individuals became increasingly more promotionally oriented, dedicating more of their time and resources to it. The 'need to promote' became inculcated unconsciously not only by companies and brands but also by institutions and individuals.[74]

The Levi Strauss campaign was one of the first examples of corporate rebranding in the modern sense: an idea that could be used to deliver a consistent emotional proposition through the myriad of emerging channels. Nike's arresting 'Just do it' tagline, introduced in 1988, was the epitome of this new approach. Imperative, impatient, presumptuous, and even a little rude, it was not the sort of thing consumers had heard before. It suggested something more than its literal meaning was going on, yet allowed people to interpret it as they wished in the knowledge that by doing so they were establishing a personal connection with the brand. Three words upon which an entire corporate strategy could be built, 'Just do it' underpinned Nike's brand communication as it increased its share of the North American sports-shoe business from 18 per cent to 43 per cent over the next ten years.[75] Brand communication based on emotional appeals may not have been the start of 'advertising creating culture' that many commentators believed at the time, and the relationship between persuasion and popular culture is probably symbiotic rather than causal. However, the Levi's campaign was one of the first examples of persuasion's ability successfully to reposition an established brand into the emergent consumer culture by using emotional rather than rational appeals.[76]

[73] S. West, *Playing at Work: Organizational Play as a Facilitator of Creativity*, <http://www.thecreativeindustries.co.uk/uk-creative-overview/facts-and-figures/employment-figures>.
[74] Davis, *Promotional Cultures*, 3–5; Wernick, *Promotional Culture*.
[75] 'The History of Advertising in Quite a Few Objects—No 118: Nike's "Just do it" Tagline', *Campaign*, 23 January 2015.
[76] Mort, *Cultures of Consumption*, 7–18.

5

Lifestyle Choices

Branding and Public Relations, 1980–1997

Branding: Brands with Personality

The role of marketing within major corporations changed profoundly during the 1980s. The impact of these changes was so great that it was still being felt well into the twenty-first century. Throughout the 1970s it became increasingly apparent that many successful consumer-facing companies were beginning to view marketing as a strategic discipline in its own right, one that could drive business growth, rather than merely as the slicker end of the sales department. In the immediate post-war period—a time when trade was fragmented, dominated by small, independent high-street retailers, and consumers bought whatever they could get hold of—there was little discussion about marketing and few marketing departments. Many issues that have since come to be addressed by marketing were assumed to fall within the basic concepts of economics—for example, price setting was viewed as a simple supply–demand issue—and manufacturers of consumer goods generally succeeded by focusing on effective sourcing, increasing production capacity, and improving productivity.[1] The primary concern of the business was that its products were distributed as equitably as possible, and this was the responsibility of the sales department. As a result, although marketing science had its origins in the 1950s, the earliest contributions came from outside the field, from the various disciplines of management science, which were typically part of engineering faculties rather than business schools at the time.[2] The effectiveness of marketers in the 1960s and 1970s was also limited by the paucity of

[1] R. Winer and S. Neslin (eds), *The History of Marketing Science* (Singapore: World Scientific NOW, 2014), 1–17.
[2] R. Bartels, *The History of Marketing Thought* (Columbus, OH: Publishing Horizons, 1988), 177; Winer and Neslin (eds), *The History of Marketing Science*, 2.

consumer research data available to them. Anyone trying to model consumer choice at this time would have been limited to a small number of diary panel datasets.[3] For example, the market research conducted by JWT on behalf of its clients during the 1960s was extensive for the period—and, in all probability, expensive—but shallow. Typically, a large number of interviews about a product were conducted with respondents from within the target audience. A summary of their answers would be collated into a report from which limited conclusions could be drawn. For example, in the case of Mr Kipling, although JWT was able to establish that there was a market demand for packaged cakes, it could not deduce that the reason for this was that the lives of women were changing. More women were entering the workplace, which meant they had less time for activities such as baking. Consequently, the initial campaign targeting a declining group of full-time housewives resulted in disappointing sales.[4]

The emergence of consumer culture in the 1960s compelled companies to become more customer oriented. At the start of the decade companies were still cosseted by the restrictive practice of retail price maintenance. This policy (sometimes called 'resale price maintenance') allowed a manufacturer and its distributors to set a minimum price below which its products would not be sold. If a reseller failed to maintain prices—for whatever reason—the manufacturer could stop supplying them with further products. Businesses at this time can generally be regarded as sales-led, reactive, short term in their thinking, and focused exclusively on the goods they were producing. Advertising was the primary marketing activity, normally supported by a mobile travelling sales force to build distribution, but price maintenance was the key marketing tool, effectively managing the relationship with retailers which the field sales force could then police.[5] Market growth and healthy margins meant there was plenty of room for competition. In this environment, the impact of advertising on business performance was relatively easy to understand and to measure: good advertising was quite simply the kind that led to an increase in sales. This cosy equilibrium was initially disrupted by the 1964 Resale Prices Act, which considered price maintenance to be against the public interest and declared the practice illegal.[6] As well as consumers, the Resale Prices Act was intended to help the retail sector, then predominantly made up of small-to-medium-sized enterprises. However, it was to confer a huge commercial advantage to the burgeoning supermarket chains whose business models were based on discounting. The removal of

---

[3] Ibid. 1.   [4] HAT 50/1/21/2.
[5] OECD, Policy Roundtables: Resale Price Maintenance, <http://www.oecd.org/competition/abuse/1920261.pdf>.
[6] *Resale Prices Act* <http://www.legislation.gov.uk/ukpga/1976/53>.

price maintenance helped to fuel their rapid expansion and over the next fifteen years the grocery trade became increasingly dominated by the chain stores. Between 1961 and 1997, the number of independent retail grocers in the UK fell from 116,000 to just 20,900.[7] By 1990, supermarkets accounted for 80 per cent of the grocery market and were rapidly expanding into other multiple retail categories such as apparel, financial services, homeware, electrical goods, and furniture.[8] There was a similar trend towards multiple retailers across almost every retail sector from electrical goods to clothing. Retail chains invariably sought to achieve market share through competitive pricing, extensive advertising, and investment to build up their store franchises.[9]

For manufacturers this constituted a radical shift in business focus. Rather than dictating terms to small independent retailers they were now more likely to have a route to market through a handful of key accounts, each with hundreds or even thousands of stores across the country. Many independents were either absorbed into bigger concerns or simply went out of business. The balance of power shifted away from the manufacturers. With so much control over market access retailers were able to compel suppliers to subsidize lower shelf prices thereby drastically reducing profit margins and forcing them to chase turnover. Manufacturers also faced the additional challenge of private brands—the retailers own-label products sold exclusively in their own stores, which often emulated the look and feel of the competing name brands they piggybacked. Private branding was pioneered in the UK by Marks and Spencer, which created St Michael as an overarching 'own label' that provided a blanket guarantee of quality across a range of categories from apparel to packaged food.[10] Private brands invariably enjoyed lower price points than their name brand competitors.[11] In this climate of downward pressure on pricing and profit erosion, sales-led strategies were no longer adequate, as they presented few options beyond reducing either product quality or advertising budgets (or both) in an attempt to preserve margins. In this aggressive, new trading environment success required more than pumping out ranges and supporting them with a few advertisements plus some product management.[12] By the end of the 1970s, many businesses had recognized the need for change and were trying to develop marketing strategies.

The research and ideas of Bartels represented a watershed in attitudes to the study of marketing, proving influential on subsequent academics, who almost unanimously adopted his approach—which imitated economics—of

---

[7] J. Blythman, *Shopped: The Shocking Power of British Supermarkets* (London: Harper Perennial, 2007), 5.
[8] Ibid. 4.   [9] W. Kay, *Battle for the High Street* (London: Corgi, 1989).   [10] Ibid. 271.
[11] Blythman, *Shopped*, 271–8.   [12] Ibid.

distinguishing between theory and practice.[13] Two fields of study emerged: the *history of marketing thought*, which was concerned with theory, and *marketing history*, which was focused on its practice. The significance of history for academics was that it helped to identify baselines from which future marketing theory could evolve and new strategies could be extrapolated.[14] Foy and Pommerening highlighted many of the main issues facing the discipline and predicted that in the new trading environment marketing rather than sales would become 'the corporate pacesetter'.[15] Rather than concern themselves with a single focus (the end user), companies were now obliged to deal with a range of stakeholders. Individual trade customers had achieved such a scale that they had effectively become profit centres of the business, requiring the same management attention as the companies' own products. The implications for new product development (NPD) were also significant. Delisting was a major concern even for established brands: if one or more key retailers felt that some rising star brand fitted in better with their own aims and objectives, that new brand would be stocked instead.[16]

By the early 1980s, the trading environment was characterized as aggressive, complex, and highly competitive. It was clear that a new approach was required, but in most organizations the role of brand or product manager was still fairly junior, largely concerned with the four Ps of product, promotion, place, and price, but not much else. Marketing was still essentially just a service provided to the sales team, responsible for ensuring products were attractive and that they stood out on the shelves.[17] Foy and Pommerening argued that the integrated marketing/sales/production approach that the new trading conditions encouraged also required a change in the organizational structure and information requirements of the business.[18] They noted that in market-led organizations the marketing function cut through all the other departments rather than operating in its own silo. Here brand managers were at the heart of the business and responsible for all aspects of the product from conception through launch to maturity, assessing the trade-offs between the demands (actual or potential) of the market and the capabilities of the company, balancing the possible solutions, and recommending a response.[19] However, these more nuanced forms of marketing activity were much less easy to understand or measure, and within segmented markets sustaining

---

[13] Bartels, *The History of Marketing Thought.*; B. Weitz and R. Wensley, *Handbook of Marketing* (New York: Sage, 2006), 47.

[14] Ibid. 7.

[15] P. Foy and D. Pommerening, 'Brand Marketing: Fresh Thinking Is Needed', *Management Review*, 68/11 (1979), 20.

[16] K. Davies, C. Gilligan, and C. Sutton, 'Structural Changes in Grocery Retailing: The Implications for Competition', *International Journal of Physical Distribution and Materials Management*, 15/2 (1985), 3–48.

[17] Foy and Pommerening, 'Brand Marketing'.   [18] Ibid. 21–3.   [19] Ibid. 23–4.

success over the long term became a much more complex exercise. Marketing activity was no longer aimed exclusively at new users but also designed to deepen relationships with retailers and to develop brand loyalty with existing consumers. Such long-term initiatives might not pay off immediately. This issue was addressed by Jacoby and Chestnut.[20] Their aim was to 'provide the marketing manager with an understanding of what brand loyalty is and is not and how it can be measured and used', but they also provided greater focus and direction to further academic thought.[21] By analysing fifty-three research approaches, they made the case that marketing activity should be focused not on achieving repeat purchases but on achieving true brand loyalty instead.

Brands are different from products. Defining a product is not straightforward. It is not just a consumer good; it can also be a service. For the purposes of this discussion, Doyle provides a helpful definition, arguing that a product's value lies not in what the producer produces but in how the consumer benefits. In essence, people do not necessarily want the things that they buy—such as power drills, computers, or motorcars—what they actually want is the ability to make holes, to surf the Internet, or to go places and visit people. In this context, a product can be thought of as 'anything that meets the needs of customers'.[22] Black & Decker, Apple, and Jaguar are brands with a reputation for high quality, associated, respectively, with products like power drills, computers, and cars. Unlike products, brands are intangible—figments of our collective imagination—so we cannot point at brands in the real world because they do not occupy physical space; they are neither entities like Winston Churchill or Madonna, nor objective phenomena like gravity or radiation. Yet, brands are not entirely subjective either. The Black & Decker, Apple, or Jaguar brand will not cease to exist just because one stops believing in them or chooses to view the products they produce simply in terms of their utility— namely, as nothing more than power drills, computers, and motorcars. Harari argues that brands occupy a space called the inter-subjective—that is to say, they exist within the communication network that links the collective, subjective consciousness of many people.[23] The majority of cultural and social drivers are inter-subjective—government, religion, law, commerce, economics—and, like them, brands do have both a presence and a narrative. That narrative is a fiction, but nevertheless there is a general understanding among consumers about what the brand Black & Decker, Apple, or Jaguar means or stands for.[24]

---

[20] J. Jacoby, *Brand Loyalty: Measurement and Management* (New York: Wiley, 1978).
[21] Ibid., p. xi.
[22] P. Doyle, 'Building Successful Brands: The Strategic Options', *Journal of Consumer Marketing*, 7/2 (1990), 5–20.
[23] Y. N. Harari, *Sapiens: A Brief History of Humankind* (London: Vintage, 2015), 32–6.
[24] Ibid. 115–19. See also C. Levi-Strauss, *Myth and Meaning* (Toronto: Toronto University Press, 1978).

Therefore, if a product is anything that meets the needs of customers, then a brand can be considered a concept that customers engage with collectively at an emotional level, and branding is a process that involves telling stories about those concepts and persuading people to believe them.

Branding is a highly effective means of selling products. For Jacoby and Chestnut, brand loyalty is a deterministic subset of repeat purchase behaviour.[25] A brand works by facilitating the consumer's choice process, giving them the impression that it is the most effective option among the choices on offer. On a daily basis, consumers must make a large number of purchasing decisions; consequently they are besieged by an even larger number of products and messages vying for their attention. Brands appear to simplify this decision-making process by removing the need for difficult, rule-governed System Two thinking and providing the individual with a familiar short cut.[26] For example, as a result of branding, 'I'm thirsty—I need a drink' might become 'I'm thirsty—I need a Pepsi'. Brands also rely on habit, as consumers tend to stick with things that have proven satisfactory in the past. This is especially true for low-involvement purchases, which constitute the majority of transactions. Brand loyalty cannot be categorized as rational behaviour. A 1988 survey by *The Economist* concluded: 'People all over the world form irrational attachments to different products. Humans like to take sides . . . By most "tangible" measures, BMW cars and IBM computers are not significantly better than rivals, but customers will pay significantly more for them.'[27] In truth, this behaviour is borne out of expediency rather than loyalty. There is usually more than one brand that will satisfy a consumer's need, which is why few people who ask for a Pepsi are genuinely disappointed if they are offered Coke instead.

Marketing: Into the Vanguard

The market-led approach to business had been pioneered successfully during the 1970s by companies such as Apple, McDonalds, Virgin, and Nike. However, a theoretical basis for understanding how successful brands were created within the 'new commercial reality' was ultimately provided by Levitt.[28] Levitt's persuasive and hugely influential essay 'The Globalization of Markets'

---

[25] Jacoby, *Brand Loyalty*.
[26] A. Tversky and D. Kahneman, 'The Framing of Decisions and the Psychology of Choice', *Science*, 211/4481 (1981), 453–8.
[27] 'The Year of the Brands', *The Economist*, 24 December 1988.
[28] T. Levitt, *The Marketing Imagination* (New York: Macmillan, 1983); T. Levitt, 'The Globalization of Markets', *Harvard Business Review*, 61/3 (1983), 92–102. Although Levitt did not coin the term 'globalization' himself, he was responsible for its subsequent popularization.

appeared in the May 1983 issue of the *Harvard Business Review* and dealt with the implications of what he described as 'the emergence of global markets for standardized consumer products'.[29] Levitt claimed that new technology had 'proletarianized' communication, transport, and travel.[30] The world was becoming more affluent: people enjoyed having money and wanted to spread it over as many goods as they could. Even in the developing world 'nobody takes scarcity lying down—everybody wants more'.[31] Consequently, consumers across the globe now wanted much the same things: the latest goods they had seen, heard about, or experienced via this new technology. Gone were the days when a company could sell last year's products to less developed parts of the world and enjoy higher profits in these foreign markets than they did at home. Instead, there was now a single, global mass market for standardized consumer products.

This global market potentially offered a huge opportunity, but Levitt argued it was one that only companies with the right strategy would be able to exploit. Levitt drew examples from high-touch and high-tech business sectors in support of his argument, such as McDonalds restaurants, Coca Cola, Pepsi, Revlon cosmetics, Levi Strauss jeans, Hollywood movies, IBM computers, and Sony televisions. High-touch businesses were those characterized by a high degree of human interaction with their customers, as opposed to those that transacted through high-technology.[32] He made a distinction between multinational (foxes) and global (hedgehogs) corporations. Foxes operated in many countries at high relative costs, adjusting and tailoring their products and practices in each one to suit perceived local tastes. Hedgehogs, on the other hand, treated the entire world as a single entity; they sold the same things everywhere and benefited from much lower operating costs. Hedgehogs recognized the truth: that people everywhere were united in a desire for modernity and were driven by price more than notional national characteristics.

In Levitt's opinion, businesses did not have a choice. There was no place for product-obsessed multinationals; they would have either to adopt the global model—'offering everyone simultaneously high-quality, more or less standardized products at optimally low prices'—or to go out of business.[33] No sector would be exempt: all would be affected, from steel and automobiles to food and fashion. Fortunately, producing market-standardized products was not only achievable but also desirable, because it would lead to 'enormous economies of scale in production, distribution, and management'.[34] He contrasted the differentiated strategy of foxes with the distinctive strategy of hedgehogs. Foxes tended to be overly obsessed with the products they produced and 'thoughtlessly accommodating' to the perceived nuances of individual markets.[35] In contrast,

---

[29] Levitt, 'The Globalization of Markets', 92.   [30] Ibid. 93.
[31] Ibid. 96.   [32] Ibid. 93.   [33] Ibid. 96–7.   [34] Ibid. 92.   [35] Ibid. 96.

hedgehogs focused on the 'one great thing' that made their brand distinctive and thereby allowed them to be competitive on a world basis. Levitt advocated that, rather than promoting product differences, companies should be understanding and meet the needs of their customers. Marketing should be used to support brand distinctiveness and work vigorously towards global convergence.

Levitt's basic contention that companies spent too much time producing products and too little time satisfying customers was compelling. Written only a year after he had joined the Harvard Business School, his follow-up book *The Marketing Imagination* went on to sell almost one million copies, and, together with his article, can be seen as a turning point in the acceptance and respectability of marketing.[36] Many followed Levitt—most notably Kotler, who provided a much more rigorous academic analysis of global marketing and a framework for taking it further—but prior to the publication of 'The Globalization of Markets' the typical marketing department had been a minor corporate concern.[37] Levitt and Kotler can be regarded as raising the status of marketing from comparative disrepute to a strategic function in its own right. Following Drucker, Levitt argued that the purpose of a business was not simply to make money but 'to create and keep a customer'.[38] Kotler had long argued that marketing was a business function that evolved over time.[39] Initially his work was focused on transactional marketing, but he came to much the same view as Levitt: that, rather than merely commerce, marketing was a social activity—the exchange of values between two parties. (It was also Kotler who first coined the term 'social marketing' in 1971.[40]) His vision of marketing was entirely customer focused—it was a strategic business function not a product development afterthought: 'Marketing is not the art of finding clever ways to dispose of what you make. Marketing is the art of creating genuine customer value. It is the art of helping your customers become better off.'[41] Although Levitt did not discuss branding specifically, the broad interpretation of his ideas (which gained wide acceptance) was that to be effective across many different cultures transnational companies should standardize products,

---

[36] *Guru: Theodore Levitt*, < http://www.economist.com/node/13167376>.

[37] K. Philip and K. M. Murali, 'Flawed Products: Consumer Reponses and Marketer Strategies', *Journal of Consumer Marketing*, 2/3 (1985), 27–36. See also P. Kotler, 'Global Standardization: Courting Danger', *Journal of Consumer Marketing*, 3/2 (1986), 13–15; P. Kotler and W. Mindak, 'Marketing and Public Relations: Should they Be Partners?', *Journal of Marketing*, 42/4 (1978), 13–20.

[38] Levitt, 'The Globalization of Markets', 101–2.

[39] P. Kotler, *Marketing Management: Analysis, Planning, and Control* (Englewood Cliffs, NJ: Prentice-Hall, 1967); P. Kotler, *Principles of Marketing* (Englewood Cliffs, NJ: Prentice Hall, 1980); P. Kotler, *Marketing: An Introduction* (Englewood Cliffs, NJ: Prentice Hall, 1987).

[40] P. Kotler and G. Zaltman, 'Social Marketing: An Approach to Planned Social Change', *Journal of Marketing*, 35/3 (1971), 3–12.

[41] P. Kotler, *Marketing Insights from A to Z: 80 Concepts Every Manager Needs to Know* (New York: Wiley, 2003), p. xii.

packaging, and communication to achieve a lowest-common-denominator position. From that common-sense viewpoint, the previously woolly activity of branding looked not only like the vehicle to ensuring consistent customer communication, but also a genuine exercise in reducing costs.

There was significant academic interest in Levitt's ideas. Research into both branding and marketing increased concurrently with their rising commercial prominence. However, not all findings were positive, and global branding was not without its critics. For example, an empirical study of US brands overseas undertaken by Rosen, Boddewyn, and Louis found that, 'despite all the talk about the internationalization of marketing efforts, [aside from a few stars], the international diffusion of US brands is actually rather limited'.[42] This dissent did little to prevent the practical application of product standardization. Following the collapse of communism in the former Eastern Bloc countries at the end of the 1980s, new markets opened up to western brands, which enabled the rapid extension of globalization into a truly global philosophy. Marketing was now identified as the key business discipline that could unlock a cornucopia of opportunities. During the 1990s there was an ongoing effort to adapt or reinvent established marketing theory to address the challenges presented by globalization. For example, there were attempts to expand the four Ps to seven (by adding physical evidence, people, and process to product, price, promotion, and place) or replace them altogether with a more customer-focused four Cs (notably, Lauterborn's consumer, cost, communication, and convenience, and Shimizu's commodity, cost, communication, and channel).[43] From the mid-1980s, marketing became an increasingly integrated business function: not simply a department but a culture.

Attitudes to advertising had also changed. It was less frequently viewed simply in terms of its ability to shift boxes; it could be used to communicate and position the brand. However, advertising could not create brands on its own, and it was not the basis of the brand itself. Bartle Bogle and Hegarty's 501's campaign had persuaded consumers to think about Levi's jeans in a different way, but it did not change either the product or Levi's brand values. It employed existing brand equity to tell a new, evocative, and compelling version of the American heritage story, but from the consumer's perspective it was as if Levi's had acquired a fresh, vastly more interesting personality. Competitors can quickly copy a pair of jeans, a cigarette, a soft drink formula,

---

[42] B. Rosen, J. Boddewyn, and E. Louis, 'US Brands Abroad: An Empirical Study of Global Branding', *International Marketing Review*, 6/1 (1989), 18.

[43] R. Lauterborn, 'New Marketing Litany: Four Ps Pass 7Cs Words Take Over', *Advertising Age*, 61/41 (1990), 26; A. Shimizu, *Advertising Theories and Strategies* (Tokyo: Souseisha, 1989); Professional Academy, *Marketing Theories: The Marketing Mix—from 4 Ps to 7 Ps* <http://www. professionalacademy.com/blogs-and-advice/marketing-theories—the-marketing-mix—from-4-p-s-to-7-p-s>.

or a computer specification, but what they cannot copy is a brand's personality. Competing products might to all intents and purposes be identical (chemically so in the case of Pepsi and Coke), but in the all-important opinion of the consumer no two brands are exactly the same. Differentiation is achieved entirely by the process of branding—intangible and difficult to define or measure in principle, but undeniably effective in practice.

Doyle identified four brand strategies that could be used to build sustainable differentiated advantages for consumers, which he summarized as quality, service, innovation, and differentiation.[44] In this model, brands were built from the inside out—for example, Apple's *Think Differently* advertising campaign for its new Macintosh computer *told* consumers what it stood for, but the company also needed to *show* them what it stood for. Claims needed to be backed up—demonstrably so—and consistency maintained across all points of contact. From launch advertising and public relations, through the retail purchasing experience to the post-sales customer service and customer loyalty programmes, the brand question for Apple was how the concept of *Think Differently* could be applied to that entire process at all stages. Similarly, through its brand advertising, Nike told consumers that it stood for 'sporting excellence', but it also demonstrated this commitment to them through its sponsorship of elite athletes, leading sports teams, and top sporting events.[45]

The investment required to build a brand in this way was high, but the pay-off for success was not insignificant. Doyle argued that leading brands enjoyed higher customer loyalty. Challenger or new brands needed to attract customers, which affected net margin, because to do so required expenditure on advertising and other forms of promotion. It could cost a business up to six times more to attract a new customer than to retain an existing customer.[46] Consumers were also willing to forgive or overlook occasional aberrations where strong brands were concerned. A poor product or experience might turn consumers off a weak brand forever, but the likes of Heinz, Ford, or British Airways were more likely to be forgiven. Doyle recounted an anecdote involving a colleague who rang Federal Express, which then had an impeccable reputation for customer service, twenty-seven times over a six-month period:

> Twenty-six times a FEDX employee answered during the first ring of the telephone. On the twenty-seventh time the telephone rang repeatedly without any response. After repeated rings, he put the phone down because he assumed that *he* had made the mistake of calling the wrong number! Of course, if this had been a neutral or negative brand this episode would have simply reinforced one's current image of the brand.[47]

---

[44] Doyle, 'Building Successful Brands'.   [45] Ibid.   [46] Ibid. 10.   [47] Ibid. 10–11.

153

A theory of modern branding was formalized by Aaker.[48] In this model, brand equity is viewed as a combination of brand awareness, brand loyalty, and brand associations, which combine to give the value provided by a product or service. Aaker found that companies skilled at operating outside the normal media channels (those using attention-getting approaches including publicity, sampling, event promotions, and sponsorships) would ultimately be the most successful at building brand awareness.[49]

In Britain the corporate world did not require too much convincing. The news pages of *Campaign* from the mid-1980s highlight the increase in brand promotion. During the 1970s little editorial coverage was dedicated to branding, as it was an activity in which few companies were engaged. However, after 1986 there was a significant increase in the number of stories concerning brand building, as company spending increased. Brand strategies usually emerged as the consequence of a strategic review, and it is possible to track their relative success through the archive.

The adoption of a brand strategy in 1987 by Vauxhall, the British arm of General Motors, provides a good example. By the mid-1980s, Vauxhall, long synonymous with the corporate fleet sector, was languishing some distance behind its main competitor Ford—the market leader. In 1986, Ford's sales amounted to around 31 per cent of the UK market, while Vauxhall's share had fallen to 13.5 per cent.[50] In order to develop an effective turnaround strategy, Vauxhall engaged advertising agency Lowe Howard-Spink to undertake a wide-reaching company review. Their findings revealed that the Vauxhall brand was synonymous with the Cavalier, its most popular model, but the rest of its range lacked the same recognition.[51] A new corporate objective was identified—to establish Vauxhall as an aspirational motoring brand in its own right—which was some distance removed from its then current reputation as a one-product business.[52]

On Boxing Day 1987, Vauxhall launched six separate commercials for a number of vehicles in its range during the advertisement breaks in *Ghostbusters*, a family film that was broadcast on ITV to a huge audience. Rather than focus on the cars themselves, the adverts instead concentrated on the owners' relationships with their vehicles, signing off with a brand new slogan: 'Once driven, forever smitten.' Like Levi's before it, rather than producing a bespoke jingle, Vauxhall instead licensed a classic rock track, Eric Clapton's 1971 hit

[48] D. A. Aaker, 'The Value of Brand Equity', *Journal of Business Strategy*, 13/4 (1992), 27–32.
[49] Ibid. 10–11.
[50] G. Amber, 'Old Class, not New Flash: A Four-Wheel Ad Backlash?/Advertising's Use of Cars', *Campaign*, 25 July 1986; L. Ludwick, 'Vauxhall Puts 10 Million Pounds into New Strategy', *Campaign*, 8 January 1988.
[51] Ibid.
[52] S. Birch, 'Can Vauxhall's New Man at the Helm Beat off Ford's Attack?', *Campaign*, 5 December 1986; I. Fraser, 'Vauxhall Makes its Marque', *Campaign*, 7 June 1991.

'Layla', to set the tone.[53] The campaign was based on an emotional appeal about a passion for motoring rather than any tangible product benefit, and the emphasis was on the brand rather than individual models. It also established a core theme that was to take the company into the 1990s: that some men loved their Vauxhalls more than their partners.[54]

The brand building strategy was not restricted to advertising alone. In 1990, Vauxhall launched the Calibra, a coupé with a sleek exterior that shared the same floor plan and interior as the best-selling Cavalier.[55] Produced in small quantities with sales volumes that were uneconomic, the Calibra was created for no other reason than to change Vauxhall's brand image. A launch film was commissioned and shown in Germany, France, and the UK, which employed key historic events from the 1980s (such as the fall of the Berlin Wall) to reflect the shock that a company famous for producing mass-market saloons could produce such a good-looking coupé.[56] Later the same year Vauxhall also launched the Lotus Carlton. Built in collaboration with the UK sports-car manufacturer Lotus, this was a high-performance version of Vauxhall's executive saloon. Boasting a top speed of 180 mph and costing £49,000, the car was an even rarer sight on the roads than the Calibra, but it served the same brand-building function.[57]

Vauxhall's long-term strategy paid off. Between 1987 and 1991 Ford's share of the lucrative fleet car market, which accounted for almost a third of all new car sales in the UK, fell from nearly 50 per cent to below 36 per cent. In November 1990, Ford lost its position as fleet car market leader for the first time and announced UK losses of £247 million before tax the following year. It was the company's first loss for two decades. During the same period Vauxhall posted a $240 million profit.[58]

For brand managers trying to engage with an audience, there were now far more strategic and tactical options available. In terms of brand building, advertising continued to play an important role throughout the 1990s, but other elements of the marketing mix were rising in prominence. As Aaker identified, there was much more to branding than advertising, and companies increasingly looked beyond it when launching new products or initiating promotions: events, sponsorship, direct marketing, loyalty schemes, and

---

[53] D. Midgeley, 'The Cavalier—Coming out Laughing: Vauxhall Reveals its 10 Million Pounds Blockbuster', *Campaign*, 14 October 1988.

[54] I. Fraser, 'Vauxhall Makes its Marque', *Campaign*, 7 June 1991.

[55] 'Vauxhall Steers Calibra into UK and Germany', *Campaign*, 8 June 1990.   [56] Ibid.

[57] I. Fraser, 'Vauxhall Makes its Marque', *Campaign*, 7 June 1991; L. Ludwick, 'GM Launches Carlton in 2 Million Pounds', *Campaign*, 14 November 1986.

[58] I. Fraser, 'Vauxhall Makes its Marque', *Campaign*, 7 June 1991; 'Special Report on Top Advertisers and Brands: Key Market Focus—Motors', *Campaign*, 3 May 1991.

public relations were other important components of a broader brand strategy.[59] Public relations ensured that news of Vauxhall's partnership with the exotic specialist manufacturer Lotus reached a much wider audience than any vehicles produced by the partnership and did much more to improve its brand image than the 275 models sold.[60]

The wide-scale adoption of standardized global product and corporate marketing strategies was arguably the biggest contribution to the emergence of promotional culture identified by Wernick and Davies.[61] The shift in political and economic focus from common societal good to individual freedom created the opportunity, and globalization provided the commercial imperative, but it was the elevation of marketing at a corporate level and the adoption of standardized branding that most profoundly shaped consumer society. Persuasion during the 1990s was not only more persuasive than ever before but also much more pervasive, as commerce became ingrained into lifestyles. For at the heart of all this activity was the consumer—unceasingly bombarded with messages, every year, each one reinforcing the view that everything he or she felt, thought, wanted, and needed, was vitally important—and around whom an infinitely centred universe of products and brands appeared to be revolving.

Public Relations: Out of the Shadows

Although the word 'explosive' lends itself all too readily to hyperbole, it can be applied unreservedly to describe the growth of public relations in Britain during the 1980s and 1990s. In 1979 barely 20 per cent of the top 500 British companies were taking public relations consultancy advice, but five years later 69 per cent were retaining public relations consultancies, including forty-five of the Top 50 businesses.[62] The question posed by the Public Relations Consultants Association (PRCA) chairman Douglas Smith in his introduction to the organization's 1985 handbook was no longer whether 'companies should make use of consultancy communication skills, but rather how best to develop the relationship, to strike the right working balance within the respective

[59] D. A. Aaker, *Building Strong Brands* (New York and London: Free Press, 1995); D. A. Aaker, *Managing Brand Equity: Capitalizing on the Value of a Brand Name* (New York: Free Press; Toronto: Collier Macmillan Canada, 1991).

[60] P. Hudson, 'Lotus Carlton Review: Vauxhall Super Saloon Turns 25', *Daily Telegraph Cars*, 13 January 2015; L. Ludwick, 'GM Launches Carlton in 2 Million Pounds', *Campaign*, 14 November 1986.

[61] A. Wernick, *Promotional Culture: Advertising, Ideology and Symbolic Expression* (London: Sage, 1991).; A. Davis, *Promotional Cultures: The Rise and Spread of Advertising, Public Relations, Marketing and Branding* (Cambridge: Polity, 2013).

[62] D. Smith, 'Consultancy and Client: A Problem Shared is a Problem Solved', *Public Relations Year Book 1985* (London: FT Business Information, 1984).

organisations to monitor performance in a properly sophisticated manner'.[63] This rapid expansion of public relations gathered speed throughout the 1980s. Despite tighter controls on admission, PRCA membership roughly doubled between 1979 and 1984. The fee income of UK agencies rose in real terms per annum by 30 per cent, 35 per cent, and 40 per cent between 1984 and 1986.[64] The industry hit an initial peak in 1990, whereafter it suffered a sharp two-year decline before recovering strongly to reach a new high in 1997. By the beginning of 1998, the sector had expanded by a factor of thirty-one since 1979, it employed over 48,000 people—working either as consultants or in-house within press offices and public relations departments—while the Top 150 PR agencies were generating an annual fee income of £366 million (£654 million at 2018 values).[65]

The growth of the public relations industry in the UK is unusual in several respects, and not just in the rate of its development. There was not a breakthrough in theory, practice, or delivery to account for the rise, nor was there any technological innovation that suddenly made public relations much more effective than ever before. As L'Etang has identified, the discipline did not suddenly become more professional, nor did it become noticeably better at marketing itself to industry. While the emergence of 'promotional culture' during the 1990s, as described by Wernick, played some part, Miller and Dinan have argued that the growth owed 'incomparably more' to the changes in political and economic circumstances.[66] Globally the size and power of transnational corporations increased, which in turn increased demand for promotional services, as enterprises aspired systematically to extend their influence over policymakers and interest groups as well as consumers. In the UK specifically, demand for public relations was also driven by a series of changes to the regulatory framework of the market by Conservative administrations during the 1980s and 1990s. The privatization of public utilities, deregulation of financial markets and professional services (such as law and accountancy), and the increasing number of publicly listed enterprises drove both the demand for promotional services and also expenditure on promotional activity.[67]

There is much evidence to support this view, not least the fact that the three countries that engaged in the most profound privatization and financial deregulation during the 1980s—USA, UK, and Japan—emerged with the biggest public relations sectors in the 1990s.[68] In Britain's privatizations, public relations consultancies were routinely appointed to promote the benefits of

---

[63] Ibid.   [64] 'IPR Puts Industry in Perspective', *PR Week*, 19 November 1992.
[65] D. Miller and W. Dinan, 'The Rise of the PR Industry in Britain, 1979–98', *European Journal of Communication*, 15/1 (2000), 5–35.
[66] Ibid. 28–35.   [67] Ibid. 14–23, 23–4, 24–7.   [68] Ibid. 8.

share ownership in the utility and to make it attractive to potential investors. The fees for these services were substantial. Excluding advertising, the public relations and marketing budget for British Gas, which was handled by Lowe-Bell, was £15.4 million (£44 million at 2018 values), while Dewe Rogerson received a reported £2.0 million in fees (£5.9 million at 2018 values) for leading advice on the privatization of the regional electricity boards.[69] Globalization, privatization, and deregulation also increased the level of corporate activity in the form of mergers and acquisitions. In this area the role of the PR specialist changed enormously. Prior to the Big Bang of 1986, investor relations were relatively informal and companies were able to rely on their corporate financiers for communication advice.[70] Public relations was employed almost exclusively for media management, if it was used at all.[71] Following deregulation, public relations quickly became a strategic function of the takeover bid (or the defence against it) and a primary concern in the preparation and planning of finance proposals and flotations. Arfin argued that the 1980s was 'littered with the vanished or absorbed companies that didn't catch on fast enough' to the need for corporate public relations.[72]

Miller and Dinan's analysis is thorough and compelling—as far as it goes. Echoing Davies, they do not deal 'with the specific strategies or tactics of the PR industry or with general questions of success'.[73] Their paper also contains a noteworthy caveat in its closing statement: 'We are not suggesting that the factors we have outlined here are the only relevant factors in explaining the rise and specific form of the PR industry.' They go on to outline three additional causes that they believe had a bearing and that are worthy of further investigation: the decline in effectiveness of advertising, the dwindling resources for newsgathering from the late 1980s, and the expansion of the media and demand for content.[74] Furthermore, their focus was almost exclusively on financial public relations—with a nod towards corporate reputation management—ignoring all other applications (such as crisis management and corporate image building) and areas of significant growth (most notably consumer relations). Miller and Dinan are also correct in their assertion that the nature of public relations and the manner in which it was conducted did not markedly change during the period.[75] It would also be wrong to assume that public relations became more effective over time. There is in fact more evidence to support the opposite view—that a great deal of the money spent

---

[69] Ibid. 19–20.
[70] F. N. Arfin, *Financial Public Relations: Lessons from the Corporate Leaders* (London: Financial Times, 1994), 5.
[71] K. Newman, *Financial Marketing and Communications* (London: Holt, 1984).
[72] Arfin, *Financial Public Relations*, 6.
[73] Miller and Dinan, 'The Rise of the PR Industry in Britain', 27.   [74] Ibid. 30.
[75] Ibid. 29.

on promotional services during the 1980s and 1990s was undoubtedly wasted. However, what did change was the value of public relations to enterprises, the opportunities for its effective application, and the scale of public relations activity. Kotler recognized that market-facing enterprises were confronting formidable new communication challenges, all of which required insightful public relations handling—namely, consumerism, environmentalism, energy conservation, inflation, shortages, employment discrimination, and safety. He predicted that this would lead to a more active role for public relations within companies but also identified a skills gap between the market need and the supply of advice. In his view, the current education and training available to both new entrants and more experienced practitioners were wholly inadequate.[76]

Within the sector the pace of growth compounded this issue of competency. Barriers to market entry were low. Setting up a public relations agency was very inexpensive, with would-be practitioners needing little more than access to a phone, typewriter, and photocopier before they were in business. Good media contacts and an understanding of how the media worked were a bonus but by no means essential.[77] Unlike advertising agencies, whose credentials were highly visible, the potential of individual public relations agencies was much more difficult to evaluate. The proof of the pudding was all too often in the eating (a problem that the industry has never been able to address satisfactorily). The question of where new talent could be found to meet the demand was another perennial challenge. In the leader of its October 1984 launch issue, *PR Week* identified recruitment as 'the most pressing issue . . . [facing] one of the fastest growing businesses in the whole of the UK economy.'[78] Given projected growth rates, *PR Week* estimated that the sector, which then employed approximately 10,000 people in 1984, needed to recruit around 2,000 people and create 3,000 new jobs over the coming twelve months.[79] The pressure to increase capacity by almost one-third also drove the costs of recruitment. Salaries rose by 58 per cent between 1980 and 1985, but this was no reflection on improving levels of competence.[80] On the contrary, a dearth of talent led to the hasty promotion of inexperienced and less able staff into positions they were ill equipped to handle. This development further compounded the issue in two ways. First, the limited numbers of capable and experienced practitioners were able to command vastly inflated salaries and, secondly, the influx of willing but untrained novices was to prove

---

[76] Kotler and Mindak, 'Marketing and Public Relations', 16, 20.
[77] 'Taking the Plunge and Making it Work', *PR Week*, 23 May 1985, pp. 9–10; 'PRCA Survey Reveals Number of Problems', *PR Week*, 21 May 1987, p. 3.
[78] 'Keeping Tabs on the Bounty Hunters', *PR Week*, 1 November 1984, p. 4.   [79] Ibid.
[80] 'Salaries Rise 58 per cent since 1980', *PR Week*, 12 September 1985, p. 2.

damaging to the reputation of the sector.[81] Other than throw money at experienced executives, companies did very little to address the problem. Demand for public relations was high, and agencies were profitable, but it is likely that in many cases the service that their clients received was poor. This is highlighted by the fact that most new entrants felt that the training they received in post was insufficient for them to carry out the responsibilities of their jobs.[82]

Little changed. Over ten years later in a June 1995 leader, *PR Week* reported that the sector was still wrestling with much the same concerns 'There is ... intense pressure to recruit talent, which, after all, is a consultancy's only real asset ... [but] Agencies need to look for new ways of attracting and retaining staff, other than adding noughts to their salaries.'[83] The industry's trade bodies—the IPR and PRCA—did make some attempts to address the problem, most notably through the launch of a blueprint for education and training in 1988 and the introduction of the first BA courses in public relations at Bournemouth Polytechnic and the College of St Marks and St John in 1990.[84] However, the impact of these initiatives at an industry-wide level was limited. In *PR Week*'s 1997 industry survey, more than half of all staff working in-house and almost two-thirds of those working in consultancies reported that they had received no structured training.[85] The sector continued to suffer the consequences of inexperienced account handling during the 1990s but to a lesser degree than during the previous decade.[86]

Another issue was that few people—including clients—understood what public relations actually was or misunderstood what it could be used for.[87] The vast majority of respondents in a 1985 survey of the general public and media either did not know what public relations was at all or confused it with advertising. The minority of respondents who did demonstrate some knowledge of what public relations actually was also added that they did not like it

---

[81] 'A New Status, a New Voice', *PR Week*, 4 October 1984, p. 4; 'Editorial: Investing in PR Talent', *PR Week*, 28 March 1997.

[82] 'PR Salary Survey', *PR Week*, 28 March 1987, pp. 1, 6, 9–11.

[83] 'What Price PR Talent?', *PR Week*, 30 June 1995.

[84] 'Training: The Art of Course Fishing—If You Can't Run your own Training Drop a Line to the Specialists, who can Sharpen up your Top People or Knock Sense into your Up and Coming Talent', *PR Week*, 27 September 1990; 'PRCA and IPR Launch Joint Industry Training Blueprint', *PR Week*, 3 November 1988, p. 1.

[85] R. Dowman, 'Salary Survey: Career Moves—the New Breed of PR Professionals are Less Interested in Hard Cash than they are in Job Satisfaction and Recognition', *PR Week*, 28 March 1997.

[86] S. Horner, 'Training: Staff Training, Improving your Minds', *PR Week*, 27 September 1990; A. Hall, 'Failure to Win Editors' Respect', *PR Week*, 7 November 1991; V. Kinross, 'Platform: How you Fend off a Nightmare—Is Clumsy Client Handling Losing you Future Business?', *PR Week*, 8 February 1990; J. Abbot, 'Focus: Presentation Training: Time to Stand up and be Counted/In the PR Industry, Extrovert Professionals are Often Expected to be Natural', *PR Week*, 12 September 1997.

[87] J. Rafferty, 'Clients Know Nothing about Us', *PR Week*, 14 August 1986, pp. 6–7.

at all.[88] A contributing factor to this opaqueness and poor public image was the sector's persistent reticence when it came to self-promotion. While PR specialists were happy to talk about and on behalf of their clients, they were far more reluctant to talk about either themselves or their activities—even to their own trade paper.[89] In the mid-1990s, the lack of understanding about the role of public relations among marketing and branding professionals remained a major concern, leading to unsuitable briefs, inappropriate activity, and ineffective coverage (if any was achieved at all).[90] In 1995, the UK's first professor of public relations, Norman Hart, wrote: 'Their [marketing professionals] lack of understanding leads them to expect an ongoing programme of free editorial publicity which will be brought about by news releases, if there is any news, or by creative, and sometimes cranky, activities which will gain media attentions in their own right.'[91]

It was not just the clients who suffered the consequences. The focus for almost all this public relations activity was the researchers, writers, journalists, and editors working in the media. An extensive independent survey of the UK's public relations and media industries carried out by Gallup in 1991 highlighted the strides that public relations had taken during the previous decade but also its shortcomings.[92] The poll, based on two parallel pieces of research—a qualitative study of 26 editors and a quantitative study of 100 directors of public relations consultancies and 100 heads of in-house departments—revealed that more than 80 per cent of editors thought that the public relations industry provided a useful and informative service for the media. Public relations was estimated to be responsible for between 25 and 40 per cent of all coverage generated. However, around 66 per cent of editors also believed that PR speicalists lacked an adequate understanding of how the media operated.[93] *PR Week* declared the results of the survey to be 'depressingly familiar'.[94]

Yet, despite all these drawbacks, public relations not only thrived but positively triumphed in the UK. Notwithstanding the competence or otherwise of individual consultants, there was a lot more public relations activity taking place than ever before, so the number of successful campaigns increased numerically, if not necessarily as a proportion of the whole. At a broader

---

[88] L. Vee and L. McLaughlin, 'You Are Awful (some Say) but Others Like You', *PR Week*, 19 December 1985, pp. 8–9.

[89] 'Come on Spill the Beans', *PR Week*, 29 November 1984, p. 7.

[90] 'Sign up for a Crusade', *PR Week*, 28 October 1993.

[91] N. Hart, 'Platform: Marketers Miss Central Role of Public Relations—Marketing Professionals, unlike Board Directors of the UK's Top Companies, Still Underrate PR's Potential', *PR Week*, 12 May 1995.

[92] *The Media and the PR Industry: A Partnership or a Marriage of Convenience? Gallup Survey for Two-Ten Communications* (London: Gallup Social Surveys, 1991).

[93] Ibid.   [94] A. Hall, 'Failure to Win Editors' Respect', *PR Week*, 7 November 1991.

level, public relation's general effectiveness became increasingly apparent, as too did the consequences of trying to manage without it. Throughout the 1980s, the market became an increasingly turbulent and competitive environment, placing demands on enterprises to become more sophisticated in their relations with key publics. In 1984, a series of major industrial disputes and strikes affected four of the UK's leading car manufacturers—Austin Rover, Jaguar, Ford, and Vauxhall. The companies each acknowledged that the disputes were doing a great deal of damage to the reputation of the UK car industry at a time when it was losing ground to fierce competition from Europe and the Far East.[95] However, not one of the firms had any specific public relations operations, either planned or implemented, to counteract the negative effects of the strife. Rather than act in concert, they sought to distance themselves from each other's problems in the media. The result was a picture of a fragmented and fraught industry, beleaguered by industrial strife, low on productivity, and as unattractive to consumers as it was to investors.[96]

Others were quicker to recognize that public relations was the communications vehicle to deal with this kind of issue. A 1986 *Times* survey of the Top 200 UK businesses revealed that 82 per cent considered corporate communications a high priority and 56 per cent expected it to increase in importance.[97] Marketing could promote the business and advertise its products. Public relations could perform a similar function, but it was also able to address the various challenges emerging from interest groups, changing market conditions, and the rise in consumer information. It could influence policymakers, shape public opinion, and make or break corporate reputations. Moreover, it was a comparatively cheap service with few cost issues for any enterprise wanting to give it a try.

Food was one sector where producers increasingly turned to public relations. A combination of legislation and increased consumer awareness had made the blithe pronouncements of the past more difficult to support, as people paid much greater attention to the food on their plates and the effect it was having on their health and well-being. During the early 1970s, milk had a healthy, nourishing image and was considered such an essential part of daily diets that it was given free to schoolchildren. However, from 1980, public health concerns resulting from research that linked high levels of fat consumption with heart disease had seen full-fat milk appear on a growing list of dangerous foods, as those advocating lower-fat diets focused on dairy products, the most identifiable source of fats. In 1983, following a similar action in the USA, the UK government introduced nutritional guidelines

---

[95] D. McCrystal, 'Crisis for Car Firms', *PR Week*, 18 November 1984. [96] Ibid.
[97] 'Public Relations Special Report', *Campaign*, 14 November 1986.

recommending a reduction in dietary fat intake to 30 per cent of total energy intake and a decrease in saturated fat consumption to 10 per cent of total energy intake.[98] At this time, as much as one-fifth of the average British diet was in the form of saturated fat such as butter, full fat milk, cheese, cream, and fattier cuts of meat.[99]

In an attempt to halt the decline in sales of liquid milk (from 4.95 pints per person per week in 1977 to 4.33 pints in 1984) and also of butter and cheese, the Milk Marketing Board (MMB) and National Dairy Council (NDC)—the two non-governmental bodies responsible for marketing UK farmers' dairy produce—were compelled by their members to respond.[100] The government message 'Too much fat is bad for you' had been translated by the media into 'All fat is bad for you', and, as the most visible source of saturated fats, dairy was a particularly easy target.[101] It was very difficult to see how this challenge could be addressed via traditional advertising, which was then focused on the generic 'pinta, butter, and cheddar'.[102] No product feature or benefit could be rolled into a proposition that would offset popular sentiment—however misguided—that full-fat milk was bad for you because it was 'full of fat'.

The radically different market conditions demanded a new marketing strategy. A much more holistic approach was developed. Instead of challenging the basic arguments (a strategy employed by tobacco companies in the1950s and early 1960s), the market need for a diet containing less saturated fat was put at the heart of the business. In 1983, the Milk Marketing Board (MMB) replaced its long-standing advertising provider McCann-Erickson with the creative boutique Allen Brady Marsh (ABM), with the brief to develop a more contemporary image for milk. The resulting campaign—'Milk's Gotta Lotta Bottle', which ran for six years—attempted to maintain the links between milk, health, and vitality. To the same end, the MMB also sponsored the Football League Cup between 1982 and 1986, during which time it was known as 'The Milk Cup'.[103] However, the issue was not simply a matter of image but also one of education, so public relations featured much more prominently in the brand communication mix than it had in the past. One of public relation's

---

[98] *A Discussion Paper on Proposals for Nutritional Guidelines for Health Education in Britain* (London: National Advisory Committee on Nutritional Education (NACNE), 1983).
[99] Ibid.
[100] G. David, 'Milk: Still a Lot of Bottle: Britain's Milk Industry is under Attack', *Observer*, 30 June 1985, p. 29.
[101] L. Vee, 'When the Media, Medics and Market Attack the Milk Men', *PR Week*, 4 October 1984, p. 19.
[102] Ibid.
[103] C. Wilkins, 'Chris Wilkins on Peter Marsh', *Campaign*, 13 July 1993; G. Kemp, 'Dairies Unite to Give Milk a Lift—Peter Crowe Is Determined to Make Milk Fashionable again', *Campaign*, 9 June 1985; S. Outhwaite, 'Great Ads I had Nothing to Do with #23: On Milk Marketing Board, John Smith's and McDonald's', <http://www.brandrepublic.com/article/1347132/3-great-ads-i-nothing-23-stuart-outhwaite-milk-marketing-board-john-smiths-mcdonalds#rYCqtwCz0KF78LhM.99>.

great benefits is that it is versatile and multifaceted: able to send different messages to different audiences with unilateral effectiveness. In the case of milk, public relations was employed in support of advertising to raise awareness of new products, but it also played the lead role in informing and educating consumers, policymakers, and health professionals. It was used as a vehicle for rebutting popular misconceptions and could also be employed to communicate directly with the internal audience—the farmers themselves. Public relations also allowed the dairy industry actually to take advantage of the change in public tastes by raising awareness of new product development and helped stimulate demand for skimmed and semi-skimmed milk. Skimmed milk had been legally available since 1973, but at that time test marketing had suggested there was no demand for it. Following the nutritional advice on saturated fat, it became economical to produce skimmed and semi-skimmed varieties, which were sold in uniquely branded cartons and were positioned as lower-fat and low-fat alternatives to the traditional silver top.[104] In 1984, the Butter Information Council ran a successful public relations campaign that drew attention to the fact that butter and margarine—to which it was losing market share—contained the same amount of fat. Farmers were educated about the benefits of cartons over bottles through the agriculture trade press and in-house publication *Milk Producer*. Changes in government policy were also addressed. The threat of cheap imports of UHT milk from the EEC was faced off with the dual message that this presented a threat to doorstep sales (which still accounted for 81 per cent of the market in 1984) and moreover that fresh milk—that is, milk produced in the UK—was much more pleasant than 'Ultra Horrible Tasting' French milk—a point endorsed in the media by politicians, celebrities, and the general public.[105]

The growing importance of public relations can be attributed in part to the emergence of new forms of social, political, and consumer pressure that were being placed on enterprises. Public relations was identified as the brand communication discipline best able to meet those challenges.[106] A second significant factor in the sector's development was the issue of advertising inflation. From 1980 onwards, there was a significant increase in the number

---

[104] G. Kemp, 'Dairies Unite to Give Milk a Lift—Peter Crowe Is Determined to Make Milk Fashionable again', *Campaign*, 9 June 1985. For some other examples of this PR activity, see: 'Good Food Guide: A Good Spread', *Guardian*, 11 November 1983, p. 12; G. David, 'Milk: Still a Lot of Bottle: Britain's Milk Industry is under Attack', *Observer*, 30 June 1985; M. Dineen, 'Price Cut War Threat to Doorstep Milkmen', *Observer*, 29 January 1984; M. White, 'Peta's Gotta Lotta Bottle', *Guardian*, 10 February 1983, p. 3; M. Nally, 'Doorstep Pinta at Risk', *Observer*, 25 September 1983, p. 5; 'Euro Milk not Fit for Dogs', *Daily Mirror*, 10 February 1983, p. 5; P. Leith, 'Here Today, Gamma Tomorrow', *Guardian*, 21 February 1986, p. 20.

[105] L. Vee, 'When the Media, Medics and Market Attack the Milk Men', *PR Week*.

[106] H. F. Moore and F. B. Kalupa, *Public Relations: Principles, Cases, and Problems* (Homewood, IL: Irwin, 1985); J. E. Grunig, *Excellence in Public Relations and Communication Management* (Hilldale, NJ: L. Erlbaum, 1992).

of media channels. The launches of Channel 4 in 1982 and then on Sky TV in 1989 were simply the two biggest events in a continuing process of erosion affecting ITVs hegemony over the UK's commercial viewing audience. Digital print and design technology reduced production costs for newspaper and magazine publishers. Newspapers expanded, increasing pagination and introducing new sections. Desktop publishing—using computers and software to produce pages rather than the expertise of print specialists—reduced the costs of production and barriers to market entry.[107] By the mid-1980s magazines were not only cheaper to produce but livelier, better constructed, and better designed.[108] New market niches became commercially viable, opening up a range of successful consumer media dedicated to specialist interests such as football, music, and video games. For example, in the field of video games, bedroom start-ups such as Newsfield (1983) and Future (1986) expanded to become significant publishing concerns with titles such as *ZZap!* and *Amiga Format* selling between 80,000 and 160,000 copies each month.[109] Advertising funded all these media ventures either wholly or significantly. As a result, although individual advertising slots became relatively less costly, achieving the kind of penetration enjoyed by television advertisers prior to 1980 was significantly more expensive, and campaigns were typically spread across a greater number of channels and outlets. Not only was reaching the audience now more expensive, but there was also more competition for their attention. The reduced costs encouraged many new advertisers to take up the space, and—along with the usual mix of brands, products, and services—increasingly there was also the promotion of corporate, financial, or socio-political issues to consider.[110] Furthermore, the number of advertisements competing for the attention of readers and viewers was growing at a time when remote controllers, VCRs, and time-shift viewing were making them easier to ignore.

Public relations was increasingly seen by managers in large corporations as not so much a replacement for advertising in these circumstances, but an increasingly significant support to the traditional methods of mass communication.In the run-up to its peak between 1987 and 1989, the growth rate of public relations agencies was well above that of advertising agencies: some

---

[107] Q. Randall, 'A Historical Overview of the Effects of New Mass Media: Introductions in Magazine Publishing during the Twentieth Century', *First Monday* (September 2001).

[108] Ibid.; G. Hallett, 'Market Overview in Desktop Publishing', *Data Processing*, 28/9 (1986), 488–92; P. J. Gray, 'Desktop Publishing', *Evaluation Practice*, 7/3 (1986), 40–9.

[109] *Newsfield Limited*, *Companies House* <https://companycheck.co.uk/company/01758989/ NEWSFIELD-LIMITED/about>; *ABC Certificate ZZAP!, July–December 1986: 82,933* (London: Audit Bureau of Circulation, 1987); *ABC Certificate Amiga Format, January–June 1992: 161,256* (London: Audit Bureau of Circulation, 1992).

[110] P. J. Kitchen and R. A. Proctor, 'The Increasing Importance of Public Relations in Fast Moving Consumer Goods Firms', *Journal of Marketing Management*, 7/4 (1991), 357–70.

66 per cent versus 29.7 per cent.[111] Moreover, Kitchen and Proctor estimated that almost as much public relations activity at this time was operated in-house, with agency fees accounting for only half of the probable overall expenditure.[112] Public relations' adaptability allowed it to become entrenched in more and more areas of business activity. It could be geared towards most communication challenges, from publicity generation to crisis management. However, it would be misleading to suggest that the adoption of public relations was uniform across all sectors of industry. For example, Moss, Warnaby and Thame argued that in the fast-moving consumer goods (FMCG) sector during the early 1990s public relations still tended to be seen as merely a tactical component within the marketing mix that could be used to generate extra publicity.[113] Nor by any means were all public relations campaigns effective. Even a cursory analysis of media reveals that most were not, but, despite these caveats, its growth and penetration continued. Public relations also remained relatively cheap. Regardless of the comparative increase in the use of public relations, the FMCG sector's expenditure on its services in 1990 was estimated to be just 10–12 per cent of that spent on advertising. Increasing the public relations budget by 20 per cent was small beer in comparison with the same increase in advertising spend, which made it particularly attractive during a period of spiralling marketing costs.[114] Kitchen and Proctor revealed that all UK public relations agencies reported that their FMCG clients were spending more in real terms in 1991 than they had done in 1986.[115]

A third factor in the growth of public relations was the continuing change in the nature of the retail environment. As high-street multiples proliferated, retail concentration and retailer power increased, but so too did the need for differentiation in terms of less tangible, image-related brand attributes. This required a more academic approach to retail strategy and management. Increasing numbers of retailers and brands were beginning to see the benefits of using public relations in a strategic manner.[116] McDonalds set up its UK operation in 1974, but its growth picked up pace considerably during the mid-1980s, when nationwide advertising was targeted at families.[117] It did not open its 100th restaurant (in Manchester) until 1983, but by 1988 it was

---

[111] *Campaign's Data Marketing Yearbook 1989/1990* (London: Haymarket 1989); *Campaign's Data Marketing Yearbook 1990/1991* (London: Haymarket, 1990); 'Special Advertising Report', *PR Week*, 4 May 1990.

[112] Kitchen and Proctor, 'The Increasing Importance of Public Relations', 359, 361.

[113] D. Moss, G. Warnaby, and L. Thame, 'Tactical Publicity or Strategic Relationship Management? An Exploratory Investigation of the Role of Public Relations in the UK Retail Sector', *European Journal of Marketing*, 30/12 (1990), 69–84.

[114] Ibid. 69.   [115] Kitchen and Proctor, 'The Increasing Importance of Public Relations'.

[116] Moss, Warnaby, and Thame, 'Tactical Publicity or Strategic Relationship Management?'.

[117] McDonald's, *McDonald's Company History: The 1980s* https://www.mcdonalds.co.uk/ukhome/Aboutus/Newsroom/History/1980s.html.

operating over 300 outlets nationwide.[118] McDonald's popularity with a large proportion of the UK public during this period is undeniable. It offered consumers cheap, tasty, reliably standardized meals, but the opportunity to sample an authentic piece of American pop culture was also compelling, especially during the early years of expansion. However, McDonald's rise was not universally welcomed. It was criticized by a range of health, environmental, and consumer organizations for a number of business practices, including: exploiting workers, damaging the environment, farming animals under cruel conditions, promoting food linked with a greater risk of heart disease, cancer, diabetes, and other diseases, causing environmental damage because of its food packaging, and manipulating children through advertising.[119]

McDonald's public relations response to these potentially damaging challenges was strategic, significant, and systemic. The communication goal was to position the company as an organization concerned with the environment and personal well-being of its customers, but also to make McDonald's synonymous with helping young people in need and the promotion of a healthy and active lifestyle.[120] Given the incongruous relationship between fast food and the promotion of healthy and active lifestyles, this strategy seems counter-intuitive. However, there was a compelling rationale to support it. Since 1976, when the company had become an official sponsor of the XXI Olympiad Games in Montreal, McDonald's had sought to associate itself with elite sporting events. It continued its involvement with the Olympics well into the twenty-first century and also became a long-running sponsor of the FIFA World Cup in 1994.[121] McDonald's also invested in sport at a grass-roots level, supporting coaching programmes, providing equipment, and encouraging broader participation for boys and girls.[122] In 2010, McDonald's admitted that, despite decades of involvement, it had gained very little in terms of either brand awareness or increased sales from this form of sports sponsorship.[123] This position was supported by research into

---

[118] Ibid.

[119] *The Surgeon General's Report on Nutrition and Health* (Bethesda, MD: Public Health Service, National Library of Medicine, 1988); G. Cannon, *Food and Health: The Experts Agree. An Analysis of One Hundred Authoritative Scientific Reports on Food, Nutrition and Public Health Published throughout the World in Thirty Years, between 1961 and 1991* (London: Consumer Association, 1992).

[120] McDonald's, *McDonald's Fact File: Policy Statement* (London: Communications Department, McDonald's UK, 1995).

[121] McDonald's, *Mcdonald's Company History: The 1990s*, <https://www.mcdonalds.co.uk/ukhome/Aboutus/Newsroom/History/1990.html>; McDonald's, *Mcdonald's Company History: The 1970s*, <https://www.mcdonalds.co.uk/ukhome/Aboutus/Newsroom/History/1970s.html>.

[122] McDonald's, 'Sponsorships', *McDonald's Fact File* (London: Communications Department, McDonald's UK, 1995).

[123] B. Wilson, 'Football and Fries: Why Mcdonald's Sponsors Sports', *BBC News*, <http://www.bbc.co.uk/news/business-11332724>.

sport sponsorship conducted by Devlin, which found that sponsors who are perceived to be functionally incongruent to the sport receive less favourable evaluations than those perceived as functionally congruent.[124] In other words, McDonald's programme of sports sponsorship would not increase sales of burgers. McDonald's official position that 'many of our customers and our staff love the Olympics and our sponsorship means that they can get involved' was certainly true, but it was not in itself the driving commercial rationale.[125]

Like much of McDonald's corporate and social communication activities during this period, sports sponsorship was an exercise in brand positioning rather than brand awareness. For example, in 1988, under considerable pressure from environmental groups, McDonald's ditched all packaging containing CFCs and launched 'Bin it for Britain', a road-show targeting twenty-five towns and cities that was run annually in partnership with the Tidy Britain Group.[126] There was also a series of child welfare and wellbeing initiatives. In 1988, it became the main sponsor of the UK's Children of Achievement Awards. In 1989, Ronald McDonald Children's Charity, dedicated to child welfare fundraising, was registered in the UK. The following year the first Ronald McDonald House opened at Guy's Hospital, London, providing overnight accommodation for the families of sick children.[127] For all of these activities, the corporate objective was neither to sell more burgers, fries, and Happy Meals nor to increase the number of restaurant customers. Instead, they contributed to the corporate image of McDonald's as a caring, socially responsible business. Moreover—just like the sports sponsorship— they helped to communicate the company's key message that McDonald's meals could be enjoyed as part of a balanced diet and a healthy, active lifestyle. The most important facet of this campaign is that emphasis was always on what consumers should be doing when they were not eating at McDonald's. The company's 1993 leaflet, *Nutrition—A Question of Balance*, which was available for consumers to read in restaurants, is a typical example.[128] The advice contained within the pamphlet is sound: 'Staying fit and healthy is a priority nowadays for everyone. A leading concern is how the food we eat affects our health … At McDonald's we have a responsibility to help our customers eat

---

[124] M. Devlin, *Measuring Sponsorship Effectiveness: Examining the Connection between Fan Identification and Physiological Response to Sports Sponsorship Evaluation after Exposure* (Birmingham, AL: University of Alabama, 2013).

[125] McDonald's, *McDonald's Fact File: Policy Statement*.

[126] McDonald's, *Environment—Facing the Challenges: 14 Things that McDonald's is Doing* (London: Communications Department, McDonald's UK, 1994).

[127] McDonald's, *McDonald's Annual Review* (London: Communications Department, McDonald's UK, 1993); McDonald's, *Mcdonald's Annual Review* (London: Communications Department, McDonald's UK, 1994).

[128] McDonald's, *Nutrition: A Question of Balance* (London: Communications Department, McDonalds UK, 1993).

a healthy balanced diet... Fattier foods should be eaten sparingly, and we should choose lean meat and low-fat dairy products where possible.'[129] Yet, McDonald's also recognizes that, 'no matter how wide the choice, we know that most of our customers come to McDonald's for our traditional menu items, like a Big Mac, or a Cheeseburger and French Fries'.[130] The onus, therefore, is on customers to manage their lifestyles in between visits to the restaurant: 'Just as important as eating the right food is taking regular exercise... An ever-wider range of activities are available at sports clubs and gyms, but even if organised sport or aerobics doesn't appeal, you should at least try to walk as much as possible and slowly build up a routine of exercises to do at home.'[131]

Throughout all the corporate communication, the message is consistent: be reassured that eating at McDonald's is fine—sure, you will also need to exercise regularly to burn off those calories and also eat less fat and more fruit and vegetables in the future, but for now enjoy your Big Mac in peace.[132] It was a message that proved to be remarkably durable. In a 2010 interview with the BBC, McDonald's UK CEO Steve Eastbrook was still arguing along the same lines: 'I do not think sponsoring sport would have any impact [on obesity]. People come into McDonald's two to three times a month—to extrapolate that to the cause of obesity is a real stretch... We can help young people to burn the calories off.'[133] As Offer identified, the problem with starting this healthier lifestyle tomorrow is that for the vast majority of people tomorrow never comes, 'Time inconsistency means that the wish to be virtuous tomorrow may not be sustained when tomorrow arrives.'[134] Time inconsistency is a concept from behavioural economics describing a situation in which a decision-maker's preferences change over time in such a way that a preference can become inconsistent at another point in time. It is a situation that arises when an individual makes a commitment to take an action in the future. For example, a person might make a commitment to go on a diet, starting tomorrow. However, when tomorrow comes he finds himself at a party serving delicious chocolate cake and he finds he cannot resist. This is because his incentive to keep the commitment today is weaker than yesterday's incentive to make that commitment. It the case of McDonald's, the public relations messages stimulate ephemeral good intentions among consumers, which are often more than enough to offset underlying anxiety about their diet. There may be many consumer rationalizations for eating at a fast-food restaurant—a treat, time pressures, convenience, price, and so on—but all can be supported by a variation on the rationale 'I can enjoy a burger and fries today, but the

---

[129] Ibid.   [130] Ibid.   [131] Ibid.   [132] Ibid.   [133] Wilson, 'Football and Fries'.
[134] A. Offer, *The Challenge of Affluence: Self-Control and Wellbeing in the United States and Britain since 1950* (Oxford: Oxford University Press, 2007).

diet starts tomorrow' or '... but tomorrow, I hit the gym'. Yet, when tomorrow comes and the fast-food meal is in the past, these good intentions are typically forgotten, and life carries on as before. Offer argued that people find the present so compelling that any commitment to the future is very difficult for most and, for some, virtually impossible.[135]

These activities may not have contributed tangibly to sales, but they did contribute intangibly to the brand. McDonald's was able to remove itself from much of the negativity associated with its business by encouraging consumers to make positive emotional connections with its brand. If a brand's appeal is intangible, it is extremely difficult for rivals to dislodge. In 1990, *The Economist* reported that consumers associated McDonald's with many things, including cleanliness, athletics, 'and even Ronald McDonald homes for sick children before they think about food'.[136] This meant that rivals such as Burger King, focusing on the rational proposition that their burgers tasted better, could advertise as much as they liked without affecting the warm feelings induced by McDonald's non-product marketing activities.[137] If advertising was the means to increase footfall in store and sell more products, public relations was the means to control how and what people actually thought about the company.

For enterprises operating in a more volatile and complex market, within which communication often seemed like an objective as much as a process, the distinction between marketing 'the business' and 'its business' was becoming important. Brand positioning might not lead directly to sales, but the platform it provided through intangible benefits such as goodwill, trust, and loyalty clearly provided businesses like McDonalds with a competitive edge. In this regard, the subtleties and versatility of public relations proved hugely appealing. Between 1984 and 1990, the news pages of *PR Week* are filled with companies announcing the first ever appointment of a public relations agency.[138] No longer the poor relation of advertising, public relations' claim for a seat at the top table within marketing communication was gaining wider recognition from major players in the advertising industry. In 1987, Tim Lefroy, UK chairman of leading advertising agency Young & Rubicam, said: 'Advertising works like a blitzkrieg attack. Public relations is more like guerrilla warfare, subtle and insidious where advertising might be considered

[135] Ibid. 28–42, 48, 66.
[136] 'The Advertising Industry: The Party's Over', *The Economist*, 9 June 1990, p. 7.   [137] Ibid.
[138] Examples are numerous, but, for an indication, across a variety of sectors, see 'Barclays Opts for Oracle', *PR Week*, 1 November 1984, p. 2; 'Broad Street Wins BA Float', *PR Week*, 8 November 1984, p. 3; 'Consultancy Boost for Miners Campaign', *PR Week*, 9 May 1985, p. 1; 'Fashion House Models Labour 'S Job Message', *PR Week*, 25 May 1985, p. 1; 'Anyone for Biscuits (Nabisco)?', *PR Week*, 14 March 1985, pp. 6–7; 'Street Wins Virgin Float', *PR Week*, 23 October 1986, p. 5; 'Food Giant Embarks on Communications Drive', *PR Week*, 1 September 1988, p. 3.

straightforward and even blunt.'[139] Lefroy echoed the thoughts of many in the sector by recognizing the need for the two disciplines to work more closely together.

Not surprisingly, some in the public relations sector went even further. In 1990 a special report in *The Economist* entitled 'The Party's Over' brought the challenges facing the advertising sector into sharp focus.[140] It argued that advertising was 'probably much less powerful than both its proponents and critics make out', that it had become 'only one out of many marketing weapons, and a relatively expensive one at that'.[141] The report predicted that over the coming decade direct marketing and public relations would increase their share of the marketing budget, as companies placed 'a higher premium on influencing the "opinion former" audience of the rich and powerful. Miss Anita Roddick has built up...Body Shop without a single advertisement. Those that have suffered at the hands of the green lobby such as Exxon, presumably wish they had paid more attention to their image.'[142]

The conclusions of 'The Party's Over' provided the starting point for a 1991 paper by Robert L Dilenschneider, then global CEO of PR agency Hill and Knowlton.[143] Dilenschneider called his report—provocatively and somewhat prematurely—'Marketing Communications in the Post-Advertising Era' and, under the auspices of establishing a new framework for marketing communications, challenged what he described as four widely held 'myths about advertising and marketing effectiveness'.[144] Defining marketing communication as 'the broad assortment of communications methods which can persuade people to act', Dilenschneider believed that media diversity and fragmentation were at the heart of the problem, presenting insurmountable problems in terms of logistics and cost for enterprises trying to reach audiences via traditional advertising campaigns.[145] He argued that marketing no longer meant 'advertising' alone and called for integrated marketing departments. This was not simply pulling teams together under the head of advertising but ensuring that public relations and other non-advertising disciplines were part of the process and most importantly developing a culture of marketing across the whole company: 'Build bridges to the accountants and attorneys...Everyone in the organization should be trained and incentivised to be a marketing spokesperson for the business.'[146]

By the mid-1990s, public relations was firmly ensconced as a key function of the business, accounting at its 1994 peak for 10 per cent of company

---

[139] 'The Blitzkrieg Approach to PR', *PR Week*, 24 September 1990.
[140] 'The Advertising Industry: The Party's Over', *The Economist*.   [141] Ibid. 1, 7.
[142] Ibid. 8.
[143] R. L. Dilenschneider, 'Marketing Communications in the Post-Advertising Era', *Public Relations Review*, 17/3 (1991), 227–36.
[144] Ibid. 227.   [145] Ibid. 228.   [146] Ibid. 234.

Table 5.1. Top 20 UK public relations consultancies, 1985

Rank	Company	Billings (£)	Billings (£m, 2018 values) (2016 value)
1	Good Relations Group	5,100,000	15.6
2	Charles Baker Group	4,551,000	13.9
3	Shandwick Group	2,900,000	8.8
4	Burson-Marsteller Group	2,848,000	8.7
5	Dewe Rogerson Group	2,114,000	6.5
6	Wellbeck PR	1,895,000	5.8
7	Hill & Knowlton	1,784,000	5.5
8	Daniel J. Edelman	1,610,000	4.9
9	Kingsway Group	1,460,000	4.5
10	Carl Byoir & Associates	1,400,000	.3
10	Harrison Cowley Group	1,400,000	4.3
12	Biss Lancaster	1,325,000	4.1
13	Excel PR	1,260,000	3.9
14	Countrywide Communications	1,250,000	3.8
15	Leslie Bishop	1,200,000	3.7
16	Granary Communications	1,146,000	3.5
17	Communications Strategy	1,121,000	3.4
18	Streets Financial	1,100,000	3.4
18	Lopez PR	1,100,000	3.4
20	Vallin Pollen	1,080,000	3.3

Source: PR Week, 12 September 1985, p. 85.

budgets.[147] Although this figure fell to 7 per cent during the next three years, these losses were offset to a large extent by the influx of new clients, as awareness of the power of effective public relations continued to increase.[148] Despite the softening in demand, ten years after the first *PR Week* league table was launched in 1985, the biggest agencies were all significantly larger concerns.[149] Billings at Daniel J. Edelman had grown by 719 per cent, Hill and Knowlton by 464 per cent, Dewe Rogerson by 399 per cent, Biss Lancaster by 283 per cent, and Burson-Marsteller by 248 per cent (see Tables 5.1 and 5.2). The dip in demand was only temporary, and, by 1997, the sector was again growing rapidly, with income from the Top 150 agencies rising by 20 per cent year on year.[150] A 1998 survey of 521 leading companies by the Marketing Forum revealed that 45 per cent of businesses expected to increase public relations spending within the coming year.[151] By the end of the period, communication experts were also making it to the top of the corporate ladder—for example, Glaxo Wellcome's CEO Robert Ingram, who described his route to the top as through government/public affairs; Simon Lewis, who in 1998 became CEO of a business unit at Centrica following a career in corporate communications; and, in the public sector, former local

---

[147] 'UK Firms Increase PR Allocation Says Marketing Forum', *PR Week*, 11 December 1998.
[148] Ibid.   [149] 'The Top 150 UK PR Consultancies 1998', *PR Week*, 24 April 1998.
[150] Ibid.   [151] 'UK Firms Increase PR Allocation Says Marketing Forum', *PR Week*.

Table 5.2. Top 20 UK public relations consultancies, 1996 and 1997

Rank 1997	Rank 1996	Company	Billings (£m., 20186 values) 1997	Billings (£m., 20186 values) 1996	Increase (%)
1	1	Shandwick UK	44.7 million	43.6 million	2.5
2	2	Bell Pottinger Communications	41.6	£38.2	9.0
3	3	Hill & Knowlton	33.0	£30.9	7.0
4	4	Countrywide Porter Novelli	30.0	£28.9	4.0
5	6	Dewe Rogerson	23.0	£22.0	5.0
6	8	Incepta Group (Citigate)	20.1	14.8	36.0
7	7	Weber PR Worldwide	18.4	16.0	14.0
8	9	Edelman PR Worldwide	14.4	13.1	9.0
9	15	Euro RSCG International Comms	12.6	8.7	43.0
10	12	The Grayling Group	12.2	10.8	13.0
11	11	Charles Barker BMSG	12.1	10.8	12.0
12	14	Medical Action Communications	11.5	8.1	42.0
13	13	Text 100	10.9	8.1	33.0
14	16	Scope Ketchum Communications	10.0	7.6	33.0
15	23	Freud Communications	9.7	7.5	29.0
16	18	GCI Communications	9.0	6.5	25.0
17	19	College Hill Associates	8.2	6.4	28.0
18	22	Fishburn Hedges	8.0	6.3	28.0
19	24	Harvard PR	7.6	5.7	32.0
20	17	Key Communications	7.5	6.7	12.0

Source: PR Week, 24 April 1998.

government PR Lorraine Langham was appointed executive director of Hackney Council.[152]

Consumer Public Relations

The sector's rapid growth helped it to mature quickly. New market niches became commercially viable, particularly in the consumer sector, healthcare, and hi-tech.[153] Specialist agencies were established targeting, initially at least, specific market segments; for example, Coalition Group (1990) targeted clients in the entertainment industry, while Bastion (1992) focused more specifically on video games, and Medical Action Communications (1988)

---

[152] 'Top 150 Uk Consultancies: Biggest Growers Led by Old Hands: A Mixture of Experience and Niche Specialism has Fostered the Success of this Year's Fastest Growing Consultancies', *PR Week*, 29 April 1993.

[153] R. Gray, 'Corporate Structure: PR Takes First Steps in Rising to New Heights: When Simon Lewis Returns to Centrica, It Will Be in a Senior Management Role', *PR Week*, 20 November 1998; S. Bevan, 'Analysis: When Small is Beautiful: Some Large PR Agencies may be Losing out to Niche Players with a Colourful Reputation and a Knack for Media Relations', *PR Week*, 30 September 1994.

specialized in healthcare.[154] Elsewhere some longer-established businesses concentrated on a single sector as part of their growth strategy—for example, Text 100 (1981) experienced rapid expansion after 1990 by targeting hi-tech companies.[155] Arguably the most significant specialist start-up of all was the entertainment public relations agency founded in 1986 by 23-year-old Matthew Freud and which bore his name in a variety of combinations. Twenty-five years after its foundation, Freud would become the UK's biggest consumer public relations consultancy, with billings of £22.5 million— greater than the combined turnover of the second, third, and fourth largest agencies.[156] Between 1994 and 1997, Freud's annual billings grew from a modest £830,000 to £5.5 million (or from £1,6 million to £9.8 million at 2018 values).[157] Impressive though these figures are, it was Freud's approach to public relations rather than its financial performance that lends it significance.

Matthew Freud's formative years were spent at some remove from the corporate finance sector that funded the rapid expansion of his competitors. After working as a press officer at the record label RCA, Freud began his agency with just one client, the Irish folk-rock group Clannad, whom he managed to get into both the *Sun* and the music magazine *Smash Hits* (then selling around 500,000 copies every fortnightly issue).[158] Early success with campaigns for The Hard Rock Cafe and Jiffi Condoms cemented Freud's reputation with prospective clients as a public relations specialist capable of securing highly effective coverage in frothy, yet hugely popular, sections of the media, but just as importantly with tabloid journalists as a reliable source of exactly the kind of content they were after.[159] Freud's expertise was also his ability to appeal to any celebrities who wished to raise their profile in a similar manner, and he proved adept at cross-pollinating his accounts. For example, pictures of pop stars and actors 'partying hard' at The Hard Rock Cafe were exactly the kind of story the newspaper gossip columns were looking for, having developed a

---

[154] *Coalition Group, Companies House*, <https://companycheck.co.uk/company/02541209/COALITION-GROUP-LIMITED/about>; *Bastion Limited, Companies House*, <https://companycheck.co.uk/company/02742050/BASTION-LIMITED/about>; *Medical Action Communications*, <https://companycheck.co.uk/company/02284094/MEDICAL-ACTION-COMMUNICATIONS-LIMITED/about>; 'Osman to Leave Redwood for Top Role at Channel 5', *PR Week*, 14 June 1996.

[155] *Text 100, Companies House*, <https://companycheck.co.uk/company/02433862/TEXT-100-INTERNATIONAL-LIMITED/about>.

[156] 'Top 50 Consumer Consultancies', *PR Week*, 28 May 2010.

[157] 'Top 150 PR Consultancies: Top Performers—Freud Communications Sees the Fastest Growth in Fee Income', *PR Week*, 28 April 1995; 'The Top 150 UK PR Consultancies 1998: Overview: Growing up: Public Affairs and Investor Relations Proved Lucrative for Most Top 10 Agencies, but the Levels of Growth Recorded in Last Year's Top 150 Survey have Steadied', *PR Week*, 24 April 1998.

[158] 'Profile: Mathew Freud', *PR Week*, 9 December 1994; 'Smash Hits Magazine Closing down'; *BBC News*, <http://news.bbc.co.uk/1/hi/entertainment/4673136.stm>.

[159] 'Profile: Mathew Freud', *PR Week*, 9 December 1994.

newfound enthusiasm for pop music following the success of Live Aid. The restaurant's consistent appearance in the *Sun*, the *Daily Mirror*, and other tabloids did a great deal to bolster the brand image of the burger bar as 'the place where the stars go to eat' but also provided the kind of unobtrusive-yet-awareness-raising coverage that the stars themselves were looking for.[160] Freud's break into the mainstream came when his youth culture credentials helped him secure Westminster City Council's 'Say No to Drugs' campaign. A significant success (combining a number of clients, which was to become a typical Freud tactic) was gaining the support of Princess Diana, who was photographed signing the 'Say No to Drugs' campaign board at the Rock Garden in Covent Garden during November 1986.[161]

In May 1990, Freud relaunched his agency as Freud Communications, with a view to taking on mainstream consultancies. Account wins—including the English Shakespeare Company, Bose audio (from Dampier Robertson Redel), and US children's TV institution *Sesame Street*—were initially modest, but in 1992 the agency acquired its most significant client to date when it was hired by production company Planet 24 to promote Channel 4's *The Big Breakfast*.[162] This client established both Freud and his agency as a serious media player, and by 1995 media brands accounted for over 40 per cent of Freud's business ,with a stream of clients arriving, including several from more established agencies: BBC Radio 1 (from Lynne Franks), BSkyB, Camelot (Britain's national lottery operator), Elton John, Pepsi (from H&K), Playboy TV, Sega (also from Lynne Franks), the Special Olympics International, and Virgin.[163]

Freud was the first agency to take entertainment publicity into the broad consumer sector, and it remained the most successful exponent until the end of the period, although many others tried to emulate its approach. This style of public relations—juxtaposing different clients for their common good—grew more appealing, as companies tried to reach out to an audience that was increasingly more youthful in outlook and lifestyle. Society was changing very quickly. Between 1988 and 1994 there were several radical developments in

---

[160] See, e.g., J. Blake, 'Slick Mick', *Daily Mirror*, 29 July 1986, p. 11; J. Blake, 'British Burgers Rock the States', *Daily Mirror*, 27 April 1987, p. 13; G. Pringle, 'White Hot Club', *Daily Mirror*, 25 June 1987, p. 13.

[161] R. Letkey, 'Princess Diana Signs the "Say No to Drugs" Campaign Board in London', *Reuters*, 27 November 1986.

[162] S. Farish, 'Freud Wins Entire Bose Marketing', *PR Week*, 13 February 1992; 'Profile: Mathew Freud', *PR Week*, 9 December 1994; S. Bevan, 'Virgin Turns to Big Breakfast PR Team', *PR Week*, 25 November 1993.

[163] 'Profile: Mathew Freud', *PR Week*, 9 December 1994; L. Goddard, 'Playboy TV Hires Freud after Six-Way Pitch', *PR Week*, 7 July 1995; 'Freud on Sky High', *PR Week*, 17 March 1994; 'Freud Communications Lands Elton John', *PR Week*, 26 May 1994; M. Kavanagh, 'Radio 1 Breaks with Lynne Franks', *PR Week*, 9 June 1995; 'Camelot Launch New Scratch Card Game', *PR Week*, 3 March 1995; 'Games Go to Freud', *PR Week*, 22 February 1990; M. Tungate, 'Sega Leaves Franks for Freud', *PR Week*, 28 April 1995; S. Bevan, 'Virgin Turns to Big Breakfast PR Team', *PR Week*, 25 November 1993.

the way that higher education was funded and structured, which resulted in a doubling of the number of 18–21-year-olds in full-time education from 15 per cent to 30 per cent.[164] People were moving out of home earlier, but also getting married and having children later. Young people were also more affluent than their 1980s forebears had been, with more disposable income: the spending power of under-18 alone reached £9.4 billion per annum in 1992.[165]

Youth Orientated Brands—the so-called YOBs—were becoming part of the mainstream. This shift was reflected in popular culture, as people were maintaining youthful interests much later into adult life: pop music, films, magazines, video games, jeans, and trainers were no longer just children's fads. For the first time, the fashion was to dress younger. Magazines for older consumers of music, film, and video games appeared. The average age of readers of video game, music, and football magazines such as Q (1986), Mo Edge (1993), Mojo (1993), Select (1993), PC Zone (1994), PC Gamer (1994), Kick It City (1994), and 442 (1994) was in the mid-to-late twenties.[166] The subtlety of public relations enabled it to play a vital role in helping to push products to this audience. It was far more effective to approach consumers indirectly through editorial in magazines and dedicated television and radio programmes rather than directly through advertising. The launch of the Sony PlayStation in 1995 was testament to this demographic shift. At the launch, the target audience for the console was males in the 18–30 age group.[167] This was reflected both in the launch line-up of adult-oriented content and in a marketing strategy that relied heavily on public relations to generate word-of-mouth endorsement. One innovative, high-profile initiative was the console's promotion in nightclubs across the UK, which literally got it into the hands of the target audience but more importantly gave the magazines and newspapers something to write about. Undoubtedly, many more people read about this activity in a magazine than actually played on a PlayStation in a nightclub themselves. The key message was communicated by the juxtaposition of a games console with a nightclub—this was entertainment for grown-ups, not kids.[168]

---

[164] R. D. Anderson, *British Universities: Past and Present* (London: Hambledon Continuum, 2006).
[165] 'The *Campaign* Report on Worldwide Advertising: The Kids Are Uptight—Advertisers Tuned in to the Teenage Wavelength', *Campaign*, 13 May 1994.
[166] 'Future Publishes New PC Magazine', *PR Week*, 31 March 1995; C. Sullivan, 'Rock of Ages; Mojo, a Glossy Monthly Aimed at Ageing Rockers, Is the Latest in a Long Line of Minutely Targeted Music Magazines', *Guardian*, 29 October 1993, p. A8; *Future Publishing Advertising Rate Card* (Bath: Future Publishing, 1997); B. Parfitt, *Retrospective PC Zone* <http://www.mcvuk.com/news/read/retrospective-pc-zone/01797>.
[167] Author's personal archive: interview with Rob Pegley, former editor, *Official PlayStation Magazine* (issues 8–42), Future Publishing, 27 July 2016.
[168] Ibid.

Persuasion and Promotional Culture

In terms of the promotional culture described by Wernick and Davies and the challenges of affluence and consumerism identified by Offer, Schor, and Skidelsky and Skidelsky, it is arguable here that British society felt the impact of persuasion most profoundly. It is a fact often overlooked that public relations also provided a service to the media. Thanks largely to the introduction of satellite and cable systems, the number of TV channels in Britain grew from just three in 1980 to several hundred in 1997, with many broadcasting twenty-four hours a day. The number of hours broadcast by the terrestrial channels also increased, and there was a similar expansion, albeit less pronounced, in radio. Digital technology allowed newspapers to swell in size as well as number, adding numerous sections and supplements dealing with a host of subjects from cars, homes, and holidays to music, film, and fashion. The same innovations allowed magazines to proliferate. Specialist magazines emerged to cover a gamut of interests. In 1990, sales of men's lifestyle magazines amounted to barely one million magazine sales per annum, but by 1997 it was one of the most influential publishing sectors, producing sales of around 2.4 million copies each month.[169] For consumer brands, the expansion of the publishing and broadcast sectors during the 1980s presented a raft of publicity opportunities, which in turn drove a need for more formal management of media relations. Specialist titles with small budgets and few members of staff often relied entirely on public relations for content. The same is true for the newspaper sections and TV or radio shows, which relied on public relations to furnish them with interview subjects, preview and review materials, feature ideas, competition prizes, funded press trips, subsidized overseas travel, and paid-for photoshoots and artwork.

A stock analogy, repeated numerous times by PR specialists over the decades with varying degrees of crudeness, is that, if advertising is like a boy going into a bar and telling a girl how great he is, then public relations is like the girl's best friend telling her how great the boy is. By the 1990s, the sector was maturing, with dedicated specialists servicing a raft of consumer sectors from beverages to video games. The power of word-of mouth recommendation even convinced a few that, on occasion, public relations alone was enough for them to achieve their brand-building objectives. In 1991, TSB paid the Quentin Bell agency £100,000 to raise awareness of its account services among the UK's 700,000 15–16-year-olds.[170] The agency arranged

---

[169] B. Archer, 'Special Report on Top Consumer Magazines: Top 100 Consumer Magazines—Consumer Magazines Have Proved Markably Resilient to the Recession in Terms of Sales and Readers if not Revenue', *Campaign*, 1 November 1991.

[170] T. O'Sullivan, 'TSB Says Yes to Quentin Bell', *PR Week*, 7 May 1991.

for the bank to go into schools and give a series of talks on money matters to teenagers. Four years later, TSB was claiming consistent leadership over its competitors in signing up young customers.[171] In June 1995, Bass opted for public relations rather than advertising to launch its brand of alcoholic lemonade 'Hooch' to an initial target audience of 'communications literate 18–30 year olds'.[172] The proliferation and fragmentation of media also helped public relations become more popular. Not only did much of the media rely on public relations for editorial content, but it often proved too expensive to incorporate all the outlets relevant to a particular target audience into an advertising campaign. There were also occasions when public relations and advertising fed off each other. Trevor Beattie, creative director at TBWA, claimed that the agency secured £50 million worth of media coverage for the first two posters of its Wonderbra campaign.[173]

Whatever the rationale, the impact on consumers of all this public relations activity was profound. Most of what they were reading, seeing, and hearing between the advertisements could no longer be regarded as pure information. Public relations might inform and entertain, but it was always a vehicle for pushing a message or establishing a position about a service, product, person, idea, or organization. It was by no means all effective or harmful, but, as Lewis and Shenk highlighted, it was ubiquitous.[174] Furthermore, the aim of public relations was not simply to generate coverage but to shape popular opinion. The most effective coverage was that which stimulated word of mouth among early adopters within the target audience. This idea was nothing new in itself. In 1962, Rogers originated the Theory of the Diffusion of Innovations, proposing that a small proportion of the population typically adopts new products, or ideas, before they achieve broad acceptance or mass-market appeal (Rogers called this group the 'Early Adopters', but they are also known as 'opinion formers', 'taste makers', or 'trendsetters').[175] It is this group's willingness to adopt an innovation—based on awareness, interest, evaluation, and trial—that ultimately determines how successful the product, service, or idea will be with the majority of the target audience. However, what was new during the 1990s was the extent to which this process was being manufactured through the vastly expanded, public-relations-driven mass media.

[171] B. Archer, 'Can PR Build Brands?', *Campaign*, 24 May 1996.
[172] J. Owen, 'Creative Consistency and Innovative Media Buying Have Put Hooch Ahead of its Rivals', *Campaign*, 8 December 1995.
[173] G. Kemp, 'Bra Wars Breaks out on Mother's Day Trip', *Campaign*, 25 March 1994; B. Archer, 'Can PR Build Brands?', *Campaign*, 24 May 1996.
[174] D. Lewis, *Information Overload: Practical Strategies for Coping in Today's Workplace* (London: Penguin, 1999); D. Shenk, *Data Smog: Surviving the Information Glut* (San Francisco: HarperEdge, 1997); N. Paton-Walsh, 'Information overload', *Observer*, 16 January 2000, p. G37.
[175] E. M. Rogers, *Diffusion of Innovations* (New York and London: Free Press, 1995).

Early Adopters are exceptional but not rare, constituting around 13.5 per cent of the population. Early Adopters are important to all forms of persuasion but particularly to public relations, because not only are they are the first group to respond to a new proposition or make a purchase (after a small number of 'Innovators', who make up just 2.5 per cent of the population), but they also tend to tell friends, family, colleagues, and other people all about them.[176] These individuals have the highest degree of opinion leadership among the other adopter categories. As such, they are a similar 'invisible' means of promotion. Stimulating word of mouth is the final but most important part of the persuasion process. A product might not necessarily succeed as a result of good word of mouth, but without it failure is as almost guaranteed. This is due to the fact that most consumers—the 68 per cent that makes up the Early Majority and Late Majority (in Rogers's model)—rely heavily upon the endorsement of Early Adopters to inform their buying decisions. The Early and Late Majorities behave differently from Early Adopters. Individuals in these groups typically do not subscribe to specialist magazines or assiduously read product reviews. They do not need to see a film, read a book, or play a game the instant it comes out, but, whether they do so sooner, later, or never relies heavily upon the opinion of the Early Adopters.[177]

Effective public relations can stimulate word-of-mouth communication between consumers by providing them with social currency. Social currency is the sociological term for information that can be shared to encourage further social encounters. The idea is derived from Bourdieu, who extended the notion of capital to social and cultural categories. In this model, social currency is information that can be shared with other people and that encourages further social encounters.[178] Bourdieu argued that individuals occupied a multidimensional space in society, and as such they were defined not exclusively by social class but by different kinds of social and cultural capital, which can be articulated through relationships. For example, Rein, Kotler, and Shields noted that young men in particular feel the need to learn about current sporting events in order to facilitate social interaction.[179] Social currency for football fans may take the form of knowledge of the transfer market, playing tactics, or even an opinion on the impending fortunes of a manager, player, or club. For somebody interested in fashion, it may involve knowing what the colours of the season are going to be or how to 'get the look' of a voguish celebrity. Social currency can increase an individual's sense of self-worth, providing status and recognition, but it is more likely simply to allow

---

[176] Ibid. 282, 283.   [177] Ibid. 283–4.

[178] P. Bourdieu, 'The Forms of Capital', in J. Richardson (ed.), *Handbook of Theory and Research for the Sociology of Education* (New York: Greenwood, 1986), 241–58.

[179] I. J. Rein, P. Kotler, and B. Shields, *The Elusive Fan: Reinventing Sports in a Crowded Marketplace* (New York: McGraw-Hill, 2006).

someone to engage in interaction with colleagues, acquaintances, and friends and build a community by establishing common ground.

For marketers, social currency is the extent to which people share their brand (or information about their brand) with other people as part of their everyday social lives at work or at home.[180] Young people feel a particular pressure to accrue and dispense social currency in order to engage with their peers. Building social currency into a brand's communication increases its levels of engagement with consumers and interaction with customers and creates an affiliation between brands and their customers. Through increasing consumer engagement, social currency provides people with enough information and knowledge to have a conversation around the brand.[181] Consumers get a feeling of belonging and an opportunity to develop their own identity within their peer group. More than half of all consumers' brand loyalty can be explained by social currency, and patrons of brands with high social currency show a significantly higher willingness to pay a price premium.[182] For example, consumers looking to purchase a pair of trainers could conduct their own research through an exhaustive trawl of sports media. A much easier way to get the information they require is to ask the opinion of family, friends, or peers who regularly purchase trainers and may already have done the hard work. If this information proves to be sound, then the value of the information and respect for the person who provided it will increase. The new purchasers may even turn into advocates for the brand, passing on their good opinion of the trainers to others, and the cycle will continue. Or, even more succinctly, a drinker in a bar considering which brand of lager to consume would be more likely to purchase a Budweiser if his friends asked him 'Whatssup?' than he would if they were to describe the beer's flavour positively when compared to the other lagers on sale.[183]

Within many categories, branding is the only difference between otherwise virtually identical products. Public relations has proved to be an effective vehicle for reinforcing brand values and carving out a position. The economy became increasingly concept based rather than product based as companies such as Nike, Coca Cola, Virgin, and Orange (and a host of other brands who did not necessarily manufacture anything themselves) devoted their marketing effort to the task of persuading consumers to select from competing sets of nebulous lifestyle choices. In this promotional culture, commerce was able to colonize more and more areas of everyday life, and consumption—rather than class, geography, religion, or occupation—was to become the primary form of self-identity and self-expression.

---

[180] E. Joachimsthaler, M. Pfieffer, M. Zinnbauer, and T. Honer, *Social Currency Study* (New York: Vivaldi Partners, 2010), 5.
[181] Ibid. 16–19.   [182] Ibid. 13.   [183] Ibid. 28–35.

Part Three
Colonization

Persuasion and Male Consumption, 1969–1997

Part Three serves as a case study of the broader developments discussed in Chapters 3, 4, and 5. It looks at the impact of the persuasion industries on male consumption in the UK through the exploitation of opportunities presented by a raft of new media channels. There was an ongoing re-evaluation of male consumer behaviour, which manifested itself through an emergent men's lifestyle magazine sector, but also an expansion of established media— that is, newspapers, television, and radio. New applications of persuasion also came to the fore, as public relations and branding began to play a salient role in the marketing mix. The result of these changes was a concerted increase in the quality and quantity of brand communication aimed at men.

A further key theme is the rapid expansion of popular culture, which gathered pace during the 1980s and led to the assimilation of many countercultural cornerstones into the mainstream. In the context of male consumption, the result was a reduction of masculinity and its symbols (in a commercial sense) to a set of homogenized lifestyle choices.

Chapter 6 looks at the changes in attitude within the persuasion industry towards male consumers and the emergence in the UK of a mass-market men's magazine sector between 1986 and 1997. It also explores the relationship between titles such as *LM, Q, Loaded* and *FHM* and the public relations industry. Chapter 7 explores the rise of corporate branding and the influence of brand equity, brand image, and brand personality upon the preferences of male consumers.

The relationship between the media and those engaged in persuasion is typically presented as adversarial. Notwithstanding their differing objectives, the relationship between editorial teams and PR specialists was in fact largely symbiotic. The persuasion industries provided the media with a subsidized or cost-effective means to create premium content—for example, by providing fully funded access to interview subjects, review, and preview materials or delivering feature ideas. In return, the media provided the opportunity for seemingly impartial, positive coverage (a much more powerful form of promotion than advertising) but also a highly effective, direct channel to a target market that had previously been fragmented and very difficult to reach.

However, while persuasion in the form of advertising, branding, and public relations contributed significantly to the success of many media outlets, it also drove editorial agendas. The result of this collusion was a significant change in the aspirations, outlook, and behaviour of 20–40-year-old male consumers during this period. The principal beneficiaries of this relationship were the publishers and consumer brands, which both enjoyed an increase in profits and turnover thanks to the creation of a new mass-media channel to a previously hard-to-reach audience.

6

'For Men Who Should Know Better'

The Emergence of Men's Lifestyle Media

Changing Attitudes

It should be stated from the outset that, while this chapter deals with developments in male consumption, its central argument should not be misconstrued. It is not my contention either that, prior to 1969, there was no brand communication aimed at men, or that such efforts were ineffective until the 1970s. On the contrary, a great deal of persuasion throughout the early post-war period was expressly targeted at men, and much of it was undoubtedly successful to some extent. Moreover, an arguably much greater quantity of brand communication produced during the 1990s was ill conceived, poorly executed, and ultimately ineffective. The final decades of the twentieth century also witnessed a huge, quantitative increase in opportunities to reach consumers through ever-expanding mass media. With that in mind, the central discussion hereafter is concerned first with changes in both the objectives and the attitudes of commerce in regard to male consumers and, second, with the emergence of innovative forms of brand communication that specifically targeted man. Together these factors contributed to the development of different totems of masculinity and a new culture of male consumption.

In comparison with female consumption during this period, male consumption has received relatively little academic attention. There are some studies concerning product categories, advertising appeals, and images of masculinity in advertising, but usually for comparison purposes in the context of a wider examination of feminine consumption.[1] In part, this may be due to

---

[1] For a thorough review, see M. McGrath and J. Heitmeyer, *The 'New' Male Consumer: Appearance Management Product Advertising and the Male Physical Ideal in Men's Interest Magazines from 1965–2005* (Tallahassee, FL: Florida State University, ProQuest Dissertations Publishing, 2006), 1–7.

the fact that overwhelmingly during the early post-war decades advertising was aimed squarely at women. In 1971, television advertising spend in the UK topped £100 million for the first time, yet more than three-quarters of that amount came from just six product categories: food, household goods, beverages, toiletries and cosmetics, household appliances, and publishing.[2] In only two of these categories, beverages and publishing, could men really be considered as part of the target audience. Within the advertising industry itself, the notion that women were the target audience for most of its output was regarded as a matter of fact. In 1970, *Campaign*'s 'Close Up/Creative' column reported that 'women are the prime target for much of the advertising we prepare—and in many cases, the only target'.[3] Written by an anonymous creative director, 'Close Up/Creative' was a long-running weekly column that provided candid, no-holds-barred, peer reviews of the latest print and TV campaigns. The column was dominated by advertising aimed at women: from the utilitarian (underwear, cleaning products, and household goods) to the aspirational (holidays, soft furnishings, and fashion).[4]

From the perspective of the advertising industry, male consumers at this time were interested in tobacco and beverages ('beer and baccy') but little else of significance.[5] Campaigns aimed at men were occasionally featured within 'Close Up/Creative', but any deeper analysis of male consumer advertising was typically presented as a departure from the norm, usually in the form of a special feature linked to a broader theme rather than across the whole issue. For example, a feature from September 1970 entitled 'The Ads Reach inside the Playboy Mind' examined products that were 'either made or their advertising is noticeably tailored to the persona of the imaginary character, the Playboy'.[6] Yet even this unashamedly masculine feature was juxtaposed, somewhat incongruously, with a display advertisement for a regional media group claiming to hold the key to reaching the real target audience: 'Border Weekly Newspaper Group—The housewife's hunting ground.'[7]

---

[2] B. Henry, *British Television Advertising: The First 30 Years* (London: Century Benham, 1986), 140.

[3] 'Well, just how Much Does Advertising Really Talk to Women?', *Campaign*, 20 February 1970, p. 17.

[4] 'Close Up/Creative' was a weekly review of the latest advertising campaigns. This section ran in *Campaign* in various guises (e.g., 'Ad Review', 'Critique') throughout the period. For some specific examples, see 'The Balloon Goes up for Yellow Pages', *Campaign*, 5 December 1969, p. 17; 'Here are Some Good Ideas but then they Always Were', *Campaign*, 14 August 1970, pp. 13, 15; 'As a Joke, Feeble; as an Ad, Pathetic', *Campaign*, 20 December 1974, p. 11.

[5] R. Chapman, 'Magazines Wait as England Fights it out in Mexico', *Campaign*, 22 May 1970, pp. 21–3.

[6] 'The Ads Reach inside the Playboy Mind', *Campaign*, 18 September 1970, p. 16.

[7] G. Monkman, *Life Lessons from Charles Saatchi* (2013), <http://www.adnews.com.au/news/life-lessons-from-charles-saatchi> (accessed 26 June 2016).

Outside of beer and baccy, there were areas within which a proportion of advertising was aimed at men—for example, wearing apparel, leisure equipment, and motoring. However, in terms of overall spend, these were niche categories accounting respectively for just 2.4, 1.23, and 3.37 per cent of the TV advertising profile in 1970.[8] Of the Top 20 television-advertised brands in that year, only four could be considered predominantly to target male consumers: Guinness (14), Shell Petrol (15), Double Diamond (19), and Gillette Platinum Razor Blades (20). Further evidence for how ineffective advertising to men was considered to be is provided by the clandestine arrangement reached in the early 1960s by British car manufacturers Ford, Vauxhall, Chrysler, and British Leyland. The four companies agreed never to advertise their products on television in the UK, under the rationale that to do so would have a negligible impact upon sales and simply erode margins. This thinking was underpinned by a belief that it was very difficult to change a man's mind where his choice of motorcar was concerned—and certainly not through something as vulgar as television advertising.[9] This moratorium prevailed throughout the decade and was broken only by Japanese manufacturer Datsun's entry into the UK market in 1969.[10] The impact of Datsun's decision to advertise on television was profound. In 1971, TV advertising spend in the motoring category was just £3.4 million (£50.8 million at 2018 values), and 2.08 per cent of the TV profile, per annum. By 1980, this had grown to £42.4 million (£204.5 million at 2018 values), and 5.56 per cent of TV profile, per annum.[11] For such an arrangement to be sustained, all parties involved would have to subscribe to the view that advertising is ineffective. If even one company involved felt that it could gain a competitive advantage or increase its market share through the execution of better marketing and advertising, it is inconceivable that it would concede that advantage to the benefit of its competitors.

The belief that male consumers were difficult to influence by advertising and marketing extended beyond the motor industry. It can also be seen in the commercial challenges peculiar to media outlets exclusively aimed at men during this period. In 1970, *Campaign* highlighted these issues in a feature concerning the burgeoning UK weekly football magazine market.[12] England's 1966 World Cup success had proven a circulation boon for established monthly soccer titles such as IPC's *Charles Buchan's Football Monthly*, which saw its circulation leap from a little over 150,000 to 250,000 copies per issue.

---

[8] MEAL digest, reported in Henry, *British Television Advertising*, 516.   [9] Ibid.
[10] Ibid. 140; L. Roderick, 'TV Ads at 60: A History', *Marketing Week*, 21 September 2015; J. Liu, J. Li, L. Feng, L. Li, J. Tian, and K. Lee, 'Seeing Jesus in Toast: Neural and Behavioral Correlates of Face Pareidolia', *Cortex*, 53 (2014), 60–77.
[11] Henry, *British Television Advertising*, 516.
[12] R. Chapman, 'Magazines Wait as England Fights it out in Mexico', *Campaign*, 22 May 2970.

This increase persuaded independent publisher Martec to launch the first soccer weekly, *Jimmy Hill's Football Weekly*, in 1967. IPC responded with not one, but three titles: *Goal* (1968), *Shoot* (1969), and *Scorcher* (1970), targeting respectively 12–34, 9–15, and 8–12-year-old males.[13] By 1970, these three titles were reporting combined sales of more than one million copies per week and almost total domination of the market with a 77.4 per cent share.[14] It was an unusual market in certain respects, as titles did not have to rely on advertising revenue in order to survive. Editorial production costs were low, and circulations were high enough to ensure a satisfactory profit margin. Yet, despite *Goal*'s high circulation, *Campaign* regarded IPC's plans to raise the title's advertising revenues from £29,000 to £35,000 per annum as 'extremely ambitious'.[15] It argued that the lack of statistical data about the audience and the large juvenile readership of even this ostensibly adult-oriented title virtually precluded any advertising from the beer and baccy categories. The magazines' existing advertisers were companies connected with the game itself— such as football boot and shirt manufacturers—and all were comparatively small spenders. One unnamed IPC ad manager admitted: 'It's very hard to get advertisers to take the plunge.'[16] Indeed, with their younger profile, IPC's two other titles deliberately restricted their advertising to 'football related products'.[17] As such, *Shoot* and *Scorcher* carried promotions for other juvenile products such as cereals or confectionery only when they were linked directly with soccer.

The question is not so much whether but rather why male consumers were being overlooked. There was a reluctance to address marketing towards men evident across the mainstream. One reason is that advertisers at the time had a limited understanding of the behaviour of all consumers and not just males. This issue was a concern for many working within advertising agencies and marketing departments at the time. UK industry was spending almost £15 million per year on market research by 1969 (£248 million at 2018 values), but little was being done in the terms of genuine academic research.[18] As a result, the market research methods employed were hopelessly outdated—for example, standard market classification methods were still based on the A, B, C1, C2, D, and E classes created in the early twentieth century to model an early industrial economy.[19] Misconceptions abounded. Within the advertisements themselves there was an overreliance on outdated tropes and stereotypes. Children were presumed to be of little economic consequence beyond sweets, cereals, and toys; men were believed to find shopping—among a whole host of other activities— emasculating or effeminate, and little thought was given to the evolving role of women in society. In the early 1970s, women remained the target audience

[13] Ibid.   [14] Ibid.   [15] Ibid.   [16] Ibid. 21–3.   [17] Ibid. 23.
[18] 'The Seven Ages of Man', *Campaign*,16 July 1968, p. 33.   [19] Ibid.

for the vast majority of advertising but were invariably depicted within the commercials as dependants—whether children, housewives, or mothers—whose place was, often literally, in the kitchen. Even when it was recognized that times were changing, the advertising industry could still manage to sound old-fashioned. As *Campaign* reported—without irony—in a 1970 feature on effective advertising to women: 'It doesn't take half an eye, squintingly applied, to detect that not only do women come in all shapes and sizes, but that the same woman is quite capable of very radical changes of aspect. She can be a miser over margarine, a courtesan choosing cosmetics and as many alliterative analogies as you can twist tongue to.'[20]

In that context, perhaps it is not too surprising that the mid-twentieth-century academic critics of affluence—such as Galbraith, Friedan, and Goodman—often demonstrated a better understanding of consumer behaviour than many so-called industry experts.[21] Recent historiography concurs with the view of these commentators that affluence was central to the emergence of new cultures of consumption. The role of persuasion (albeit conflated to 'advertising') is also of particular importance to Offer, who argued that it contributed directly to one of the paradoxes of affluence by intruding upon genuine personal relationships through an implied, but thoroughly artificial, intimacy.[22] While Offer does not have a great deal to say about the practices and applications of persuasion, other historians have attempted to make more nuanced connections between advertising and social history—for example, both Hilton and Gurney addressed the politics of advertising within market capitalism.[23] Mort also carried out a more rounded analysis, exploring the development of new symbols of masculinity to address a rise in consumerism during the 1980s, and detailing the advertising industry's growing understanding of consumer demand.[24] Yet, even within these deeper investigations, there remains a tendency for historians to focus exclusively on output rather than practice, and, perhaps as a result, applications of persuasion other than advertising are generally ignored.

[20] 'Well, Just How Much does Advertising Really Talk to Women?', *Campaign*, 20 February 1970, p. 17.
[21] B. Friedan, *Feminine Mystique: 10th Anniversary Edition* (New York: Norton, 1973); J. K. Galbraith, *The Affluent Society* (London: Penguin, 1999); P. P. D. Goodman, *Growing up Absurd: Problems of Youth in the Organized System* (London: Victor Gollancz, 1961).
[22] A. Offer, *The Challenge of Affluence: Self-Control and Wellbeing in the United States and Britain since 1950* (Oxford: Oxford University Press, 2007), 104–6.
[23] P. Gurney, 'The Battle of the Consumer in Post-War Britain', *Journal of Modern History*, 77.4 (2005), 956–87.
[24] F. Mort, *Cultures of Consumption: Masculinities and Social Space in Late Twentieth-Century Britain* (London: Routledge, 1996); F. Mort, 'The Commercial Domain: Advertising and the Cultural Management of Demand', in P. Jackson, M. Lowe, D. Miller, and F. Mort (eds), *Commercial Cultures, Economics, Practices, Economies* (Oxford: Berg, 2000); F. Mort, *Capital Affairs: London and the Making of the Permissive Society* (London: Yale University Press, 2010).

Nixon conducted a detailed study of advertising and its critics in Britain during the 1950s and 1960s, during which time a sustained debate took place about advertising's economic and social role. However, this discussion was dominated by advertising's critics who were characterized by an 'almost obsessive fascination...and scrutiny' of the medium.[25] The critics argued that commercials on TV spoilt viewers' enjoyment of the programmes they interrupted. They also felt that there were too many adverts, that they were intrusive and repetitive, and that their claims were subjected to too little regulation. These attacks were a source of considerable concern for the industry, which was, in Nixon's words, 'locked in a constant struggle to limit the effects of government intervention on the operation of their business'.[26] However, the moralism at the heart of the critics' arguments prevented them from engaging with the utility and popularity of goods being promoted and allowed advertisers to popularize a counter-view of their output: that it was the legitimate expression of people's desire for a better life through the consumption of products and services.[27] For Nixon, this is a key development in a process that sees the status of advertising men and women move from cultural pariahs to celebrated heroes in the UK by the end of the century. Crucially, Nixon also argues that the intellectual gap between the advertising industry and its critics points to an even wider division within the minds of individual consumers. People were typically anxious about the effect of advertising on others but were happy to be drawn to the world of consumer goods themselves, which they identified with personal freedom.[28]

Certainly, advertising did become much more popular with consumers after 1970. As the quality of television advertising increased steadily throughout the decade, commercials were increasingly accepted as part and parcel of an evening's viewing. Rather than an intrusion, they were often seen as an enhancement—almost as a separate entertainment form—with many long-running campaigns becoming popular with viewers in their own right.[29] The increased effectiveness of advertising as both a sales and an entertainment medium is crucial to the development of the male consumer. The persuasion industries' key developments of the 1970s—the creative revolution, planning, positioning, and market research—allowed companies fully to exploit the opportunities presented by a consolidating retail environment that was becoming increasingly dominated by high-street multiples. It also provided them with the capability to reach out to new market niches with fresh products through an expanding and fragmenting mass media. In its initial stages,

---

[25] S. Nixon, 'Salesmen of the Will to Want: Advertising and its Critics in Britain 1951–1967', *Contemporary British History*, 24/2 (2010), 216.

[26] Ibid. 213.   [27] Ibid. 227–8.   [28] Ibid. 233.

[29] For numerous examples, see *The Gunn Report Top 100 Commercials of the 20th Century*, <https://www.gunnreport.com/content/the-100-best-commercials-of-the-20th-century/>.

this media expansion occurred primarily on the newsstands and radio waves, but not on television. Other than the extension of the children's television schedule (into weekday mornings during school holidays from 1971 and Saturday mornings from 1974), the actual number of broadcast hours rose very little until the launch of Channel 4 in 1982.[30] The number of hours viewed also remained relatively constant: 2.9 hours per day in 1974, reaching a low of 2.4 in 1982, and rising to 2.8 hours per day in 1984.[31]

Mort charted the British public's evolving relationship with consumption during the 1980s and put these changes into a broader historical context with a particular emphasis on male consumers.[32] As consumption now occupied a hitherto unimaginably central role in the fabric of everyday life, products and brands had become increasingly important components in the determination of social identities, including masculinity. The focus of the economy shifted away from manufacturing towards finance and commercial services, and consumer spending became synonymous with personal freedom. It was also during this period that the persuasion industry was developing a much greater understanding of the mind and motivations of consumers, thereby realizing the potential offered by marketing based on emotional appeal and brand positioning. The increases in consumer choice, media channels, and attempts to influence them that occurred as a result of these developments had their most profound effect on the specialized discipline of consumer public relations.

Willis described consumer public relations as a vehicle for delivering attitudinal and behavioural change that can enhance the sales environment and help to drive purchases in a manner that is 'often more subtle and sophisticated than more direct forms of communication'.[33] The goal of consumer public relations is to build relationships between an organization and existing or potential customers. In practice, it is a specialized discipline that focuses upon the formation of meaningful connections between consumers and brands in order to stimulate the sale of goods or services. In essence, publicity is generated within a number of relevant media channels that can present the product or service in a manner that makes it attractive to the target audience.

Although consumer public relations is a vehicle to promote products and services that results in sales, its methods have little in common with marketing.[34] For those engaged more broadly in persuasion, the benefit of consumer pubic relations is its point of critical intervention in the consumer's decision-making process. It provides an opportunity, as Theaker said, 'to interact with the consumer, build relationships and converse meaningfully with

---

[30] Henry, *British Television Advertising*, 229.   [31] Ibid.

[32] Mort, *Cultures of Consumption*.

[33] P. Willis, 'Public Relations and the Consumer', in R. Tench and L. Yeomans (eds), *Exploring Public Relations* (2nd edn; London: Financial Times/Prentice Hall, 2009), 409–24.

[34] A. Theaker, *The Public Relations Handbook* (London: Routledge, 2004).

them'.[35] These interventions usually take the form of editorial coverage (articles) in print and broadcast media that has resulted from public relations activity. Articles can take many forms—news stories, interviews, previews, reviews, features, and so on—but the brand's message must always be contained within them. Consumer PR's ability to influence buying decisions is governed by several factors, most notably the quality of both the medium and the article, the article's prominence or position within the medium, the reach of the medium, the quality and quantity of the medium's audience, and the clarity of the brand message (regardless of whether it is subtle or explicit). However, despite its strengths, public relations is most effective when it is working in concert with other marketing activities such as advertising, sales promotion, direct marketing, and sponsorship. The media outlet is critical to the success of almost all consumer public relations activity. Without stories in the media, the reach of a publicity stunt, launch event, or press conference extends only as far as the live audience in attendance.

During the 1970s, media opportunities for consumer public relations as a whole were limited, but this was particularly true where campaigns that targeted men were concerned. Newspapers were still largely concerned with news rather than the analysis, reviews, and lifestyle features that would fill burgeoning sections over the following decade; meanwhile, the scope for public relations within tightly regulated broadcast media was extremely limited.

The most popular format for the print and broadcast media expansion of the 1980s and 1990s was the magazine. Magazines could be themed around a single vertical subject (for example, music, football, fashion, television, film, video games, motoring, foreign holidays, cosmetics, or home improvement); alternatively a wide range of subjects could be combined to create a more general 'lifestyle' offer. In both cases the magazine provided the audience with essentially 'the same, but different' on a weekly, fortnightly, or monthly basis. National newspapers also assiduously adopted the magazine format during the 1980s, as dedicated specialist sections covering subjects that had often been hitherto overlooked, such as popular music and football, were seen as a means of driving advertising revenue. Cox and Mowatt highlighted a number of notable changes that were to have a profound impact on the business of magazine publishing during the 1980s.[36] Most important of all was the introduction of digital desktop publishing—using computers and software to produce pages rather than the expertise of print specialists— which not only reduced the costs of production but also removed barriers to

[35] S. Hutchinson, 'Consumer Public Relations', in A. Theaker (ed.). *The Public Relations Handbook* (4th edn; Abingdon: Routledge, 2012), 354.
[36] H. Cox and S. Mowatt, *Revolutions from Grub Street: A History of Magazine Publishing in Britain* (Oxford: Oxford University Press, 2015), 135–41.

market entry.[37] The print industry had been forced to accept the reality of convergent digital media production processes and was much less unionized than it had been in previous decades. The end of the closed-shop agreement meant printers could take in material from any source, regardless of whether union staff were involved in its production or not. Further changes to wholesale distribution and retail agreements persuaded publishers to innovate and attempt to unlock new markets—for example, the rise of sale-or-return allowed low-budget magazines to launch and take leading positions in the market. European publishers, benefiting from superior scale and efficiency, were able to take advantage of these opportunities and enter the UK market with English versions of established titles—such as *Hola* (Spain) with *Hello!* in 1988—or in mature markets—for example, Bauer (Germany) with *TV Quick* in 1991.[38] This increased competition contributed to sector growth. In 1980, after several years of decline, the *British Rates and Data Directory* (*BRAD*) listed a total of 1,367 consumer titles published in the UK, but, by 1996, the number had almost doubled to 2,672.[39]

By the mid-1980s, magazines were not only cheaper to produce but livelier and better designed.[40] New market niches became commercially viable, opening up a range of successful consumer media dedicated to specialist interests such as football, music, film, and video games. For example, in video games, bedroom start-ups such as *Newsfield* (1983) and *Future* (1986) expanded to become significant publishing concerns with a number of individual titles within their portfolio regularly selling 100,000–200,000 copies each per month.[41] With low production budgets and more pages to fill, editorial teams relied heavily on the public relations activities of third parties for creation of cost-effective content. To manage the opportunities presented by burgeoning specialist media, most video games publishers were operating an internal public relations function of some description by the 1990s. Specialist independent public relations consultancies dedicated to the games media also began to emerge, such as Barrington Harvey (1988), Coalition Group (1990), and Bastion (1992). By 1995, these three consultancies were representing significant players such as Sega, Sony, Nintendo, Gremlin, Psygnosis, Sales Curve, Activision, Ocean, and Eidos, with each account bringing in fees of more than £60,000 per annum (£114,000 at 2018 values).[42]

---

[37] Q. Randall, 'A Historical Overview of the Effects of New Mass Media: Introductions in Magazine Publishing during the Twentieth Century', *First Monday* (September 2001).

[38] E. Bell, 'One Year on, it is Still Hello!', *Campaign*, 26 May 1989; 'Bauer Launches TV Quick into Listings Arena', *Campaign*, 22 March 1991.

[39] *British Rate and Data Directory 1981* (London: Brad Group, 1980).

[40] G. Hallett, 'Market Overview in Desktop Publishing', *Data Processing*, 28/9 (1986), 488–92.

[41] *Video Game Magazine Preservation*, <http://retroactionmagazine.com/retrolinks/video gaming-magazine-preservation/>.

[42] *Barrington Harvey Limited*, <https://companycheck.co.uk/company/02230474/BARRINGTON-HARVEY-LIMITED/about>; *Coalition Group, Companies House*, <https://companycheck.co.uk/company/02541209/COALITION-GROUP-LIMITED/about>; *Bastion Limited, Companies House*,

For consumer public relations in general, the expansion of the consumer magazine sector during the 1980s and 1990s presented a growing raft of publicity opportunities, which in turn drove the need for more formal management of media relations. In many cases almost all of a consumer magazine's content was the result of public relations activity to some degree. Public relations departments and specialists provided news stories, photographs, and artwork, review and preview materials, access to interviewees, and competition prizes, and also funded press trips to create news and feature content. The public relations specialist, whether working for an agency or an in-house press department, was a conduit between the journalists and the things they needed to get their job done: review materials, interview subjects, release schedules, press passes, and invitations to newsworthy events. For the clients, public relations offered a means of control; news, reviews, interviews, and other coverage could be planned to appear at a point when it would have the optimum impact on sales.

The magazine format was also adopted by television. Perhaps surprisingly, it was successfully pioneered in children's television, one of broadcasting's most heavily regulated areas. During the 1960s, there was very little in the way of children's TV. Programming was limited to just over one hour per day on weekdays, typically beginning at 4.45p.m. and finishing at 5.55 p.m.[43] At weekends there was a blurring of 'family viewing' in this late afternoon slot, which might variously include pop music show *Juke Box Jury*, the sci-fi series *Dr Who*, or police drama *Dixon of Dock Green*, all of which were very popular with children.[44] In truth, there was little appetite to provide more children's programming from either the BBC or companies within the ITV network. Between 1964 and 1967, the BBC did not even operate a dedicated Children's Department, with output for the under 16 age group reduced to a function within the broader Family Department.[45] The strategy was in part an attempt to claw back the audience lost to ITV, whose more populist schedule—featuring cartoons and imported American material—had proven appealing. Children's television held little appeal to advertisers. As such, ITV had viewed its responsibility to provide such content as nothing more than a loss-making requirement of its broadcast licence. Attitudes changed following the publication of the Pilkington Committee on Broadcasting's report, published in 1962, which levelled criticism at the quality of ITV's programming.[46] By the

---

<https://companycheck.co.uk/company/02742050/BASTION-LIMITED/about>. Account values: author's personal archive: email correspondence with Ciaran Brennan, former director at Bastion, Tim Vigon, former director at Coalition Group, and Simon Byron, former director at Barrington Harvey.

[43] D. Buckingham and H. Davies, *Children's Television in Britain: History, Discourse and Policy* (London: British Film Institute, 1999), 8.
[44] Ibid. 84–5.   [45] Ibid. 29–32.   [46] Ibid. 32.

1970s, ITV's output ceased to be a markedly different alternative to that of the BBC, although it was broadcasting less content: an average of just over 60 minutes per day in comparison with the BBC's 105 minutes.[47]

Despite that apparent lack of commitment, it was ITV that notably pioneered the magazine format on Saturday mornings with the anarchic magazine show *Tiswas* (launched by ATV in 1974 and nationally in 1976).[48] The success of *Tiswas* was quickly countered by the BBC. In October 1976, it launched the similar, though altogether more somber, *Multi-Coloured Swap Shop*.[49] Both programmes were initially conceived as low-cost scheduling devices, seamlessly linking cartoons and serials in a singular entity that discouraged channel hopping during a period when it was believed, without much evidence, that older viewers would be unavailable.[50] Together *Tiswas* and *SwapShop* (as it later became known) not only helped to establish Saturday morning as prime viewing time for children, but also established both the magazine format and a style of playful presentation that was to prove perennially popular across adult programming during the 1980s and 1990s. *Tiswas,* for example, gave the impression of organized chaos. The cartoons, comedy sketches, live music, and interviews together with the flan flinging and buckets of water—all of which were interspersed with knowing references from sassy presenters aimed at the watching parents—gave life to the conceit that it treated everything with irreverence: its guests, its audience, itself. This approach thrived long after *Tiswas* had ceased broadcasting in 1982, providing the template not only for Saturday evening family viewing with series such as *Surprise Surprise!* (1984–2015) and *The Late, Late Breakfast Show* (1982–6), but also for live magazine shows aimed at young adults, for example Channel 4's *The Word* (1990–5) and *TFI Friday* (1996–2015).[51]

Studio guests for these shows—typically drawn from the fields of entertainment, music, or sport—provided interviews to fill screen time, which could be supplemented by performances, short film clips, and other content where appropriate. News sections highlighted forthcoming events. Products of interest to the audience—the latest music, film, TV, book, and (later) video game releases—were reviewed or previewed in the studio to provide an interesting segment. These were popular with the viewers and very cheap to put together. Further impetus was provided by live links or recorded reports from external events. Each of these segments provided a different opportunity for promotion.

---

[47] Ibid. 85.   [48] *Tiswas*, <www.screenonline.org.uk/tv/id/562178>.
[49] *Multi-Coloured Swap Shop* <http://www.screenonline.org.uk/tv/id/442768/>.
[50] Buckingham and Davies, *Children's Television in Britain*, 87.
[51] R. Demaris, 'Positioning: The Battle for your Mind (Book Review)', *Journal of Marketing*, 56/1 (1992), 122–5; *Surprise! Surprise!* <http://www.imdb.com/title/tt0086810>; *The Word*, <http://www.screenonline.org.uk/tv/id/569118/>; *TFI Friday*, <http://www.imdb.com/title/tt0115383/?ref_=fn_al_tt_1>.

For example, a musician might perform the latest song from a new album and then announce the dates for a forthcoming tour during an interview, an actor would talk about a forthcoming film and a clip of footage would be shown, or a footballer might be interviewed about an important match before giving details of how to get tickets. New products could also be submitted for review sections.[52]

The opportunity to promote a toy, book, play, film, record, or live event was not lost on publicists working in the publishing, sports, and entertainment industries.[53] Children could see an item featured on *SwapShop* in the morning and then buy it from the shops in the afternoon. Appearances often had a measurable effect upon sales. Without any advertising support, the Rubik's Cube became the most popular toy of 1981 in the UK following TV appearances on BBC1's *SwapShop* and *Blue Peter* (the channel's midweek magazine).[54] Guests could also benefit from a tangible impact on their public perception. Certainly, Gordon Reece recognized the opportunity that magazine programmes represented when he secured an interview slot on BBC1's *Jim'll Fix it* for Margaret Thatcher in 1978. This was, according to Tim Bell, 'one of the first steps in that radical message modernization process'.[55]

The Emergence of Men's Lifestyle Media

Historians have described the 1990s as 'a truly golden era' for UK consumer magazines.[56] The developments of the 1980s in print and digital production were beginning to have an impact, barriers to entry were low, and the new technological processes invigorated editorial teams, allowing publishers to take creative risks and undertake low-cost launches. In combination, these conditions provided the sector with a platform for unprecedented and explosive growth.[57] However, although the 1980s witnessed a huge increase in the number of individual titles, the total number of copies sold per year in 1990 was almost half of the 2.5 billion peak enjoyed in the early 1970s.[58] The Top 100 best-selling titles were all produced by just a handful of publishers, the

---

[52] For examples of consumer public relations tactics, see C. Barker, 'Special Report on Consumer PR: Now that's the Way to do it—What Makes a Hit Consumer PR Programme?', *PR Week*, 5 December 1990; M. Fearnley, 'Special Report on Consumer PR: Keeping up with the Jones's', *PR Week*, 5 December 1991; A. Hall, 'Agencies' Growing Flexibility is Ignored', *PR Week*, 25 November 1993; E. Charles, 'Focus on Marketing Communications: PR Adds Lift to your Brand Assets', *PR Week*, 3 February 1995; D. Rogers, 'Focus: Marketing Comms—the Faces behind the Brand Names', *PR Week*, 16 May 1997.
[53] For further insight into entertainment public relations during the early 1990s, see J. Foley, 'Showbusiness: Putting on a Performance', *PR Week*, 27 February 1992.
[54] N. Hammond, *How to Solve the Cube in 37 Seconds* (Derby: Blackhall, 1981), 19.
[55] T. Bell, *Right or Wrong: The Memoirs of Lord Bell* (London: Bloomsbury, 2014), 42.
[56] Cox and Mowatt, *Revolutions from Grub Street*, 141.   [57] Ibid. 142.   [58] Ibid. 142.

biggest of which, IPC, enjoyed a 45.6 per cent market share.[59] There remained a conspicuous gap in the market. The most profitable titles—those with the largest circulations and most lucrative advertising—were all aimed at women: there was no analogous market for men's magazines.

At this time, the UK women's magazine sector was a mature market, heavily segmented, with titles catering for all ages, tastes, and lifestyles selling in significant numbers. The biggest sellers of all were the weeklies—*Woman*, *Woman's Weekly*, *Woman's Own*, and *Woman's Realm*—which were all aimed at housewives and had changed very little since the 1950s. They remained formulaic but were still achieving sales of between 500,000 and 1.5 million copies per issue at the end of the century.[60] There was also a newer, lucrative monthlies market targeting working and younger women, which was dominated by titles launched in the 1970s such as *Cosmopolitan* and *Company*.[61] Handled by the newly formed advertising agency Saachi & Saachi, *Cosmopolitan* had proven a pivotal launch. Under its editor, Joyce Hopkirk, the magazine dealt with genuine concerns of its target audience (women in their twenties) and reflected the more permissive attitudes towards sex and relationships that had developed during the 1960s. The second issue promised the first male nude and sold out of its 450,000 print run in just a couple of days.[62] *Cosmopolitan* did not have the market to itself for long. By the mid-1980s, the likes of *Elle*, *Company*, *Prima*, and *Cosmopolitan* itself were doing almost as well as the more established weekly titles.[63] Later magazine launches into this sector could afford to be ambitious yet remain realistic. For example, in August 1988, IPC Magazines launched the British version of *Marie Claire*, then France's leading fashion and general interest monthly. Positioned as 'the multi-faceted magazine for multi-faceted women', targeting ABC1 females between the ages of 20 and 34, the launch edition of *Marie Claire* had a print run of 375,000.[64] This would be continued for the first three issues, with projected settle-down sales of 225,000 copies per month, with each containing approximately 50 pages of advertising (out of a total of 220 pages). With full colour ads costing £4,250 per page, this gave a potential gross yield of £212,000.[65] For publishers looking at that level of copy sales and advertising revenue, the creation of a comparable product for men was a tantalizing opportunity. At the time it was widely regarded as 'the Holy Grail' of magazine publishing.[66] However, there was no analogous men's magazine market. Extant magazines targeting men tended to focus on special

---

[59] Ibid.   [60] Ibid. 125–8.   [61] Ibid. 109.   [62] Ibid.

[63] 'Why Women Are No Longer a Captive Audience for Weeklies', *Campaign*, 26 September 1986; Y. Roberts, 'Special Report on Consumer Publishing', *Campaign*, 25 August 1989.

[64] P. Nathanson, 'August Launch Set for UK Marie Claire', *Campaign*, 19 February 1988.

[65] Ibid.

[66] Many examples of the term 'Holy Grail' being used include: 'Publishing Trio Plot Men's Lifestyle Title', *Campaign*, 8 August 1986; 'Emap Make Bid to Launch Glossy Men's Magazine', *Campaign*, 23 May 1986; L. White, 'The Custodians of Style/Focus on the Magazines, The Face, i-D,

interests and hobbies—such as motoring, model-making, sport, or DIY—rather than lifestyles and attracted little in the way of mainstream advertising.

It is perhaps worth briefly considering a somewhat tawdry exception to this rule, because there was one category of magazine that men were buying in large numbers. By the mid 1970s, so-called soft-core pornographic magazines were selling in large quantities, with major titles such as *Penthouse, Mayfair,* and *Men Only* shifting around 450,000 copies per month.[67] Despite any claims to the contrary, these magazines were certainly not bought for the articles. Notwithstanding the fact that this alone meant that editorial coverage offered no public relations value, these magazines were destined never to attract advertising from a mainstream brand, regardless of the number of 'readers'. As a result, this category can be considered an entirely separate market to conventional publishing and sits outside of the discussion.[68]

Owing in part to magazine publishing's focus on the women's market, Cox and Mowatt identified a prevailing lack of innovation within the industry at this time, highlighted by the success of a number of small independent publishers.[69] These publishers were able to cater for consumers not served by traditional magazines. Felix Dennis, an erstwhile co-editor of *Oz* alongside Richard Neville, launched Dennis Publishing in 1973 with this market-reactive strategy. Dennis made £60,000 on sales of its first title, *Kung Fu Monthly,* in 1974 (£691,000 at 2018 values) and continued to publish successfully in similar niche markets throughout the decade, following fashions and fads with such diverse titles as *TV Sci Fi Monthly, Which Bike?,* and *Skateboard! Magazine.*[70] Again, these titles held little appeal to mainstream brands in terms of either advertising or public relations.

Throughout the 1980s, UK publishers large and small engaged in numerous, fruitless efforts to produce a men's lifestyle magazine. Despite a growing list of failures, many were prepared to persevere. Their rationale was not difficult to understand. Magazines were fairly straightforward business units to run, with only two main revenue streams: advertising and copy sales. Publishers would know a magazine's target audience, its cover price, and also how much advertising space was available for sale. How much they could charge for that space was incumbent upon the volume of copy sales (or its 'reach' into that audience). From here it was fairly easy to forecast turnover, determine editorial and production costs, and set profit margins. For new launches the main risks related to how many copies the magazine would eventually sell (the settle-down

and Blitz', *Campaign,* 27 June 1986; N. van Zanten, 'In Search of Elusive Youth', *Campaign,* 16 March 1984; S. Buckley, 'How to Talk to More Men', *Media Week,* 12 February 1988.

[67] *Periodicals and the Alternative Press* (London: Royal Commission on the Press, 1977), 46.

[68] M. Collins, *Modern Love* (2001; London: Atlantic, 2004).

[69] Cox and Mowatt, *Revolutions from Grub Street,* 107–13.   [70] Ibid. 111.

sales figure), what advertising it could attract, and what advertisers would be prepared to pay for it.[71] It did not take an expert to conclude that a magazine enjoying high sales with affluent 18–30 males would attract a high volume of advertisers prepared to pay a premium price.

It was not only the publishing industry that was eager to open up this new market; brands were also frustrated at the lack of a successful men's lifestyle magazine.[72] Male consumption increased throughout the 1980s. Mort argued that these changes were 'specific rather than general', as brands sought out particular markets and distinct niches.[73] The character, behaviour, wants, and needs of young men were the subject of particular scrutiny, which resulted in commerce and masculinity becoming entangled. More and more brands were trying to reach males aged 18–35 from categories such as cars, personal finance, watches, male grooming, sportswear, cameras, clothes, alcohol, footwear, home entertainment, food, holidays, video games, films, and music. However, in terms of how that reach could be achieved, they were faced with a set of limited options and unsatisfactory choices. These amounted to running advertisements either in highly expensive television or newspaper campaigns or across a disparate bunch of specialist interest and hobby titles, bolstered perhaps by billboards and posters. This pent-up demand was reflected in some desperate-sounding schemes to reach male consumers through seemingly inappropriate media. Some even contemplated advertising within women's magazines. In 1986, Brylcream's marketing manager Graham Neale informed *Campaign* that he was 'currently considering [placing advertisements in] women's magazines like *She* with a strong male readership'.[74]

With such high demand, it is no surprise that attempts to unlock this market were frequent. Tactics surrounding each launch varied, but two distinct strategies did emerge. The success of mass-market men's titles in the USA and Australia convinced many to remain optimistic; to take the view that it was just a question of getting the right content mix, look, and feel. For others, the problem was simply that most men did not want a general read. As Zed Zewanda, advertisement director at Emap, said in August 1986: 'Men don't define themselves as men in what they read, they define themselves as people who are into cars, who play golf or fish... As a publisher what you're really looking for are interests popular enough to support new titles.'[75] Zewanda's view was shared by the auteur of one of the sector's few (relative) successes.

---

[71] S. Taylor, 'Magazines for Men: On the Trail of the Typical British Male', *Campaign*, 29 August 1986.

[72] A. Jivani, 'British Males Give yet Another Hopeful Suitor the Cold-Shoulder: Why Men's Magazines Are not for Men', *Campaign*, 5 June 1987.

[73] Mort, *Cultures of Consumption*, 2.

[74] S. Taylor, 'Magazines for Men: On the Trail of the Typical British Male', *Campaign*, 29 August 1986.

[75] Ibid.

In 1980, Nick Logan launched the *Face*, published by his own company Wagadon.[76] Logan had a background in music magazine publishing. Two years earlier he had been one of the team behind the successful launch of Emap's pop music fortnightly *Smash Hits* and drew upon this experience to create his own independent title targeting men and women, 'When I started [the *Face*] I believed people like IPC, who told me that there was no market for a general title. Therefore I made it music-based and gradually brought in the other stuff to make it, after a couple of years, what I had wanted it to be in the first place.'[77]

The *Face* became the first and most important of a trio of publications— along with *I-D*, published by Time Out and *Blitz*, published by Jigsaw—that became known collectively as the style press.[78] This description was useful to distinguish these magazines from traditional titles such as *Vogue* or *Harpers and Queen*, but was somewhat misleading in terms of their content—a combination of pop music, fashion style, and art aimed at the young urban cognoscenti. The popularity of the style press within the media (and its influence upon them) was never matched in terms of sales.[79] The *Face*'s 1986 audited circulation figure was 98,208—approximately the same amount as the combined, unaudited sales claims of its two rivals.[80] While this figure is certainly impressive for a small, tightly run, independent operation like Wagadon, it fell way short of the circulation enjoyed by the women's weeklies (in the millions) and Top 20 best-selling women's monthlies (in the hundreds of thousands).

The target audience for the style press included both men and women, and its commercial objective was to occupy a niche rather than to reach the mass market. For advertisers and public relations specialists, these media offered a useful starting point rather than a means to an end. For a brand like Levi's, looking in 1985 to reinvigorate the tired image of denim jeans among 18–30-year-olds, the creative values and specific targeting of the style press was an ideal place to launch its press campaign for 501s.[81] The creative work of the advertising agency of Bartle Bogle and Hegarty fitted perfectly within its pages. As the media buyer responsible for placing these advertisements said: 'We were after a style-conscious market. Street credible or whatever you want

---

[76] L. White, 'The Custodians of Style/Focus on the Magazines, The Face, i-D, and Blitz', *Campaign*, 27 June 1986.

[77] S. Taylor, 'Magazines for Men: On the Trail of the Typical British Male', *Campaign*, 29 August 1986.

[78] Mort, *Cultures of Consumption*, 22.

[79] L. White, 'The Custodians of Style/Focus on the Magazines, The Face, i-D, and Blitz', *Campaign*, 27 June 1986.

[80] *ABC Certificate, The Face, January–June 1986: 98,208* (London: Audit Bureau of Circulation, 1986).

[81] L. White, 'The Custodians of Style/Focus on the Magazines, The Face, i-D, and Blitz', *Campaign*, 27 June 1986.

to call it—and those magazines cut across class, age and gender divisions. Their total circulation is small but you can't quantify that sort of opinion leading.'[82] Yet, for all its tactical appeal, when it came to reaching a wider audience, the style press failed to pass muster. In 1986, the Law Society ran a press campaign targeting 'young, male downmarket . . . not yuppies' that aimed to explain the civil right to legal aid on arrest.[83] Maitland Hards Gill, the media buying agency responsible for the campaign, selected a diverse media portfolio—including the rock music weekly *Sounds* and *the Sun* as well as the Conservative party organ *the Spectator*—but bypassed the style press altogether. The implication was that style-press readers were 'more likely to be radical young lawyers than their emergency clients'.[84]

In 1986, the two contrasting strategies—to reach a mass market of male readers either vertically via general interest, or horizontally via a specialist interest—were put to the test in the launch of two monthlies that occurred almost simultaneously. First up was *Q*, launched by Emap in October. Its editor, Mark Ellen, and publisher, David Hepworth, had much in common: both had a history in music magazines, both were former *New Musical Express* (*NME*) journalists, and, like Logan, both had been instrumental in the success of *Smash Hits*, which was regularly selling over one million copies every month by this time.[85] *Q* was an attempt to capitalize on the popularity of the compact disc, then still considered a new technology, which was proving most popular with an affluent, older generation of largely male music fans whose tastes were being ill served (if not ignored entirely) by the existing music press. *Q* immediately set itself apart from the traditional rock weeklies and pop magazines through high production values that were designed to appeal to mature readers and premium advertisers alike. The title itself, *Q*, was contrived to be 'an empty cipher . . . so that readers can fill in the spaces themselves' and its strapline, 'The modern guide to music and more', attempted to communicate its more general content offer.[86] By persuading enough music-loving men to buy *Q*, Emap aimed to create a de facto mass-market men's magazine that would be attractive to advertisers. In the reckoning, the 'and more' promised in the strapline amounted to only a tiny proportion of the overall content offer. Music news, interviews, features, and reviews dominated, with non-music content relegated to a short films, books, and videos section, a monthly consumer electronics column, and the occasional interview with a non-musical celebrity. The launch was a relatively low-key affair. By starting small and relying on word of mouth, Emap could afford to spend in direct support of the magazine itself

---

[82] Ibid.   [83] Ibid.   [84] Ibid.
[85] Smash Hits *Magazine Closing down*, <http://news.bbc.co.uk/1/hi/entertainment/4673136.stm>.
[86] A. Jivani, 'Can LM and Q Survive in a Field Littered with Corpses?', *Campaign*, 19 September 1986.

rather than on marketing activity in the hope of delivering a long-term success. Q quickly became established as a grown-up music magazine and was selling 147,174 copies per month by 1990.[87]

Despite a similarly anodyne moniker, Newsfield's *LM* was an entirely different proposition from Q. Founded in 1983, Newsfield was a young publisher that had enjoyed a great deal of success with computer and video games magazines such as *ZZAP!* and *Crash*. By 1986 *Crash* was selling 101,483 copies per month largely to teenage boys and young men.[88] Fired by this success, the company took the decision to leverage its apparent understanding of the young male market and publish a general lifestyle magazine. As a result, *LM* was launched in December 1986. Although *LM* was described variously as standing for *Lads' Monthly*, *Loadsa'Money*, *Lonely Males*, and *Leisure Magazine*, the initials were probably meaningless.[89] In an attempt to generate awareness and stimulate demand from the audience, a dummy issue was produced prior to the newsstand launch and distributed free to the 200,000-plus readers of *Crash* and *ZZAP!*. A TV commercial was also produced and ran in a selection of ITV regions.[90] With a budget of £500,000 (£1.4 million at 2018 values), *LM* was the largest project ever undertaken by Newsfield. It also required the opening of a London office (the company's HQ was in Ludlow, Shropshire) and a dedicated team of seven full-time editorial staff.

LM's content offer was not so much broad as disparate. Music featured heavily in the dummy issue, with articles on David Bowie (but notably, no interview) and cult bands The Fall and Stump (neither of whom were likely to receive much coverage in Q outside the reviews section). There was an interview with Liverpool footballer Ian Rush; features on graphic novelist Frank Miller's reboot of *Batman* as *The Dark Knight*, Stanley Kubrick's 1971 movie *A Clockwork Orange*, martial arts weapons, personal stereos, and video-game joysticks; and reviews of the latest movie, book, music, video, and video game releases.[91] The first issue also included: 'A run-down of the fashion's [*sic*] that are going to hit the high-street stores in the spring, a guide to jumble-sale bargain-spotting.'[92] There was also a serial feature called 'Man in a Suitcase', in which a writer stayed in a city for a week (in this case, Birmingham) and produced 'an in-depth report of what he's been up to, who he's met, what bands are emerging, what haircuts are in, what are the best shops, what are the

---

[87] *ABC Certificate, Q, July–December 1990* (London: Audit Bureau of Circulation, 1990).
[88] *ABC Certificate Crash, July–December 1986: 101,483* (London: Audit Bureau of Circulation, 1987).
[89] S. Poulter, 'Inside LM Towers', *Crash* (December 1986); *Liquidators Report: Newsfield Limited Trading History* (Manchester: Messrs Kidsons, Impey & Partners, 1991); *LM magazine—The Proto Lads* [*sic*] *Lifestyle Magazine (1986–1987)*, <https://thoseweleftbehind.co.uk/2008/06/22/lm-magazine-the-proto-lads-lifestyle-magazine-1986-1987/>.
[90] *Liquidators Report.*   [91] S. Poulter, 'Inside LM Towers', *Crash* (December 1986).
[92] Ibid.

best nightclubs, what sports facilities there are, what the local radio station is up to and what's happening on the street'.[93] Issue one of *LM* appeared on the newsstands in December 1986 with an introductory £1 cover price. Newsfield predicted that around 160,000 boys aged between 14 and 18 would buy the title and, like Emap, was relying on word of mouth rather than an above-the-line spend on advertising to push the title to an ambitious settle-down target of 250,000.[94]

The fortunes of the two magazines differed enormously. Q quickly established itself as the UK's leading music title, attracting the calibre of lifestyle advertiser that Zewanda had predicted. For example, in issue 43 of *Q*, which appeared in September 1990, there were colour advertisements for fashion brands (Converse, Fruit of the Loom, Levi's), cigarettes (Silk Cut, John Player, Marlboro), beverages (Teachers, Ballantine's Whisky, Budweiser, Jack Daniels, Stella Artois, Kingfisher), cars (Mazda, Rover-Mini, Ford), personal finance (Barclays), consumer electronics (Kenwood, Kodak, Hitachi, Panasonic, Maxell), cycling (Halfords), and diamond engagement rings.[95] Q's success resulted in a number of new magazines launches adopting a similar strategy. Like Q, some relied on music for the hook, such as *Select*, launched in July 1990 by United Newspapers, and *Vox*, launched in October 1990 by IPC; while others relied on fashion, such as *Arena*, from Wagadon first published quarterly in November 1986; or film, such as *Q*'s sister title *Empire*, launched by Emap in July 1989.[96]

Notwithstanding assurances from Newsfield's co-founder Roger Keen prior to launch that it was not 'going to jump into the market only to jump out again when things begin to look bad' and that, whatever the sales figures, 'we will keep it going for at least a year', *LM* folded after just four issues.[97] A trading statement from the company's liquidators revealed that, although the circulation figures had fallen significantly short of expectations, they were on an upward trend. The real issue was that *LM* did not attract enough advertising, and promises made prior to launch by major national consumer advertisers and media agency account handlers were not forthcoming. There was a feeling among potential advertisers that *LM* was not presenting the right image; it was certainly a long way from *Q*, let alone its more direct competitors

---

[93] Ibid.

[94] A. Jivani, 'Can LM and Q Survive in a Field Littered with Corpses?', *Campaign*, 19 September 1986.

[95] *Q issue 48* (London: Emap, 1990), pp. 8–9, 15, 16–17, 24–5, 31, 32–3, 38–9, 40–1, 51, 59, 60–1,70–1, 78–9, 80, 86–7, 111, 114, 116–17, 122, 126–7, 143.

[96] L. White, 'The custodians of style / Focus on the magazines, The Face, i-D, and Blitz', *Campaign*; 'IPC music monthly drops price for launch '*Campaign*, 31 August 1990; B. Archer, ' "Wally of the Year" makes his mark in magazines: Jonathan King, the man everyone loves to scorn, is back—and he's aiming to fill a "yawning gap", in the music magazine market', *Campaign*, 31 May 1991; R. Ashton, 'TBWA wins task to build Emap Empire', *Campaign*,17 February 1989.

[97] A. Jivani, "Can LM and Q Survive in a Field Littered with Corpses?', *Campaign*, 19 September 1986.

in the style press. With very little advertising revenue and no upturn in sight, *LM* was haemorrhaging so much money that the plug was pulled.[98]

Despite the failure, there was, as Jivani pointed out in *Campaign*, 'no shortage of new candidates willing to learn from Newsfield's experience and take the test in their turn'.[99] For those candidates there was much to learn. *LM*'s dismal performance was by no means unique. A list of costly failures and shelved projects—including the *Hit* from IPC and *Cosmo Man* from the National Magazine Company—were a stark warning to publishers bent on achieving the seemingly impossible goal of establishing a men's general interest title. This left only the tangential route to the same readership of producing a men's magazine but avoiding calling it a men's magazine at all costs. As then editor of *Q* Mark Ellen said: 'The magazine is for people interested in music, which is predominantly a male leisure pursuit but we would never call it a men's magazine.'[100] What appears to be an assumption about the different patterns of music consumption is borne out somewhat by the fact that *Q* sold prodigiously to a predominantly male audience.

There is, however, an alternative reading of *LM*'s failure and *Q*'s success. Launching any general interest magazine was a hugely expensive undertaking. The aforementioned launch of *Marie Claire*, into an established market with proven demand, was supported by a £2.5 million marketing spend above and beyond the magazine's significant production budget.[101] In comparison, Newsfield's £500,000 budget for *LM* looked modest and was arguably inadequate. Given the high cost of failure, it was imperative that any new magazine's content offer must be compelling for its potential readers. In this regard, *Q*'s proposition was very easy to understand: music news, reviews, and features for the discerning, older male listener. In stark contrast, *LM*'s content in its launch issue was all over the place. It confused general interest with a lack of coherence and seems to have no idea who its target audience were: martial arts enthusiasts considering a weekend break in Birmingham with a passion for esoteric music, cult films, and jumble sales perhaps? *Q* also benefited from a further advantage: despite being content rich, with an average of more than seventy pages of editorial, it was comparatively cheap to produce because it relied upon, and was able to rely heavily upon, public relations.

The commercial realities of generating editorial are universal. One 500-word article looks very much the same as another on the page, but the costs of putting

---

[98] *Liquidators Report: Newsfield Limited Trading History* (Manchester: Messrs Kidsons, Impey & Partners, 1991).

[99] A. Jivani, 'Can LM and Q Survive in a Field Littered with Corpses?', *Campaign*, 19 September 1986.

[100] A. Jivani, 'British Males Give Yet Another Hopeful Suitor the Cold-Shoulder: Why Men's Magazines are not for Men', *Campaign*, 5 June 1987.

[101] P. Nathanson, 'August Launch Set for UK Marie Claire', *Campaign*, 19 February 1988.

them together can vary enormously. For example, investigative journalism is usually very expensive; executing an exposé of corporate corruption or an elaborate sting can be an expensive undertaking often involving days, weeks, or even months of potentially worthless endeavour. Towards the other end of the scale, a review of a CD, film, or concert of similar word-length can be produced in half an hour. Rewording a press release, topped and tailed with some analysis, takes a matter of minutes. In media terms, nothing is cheaper than opinion and analysis: they require little research, there is no time-consuming chase for quotes from third parties, and can be produced almost instantly.

In Q's case, the materials to produce its copy invariably came either from the public relations departments of record labels and concert promoters or from publicists working on behalf of the musicians themselves. Q was little more than one big buyer's guide. News items, inspired by press releases, were used to drive awareness of forthcoming tours or releases; features, interviews, and reviews were used to promote (then) current activity. Almost no one appeared in Q unless they had something to sell; even the occasional retrospectives were designed to stimulate purchases of back catalogue. For the music brands, artists, and bands, Q was an important platform from which to reach the target audience (fans), and coverage within was highly valued. As such, the cost of flying a journalist and photographer to New York to give a favourable review of a concert or interview a priority act was a small price to pay for a guarantee of three or four pages of influential editorial coverage—certainly a fraction of the cost of their advertising value and substantially more persuasive. For example, in Q issue 48, which appeared in September 1990, there were interviews with Candy Dulfer in The Hague, The Pixies in Boston, and Jean Michel Jarre in Paris. There was also a diary of Bruce Springsteen's European tour and a report from Berlin about Pink Floyd.[102] In all cases, the magazine's expenses will have been covered by corporate public relations budgets. Furthermore, all the CDs, books and concert passes used for review (and accompanying promotional photos) would also have been provided free of charge.

This effective subsidy was by no means new or even unique, but, as with advertisers, the attractiveness of a publication to public relations teams and departments depends on the profile and the qualities (over and above the quantity) of its readers. For example, in 1986, *Street Machine*, a magazine devoted to car customization widely available in high-street newsagents such as W. H. Smith and John Menzies, boasted a higher coverage of 15–19-year-old males than all the music press, yet it attracted no mainstream advertising. Despite its publisher's claims that it was speaking to its readers

---

[102] *Q, 48* (1990), 12–14; 18–19; 28–30; 42–50; 62–75.

in a language they could understand, editorial covering 'superb examples of the street rodding art' fell somewhat short of the image that most major brands were aiming to project.[103] Newsfield's stable of computer and video games magazines were, like *Q*, entirely public relations driven (which is why they could be produced so cheaply in Ludlow). However, they suffered from the same reluctance that mainstream advertisers had shown to *Street Machine*. To succeed with *LM*, Newsfield would have had to convince advertisers that the title was worth investing in and persuade the public relations specialists that it was worth their while to provide it with the materials for editorial.

If the magazine's early demise is evidence for a lack of the former, an analysis of the editorial content shows there was very little public relations support either. It is an enduring truth within the media, first noted by Alfred Harmsworth, founder of the *Daily Mail* and *Daily Mirror*, that it is much easier to write about people rather than objects, because 'people are so much more interesting than things'.[104] For that reason, companies with products to promote tried wherever possible to communicate their brand stories through people. This typically involved the engagement of a celebrity to provide product endorsement. Public relations teams would offer media outlets exclusive interviews with a celebrity in return for a guarantee that some discussion or mention of the product would appear in print. For example, footballers had very little to gain personally or professionally from giving an interview, because, unlike musicians or actors, their success did not rely to any extent upon this kind of promotion. Yet demand for interviews by footballers remained high. Publications would usually (but not always) refuse to pay directly for interviews, so an indirect arrangement with a public relations representative often constituted the only means to gain the desired access.[105] From the brand's perspective, however it is presented to the readers the footballer's interview becomes nothing more than a promotion vehicle. Any failure on the part of the media outlet to comply would result in the denial of access further down the line.

In this context, the claim that *LM* was simply ahead of its time looks to have little founding.[106] There is a visible lack of ambition where the editorial is

---

[103] Ibid.

[104] A. Bingham, 'Monitoring the Popular Press: An Historical Perspective', in M. Temple (ed.), *The British Press* (Maidenhead: Open University Press, 2008).

[105] There are numerous examples of this. See P. Costanzo and J. Goodnight, 'Celebrity Endorsements: Matching Celebrity and Endorsed Brand in Magazine Advertisements', *Journal of Promotion Management*, 11/4 (2006), 49–62; V. Ekant, B. Ilda, and A. S. M. Brett, 'If Kate Voted Conservative, would you? The Role of Celebrity Endorsements in Political Party Advertising', *European Journal of Marketing*, 44/3–4 (2010), 436–50; M. Mitka, 'Celebrity Endorsements', *Journal of the American Medical Association*, 299/6 (2008), 625.

[106] *LM magazine—The Proto Lads [sic] Lifestyle Magazine (1986–1987)*, <https://thoseweleftbehind.co.uk/2008/06/22/lm-magazine-the-proto-lads-lifestyle-magazine-1986-1987/>.

concerned. Other than an interview with Ian Rush (then one of the top footballers in the UK), which may have been set up via a sportswear manufacturer, there is little evidence of the kind of heavyweight public relations support that success would have demanded. The David Bowie and Stanley Kubrick articles are retrospective 'essays' rather than exclusive interviews. The interview with Stump, whose debut album for major label Phonogram failed to make the UK Top 75, was hardly a hot prospect to draw in the readers.[107] The articles on martial arts and jumble sales bear all the hallmarks of being conceived by an editorial team on a limited budget rather than pitched by a well-funded public relations department. Most telling of all is *LM*'s Man in a Suitcase series. Sending one-seventh of the editorial team to Birmingham for a whole week may not have been financially onerous, yet in terms of time spent to produce an article not only lacking in aspiration but arguably of little interest to all but a tiny proportion of the readership, it was a cost that the publication could ill afford to bear. Newsfield's belief that it understood the demands of this audience was misplaced, but so too was its evaluation of its own strengths and weaknesses. It should have been evident that its current stable of magazines relied heavily upon public relations support for their success. While there was nothing inherently wrong with that model, the failure to leverage that support to produce a more compelling consumer proposition (perhaps playing to its strengths and using video games as a hook) was a key component in its failure.[108]

Following the closure of *LM*, there was a prevailing view among publishers and advertisers that British men were served well enough by their specialist 'stealth' titles, such as *Q, Select* (both music), or *Empire* (film). The belief was that, in comparions, any general title, such as *Unique, For Him*, or *Arena* could reach only the relatively small number of men who want to buy a lifestyle magazine unreservedly aimed at them. This line of thinking was supported by the arrival of *GQ* (*Gentleman's Quarterly*) in December 1988, which was publisher Condé Nast's first independent British launch for thirty years.[109] Given that it was such a risk-averse publisher, it is perhaps no surprise that Condé Nast's introduction of its men's title was a drawn-out affair. The publisher first tested a men's magazine in the mid-1970s and continued to do so with varying degrees of enthusiasm for the next ten years.[110] *GQ*, a UK version of an established US style and features magazine, was first considered as one-half of a dual launch scheduled for spring 1987 that would cover both ends of the men's market. The second title was described as

---

[107] M. C. Strong, *The Great Indie Discography* (Edinburgh: Canongate, 2003), p. 889.
[108] A. Jivani, "British Males Give yet Another Hopeful Suitor the Cold-Shoulder: Why Men's Magazines Are not for Men', *Campaign*, 5 June 1987.
[109] Reporter, 'GQ UK Launch Date', *Campaign*, 14 March 1988.
[110] 'Conde Nast Shelves Title for Young Men', *Campaign*, 29 May 1987.

less 'glossy and sleek' with a 'quirkier approach'.[111] Confident that at least one title would prove successful, Condé Nast was disappointed when both concepts fared poorly during the research phase. MD Richard Hill said that the results revealed thar either title would 'have great difficulty in achieving 50,000 copy sales'.[112]

Condé Nast regrouped and, after dropping the sister publication, finally scheduled *GQ* for standalone launch on 10 November 1988, 'targeted exclusively at the 700,000 or so men with a net income of £15,000 or more' (£40,000 at 2018 values).[113] With a bi-monthly publication and print run of 80,000, sales were predicted to settle down at 50,000. The budget for year one was £1 million (£2.68 million at 2018 values) with a three-year plan to reach at least ten issues per annum and a trading profit by year three.[114] Editor Paul Keers predicted: 'An element of wickedness . . . with a bit of sex from the waist up.'[115]

A more fitting description of the launch issue would have been 'dead from the waist down'. A startlingly sober affair, the cover featured Michael Heseltine, erstwhile Conservative government Secretary of State for Defence, and promised in-depth features on business expenses and 'The Death of the Honourable Englishman'. In his Savile Row suit, Heseltine was, to say the least, an odd choice of cover star. Nicknamed 'Tarzan' by the popular press, he might well have looked like a man who bought his own furniture to crustier colleagues in the Commons, but he was hardly the kind of figure likely to resonate with legions of young British males, flushed with the hedonism of the Second Summer of Love and looking for something colourful to read.[116] The launch issue *GQ* looked more like *Management Today* than the *Face*; nevertheless, although out of step with the zeitgeist, issue one struggled to sales of 44,700 copies in its first month and had crawled past its 50,000 target by the time issue two appeared on 2 January 1989. This modest success persuaded Condé Nast to double its promotional budget to £200,000 per edition (£510,000 at 2018 values) and immediately address the issue of its cover stars.[117]

For the five years following its launch *GQ* was unquestionably the highwater mark in the men's magazine sector. Its ABC of 91,325 recorded for the first quarter of 1993 put it some 25,000 sales ahead of the number two title in the market, *Esquire*. Yet, however impressive this figure appeared at the time, it

---

[111] A. Jivani, 'British Males Give yet Another Hopeful Suitor the Cold-Shoulder: Why Men's Magazines Are not for Men', *Campaign*, 5 June 1987.
[112] Ibid.   [113] R. McKay, '*GQ*—for the 40 per cent Well-Fed Man', *Campaign*, 13 May 1988.
[114] A. Senter, 'The *GQ* Man's Goal is Quality: Paul Keers New Editor of *GQ*, a UK Version of the US Men's Magazine', *Campaign*, 22 April 1988.
[115] Ibid.
[116] The Second Summer of Love was the name given to the period 1988–9 in Britain, in which unlicensed rave parties, acid house music, and the drug MDMA became part of popular culture and the subject of much tabloid hysteria.
[117] '*GQ* on Target as Ad Spend Doubles', *Campaign*, 9 December 1988.

would be wrong to suggest that *GQ's* was an unqualified success, nor was it the breakthrough title that the sector had been looking for. During the same period *Cosmopolitan*, a similarly positioned magazine targeting women, was routinely selling 472,770 copies per month.[118] Perhaps more tellingly, at sales of 95,482 copies per issue, even the *Face*, now well into its second decade, was outselling *GQ*.[119] Not that any of this was of too much concern to Condé Nast; *GQ* was full of the kind of premium advertising—for fragrances, fashion brands, watches, and cars—that the UK's biggest magazine publishers IPC and Emap were desperate to secure. Both, however, lacked a competing title.

The Lads' Magazines: A New, Mass-Market Readership

The inception of IPC's 'publishing phenomenon' *Loaded* is usually recorded as a matter of legend.[120] According to its co-founders James Brown and Tim Southwell, the idea for a magazine 'about all the best moments you've ever had' was conceived in Barcelona in 1992, during a drunken evening spent watching Leeds United play in a Champions' League football match.[121] The probable truth is somewhat more prosaic. Despite the publications' modest sales, the advertising revenues enjoyed by the three leading men's magazines *GQ*, *Esquire*, and *Arena* had not gone unnoticed. Both IPC and Emap had been developing ideas for a men's title since the late 1980s. There is also evidence to suggest that both had also considered the same strategy of acquisition. Their target was a title owned by the small, independent publisher Tayvale called *For Him*.

Launched in 1985 as a bi-annual publication for the fashion industry, *For Him* was initially distributed through men's outfitters.[122] It appeared irregularly at first, achieving a small readership estimated to be around 25,000.[123] In June 1989, *Campaign* reported that IPC had attempted to purchase *For Him* in an attempt to break into the men's magazine market. Although IPC's CEO, John Mellon, denied that he was in negotiations to buy the title, other sources at IPC and Tayvale confirmed that an initial bid to buy a 45 per cent stake had been made. The bid was rejected, but discussions regarding a sale remained ongoing.[124]

Although the talks did not lead to a purchase on this occasion, IPC's interest was enough to persuade Tayvale to invest in the title with a view to selling it

---

[118] Ibid.   [119] S. Hatfield, 'Old Style Bibles for the 90s', *Campaign*, 17 September 1993.
[120] *Loaded* is described by many people as a 'publishing phenomenon'; see, e.g., 'Loaded has a New Editor and the Lad's Mag is Growing up', *Campaign*, 2 February 2001; J. Brown, 'The Decline of Lads' Mags: Unloaded, and now the Party is over', *Independent*, 18 August 2006.
[121] Ibid., T. Southwell, *Getting away with it: The Inside Story of* Loaded (London: Ebury, 1998), 2.
[122] A. Fraser, 'IPC in Surprise Bid for Men's Title', *Campaign*, 30 June 1989.   [123] Ibid.
[124] Ibid.

on at a later date. In August 1990, on the back of an ABC figure of 64,325 (not including 40,000 or so copies distributed via men's outfitters), Tayvale announced that the magazine would be published monthly, a decision reflected in the new title of *FHM* (an abbreviation of *For Him Monthly*).[125] The changes were successful in shifting perceptions of the magazine from a fringe specialist that 'added value' for fashion retailers into a more coherent consumer proposition that was capable of competing directly on the news-stand with *Arena*, *Esquire*, and *GQ*. Further rumours surrounding its sale continued to appear, and it is likely that loose discussions with both IPC and Emap took place during the early 1990s.[126] Certainly the purchase of *FHM* made sense strategically for both companies. The publishing clout of either IPC or Emap would undoubtedly make a difference to copy sales and advertising revenues, while purchasing and relaunching an established title could be less risky—and almost certainly less expensive—than launching a completely new magazine. There was also a precedent. In December 1989 Nick Logan had sold a 40 per cent stake in Wagadon to Condé Nast. The deal eased cash flow concerns and allowed the *Face* and *Arena* to benefit from Condé Nast's vastly more substantial sales, production, and distribution capabilities, but Logan was also able to retain his all-important creative control.[127]

Whatever its intentions were towards *FHM*, by late 1992 IPC was research-ing its own launch into the market. The move was entirely driven by a desire to tap into the advertising revenues being generated by the men's lifestyle titles. The project was headed up by Alan Lewis, a highly respected former editor of music weeklies *Sounds* and *NME* with a track record for two successful launches to his credit—the rock fortnightly *Kerrang!* (1981) and *Vox* (1990)—the latter being IPC's response to the success of *Q*. Initially Lewis looked at putting together a young men's weekly in a similar vein to Emap's *Sky*.[128] *Sky*'s emphasis was on entertainment—a light mix of music, TV, film, and literature—rather than style or fashion. Looking around for a potential editor, Lewis approached James Brown. Born in Leeds in 1965, Brown had arrived at the *NME* in 1986 and over the next five years rose through the ranks to become deputy editor. Brown had a reputation as a brilliant ideas man with a great eye for talent. He was largely responsible for transforming the *NME* from an earnest, rather po-faced publication into a much broader and more entertaining read by recruiting talented new writers such as Andrew Collins and Stuart Maconie.[129] Despite his obvious capabilities, Brown was

---

[125] 'Men's Fashion Mag Gears up to Go Monthly', *Campaign*, 24 August 1990.
[126] M. Toor and C. Beale, 'FHM Editor Denies Sell-off', *Marketing*, 3 September 1992.
[127] S. Clarke, 'Logan's Run of Luck at Conde', *Campaign*, 9 December 1988.
[128] Southwell, *Getting Away With It*, 16–19.
[129] S. Maconie, *Cider with Roadies* (London: Ebury, 2003); A. Collins, *Heaven Knows I'm Miserable Now: My Difficult 80s* (London: Ebury, 2005).

also perceived as a maverick—someone who, according to Lewis, was 'not exactly management material' and lacked both the organizational skills and the right personality to run a weekly newspaper with a staff of thirty-five people.[130] As a result, Brown was passed over for the editor's job at *NME* on two occasions and left IPC in 1992. Lewis, however, remained impressed by his ideas and invited him to lead his nascent men's magazine project at the beginning of 1993.[131]

Launched in April 1994 and billed as a magazine 'For Men who Should Know Better', *Loaded* appeared to be at odds with every other title in the market. Rather than fashion or some other product hook, *Loaded*'s focus was experiences. It was written without claims to objectivity in the so-called gonzo style. Pioneered in the late 1960s by US writers such as Hunter S. Thompson, Lester Bangs, George Plimpton, and Tom Wolfe, gonzo was an energetic form of journalism in which the writer was an active participant and often the main protagonist. It lent itself especially well to self-deprecating humour and social commentary.[132] The front cover of issue one featured a provocative close-up of iconic British actor Gary Oldman. Inside were articles about hotel sex, skydiving, and going on tour with musician Paul Weller. All articles—even the video reviews—were written in the gonzo style. There was no attempt at impartiality or objectivity. The result was a surprisingly coherent and aspirational package. The conceit was that the members of the editorial team putting the magazine together were having the time of their lives, but they were not experts handing out pearls of wisdom in the manner of Peter York or Robert Elms in *the Face* and *Arena*. The writers were presented as 'ordinary lads', just like the magazine's readers, or rather as ordinary lads who could not believe their luck.[133] Through its identity, tone, and values, *Loaded* invited readers to form a strong empathetic bond with its brand; from the premise *we are just like you*, drawing the conclusion that *this could be me* did not require a leap of faith.[134]

Loaded's differentiation within the market is highlighted by a comparison with competing editions of other men's magazines available on newsstands in April 1994. Issue 45 of *Arena* featured singer Chris Isaak on the cover, while inside were features on the difficulties facing couples after the birth of a child, an exposé of the Las Vegas underworld, and '24 pages of Spring fashion'.[135] *GQ*'s May 94 issue contained 'Fools for Love', a self-help feature on how to

[130] Southwell, *Getting away with it*, 17.   [131] Ibid. 16.
[132] For examples of gonzo writing, see L. Bangs and G. Marcus, *Psychotic Reactions and Carburetor Dung* (London: Heinemann, 1988); H. S. Thompson and R. Steadman, *Fear and Loathing in Las Vegas* (London: Paladin, 1972); T. Wolfe, *The Pump House Gang* (1968; London: Black Swan, 1989).
[133] Southwell, *Getting away with it*, 37–44, 80–91, 99; H. Birch, 'Triumph of the New Lad: Stylish? Clever? Sophisticated? Don't be Silly: The Men's Magazine of the Moment is about Football, Booze and Babes. And it's Laughing All the Way to the Bank', *Independent*, 8 September 1994.
[134] *Loaded*, 1 (1994).   [135] *Arena*, 45 (1994).

Table 6.1. UK men's magazines, January–June 1995 and January–June 1996

Title	Publisher	Average circulation per issue		% change year on year
		January–June 1995	January–June 1996	
Arena	Wagon	76,879	93,513	+21.6
Esquire	NatMags	110,798	107,058	−3.4
FHM	Emap	90,607	181,581	+100.4
GQ	Condé Nast	127,276	131,074	+3.0
Loaded	IPC	127,677	238,955	+87.2
Maxim	Dennis	n.a.	113,264	n.a.
Men's Health	Rodale	114,975	131,887	+14.7

Note: n.a. = not applicable.
Source: Audit Bureau of Circulations.

gain a better understanding of women, 'How Men Handle Being Pregnant', and articles on the Mexican Peasants' Revolt and eco-terrorism.[136] *Esquire*'s lead features were an interview with French actor Gerard Depardieu and a self-help guide entitled 'Relax! 50 Reasons why you're Better off than you Think'. There were also extended articles on male grooming, spring fashion, and classic cars.[137] In comparison to *Loaded*, the combination of fashion, male grooming, self-help, and interviews with actors and sports stars looked tired and formulaic, if not to say boring—a fact that was immediately reflected in sales performance. Within twelve months, *Loaded* and its innovative editorial style was outselling the established market leader *GQ* (see Table 6.1). However, *Loaded* was not simply increasing its market share; it was creating an entirely new market. While the existing men's titles might have had their circulations eclipsed, it is important to note that they did not fall. In fact, they all appeared to have hit a glass ceiling in terms of sales, which remained fairly flat up until 1998. Rather than taking market share, *Loaded* and the titles that followed its lead appeared to stand for something completely different and were selling magazines to people who had never bought—or even considered buying—*Arena*, *Esquire*, or *GQ* before. To differentiate between these two categories, the new media became known collectively as lads' magazines as opposed to men's magazines.[138] In recognition of this achievement, *Loaded* received the top two

---

[136] *GQ* (May 1994).   [137] *Esquire* (May 1994).
[138] There are numerous examples of this distinction: e.g. H. Birch, 'Triumph of the New Lad: Stylish? Clever? Sophisticated? Don't be Silly: The Men's Magazine of the Moment is about Football, Booze and Babes. And it's Laughing All the Way to the Bank', *Independent*, 8 September 1994t; S. Armstrong, 'Profile: Sorting the Men from the Lads—Nigel Ambrose, Editor, *Maxim*', *PR Week*, 23 May 1997; 'Perspective: It won't Take Long for Lads to Change into Dads', *Campaign*, 9 August 1996; C. Beale, '*Loaded* has a New Editor and the Lad's Mag is Growing Up', *Campaign*, 2 February 2001; E. Trickett, '*Loaded* Co-Founder Returns to Put Lads' Mag back on Top', *Campaign*, 4 December 1998; D. Teather, 'Father of Lads' Mags Still Loaded with Ideas', *Guardian*; J. Brown, 'The Decline of Lads' Mags: Unloaded, and now the Party is Over', *Independent*, 17 August 2006, <http://www.independent.co.uk/news/media/the-decline-of-lads-mags-unloaded-and-now-the-party-is-over-5330178.html>.

consumer prizes—magazine and editor of the year—at the industry's Professional Publishers Association (PPA) Awards in both 1995 and 1996. For his part, Brown was voted the British Society of Magazine Editors' Editor of the Year, also for two years running.[139]

In April 1994, Emap finally completed its long-mooted purchase of *FHM*.[140] Coincidentally, *FHM*'s May 94 edition was the first to be published following this agreement, which saw it go head to head with the launch issue of *Loaded*. Emap announced that the title would be relaunched under the aegis of newly appointed editorial director David Hepworth.[141] Where *FHM* was concerned, there was a considerable amount of work to be done. With sales of 60,298, *FHM* was lagging well behind *GQ* and *Esquire* with content that was more of the same.[142] The May 94 issue featured boxer Billy Schwer on the cover (looking as though he had just finished a particularly testing fight) and it contained an article on buying the perfect suit, a self-help guide to the art of flattery, and an extended feature on 'Summer Grooming'.[143] Mike Soutar, then editor of *Smash Hits*, was Hepworth's first senior appointment. Soutar was a very different character from Brown. A graduate of the University of Michigan Business School, he was almost immediately identified as management material and fast-tracked to become Emap's youngest ever editor when, in 1991, he took over *Smash Hits* at the age of 24.[144] Emap took its time over the relaunch, announcing a £400,000 (£757,000 at 2018 values) redesign for the title in February 1995. With around £250,000 (£473,000 at 2018 values) of the total amount allocated for media promotion, the new *FHM* would be repositioned away from the established men's titles as a direct competitor to *Loaded* in the lads' magazine sector.[145] The first issue to benefit from the new look was the October 1995 edition, which hit newsstands early in September.

If Emap's response to *Loaded* seemed tardy rather than considered, the same could not be said for the arrival of the third magazine into the sector. *Maxim*, launched in April 1995 by Dennis publishing, was the result of extensive market research. Under editor Gill Hudson, a veteran of women's magazines, its focus was to be upmarket consumer goods and product reviews. Dennis was predicting a settle-down circulation of 50,000 copies.[146] Whether *Maxim* and

[139] 'Top Performers of 1996: Medium of the Year: Sky Television', *Campaign*, 10 January 1997; '*Loaded* Breaks Tradition to Take Double Honours at PPA Awards', *Campaign*, 5 May 1996; 'Lads' Mag *Loaded* Scoops Top Prize at the PPA 1995 Awards', *Campaign*, 5 May 1995.

[140] 'Emap Selects Chief to Promote Special Value Magazines', *Campaign*, 20 May 1994.

[141] Ibid.

[142] *ABC Certificate, FHM, January–June 1994: 60,298* (London: Audit Bureau of Circulation, 1994).

[143] *FHM* (May 1994).

[144] C. Gourlay, 'Youngest Ever Editor Set to Revive a Flagging *Smash Hits*', *Campaign*, 31 January 1991.

[145] 'Emap Overhauls FHM', *Marketing*, 2 February 1995.

[146] 'Men's Monthly Will Focus on Upmarket Goods', *PR Week*, 13 January 1995.

the redesigned *FHM* took market share from *Loaded* or contributed to further growth of the lads' sector is unclear. Certainly, the look and feel of the new entrants were different from that of *Loaded*. The early issues of *Maxim*, as might have been expected, felt very much like a women's magazine targeting men. Its short, punchy articles and features were a long way from the first-person adventures spread over five or six pages that dominated *Loaded*, and it seemed to be aiming at an older, more assured audience. For example, Issue 5, which appeared in September 1995, contained several articles that would not have looked out of place in *Cosmopolitan* or *Marie Claire*—on infertility, whether or not to have sex on a first date, how to have the perfect picnic, and the moral dilemma of posing for topless photos.[147] In combination with an extensive reviews section of gadgets and technology (playing to one of publisher Dennis's key strengths), along with the usual self-help and how-to guides—and the even more usual photos of scantily clad women—*Maxim* was able to differentiate itself and carve out a lucrative niche within the market.

If *Maxim*'s achievement was to carve itself out a considerable niche, *FHM*'s success was no less than total market domination. By the end of 1997, its sales were greater than *Maxim* and *Loaded* combined (see Table 6.2). Accusations that in *FHM* Emap had merely produced a facsimile of *Loaded* appear largely unfounded. While pictures of attractive young women in some state of undress were clearly a compulsory component of all three of the bestselling lads' mags, their importance in terms of the success of individual titles can be overstated. For these features the magazines were all pulling subjects from the same pool. There was relatively little qualitative difference, and several models appeared regularly on the covers or within the pages of all three titles at different times. *FHM*'s success was due to how it incorporated this kind of

Table 6.2. UK men's magazines, January–June 1998

Title	Publisher	Average circulation per issue	% change year on year
Arena	Wagon	65,010	+21.6
Esquire	NatMags	112,161	+20.7
Face	Wagon	78,173	−27.7
FHM	Map	775,451	+53.6
GQ	Condé Nast	130,152	−4.0
Loaded	IPC	456,373	+20.04
Maxim	Dennis	300,786	+63.0
Men's Health	Rodale	245,659	+30.5
Sky	Map Metro	171,101	−1.4
Stuff	Dennis	64,183	+11.3

Source: Audit Bureau of Circulations.

[147] *Maxim* (September 1995).

content into its proposition. An issue of *Maxim* or *Loaded* would not outsell *FHM* simply because it had a higher profile cover star that month. Behind its 'babes in bikinis' façade, *FHM* was more like *Q*—little more than a buyers' guide. In this case, however, rather than just music, *FHM* purported to advise on the reader's entire lifestyle.

FHM's tone was a complex and often contradictory mix of uber-confidence and knowing incompetence. The implication was that its readers, possessed of the same insecurities, were in need of guidance. Its tone of voice was everyman rather than alpha male. If *Loaded*'s aim can be described as to entertain and inspire its readers, then *FHM*'s was to entertain and inform them. *Loaded*'s emphasis was on the hedonistic and excessive. For those aspiring towards a 'rock n roll' lifestyle, this was a compelling fantasy, but, for most people with a job to hold down and bills to pay, a fantasy nonetheless. *FHM*'s emphasis was commerce, dressed up as empowerment or enablement. It gave its relatively affluent readers plenty of ideas for what they could do with their disposable income.

This differentiation is best illustrated in the contrasting manner that the two magazines tackled similar subject matter. For example, an article called 'Up Shit Creek', which appeared in *Loaded*'s August 1995 issue, is typical of the magazine's approach.[148] This is essentially a straightforward travel feature about outdoor activity holidays. It features information and detailed costs about hiring canoes and where to buy tents, other specialist gear, and outdoor clothing. It also provides the requisite editorial for the brands that funded the trip and whose public relations teams almost certainly came up with the idea. However, the story is given a twist and presented in the style of a first-person adventure about 'six men, three canoes and a mission to get to Mushroom Island', which starts one 'drug crazed evening'.[149] The 'six men' who star in the story are all members of *Loaded*'s editorial team. The impression given is that they have thrown themselves into the activity with little preparation or training and spent most of the time drinking heavily and taking recreational drugs, which is certainly the image that the magazine wanted to project. This editorial style contrasts starkly with *FHM*'s, wherein—barring a few regular columnists—the writers were generally not a major part of the story at all. For example, *FHM*'s 'Go Berserk with Bits of Wood' is a similar themed travel feature about skiing holidays. It is humorous, irreverent in tone, and entertaining, but rather than a 5,000-word gonzo adventure involving 'the team', a pithy 500-word anecdote sets up an extensive list of essential information. Details are provided for where to go and what to wear in a feature that is part travel guide/part fashion guide/part consumer reviews round-up, with prices

---

[148] M. Deeson, 'Up Shit Creek', *Loaded* (August 1995).   [149] Ibid. 43.

and contact details for retailers and travel agents helpfully provided.[150] Both are lengthy features—seven pages of editorial in *Loaded* and eleven and a half pages in *FHM*—but, while *Loaded* gave its readers inspirational ideas about how they could spend their free time, *FHM* showed theirs exactly how to do it, where to do it, and precisely how much it would cost.

It is undeniable that *Loaded* was the first magazine truly to open up the broader men's market, but above and beyond the role played by its inspirational launch editor there were several key factors that contributed to the category's success. Research into British lifestyles indicated that, with lower rates of marriage, later marriage, and higher divorce rates, a growing proportion of the male population was living in a single-person household. By 1995, as Mort identified, a distinctive market aimed at young men had developed. For the first time they were being encouraged to spend money on themselves, and shopping had become a masculine pursuit. Within the style press, the 'new man' was held up as a totem of economic prosperity, but in fact product and graphic designers, advertisers, marketers, public relations specialists, and journalists were already endeavouring to satisfy a range of new male identities. To use Mort's terms, the lads' magazines emerged fully formed and were so successful because they occupied this 'significant part in young men's narratives of self'.[151] The market became a stage upon which all aspects of men's lifestyle could be played out. And, no matter what the problem, commerce could provide the answer. Magazines such as *FHM* and *Loaded* offered not only to help readers navigate through increasingly complex lifestyles but also to feel connected or 'part of something' and 'more prepared to speak more freely on personal matters such as grooming and . . . more ready to express feelings'.[152]

By the end of 1997, the men's magazines and lads' mags were selling over 2.3 million copies per month to the 4.5 million 20–40-year-old men in the UK.[153] In 1991, ABC1 men made up 22.8 per cent of the population, rising to 25.5 per cent in 1996.[154] Given that many copies would have been read by more than one person, their actual reach into this market was almost certainly much higher. Brands were not slow to recognize the implications. The magazines gave their readers the impression that it was possible to buy an advantage and showed how that could be done by having the right clothing, looking groomed, and being seen eating and drinking in the right places; by doing all the 'right' things.

[150] P. Thorne, 'Snow Special', *FHM* (December 1996), 180–98.
[151] Mort, *Cultures of Consumption*, 205.
[152] *British Lifestyles 1996* (London: Mintel International Group, 1996). Also reported extensively in: A.-M. Crawford, 'Men at War', *Campaign*, 29 August 1989.
[153] *Post-family leisure trends—UK* (London: Mintel International Group, 2000).
[154] A.-M. Crawford, 'Men at War', *Campaign*, 29 August 1989.

The lads' magazines had a major impact on their readers' tastes and behaviour. The mass-market channel to male consumers that they provided allowed brands to target men with a host of new product categories. Moreover, they were able to do this through both advertising and public relations; the publishers relied not only on the revenue that advertisers provided but also on public relations activity, which provided their magazines with content. Brand messages often appeared to be impartial editorial. Articles in consumer magazines became increasingly commoditized, as more businesses sought to promote their products through corporate branding. Readers were much more resistant to advertising than they were to editorial, which they regarded with more credibility. As head of UK public relations agency Bell Pottinger Sir Tim Bell said in 1995: 'A strong story placed in the newspaper [or magazine], picked up by everybody else, will actually have more impact than an advertising campaign.'[155]

[155] Bell originally made this comment during a Marketing Society lunch on 8 December 1995, and he was quoted in D. Michie, *The Invisible Persuaders* (London: Bantam, 1998).

7

Symbols of Self-Expression

The Rise of Corporate Branding

The Influence of Brand Equity, Image, and Personality

A natural consequence of the rise of marketing as the key strategic function was that the discipline itself—rather than sales or product development— began to drive commercial strategies. The success of branding activities, in terms both of ensuring consistent customer communication and of genuinely reducing costs, did not go unnoticed. Aaker and Keller identified that brand- ing as a concept became important to understand at a corporate level and so developing and managing brand image became a prominent feature of a firm's marketing programme.[1] Brands helped consumers to distinguish the goods and services of a company from those of its competitors, but also simplified the purchase and provided information. As a result, branding made customers feel secure throughout the purchase decision-making process.

Companies launch new products in order to attract as many customers as possible and increase their market share. As competition increased in markets where there was little difference between products, new product launches ran a high risk of failure.[2] In these circumstances, the extension of existing brands proved to be successful, as long as consumers were willing to accept the extension of the branded product into the new category. In 1988, Tauber and Aaker stated that extending brands in this manner typically involved using the name of an existing brand to launch a completely new product

---

[1] D. A. Aaker, *Managing Brand Equity: Capitalizing on the Value of a Brand Name* (New York: Free Press; Toronto: Collier Macmillan Canada, 1991); K. Keller, *Strategic Brand Management: Building, Measuring and Managing Brand Equity* (Upper Saddle River, NJ: Prentice Hall, 1998).

[2] J. S. Panwar and D. Bapt, 'New Product Launch Strategies: Insights from Distributors Survey', *South Asian Journal of Management*, 14/2 (2007), 82.

into a different market.[3] Chen and Liu have argued subsequently that this strategy was also appealing because it not only reduced the need for market research and advertising spend but also increased the chances of success owing to the performance of the parent brand.[4] A 1993 study by Keller noted that a brand is an accumulation of relationships, and, together with Aaker in an earlier paper, he also demonstrated how initial brand relationships with consumers could be used to develop successful extensions.[5] However, for companies there was also a demographic imperative behind the rise of marketing. Issues such as the ageing population, declining birth rate, increase in the number of working women, rise in average age of marriage and fecundity, and changing tastes impacted on traditional markets and affected product sales, forcing businesses to review their brand communication strategies.

Brand extensions began in earnest during the early 1980s.[6] In the FMCG sector companies such as Coca-Cola, Heinz, and Beecham (Lucozade) started to take a corporate view of their product range and began introducing new iterations of the historic parent brand—for example, Diet Coke (1982), Caffeine-Free Coca Cola (1983), and Coca-Cola Cherry (1985).[7] Heinz's strategy differed slightly. In 1978, it purchased Weight Watchers, a manufacturer of weight loss and maintenance packaged food; products continued to bear the Weight Watchers logo but the words 'by Heinz' were incorporated into the brand. The rationale was that the values of taste and quality associated with Heinz would add value to the Weight Watchers brand; its positioning was 'good-tasting, reduced-calorie, portion-controlled food'.[8] Successful as this strategy of extension was. it effectively decoupled the brand from the product. For example. Coca Cola was no longer just a sugary soda drink; it was a family of products under one corporate brand that shared the same values and personality. However, rather than diminishing the value of the parent brand in the case of Coca-Cola, and many others, its equity was actually increased. The marketing of a company's products and services had traditionally been kept separate from the marketing of its

[3] A. M. Tauber, 'Brand Leverage: Strategies for Growth in a Cost Controlled World', *Journal of Advertising Research* (August–September 1988), 26–31.

[4] K. F. Chen and C. M. Lui, 'Positive Brand Extension Trial and Choice of Parent Brand', *Journal of Product and Brand Management*, 13/1 (2004), 25–36.

[5] K. Keller, 'Conceptualizing, Measuring and Managing Customer-Based Brand Equity', *Journal of Marketing*, 57/1 (1993), 22; D. Aaker and L. Keller, 'Consumer Evaluations of Brand Extensions', *Journal of Marketing*, 54/1 (1990), 27.

[6] There are numerous examples of successful corporate brand extension across a broad range of sectors during the period. For further reading, see D. A. Aaker and A. L. Biel, *Brand Equity and Advertising: Advertising's Role in Building Strong Brands* (London: Psychology Press, 1993).

[7] 'Diet Coke Introduced', *Wilmington Morning Star*, 9 July 1982 p. 6B; 'Soft Drinks: I Gave my Love a Cherry Coke', *Time*, 4 March 1985, <http://content.time.com/time/magazine/article/0,9171,961943,00.html>; Lucozade advertising: HAT, Smith Kline Beecham UK, HAT 59/15/10.

[8] *History of Weight Watchers* <http://www.dwlz.com/WWinfo/historyofww.html>.

corporate image or reputation, but, as a result of successful brand extensions, corporations began to recognize the possible advantages of combining the two to create an omnipresent corporate brand. The commercial success of many brand extensions compelled senior management within large organizations to regard their brands as the most important assets of the company and their extension as an effective means of increasing brand equity.[9] An analysis of studies in the field of building brand equity, carried out by Shyle and Hysi in 2012, revealed that by the end of the twentieth century (and despite there being a number of different definitions of brand equity) there was a clear consensus that its increase was considered to be one of the main corporate goals.[10]

McDonald's, the restaurant chain, provides an example of successful corporate branding during the 1980s. Whether they want a Big Mac, Filet-O-Fish, or Chicken McNuggets, customers are more likely to say something like 'I fancy a McDonalds'. The quality, taste, and experience of eating in one of their restaurants are wrapped up in and endorsed by the McDonald's name. Indeed, this branding works to such an extent that 'McDonald's' is often given a nickname by consumers such as 'Macky Dees' or 'Golden Arches'. This in turn becomes a generic term for any fast-food meal, and customers will use the phrase even when they intend to visit a different restaurant chain such as Burger King or Kentucky Fried Chicken. The same is true for a range of categories. People often use brand names such as Coke or Levi's to refer generically to different kinds soda or jeans (in much the same way that the brand name 'Biro' is used to describe different makes of ballpoint pen or 'Hoover' a vacuum cleaner). Customers may even ask for Coke or Levi's but are equally satisfied if they end up with a Pepsi or a pair of Diesel jeans instead.[11] In 1987, *Campaign* attributed the rise of corporate branding to 'the advent of . . . corporate raiders—companies going after other companies. Suddenly, a company you had never heard of would start telling you how important it was, how it was responsible for brands you couldn't do without.' The newspaper also recognized that this initial phase was over as companies woke up to the long-term advantages in corporately identifying their brands, which provided both a guarantee for consumers and a pertinent reminder of

[9] R. Dwek, 'Top UK Brands and Clients: How Far Can Brand Extensions Be Pushed?', *Campaign*, 26 April 1996.

[10] I. Shyle and V. Hysi, 'The Study of Brand Equity as a Relationship between Brand Personality and Consumer Personality', unpublished paper, Economic & Social Challenges Dedicated to Economy & Business Doctoral Students Conference, Tirana, Albania, 2012. See also M. Agarwal and V. Rao, 'An Empirical Comparison of Consumer-Based Measures of Brand Equity', *Marketing Letters*, 7/3 (1996), 237–47.

[11] D. Rogers, 'Focus: Marketing Comms—the Faces behind the Brand Names', *PR Week*, 16 May 1997.

corporate value to investors. It was also viewed as a means of supporting less heavily or non-advertised brands in the company's portfolio.[12]

This process linked business strategy more closely than ever with marketing strategy and provided the persuasion industries with a new opportunity. The more progressive marketing service providers recognized that the role of the advertising or PR agency could involve much more than simply producing advertisements and generating publicity; it could take on elements of management consultancy and become involved in product development. Many agencies repositioned themselves as cerebral communication consultancies that could do the clients' strategic thinking for them. St Luke's was typical of this new kind of operation. St Luke's launched in 1994, following a management buyout of global agency Chiat Day's London office and immediately positioned itself as a communication consultancy: 'A fast problem solver for brands.' It rarely mentioned its output, but placed great emphasis on its thoughtful, strategic consultancy.[13] The approach proved to be more than hot air. One of the nascent St Luke's pillar accounts was the Body Shop—an environmentally conscious, UK cosmetics and toiletries retailer with a reputation for ethical trading. The Body Shop was renowned for its opposition to advertising, with founder Anita Roddick even going so far as to describe it as 'environmental pollution'. For brand communication purposes, the Body Shop relied upon a combination of public relations (also used to cultivate media interest in Roddick's own life and ideals) and striking in-store marketing to generate publicity for the brand.[14]

At the time, the appointment of one of the advertising world's brightest rising stars by one of the UK's most reticent advertisers seemed a curious communion. However, as the Body Shop's marketing director Jilly Forster explained to *Campaign* in October 1994, the company 'weren't looking for an advertising agency, we were looking for a strategic communications consultant, an objective eye to help us focus on the bigger picture. But on reflection, where else would you go for that type of thing?'[15] There was initial cynicism about how any advertising agency could add value without producing any advertising. However, twelve months later, *Campaign* highlighted St Luke's successful relationship with the Body Shop as an example of an industry shift from 'doing to thinking'. The agency was working behind the scenes at a strategic, corporate level, analysing the Body Shop's brand message and advising on a range of activities from internal media opportunities to staff

---

[12] D. Bernstein, 'The Changing of Corporate Advertising', *Campaign*, 10 July 1987.

[13] K. Yates, 'Chiat Day Rechristened as St Luke's', *Campaign*, 5 October 1995.

[14] C. Cozens, 'Body Shop Reviews Anti-Advertising Policy', *Guardian*, 26 July 2001, <https://www.theguardian.com/media/2001/jul/26/advertising.marketingandpr2>.

[15] M. Martin, 'Body Shop Ends Advertising Ban to Appoint Chiat Day', *Campaign*, 14 October 1994.

training and store refits.[16] Put simply, repositioning an advertising or public relations agency as a strategic communication adviser created the opportunity to apply existing skills—market research, planning, media relations, brand identity, creativity, and so on—much earlier in the business cycle. The objective was still to influence consumer behaviour but not necessarily through advertising alone, and in some cases, at all. Results could be achieved through changes in the retail environment, customer interaction, or a sponsorship that served as a demonstration of company values. St Luke's was not an isolated example. *Campaign* reported that agencies across the board were positioning themselves as consultancies from young independents such as Howell Henry Caldecott Lury and Mother to established firms like Leo Burnett Brand Consultancy and global conglomerates like WPP.[17]

Successful corporate brands were built from the inside out. They allowed organizations to address growing consumer concerns with how they behaved and reacted to the wider world through a set of communicable brand values over and above the qualities of the individual product or service—for example, 'good customer service', 'value for money', 'safe and secure', 'promoting healthy lifestyles', 'environmentally friendly', 'playful', or 'consistently great taste'. A number of such values could be combined to develop a unique personality, which, as products and services became increasingly similar, offered a crucial point of differentiation. Often the only tangible difference between products such as burgers, sodas, beers, jeans, shirts, or trainers was the brand. Agencies tended to develop bespoke terminology to describe this process, but the ends were invariably the same. For example, in 1997 marketing consultancy Interbrand talked of building possible 'architectures'—effectively different brand strategies—that clients could adopt to achieve the appropriate corporate/ product brand balance; beneath the jargon, this approach was almost identical to that used by St Luke's.[18]

Again it should be stressed that not all attempts at corporate branding were successful. It was not a panacea. Although the benefits of success were clear, the process leading to its realization was extremely challenging. Regardless of any faux idiosyncrasies conceived by a communication agency, building a successful corporate brand in this manner made huge demands on an organization. It was no longer simply a question of advertising 'good' products or services—that was merely the starting point; the brand identity had to remain

[16] M. Martin, 'The Ad Agency Grows up: Agencies Used to Make Ads. Now Some have Forged Ahead as Cerebral Communications Consultants who Think for their Clients', *Campaign*, 13 October 1995.

[17] Ibid.; E. Hall, 'Paul Meijer to Join Saville as Latest C5 Dream Team Name', *Campaign*, 20 December 2012.

[18] D. Rogers, 'Focus: Marketing Comms—the Faces behind the Brand Names', *PR Week*, 16 May 1997.

consistent at all contact points from the boardroom to the marketplace. To achieve that, companies were required to develop integrated communication programmes with all their stakeholders, from consumers to employees, suppliers, distributors, resellers, environmental groups, government agencies, and investors.[19] Each of these stakeholders would have a nuanced but equally complex relationship with the brand. Every brand had its own personality—the set of consistent, human characteristics that also reflected the emotions and feelings evoked by the brand.[20] Brand personality allowed consumers to express an idealized sense of self and influenced their choice by exploiting a natural human tendency to anthropomorphize: to attribute human qualities, motivations, traits, or features to animals or inanimate objects.[21] This can result in the development of long-term relationships between the brand and its consumers.[22] Although there was no formula for success per se, such holistic communication demanded consistency. The core brand values had to be communicated through a multitude of channels, of which advertising was but one. Packaging, in-store presence, and customer service were now opportunities to influence and engage with consumers 'in the manner of the brand'.

Developing a sponsorship strategy—formerly a chairman's whim more often than not—also became increasingly a part of the public relations department's remit. The aim here was to match brand values with talent, events, and organizations in order to build profile.[23] Holistic communication also fell naturally within the remit of public relations owing to its distinctive advantages over advertising when it came to delivering complex messages or reaching diverse audiences. Where TV and radio were concerned, public relations invisibility could neatly circumvent strict controls on product promotion and placement. Reviews, for example, a staple of magazine shows aimed at

[19] M. Cowlett, 'Buying into Bands', *PR Week*, 24 November 2000.

[20] K. Keller, 'Conceptualizing, Measuring and Managing Customer-Based Brand Equity'; J. Aaker, 'Dimensions of Brand Personality', *Journal of Marketing Research*, 34/3 (1997), 347.

[21] S. Guthrie, *Faces in the Clouds: A New Theory of Religion* (Oxford: Oxford University Press, 1993), 120–34.

[22] J. Plummer, 'How Personality Makes a Difference', *Journal of Advertising Research*, 40/6 (2000), 79–83; A. Biel, 'Converting Image into Equity', in Aaker and Biel, *Brand Equity and Advertising*; S. Fournier, 'Consumers and their Brands: Developing Relationship Theory in Consumer Research', *Journal of Consumer Research*, 24/4 (1998), 343–53; H. F. Traci and P. F. Lukas, 'An Examination of Brand Personality through Methodological Triangulation', *Journal of Brand Management*, 13/2 (2005), 148–62.

[23] See J. Izzat, 'Special Report on Arts Sponsorship', *PR Week*, 30 November 1989; G. Waterman, 'Sponsorship: Deals', *PR Week*, 25 January 1990; R. Price, 'Letter: Sponsorship Shops Deserve Some Respect', *PR Week*, 1 March 1990; R. Cobb, 'No Holds Barred, no Blow too Low: The Rules Are there Are no Rules, as Ad Agencies and PR Shops Slug it out for the Lucrative "Fixit", Role Arranging Television Programme Sponsorship Deals', *PR Week*; J. Izzat, 'Broadcast Sponsorship: Tuning in to a Fuzzy Picture—the Pioneeers of TV Sponsorship Deals and Finding the Goalposts Keep Shifting as Regulatory Bodies Chop and Change the Rules', *PR Week*, 5 April 1990; M. Cook, 'Platform: Backing those Winning Events—Sponsorship is All about Making Money/Firms should be Supporting the Bottom Line, not Subsidising their Favourite Teams', *PR Week*, 19 July 1990.

children, young adults, and the daytime audience, were ostensibly free of editorial control. There were, it was argued, no guarantees that conclusions or coverage given to publicists would be positive (the constant supply of review copies, press passes, competition prizes, and other materials was presumably maintained on a goodwill basis). Compelling arguments could also be made in support of other forms of promotional content—for example, why wouldn't musicians, authors, or actors talk about their latest project during an interview? And wouldn't news items or features about a product, event, or exhibition that was of interest to the audience seem oddly incomplete without information about location, timings, and ticket availability?[24]

As long as editorial impartiality was seen to be maintained, these forms of promotion received little attention from either the government or the regulatory bodies: the Advertising Standards Authority (ASA), Independent Broadcasting Authority (IBA) and Broadcasting Standards Commission (BSC). The ASA's focus was squarely on the advertisements broadcast between programmes, while the IBA and BSC concentrated on programme quality and the more flagrant breaches of the rules on product placement in the shows themselves. In 1992, breakfast broadcaster TV-AM suspended its resident chef Rustie Lee after newspaper allegations, which the presenter strenuously denied, that she had taken £80,000 in backhanders in return for plugging food products.[25] Lee's misdemeanour was reported as an isolated case. However, given the opportunity for abuse this system afforded, it is somewhat surprising that such examples were so rare. In truth, providing proof of wrongdoing was difficult. *Brookside*, Channel 4's popular soap opera and most-watched show during the 1980s and 1990s, was criticized several times for giving certain brands undue prominence. However, producers insisted that the incidents were down to either dramatic realism or mistakes made during the editing process, and no further action was ever taken.[26] For these reasons, promotional content was never subjected to the same degree of scrutiny as product placement or sponsorship. Indeed, Lee herself was exposed only after an anonymous whistleblower sent a letter to the *Sun* newspaper.[27]

With little chance of detection, publicists were able to employ a variety of tactics to gerrymander the outcome of 'impartial' reviews and the content of interviews on television. For example, guest reviewers could be primed to

[24] C. Baker, 'Special Report on Consumer PR: Now That's the Way to Do It—What Makes a Hit Consumer PR Programme?', *PR Week*, 5 December 1990.
[25] B. Daniels, 'Love Fury of TV Cook Rustie', *Daily Mirror*, 4 March 1992, p. 3.
[26] H. Bonner, 'Rustie's Boiling Mad', *Daily Mirror*, 26 October 1991, p. 7; M. Kavanagh, 'Product Placement', *PR Week*, 9 June 1994.
[27] J. Izzatt, 'Broadcast Sponsorship: Tuning in to a Fuzzy Picture—the Pioneeers of TV Sponsorship Deals and Finding the Goalposts Keep Shifting as Regulatory Bodies Chop and Change the Rules', *PR Week*, 5 April 1990.

support fellow artists on the circuit, who would return the favour the following week, audience members could be planted or preselected to take part in reviews, and it was often possible to insist that interview questions were submitted in advance so that answers could be tailored to produce the maximum promotional impact. Publicists could also demand the quid pro quo of an easy ride for today's special guest in return for a pipeline of more interview subjects further down the line, while an exclusive preview, interview, feature, or review could be placed in return for a tacit guarantee of favourable coverage from the media outlet. Making these kind of deals, though very rarely if ever recorded in writing, was part and parcel of the PR specialist's lot.[28] The editorial coverage generated was both cost effective and credible. Moreover, on the BBC, where advertising was banned, this editorial coverage represented the only opportunity for brand communication to reach the biggest audiences of all. The challenge was how to ensure opportunities were exploited effectively—in other words, in a manner that would uphold the brand's values.

In 1987, *Campaign* identified three strategic approaches to corporate advertising: the explanatory, the expansionary, and the endorsement.[29] In explanatory advertising, companies talked about who they were and what they made; expansionary advertising was employed by well-known companies to tell consumers about recent developments; in endorsement advertising, each brand commercial ended with the parent company's logo and message. Advertising could be supported by additional activity in-store or at the point of sale, and brand values could also be communicated through appropriate sponsorship. Corporate public relations presented different strategic challenges from advertising, especially when products had very little to offer the media in and of themselves. Adidas trainers, cans of Pepsi Cola, and Burger King Kids Meals did not make particularly compelling interview subjects. Companies needed people—brand ambassadors—to represent them. For organizations blessed with such, a charismatic CEO could fill that role—for example, Microsoft's Bill Gates, Virgin's Sir Richard Branson, Eidos's Ian Livingstone, or Apple's Steve Jobs. However, for the majority of businesses where this was not an option, a celebrity with the necessary cachet could be engaged to perform the same function. The role of the brand ambassador in this era was much more sophisticated than the celebrity endorsees of the 1960s and 1970s, which involved having a famous personality recount the product's unique selling points in display, point of sale advertising, or even on the pack. Although this activity was perceived to add value, it was merely just a different technique for

---

[28] M. Kavanagh, 'Product Placement', *PR Week*, 9 June 1994; J. Foley, 'Showbusiness: Putting on a Performance', *PR Week*, 27 February 1992.

[29] D. Bernstein, 'The Changing of Corporate Advertising', *Campaign*, 10 July 1987.

the delivery of traditional forms of marketing. In contrast, the brand ambassador was a vital component in a much more expansive, corporate marketing strategy: the living embodiment of the brand's values. Brand ambassadors were often engaged over a period that could extend to several years.

An example of this holistic approach to corporate branding over the long term is provided by the repositioning of the soft drink Lucozade—then owned by Beecham, a British company—between 1983 and 1997.[30] Since its introduction in 1929, Lucozade had been marketed as a children's convalescence drink. It was stocked by chemists and sold in glass bottles wrapped in yellow cellophane. Its price point was much higher than other fizzy drinks, no doubt reflecting its rejuvenative properties. Owing to demographic changes within the UK, by 1983 the brand was in decline.[31] With the birth rate falling and fewer children about, a turnaround in the brand's fortunes required more than an increase in market share. The long-term solution identified was to reposition the brand by targeting a different market. However, this strategy was not without significant challenges. The obvious category to enter—mass-market sodas—was dominated by established international and domestic brands such as Coca-Cola, 7Up, Tizer, Irn-Bru, and Vimto. It was also beset with the similar demographic challenges—not least of which was the fact that, like Lucozade, these soft drinks were primarily consumed by children.[32] In order to grow, Lucozade's repositioning would have to connect it with older consumers, effectively opening up a completely new market segment.

In 1983, the advertising agency Leo Burnett carried out the brand's repositioning after securing the Beecham account following a competitive pitch.[33] Leo Burnett aimed to capitalize on the growing public interest in fitness and healthy living to reposition Lucozade as a masculine energy drink, thereby shifting the brand's associations away from 'pick-me-up', 'illness', and 'children' towards 'vitality', 'health', and 'male'. The glass bottle was retired in favour of a modern PET (polyethylene terephthalate) container— similar to that used by regular sodas—and the slogan 'Lucozade aids recovery' was replaced with 'Lucozade replaces lost energy'.[34] The advertising campaign, which ran into the 1990s, featured Olympic gold medal winner Daley Thompson (see Figure 7.1).[35] In the launch TV advertisement, Thompson provided no endorsement of the product. The commercial opens with a shot

---

[30] *Smith Kline Beecham: History* <http://www.hatads.org.uk/catalogue/corporate-marketing/48/SmithKline-Beecham/>.

[31] Ibid.; J. Dickens, 'Review-Advertising: The Ad as a Cultural Weapon/A Look at Advertisements which Have the Tide of Opinion', *Campaign*, 12 September 1996; 'Beecham Plans Foray to Boost Corporate Profile', *Campaign*, 17 April 1987.

[32] J. Dickens, 'Review-Advertising: The Ad as a Cultural Weapon/A Look at Advertisements which Have the Tide of Opinion', *Campaign*, 12 September 1996.

[33] Ibid.   [34] Ibid.   [35] HAT, Lucozade advertising, HAT 59/15/10.

Figure 7.1. *Daley Thompson breaks training for refreshment*: stills from TV and cinema advertisement produced by Leo Burnett for Lucozade, 1983. (Courtesy of Lucozade Ribena Suntory Ltd.) See also plates section.

of Thompson finishing a sprint. There is no voiceover, instead an on-screen message simply states '8.00 a.m. Daley Thompson breaks training for refreshment'. Next we see Thompson drink a Lucozade. A traffic light changes from red to green, and then Thompson resumes training, powering through a sprint in slow motion. The soundtrack is provided by the introduction to Iron Maiden's *Phantom of the Opera*, a pounding rock track, which bursts into life as Thompson breaks from the blocks. The commercial ends with a pack shot and voiceover that simply states 'Lucozade, the refreshing glucose drink'.

For a repositioning, it is interesting how little is said about the product. It is up to the viewer to infer his or her own message from the imagery. However, the advertisement is not subtle. It is difficult to infer anything other than that drinking Lucozade is an important part of Thompson's training routine. Indeed, the fact that Thompson does not say anything lends the message even greater authenticity; the style of delivery imparts the feeling that an athlete drinking a Lucozade during training is a completely natural thing. There is the sense of something being reported rather than promoted: the explicit is made to appear implicit.

The immediate success of the repositioning's initial stage persuaded Beecham to push further. In 1987, Lucozade was sold in cans for the first time, and two additional flavours (orange and lemon) were introduced. This enabled the product to be stocked alongside other canned sodas, albeit still retaining a premium price. *Campaign* described the initiative as 'a further attempt by Beecham to revitalise its core brands through line extensions'. Like Beecham's other main consumer brands—such as Bovril, Ambrosia, and Macleans toothpaste—all advertising for Lucozade now featured the company name. The rebrand resulted in a considerable turnaround in its commercial fortunes. Between 1984 and

1989, annual UK sales of Lucozade tripled to almost £75 million (£192 million at 2018 values).[36]

In 1990, Leo Burnett employed an identical strategy for the launch of a further brand extension, Lucozade Sport. This new product was a non-carbonated derivative marketed as an 'Isotonic Sports Drink'. TV adverts featuring England footballer John Barnes helped to make Lucozade synonymous with football, a relationship that was underpinned by a heavy programme of sponsorship (see Figure 7.2).[37] Unlike Thompson in his advert, Barnes is required to explain the usage occasion ('After 90 minutes of sheer hell') what isotonic means ('It's in line with your body fluids') and the product benefit ('Gets to your thirst fast'), but otherwise offers no endorsement. The closing pack shot shows two on-screen messages. The first says, 'Take sport seriously' and is followed by 'The official sport drink of British athletics'. Once again the intimation is clear: Lucozade Sport is an essential tool for elite athletes. Within two years Beecham was spending as much on the promotion of Lucozade Sport as it was on the parent brand. In 1991, Lucozade Sport announced a

Figure 7.2. *Gets to your thirst fast*: stills from TV and cinema advertisement produced by Leo Burnett for Lucozade Sport, 1990. (Courtesy of Lucozade Ribena Suntory Ltd.) See also plates section.

---

[36] J. Dickens, 'Review-Advertising: The Ad as a Cultural Weapon/A Look at Advertisements which Have the Tide of Opinion', *Campaign*, 12 September 1996.

[37] G. Davies, 'Positioning, Image and the Marketing of Multiple Retailers', *International Review of Retail, Distribution and Consumer Research*, 2/1 (1992), 13–34.

partnership with Liverpool FC, and the following year it became the official drink of the newly launched FA Premier League, a position it continued to retain at the end of the century.[38]

In that context of corporate branding, the presence of Thompson and Barnes went beyond endorsement; they were an integral part of the product positioning and brand values, effectively becoming the human embodiment of Lucozade itself. Their presence also combined with the brand's heritage to provide the repositioning with credibility. If the audience understood that Lucozade could help ill people to recover their strength, then it was not too much of a stretch to accept, first of all, that it could provide well people with energy and, secondly, with the launch of Lucozade Sport, that the energy it provided could help to improve athletic performance. Furthermore, if a brand association can be made with its ambassador—ideally to the extent that he or she become the brand personified—then the product need not be featured at all. In the case of Lucozade, consumers continued to link Thompson with the brand long after he had ceased to appear in any advertisements.[39] In 1999, Klein argued that, where branded goods were concerned, image was often the biggest component that consumers were purchasing.[40] Brand associations did much more than remind consumers to get a Lucozade if they were thirsty; they also conveyed and reinforced the brand image. The value of Lucozade's brand image is brought into stark focus when one considers the product itself. Beneath all the branding and positioning, Lucozade was nothing more than a high-sugar fizzy drink—no different from Pepsi, Coke, Sprite, or Fanta. However, the sugar content of Lucozade is exceptionally high when compared to that of other fizzy drinks at 62g of sugar per 500ml versus Coca-Cola's 54g per 500ml.[41]

For companies wishing to establish brand associations, securing the endorsement of an appropriate brand ambassador was relatively straightforward. Celebrities could be engaged easily enough, whether for just a single

---

[38] *Smith Kline Beecham: History* <http://www.hatads.org.uk/catalogue/corporate-marketing/48/SmithKline-Beecham/>; H. Milton, 'New Product Development: War on the Supermarket Shelf: When a Pack must Earn its Pay', *Campaign*, 2 May 1996; J. Dickens, 'Review-Advertising: The Ad as a Cultural Weapon/A Look at Advertisements which Have the Tide of Opinion', *Campaign*, 12 September 1996; 'Beecham Plans Foray to Boost Corporate Profile', *Campaign*, 17 April 1987; 'New Campaigns: Lucozade Moves into Cans', *Campaign*, 17 July 1987; 'Special Report on Designa Packaging: Glass Warfare', *Marketing*, 14 May 1987; C. Edward, 'Blueprints for a New Consumer', *Campaign*, 11 September 1987; 'Lucozade Woos Barnes in £2m Drinks Launch', *Campaign*, 12 April 1990; P. Meller, 'Isostar Enters the Lucozade League', *Marketing*, 2 July 1992; Susannah Richmond, 'Client's Eye View: Lucozade Strategy Calls For a Broader Approach', *Campaign*, 10 January 1992.
[39] M. Toor, 'Brands Fail to Shake Ties with Celebrities: Consumers Link Celebrities with Brands for which They No Longer Star', *Marketing*, 2 August 1990.
[40] N. Klein, *No Logo* (London: Flamingo, 1999).
[41] D. Campbell, 'Liverpool in Drive to Name and Shame Fizzy Drink Brands', *Observer*, 7 May 2016.

event or appearance or contracted on a long-term basis over many years, to appear in advertising and other marketing collateral with responsibilities for public relations. Significantly more difficult—and much more expensive—was the process of making that celebrity synonymous with the product. Speaking to the *Guardian* in 1991, Grant Duncan, an account director at Collett Dickenson Pearce (CDP), highlighted the challenge: 'Personalities have to be used intelligently. The way not to use them is in the absence of an idea to give a product some kind of impact. The important thing is to ensure there's a direct relationship between what you're selling and the person you're using, or that the relationship is an intriguing one.'[42] Nike provided perhaps one of the clearest examples from the period of how such an intriguing relationship could work in practice. During the 1990s, Nike had a brand value of 'sporting excellence' that could quite obviously be aligned with the world's top sporting athletes, so it is not difficult to see how associations with those individuals could be of benefit to the brand. Indeed, to that end, NBA superstar Michael Jordan was paid $20 million in 1992 for lending his name to the organization and its products. His fee was greater than the total wages paid to all the women in East Asia working to create the Nike Jordan range of shoes and also the entire workforce of Nike contractors in Vietnam.[43] However, it would be incorrect to think that the consumers were not deriving value from the image of Michael Jordan as well as from the shoe. If wearing Air Jordans earned the wearer esteem from within his or her peer group, then this could often be reason enough alone for the purchase.

Once a celebrity had been engaged, there were a number of possible approaches, each of which went a long way beyond old-fashioned, celebrity endorsement.[44] In 1994, Gary Lineker, another former England footballer, began a brand partnership with Walkers Crisps.[45] In the early 1990s, Walkers was established as the leading brand in the sector, claiming to hold a 33.8 per cent share of the £735m UK crisp market—more than three times that of its nearest competitor—with an annual advertising spend of around £7 million per annum (around £15 million at 2018 values).[46] Like Lucozade, Walkers' barrier to future growth was demographic, as the core market for potato crisps at the time consisted of 8–12-year-old children, whose numbers were in decline. Market domination of a declining sector is still a decline, so

---

[42] 'Money, Morals and Advertising Stars: The New Cynicism of the Soft Sell on Television', *Guardian*, 21 February 1991, p. 23.

[43] T. B. Kazi, 'Superbrands, Globalization, and Neoliberalism: Exploring Causes and Consequences of the Nike Superbrand', *Inquiries Social Sciences, Arts & Humanities*, 3/12 (2011), 1.

[44] D. Rogers, 'Focus: Marketing Comms—the Faces behind the Brand Names', *PR Week*, 16 May 1997.

[45] C. Lafferty and G. Charles, 'Why Walkers and Lineker have a Marriage Made to Last, Plus 5 of Gary's Funniest Ads', *Marketing*, 25 February 2016.

[46] 'Things you didn't Know about . . . Walkers', *Marketing*, 2 July 1992.

the brand needed to draw in older consumers. The appointment of Lineker was the central component in a strategy to reach a broader audience. As brand manager Neil Campbell explained to *Marketing*, the initial rationale was explicitly to create a living epitome of the brand and its values: 'In focus groups, when asked for the personification of the brand, they often come up with the name Gary Lineker. Walkers are seen as universal, down to earth and of the people, and so is Lineker.' Lineker also happened to be Leicester City's most famous former player, which added value for the Leicester-based Walker's, but was not the driving force behind his recruitment.[47]

Lineker was paid £200,000 (£388,000 at 2018 values) to appear in 'No more Mr Nice Guy', the first in what was to become a series of comic adverts created by BMP.[48] The central idea was that Walkers Crisps were so good that not even all-round nice-guy Gary Lineker could resist stealing them from other people. Lineker played a cheekier, mischievous, and more childlike version of himself. In the launch commercial—part of a £10m campaign (£19 million at 2018 values)—he stole a bag from a small boy who had offered him a crisp, while a follow-up saw him writing his name on a cheque found by a nun in her bag of Walkers. As *Marketing* recognized at the time, it was 'no ordinary endorsement campaign. No ordinary use of a celebrity.'[49] It was the subversive use of a recognized personality, which attracted several complaints to the Independent Television Commission and Broadcasting Advertising Clearance Centre, none of which was upheld. This simple message proved remarkably durable, and the campaign was still running at the time of writing.

The strategy to develop Lineker as the brand personified extended beyond advertising. Twenty years earlier, a celebrity endorsement would have been just that—there would have been no attempt to integrate them with the product and the marketing. Endorsements in the 1970s often felt slightly awkward, as can be seen in the examples shown in Figure 7.3, which also involved two of the top UK footballers of the time, George Best and Kevin Keegan). Walkers also used Lineker's name on the pack. However, the specially created 'Salt & Lineker' flavour built on the fictional persona of the character in the advert rather than the 'real' personality, thereby strengthening the association between the brand and its ambassador. Lineker also became involved in the company's charity work and health messaging (see Figure 7.4).[50]

There was another considerable benefit to Walkers derived from making Lineker synonymous with its brand. It was also gaining effective exposure from Lineker's regular media appearances as well as from the actual advertisements,

[47] A. Benardy, 'Advertising: Lineker to Head Walkers' Attack', *Marketing*, 24 November 1994.
[48] S. Hatfield, 'The Highs and Lows of 1995', *Campaign*, 5 December 1995.
[49] A. Robertson, 'Why Walker Ads are on a Par with a Brummie Duck', *Marketing*, 6 April 1995.
[50] T. Mason, 'Walkers Snacks Ties to Comic Relief Campaign', *Marketing*, 12 September 2002.

Figure 7.3. Pack designs for George Best Potato Crisps, *c.*1971, and Kevin Keegan Crisps, *c.*1979. (Courtesy of Walkers Ltd and Headland PR Consultancy LLP.)

Figure 7.4. Pack design for Walkers Salt and Lineker Crisps, 1995. (Courtesy of Walkers Ltd and Headland PR Consultancy LLP.)

230

owing to the fact that, as Klein identified, consumers would still continue to associate Walkers with Lineker, regardless of whether or not the brand was present.[51] In June 1995, an independent survey carried out by The Planning Partnership on behalf of *Marketing* presented consumers with a list of celebrity names and asked which brands they advertised. In first place was Gary Lineker for Walkers, with a recall of 77 per cent. In terms of the bottom line, the relationship between Walkers and Lineker was a huge commercial success, with reported sales growing from 1.34 billion to 2.75 billion packs per annum (a 105 per cent increase) between 1995 and 2002.[52]

Corporate branding was a strategy that allowed companies to extend their reach into new channels and exploit the increasing number of opportunities for brand communication beyond advertising. Sponsorship could give credence to brand values and reinforce positioning, while brand ambassadors brought products to life by providing a human face and a mouthpiece for espousal of values. Public relations controlled media access to those celebrities, sometimes completely. Interviews were not given freely. Most magazines refused to pay for interviews directly, but the celebrities themselves were compensated for their involvement in media activity by their corporate sponsors. For those in high demand, speaking to the media could be turned from a tiresome chore into a lucrative activity. For example, in October 1997, during the run-up to the France '98 FIFA World Cup, Tony Stephens, marketing director of sports agency SFX Ltd, reported that, since the start of the current season, he had received approximately 380 requests for interviews with his client Alan Shearer, a leading English footballer.[53] However, without exception, all of the requests had been turned down, as Shearer's media appearances were wholly controlled by his seven corporate sponsors—Umbro, Lucozade, Braun, McDonalds, Jaguar, Gremlin Interactive, and Asda—all of whom had incorporated a level of public relations activity into their contract. Between July and December 1997, Shearer carried out the following interviews on behalf of Gremlin Interactive alone: *Maxim*, *Total Football*, *PC Zone*, *Shoot!*, *Sainsbury's Magazine*, and *Official PlayStation Magazine*.[54] For all parties involved, the brand fit was the key to success. In

[51] Klein, *No Logo*, 57–8.

[52] 'Lineker Defends Walkers Campaign', *BBC News*, <http://news.bbc.co.uk/1/hi/uk/3756601.stm>.

[53] Author's private archive: emails exchanged between Steve McKevitt (then Head of Communications at Gremlin Interactive), George Georgiou (then Product Manager, Actua Sports, Gremlin Interactive), and Anthony Stephens (then Managing Director, Tony Stephens Associates Limited: Alan Shearer's agent), between June 1997 and October 1997.

[54] 'The Markets, Gremlin Interactive', *Mail on Sunday*, 2 November 1997, <https://www.highbeam.com/doc/1G1-110771782.html>; J. Tyler, 'Umbro Cuts Stars Down to Size', *Campaign*, 27 August 1997; T. Hunt and J. E. Grunig, *Public Relations Techniques* (Fort Worth, TX, and London: Harcourt Brace, 1994); 'Braun for World Cup Campaign', *Marketing*, 3 April 1997; J. Van Leuvan, 'Public Relations and Marketing: An Overview', *Public Relations Review*, 17/3 (1991), 215–17; G. M. Broom, *Cutlip & Center's Effective Public Relations* (11th edn; Harlow: Pearson Education, 2012); M. Danny, W. Gary, and T. Louise, 'Tactical Publicity or Strategic Relationship Management?

terms of public relations, the objective was twofold: to raise awareness about the product (in Gremlin Interactive's case, its video game *Actua Soccer 2*), but also to make the celebrity synonymous with the brand. By carefully choosing the brands they would represent, celebrities could not only make money but could also enhance their own personal brand image. For example, the connection between the English football's marquee striker Shearer and the UK's prestige car marque Jaguar made perfect sense to the brand, the celebrity, and, most importantly of all, to the consumer.

Fletcher argued that consumers need advertising to let them know what products and services are on offer and to help them make choices. For him, it is a service that the public wants, likes, 'and unequivocally needs'.[55] However, like all forms of persuasion, advertising is not an impartial information service, so the counterargument must be made that, while it is true that consumers choose the brands they want, those choices are not usually independent and are typically influenced to a large extent by some form of persuasion. In their analysis of consumption trends in the UK between 1975 and 1999, Blow, Leicester and Oldfield concluded that prices and preferences had proven more important in accounting for expenditure patterns than changes in demographics and budgets. By 1997, UK household expenditure on leisure—holidays, entertainment, catering (takeaways and restaurant meals), and leisure goods—was higher than at any point in history (see Table 7.1).[56]

Tastes had changed. A number of academics attempted to explain the evolution of new male identities. Some, such as Segal and McDowell, focused on demographic factors resulting from the decline of manufacturing and the rise of the service economy, while for others the emphasis was social and cultural—for example, Nixon and Mort both focused on the role of the style press in consumer culture. Other than the broad agreement that masculinity and male identities had changed considerably since 1980, there was little consensus.[57] For business, the academic argument was of much less importance than what these 'changes' meant in commercial terms. In 2003, the media group Emap

An Exploratory Investigation of the Role of Public Relations in the UK Retail Sector', *European Journal of Marketing*, 30/12 (1996), 69–84; Alan Shearer interviews: T. Loxley, 'Shearer: Why England will Beat Italy', *Maxim* (November 1997); S. Hill, 'Oi! Shearer', *PC Zone*, 13 February 1998; S. McKevitt, 'Shearer—Who Will You Be Watching this July?', *Total Football* (February 1998); P. Hansford, 'Shearer Find out How *Shoot!* Made Super Al Giggle', *Shoot!*, 24 July 1997; R. Pegley, 'Shear Class!', *Official Playstation Magazine* (November 1997).

[55] W. Fletcher, *Powers of Persuasion: The Inside Story of British Advertising 1951–2000* (Oxford: Oxford University Press, 2008), 254–5.

[56] L. Blow, A. Leicester, and Z. Oldfield, *Consumption Trends in the UK, 1975–99* (London: Institute for Fiscal Studies, 2004).

[57] L. Segal, *Slow Motion: Changing Masculinities, Changing Men* (London: Virago, 1990); L. McDowell, *Redundant Masculinities?: Employment Change and White Working Class Youth* (Oxford: Blackwell, 2003); S. Nixon, *Hard Looks: Masculinities, Spectatorship and Contemporary Consumption* (London: University College London Press, 1996); F. Mort, *Cultures of Consumption: Masculinities and Social Space in Late Twentieth-Century Britain* (London: Routledge, 1996).

Table 7.1. Expenditure on various commodity groups, 1975 and 1999

Commodity group	1975		1999		
	Expenditure (£/week)	Expenditure share (%)	Expenditure £/week	Expenditure share (%)	% real expenditure increase
Food	18.29	24.6	17.81	14.8	−6.1
Private transport	6.42	8.6	12.96	11.1	+101.7
Purchase of motor vehicles	3.34	4.5	9.25	8.0	+176.9
Clothing	7.47	10.1	8.99	7.7	+20.3
Catering	3.08	4.1	7.54	6.5	+145.3
Leisure goods	3.74	5.0	7.22	6.2	+93.0
Household durables	5.86	7.9	7.00	6.0	+19.5
Holidays	1.60	2.2	5.92	5.1	+270.0
Alcohol	4.41	6.0	5.84	5.0	+32.4
Domestic fuel	4.66	6.2	4.88	4.2	+4.7
Entertainment	1.91	2.6	3.99	3.4	+108.9
Private health care	1.42	1.9	3.38	2.9	+138.0
Communications	0.85	1.1	3.09	2.7	+263.5
Tobacco	3.09	4.1	2.52	2.2	−18.4
Education	0.48	0.6	2.01	1.7	+318.8
Public transport	1.75	2.4	1.94	1.7	+10.9
Domestic services	0.90	1.2	1.46	1.3	+62.2
Miscellaneous	5.06	6.8	10.95	9.4	+116.4

Note: The expenditure shares are weighted to each household's share in total expenditure. Expenditure levels are the average real per capita figures.

Source: 'Family Expenditure Survey', Institute for Fiscal Studies, London, 2004.

undertook a study into the changing lifestyles and tastes of its listeners and readers.[58] The purpose of the research was to improve advertising effectiveness and provide a context for new product development. The study followed a 1995 survey about the 15–24 youth market, which highlighted the unprecedented consumer freedom and lifestyle choice that age group was enjoying. It identified a new group of over four million, high-spending 25–39-year-old consumers (47 per cent of the population in this age group), whose tastes were practically identical to those of the then current 15–24 age group. Growing up during the years of acid house parties and Brit pop, these 'super youths' had failed to temper either their interest in or spending upon popular music, video games, and fashion—which had previously been regarded as juvenile pursuits. Clubbing was still a regular activity for 53 per cent. The largest male segment of 'super youth' comprised the 1.2 million so-called black-collar workers who, Emap claimed, had 'reject(ed) mainstream fashions in favour of an

[58] C. Goff, 'How to Spot the Top 10 New Consumers', *Campaign*, 23 August 2005.

independent sense of "boutique" style that communicates individuality and cultivated personal taste' and were drawn to aspirational brands that shared their lifestyle values such as Diesel, Paul Smith, Audi, BMW, Apple, Sony Play-Station, and XBox.[59]

This chapter has looked in detail at the widespread adoption of corporate branding strategies. Together with the developments discussed in Chapter 6— namely, a shift in commercial attitudes towards engagement with male consumers and the emergence of a specialist consumer media targeting men— corporate branding produced a new pattern of consumption by providing an effective means of reaching male consumers through a range of emergent media channels. A market generally believed to be habituated to the hard sell during the 1970s was stimulated by brands that carved out a position for themselves and communicated in a manner that allowed—or at least appeared to allow—conclusions about their values to be drawn from inference. Given the proportion of content in the new channels that was orchestrated by commerce—not just through advertising but also through public relations— it appears very difficult to counter the argument that persuasion did exert a strong influence over the preferences of male consumers in Britain.

---

[59] J. Skidmore, 'Over-50s Demand Action Holidays', *Daily Telegraph*, 29 November 2003, <http://www.telegraph.co.uk/travel/729229/Over-50s-demand-action-holidays.html>; E. Hopkirk, 'Weekend Travel Boom for Super Youths', *Evening Standard*, 12 November 2003; J. Hunt, 'Super Youths', *Sunday Mail*, 29 September 2009; T. Templeton, 'Up Front Vital Statistics: From Star-Studded Teenyboppers to US Ethics in 21 Steps', *Observer Magazine*, 14 September 2003; H. Mead, 'Worn out but Staying Young', *Newsquest Regional Press—This is York*, 8 September 2003; A. Sherwin, 'Super Youths Blur the Years to Middle Age', *The Times*, 29 August 2003; C. Goulder, 'New Breed Partying into their 30s; Rise of the Super Youth', *Express*, 29 August 2003; P. Kotler and W. Mindak, 'Marketing and Public Relations: Should they Be Partners?', *Journal of Marketing*, 42/4 (1978), 13–20.

Conclusion

Cool Britannia and the Emotional Consumer

On 31 August 1997, HRH Diana Princess of Wales died as the result of injuries sustained in a car crash while travelling through a road tunnel in Paris. The extraordinary response of the British public to this event was a huge and virtually unprecedented outpouring of grief. On 6 September 1997, over one million mourners lined the route of the funeral cortege from Kensington Palace to Westminster Abbey. The UK television audience watching the event live was in the region of 31.5 million people.[1] By 10 September, the wreaths and floral tributes left by well-wishers outside Kensington Gardens were so deep—around 1.5 metres—that the bottom layer had started to compost. Outside town halls and public libraries across the country lengthy queues formed as people waited to sign books of condolences and leave gifts or mementos. This sentiment lasted well into the twenty-first century. In 2002, a BBC poll called *Great Britons* aimed to determine whom the British public considered to be the greatest people in the nation's 2,000-year history. Diana was ranked third behind only Winston Churchill and Isambard Kingdom Brunel.[2] In another poll commissioned the same year by the UK History Channel, Diana's death was ranked as the most important event of the previous 100 years.[3] By 2004, Diana's memorial fund had raised over £100 million through a combination of charitable donations and commercial activities, and, in the same year, 75,000 people visited her grave, which was located on

---

[1] *1997: Diana's funeral watched by millions*, <http://news.bbc.co.uk/onthisday/hi/dates/stories/september/6/newsid_2502000/2502307.stm>.

[2] P. Almond, 'Poll Queries British Sense of History', *United Press International, Washington*, 27 August 2007, <http://www.upi.com/Business_News/Security-Industry/2002/08/27/Poll-queries-British-sense-of-history/UPI-69441030476098/>.

[3] 'Rue Britannia: Diana's Death Tops Poll', *Washington Times*, 31 August 2002, <http://www.washingtontimes.com/news/2002/aug/31/20020831-041721-1985r/>.

an island in the middle of a lake within the grounds of her family's estate at Althorp, Northamptonshire.[4]

Many commentators regarded this response as evidence that British society had changed. For example, in his 1998 essay 'Faking It: The Sentimentalisation of Modern Society', philosopher Anthony O'Hear explored 'the march of the fraudulent through modern society' and viewed Diana's untimely death as a defining moment in the 'sentimentalisation of Britain'—a process within which 'mob grief . . . was personified and canonised and feeling exalted above reason, reality and restraint'. O'Hear also identified the main woes of British society as 'narcissistic, godless religion . . . [government policies] obsessed with spin, image and gesture rather than substance . . . crime, broken families, failing school standards, confusion about morality and manners', attributing them to the rise of sentimentality and the decline of rationalism, 'reason, reality and restraint'.[5] Others supported this view, but also looked for a cause. Sociologist Deborah Steinberg argued that the response was due to the emergence of a more liberal society and that, rather than hysteria about the death of a Royal Family member, the outpouring of grief was due to the fact that many British people associated Diana with wider societal changes that had occurred.[6] Theodore Dalrymple, a critic of socially liberal and permissive societies, took a different view, highlighting the role of the media in the manufacture of exaggerated spontaneous sentimentality 'that was necessary to turn the death of the princess into an event of such magnitude thus [serving] a political purpose, one that was inherently dishonest in a way that parallels the dishonesty that lies behind much sentimentality itself'.[7]

Regardless of their theoretical starting point, these commentators were united in their conclusion that the public's reaction to the death of Diana was an indication that society was becoming far more expressive and emotional. Few scholars viewed this as a positive development. As Wheen argued in his 2004 critique of cultural relativism, *How Mumbo Jumbo Conquered the World*, the values of the scientific method were being betrayed by 'an insistence on intellectual autonomy, a rejection of tradition and authority as the infallible sources of truth, a loathing for bigotry and persecution, a commitment to free inquiry, a belief that (in Francis Bacon's words) knowledge is indeed power'.[8]

---

[4] J. Freedland, 'A Moment of Madness?', *Guardian*, 13 August 2007, <https://www.theguardian.com/uk/2007/aug/13/britishidentity.monarchy>.

[5] A. O'Hear, 'Diana, Queen of Hearts: Sentimentality Personified and Canonised', in D. C. Anderson and P. Mullen (eds), *Faking it: The Sentimentalisation of Modern Society* (London: Penguin, 1998), 184.

[6] D. L. Steinberg and A. Kear, *Mourning Diana: Nation, Culture and the Performance of Grief* (London: Routledge, 2002).

[7] T. Dalrymple, *Spoilt Rotten: The Toxic Cult of Sentimentality* (London: Gibson Square, 2010), 154.

[8] F. Wheen, *How Mumbo Jumbo Conquered the World* (New York: Public Affairs, 2004), 5.

Four months prior to Diana's death, on 1 May 1997, the UK Labour Party, under the leadership of Tony Blair, ended its eighteen years in Opposition. It secured a landslide victory, a 10.2 per cent swing from the Conservative government, resulting in 418 seats—the most it had ever held in its entire history. Like Diana's death, Blair's New Labour was a totem for a society that had become more emotional, expressive, and individualistic. His 'third way', initially conceived as a serious re-evaluation of policies within progressive, centre-left movements, was in essence a synthesis of right-wing economics and left-wing social policies. The 'socialism' advocated by Blair's government was ethical rather than economic. It was argued that, as contemporary social democratic governments had achieved a viable, ethical position through the provision of social welfare and regulation of more unjust features of capitalism, then there was no longer a case for the abolition of capitalism, as originally identified by Marx. The government's objective was to ensure the provision of equal opportunities rather than economic equality. As Blair said himself: 'My kind of socialism is a set of values based around notions of social justice . . . Socialism as a rigid form of economic determinism has ended, and rightly.'[9]

New Labour purported to offer a better way to run a capitalist free market economy, one that was fairer in terms of opportunity and would hopefully result in greater social mobility, but a market economy that was focused on the individual rather than society nonetheless. Driven home through the adroit use of public relations, positioning, and branding, this broad message resonated with the sensibilities of British public, many of whom were happy to buy into the concept that society could somehow be changed for the better without any of those changes impinging upon the economic or social freedoms of the individual. The promise of more of everything good and less of everything bad did not seem too good to be true. In the period following the election, public optimism was at all-time high. Blair's approval rating of 75 per cent in September 1997 was the highest enjoyed by any prime minister since records began.[10] In truth, New Labour meant different things to different people. It was conceptual, nebulous, and vague, but also upbeat, optimistic, emotionally charged, and, most compellingly, 'something good'. The epithets of New Labour could be applied just as easily to a range of popular brands, artists, or ideas as they could to the government of the day; it was all 'Cool Britannia'.

This study has addressed two key questions that have gone hitherto unanswered—namely, the extent to which the persuasion industries were responsible for bringing these changes about and the role that they played.

---

[9] N. Ascherson, 'Is it Dead or Only Sleeping?', *Independent*, 21 September 1996, <http://www.independent.co.uk/voices/is-it-dead-or-only-sleeping-1364483.html>.

[10] *Political Monitor: Satisfaction Ratings 1997–Present*, <https://www.ipsos-mori.com/researchpublications/researcharchive/88/Political-Monitor-Satisfaction-Ratings-1997Present.aspx>.

To provide a coherent response first required a thorough understanding of the processes by which consumers were making decisions. By matching the changes in persuasion industries' methodologies, strategies, and tactics that were identified to those in the political, economic, and commercial outlook of the period, it has been possible to get closer to a fuller understanding of how these societal changes came about. This has involved an examination of how evolving working practices affected output and performance, through evidence provided in the persuasion industries' dedicated historical archives, specialist media, their output, and their impact in commercial terms.

In conclusion, it can be determined that the persuasion industries' impact on the consumer society in the UK during the late twentieth century was both significant and profound. Commentators have traditionally struggled to identify with precision the role that persuasion has played: whether it shapes culture or simply follows existing trends. It is vitally important to remember that persuasion is never operating in isolation, but always in concert: it is always a means to an end, never an end in itself. Advertising, branding, marketing, and public relations are all business functions, and the persuasion industry serves the aims and objectives of its clients. These goals—whether selling toys, changes perceptions, or winning elections—ultimately become its own: don't care was paid to care.

It is practically impossible to disentangle the horizontal function of persuasion from the vertical functions of a brand or business. Yet, despite this caveat, it is very difficult to conceive how the distinctive consumer society of the1990s— typified by brand-led, emotional, concept-based lifestyle choices—would have emerged if brand communication had remained wedded to the hackneyed tropes and spurious methodologies employed widely by the persuasion industries up until the late twentieth century. Broadly speaking, persuasion in the 1960s consisted of little more than advertising, occasionally with some basic public relations support. These campaigns were aimed predominantly at women (in the roles of either mother or housewife) and based on the notions of a product-based economy dominated by fast-moving consumer goods (FMCG), wherein rational consumers responded to rational appeals that highlighted unique product benefits.

The shortcomings in this approach became apparent during the early 1970s, as Britain's commercial sector lost confidence in advertising's ability to deliver a return on investment. The sector entered a slump as spending on advertising plummeted both as a proportion of GNP and in real terms. The persuasion industries were forced to respond. Initially the emergence of more engaging forms of advertising (the result of the so-called creative revolution), pioneered by a new breed of agency that looked to the practices of the best US shops for inspiration, helped to rekindle the interest of industry, and spending increased. A more rigorous theoretical approach, driven both by the sector's own burgeoning academic literature and by developments in associated fields such as psychological and human sciences as well as behavioural economics, resulted in the adoption of more effective marketing methodologies such as planning and positioning. In turn, these developments created opportunities for other forms of brand communication to flourish, most notably public relations and branding.

At the start of the 1980s, the UK persuasion industries were in much better shape. Creatively and commercially they were starting to dominate their American rivals for the first time in their history. The change of government in Britain and the USA at the start of the 1980s could not have proved timelier. At a point when the persuasion industries were arguably more effectively geared to supporting commerce than ever before, the prevailing political leadership was in perfect alignment with its aims and objectives. In Britain, the implementation of policies such as the privatization of former public utilities, the extension of homeownership, and the provision of freer access to consumer credit created a huge demand for brand communication services, causing the persuasion industries to expand rapidly. Further changes within the commercial sector, most notably the emergence of high-street multiples and supermarket chains, and globalization created further opportunities, as marketing was catapulted from its backwater in the sales department to the strategic forefront within many leading businesses.

Following the recession at the end of the 1980s, the persuasion industries continued to increase in terms of both size and influence. One important consequence was the emergence of numerous boutique specialists, who offered expertise in a single service—such as design, creative work, media buying, branding, public relations, and planning—rather than an all-inclusive 'full service'. In theory, this development allowed clients to shop around and pull together a bespoke 'best in class' team most suited to its needs. In practice, there was a considerable churn rate, as one significant consequence of the industry's explosive growth was an ongoing shortfall in the number of competent, appropriately trained practitioners. This was a particular problem for public relations, and one that the sector showed little sign of having solved by the end of the twentieth century. As a result, the reputation of public relations suffered more than other forms of persuasion. Despite (or perhaps because of) the rapid expansion, not every campaign by any means was empirically 'better' or 'more effective' than ever before. Consumers were also changing—better educated, better informed, less biddable—and there was still a great deal of ineffective marketing advertising, branding, and public relations being produced. Yet, conversely, at its best, persuasion in the 1990s was wider reaching, more pervasive, and ultimately more effective than ever before. Its impact was often also less ephemeral. The reach of persuasion now extended way beyond selling FMCG brands to housewives. As the country came out of recession in the early 1990s, the biggest advertisers were now retailers: the supermarkets and chain stores. The myriad of new consumer media channels was also bringing down the costs of marketing, enabling many forms of persuasion to become a viable, strategic option for smaller enterprises. More and more businesses considered their corporate brand image and product positioning for the first time and appointed advertising agencies and PR specialists to help them carve out or defend a market position.

Evidence for these developments can been seen particularly clearly through the changing relationship of the brands with male consumers throughout the period. Men were not ignored completely by UK advertisers during the 1960s (notably, the focus of much of the activity in the categories of tobacco and alcoholic beverages), but they were not part of the core audience in most of the principal categories such as household products and appliances, food, toiletries, and cosmetics, which accounted for 64 per cent of television advertising. However, over the ensuing decades there was an increasing effort to reach out and engage with male consumers. This culminated in the ultimately successful, proactive efforts of publishers and brands to create a truly mass-market male consumer media during the 1990s.

Despite its poor reputation in certain quarters, public relations proved to be one of the most effective means of delivering a compelling brand message. Owing to its comparative invisibility, public relations was often indistinguishable from independent editorial endorsement. Public relations also served the objectives of media outlets themselves by providing them with a free source of good quality, editorial content (the provenance of which could easily be hidden from the readers). At the end of the 1960s, brand communication was largely restricted to advertising and easy to identify as the content between television programmes on ITV or the articles in newspapers and magazines; it was the stuff on billboards, hoardings, and handouts circulated in towns and cities. By 1997, persuasion was everywhere. It had seeped into editorial content, permeated into sporting, musical, and other cultural events, and become ingrained in private life. What people wore, drank, and ate; where they went on holiday, got married, or even how they mourned the death of a public figure—these had all become viable channels for persuasion and vehicles for self-expression. Wherever there is human communication, there is also the opportunity to push a message.

This study has focused on the development of persuasion industries in the final decades of the twentieth century with a particular interest in the changing relationship between brands and male consumers during this period. This case study provided arguably one of the more vivid examples of the inculcation of persuasion and its impact on society, but there are other subjects worthy of further investigation.

For example, there is a great deal that could be said about how the persuasion industries targeted children during the period. Similar to men, children were a group largely ignored during the 1960s by all but the toy, hobby, and confectionary sectors. Television channels were under an obligation to provide children's programming but generally considered it to be a loss leader. By the 1990s, there had been a complete sea change in attitude, which was largely due to a greater understanding of children's role within the family and the influence they exerted across a range of purchases through so-called pester power.

For the UK public relations sector, the privatization of public utilities was undoubtedly a watershed and is certainly worthy of further investigation. The challenge of selling shares to millions of individuals who had no experience of the workings of the stock market was a task that public relations was well placed to address. Success required the kind of lengthy explanation that editorial coverage is good at delivering but that advertising is not.

Much could also be learned by looking in detail at the development of a single British brand across the period. For example, founded in 1969, Virgin is a company that has not only engaged extensively and successfully in persuasion, but has also encompassed a host of diverse activities—for example, music retailing, broadcasting, video games, soft drinks, telecommunications, transport, leisure, and space travel. Interestingly, all of its activities have been delivered under the same parent brand and retaining the same values.

The emergence of the World Wide Web during the late 1990s, and in particular the rapid assimilation of social media into everyday life during the early twenty-first-century, were also a game changer for the persuasion industries. Social media are a celebration of many of the themes explored in this study (for example, emotional appeals, the use of celebrity, and consumption as a form of self-expression), but they have also provided new areas to explore, such as the increase in experiential consumption, the use of digital photography as a form of self-expression and self-publishing, the storage of memories, and the impact of connectivity on privacy. Social media have also presented the persuasion industries with a complex suite of opportunities and challenges. Online, the twentieth-century advertising model of pushing a message to a mass audience effectively became inverted. So-called viral advertising worked in reverse, with content (containing the message) seeded initially to a relatively small audience in the hope that it would reach a large audience through a network of exchanges or 'shares'. The result is a snowball effect, in which more and more shares help the message to reach a huge audience quickly. Clearly such an approach places different demands upon those involved in content creation. The Web also lends itself well to the distribution of messages via public relations, although in many cases the intermediary is no longer the traditional 'professional journalist'.

However, the challenges presented to the persuasion industry by the emergence of digital media are at least as significant as the opportunities. Audiences have become increasingly fragmented, competition for attention is fierce, and dwell times on major news channels are much shorter than in their offline equivalents. The Web is also global and open source, which makes any form of regulation very difficult. At the same time, consumers have free access to technology that blocks advertising and filters out many things that they wish to ignore (and that advertisers wish that they did not). There may well be one billion users of Facebook, but that just means there are one billion different versions of Facebook, because each consumer is, in effect, the editor of his or her own media channel.

The persuasion industries are concerned primarily with the manufacture of consent and desire. Their role in the late twentieth century, a period of significant social and economic change, was undoubtedly significant. However, the value of existing studies of public relations and advertising have to date been limited by a lack of historical perspective. In many cases there has been a tendency to focus on the contribution and output of great men and women and either to ignore altogether or to be somewhat vague and anecdotal when it comes to the role and impact of brand communication. To provide an explanation, this study has explored the changes that took place within the persuasion industries from the late 1960s until the end of the twentieth century. It has established that the persuasion industries adopted different approaches and methodologies that enabled its output to become more nuanced, engaging, and widespread to the extent that it became part of the fabric of society. It has added to the existing historiography of late-twentieth-century consumer culture by showing that, through this process, commerce became much more ingrained within both society and forms of self-expression. Not only were the persuasion industries able to meet all the challenges they faced successfully; they positively thrived as a consequence.

Bibliography

(Note: All URLs were accessed 31 December 2017)

History of Advertising Trust Archive

Boase Massimi Powel (BMP), Advertising Agency, Account Files and Other Office Papers, 1986–2005
  Collett Dickenson Pearce & Partners, Advertising Agency, Account Files and Other Office Papers, 1960–2001
  Hovis, Corporate Brand, Advertising and Marketing Material, 1886–2000
  J. Walter Thompson (JWT), London, Advertising Agency Account Files and Other Office Papers, 1960–1973
  St Luke's (formerly Chiat/Day, London), Advertising Agency Account Files and Other Office Papers, 1989–2003

Trade Newspapers, Newspapers, Magazines, and Consumer Media

Author's Personal Archive
  Arena
  Crash
  Esquire
  FHM
  GQ
  Loaded
  Maxim
  Official PlayStation Magazine
  PC Zone
  Shoot!

British Library and History of Advertising Trust Reference Library

  Campaign (1969–1986)

Gale Cengage
  Daily Telegraph
  The Independent
  Independent on Sunday

Picture Post
The Times,
Sunday Times

Nexis UK
  Advertising Age
  Adweek
  Birmingham Post Marketing
  Campaign (1986–2016)
  Herald (Glasgow)
  Marketing Week
  Media Week
  Newsquest Regional Press—This is York Sunday Mail
  Press Gazette
  Science Journal
  Travel Trade Gazette UK & Ireland
  United Press International, Washington
  Washington Post
  Wilmington Morning Star

Online
  Daily Express <www.ukpressonline.co.uk>
  Daily Mail <www.britishnewspaperarchive.co.uk>
  Daily Mirror/Mirror <www.ukpressonline.co.uk>
  Evening Standard <www.britishnewspaperarchive.co.uk>
  The Economist <www.theeconomist.com>
  Guardian <www.theguardian.newspapers.com>
  Huffington Post <www.huffingtonpost.com>
  Mail on Sunday <www.britishnewspaperarchive.co.uk>
  New Scientist <www.newscientist.com>
  Observer <www.theguardian.newspapers.com>
  Sunday Express <www.ukpressonline.co.uk>
  Sunday Mirror <www.ukpressonline.co.uk>
  Time <www.content.time.com>
  Woman's Own <www.archiveshub.jisc.ac.uk>

ProQuest Information and Learning Ltd
  New York Times

References

The 1997 Labour Party Manifesto <http://www.politicsresources.net/area/uk/man/lab97.
    htm>.
Aaker, D. A., Managing Brand Equity: Capitalizing on the Value of a Brand Name
    (New York: Free Press; Toronto: Collier Macmillan Canada, 1991).

Aaker, D. A., 'The Value of Brand Equity', *Journal of Business Strategy*, 13/4 (1992), 27–32.

Aaker, D. A., *Instructor's Resource Guide to Accompany Strategic Market Management* (New York and Chichester: Wiley, 1992).

Aaker, D. A., *Building Strong Brands* (New York and London: Free Press, 1995).

Aaker, D. A., *Developing Business Strategies* (New York and Chichester: Wiley, 2001).

Aaker, D. A., *Strategic Marketing Management* (New York and Chichester: Wiley, 2001).

Aaker, D. A., *Brand Portfolio Strategy: Creating Relevance, Differentiation, Energy, Leverage, and Clarity* (London: Simon & Schuster, 2004).

Aaker, D. A., *Spanning Silos: The New CMO Imperative* (Boston, MA: Harvard Business School Press; London: McGraw-Hill [distributor], 2008).

Aaker, D. A., *Brand Relevance: Making Competitors Irrelevant* (San Francisco: Jossey-Bass; Chichester: John Wiley [distributor], 2011).

Aaker, D., and Biel, A. L., *Brand Equity and Advertising: Advertising's Role in Building Strong Brands* (London: Psychology Press, 1993).

Aaker, D. A., and Joachimsthaler, E., *Brand Leadership: Building Assets in the information Society* (New York: Free Press, 2000).

Aaker, D., and Keller, L., 'Consumer Evaluations of Brand Extensions', *Journal of Marketing*, 54/1 (1990), 27.

Aaker, J., 'Dimensions of Brand Personality', *Journal of Marketing Research*, 34/3 (1997), 347.

'An Abbreviated History of WPP', *wpp.com* (2016), <http://www.wpp.com/wpp/about/whoweare/history/>.

ABC Certificate Amiga Format, January–June 1992: 161,256 (London: Audit Bureau of Circulation, 1992).

ABC Certificate Crash, July–December 1986: 101,483 (London: Audit Bureau of Circulation, 1987).

ABC Certificate, The Face, January–June 1986: 98,208 (London: Audit Bureau of Circulation, 1986).

ABC Certificate, FHM, January–June 1994: 60,298 (London: Audit Bureau of Circulation, 1994).

ABC Certificate ZZAP!, July–December 1986: 82,933 (London: Audit Bureau of Circulation, 1987).

Abimbola, T. M. L., *Consumer Brand Equity: A Model for the Measurement, Analysis and Evaluation of Consumer Perceived Value* (Birmingham: University of Aston in Birmingham, 2003).

Acemoglu, D., and Scott, A., *Consumer Confidence and Rational Expectations: Are Agents' Beliefs Consistent with the Theory?* (London: LSE, Centre for Economic Performance, 1993).

Adams, F. U., *Conquest of the Tropics: The Story of the Creative Enterprises Conducted by the United Fruit Company* (New York: Arno Press, 1976).

Adams, J., *Tony Benn* (London: Macmillan, 1992).

Adams, J., *Tony Benn: A Biography* (London: Biteback, 2011).

Adaval, R., and Wyer, R. S., 'The Role of Narratives in Consumer Information Processing', *Journal of Consumer Psychology*, 7/3 (1998), 207–45.

Adorno, T. W., and Horkheimer, M., *Dialectic of Enlightenment* (1997; London: Verso, 1999).

Advertising Standards Authority 13th Annual Report 1975–1976 (London: Advertising Standards Authority, 1976).

Agarwal, M., and Rao, V., 'An Empirical Comparison of Consumer-Based Measures of Brand Equity', *Marketing Letters*, 7/3 (1996), 237–47.

Alcocer, C. F., *Bringing about Strategic Thinking into Small Mexican Organisations: A Systematic Approach* (Lancaster: University of Lancaster, 1991).

Al-Khalidi, A., *Menstruation in Material and Promotional Culture: The Commodification and Mediation of Female Sanitary Products in Britain 1880–1914* (Nottingham: Nottingham Trent University, 2000).

Almond, P., 'Poll Queries British Sense of History' *United Press International, Washington*, 27 August 2007.

American Oil Chemists Society, *Thinking Small in California* (Livermore, CA: AOCS, 2004).

Anderson, R. D., *British Universities: Past and Present* (London: Hambledon Continuum, 2006).

Anheier, H. K., Glasius, M., and Kaldor, M., *Global Civil Society 2001* (Oxford: Oxford University Press, 2001).

Anheier, H. K., Kaldor, M., and Glasius, M., *Global Civil Society 2004/5* (Oxford: Oxford University Press, 2004).

Anthony, S., *Stephen Tallents and the Development of Public Relations in Britain* (Oxford: Oxford University Press, 2008).

Anthony, S., *Public Relations and the Making of Modern Britain: Stephen Tallents and the Birth of a Progressive Media Profession* (Manchester: Manchester University Press, 2012).

Arfin, F. N., *Financial Public Relations: Lessons from the Corporate Leaders* (London: Financial Times, 1994).

Arnould, E., and Wallendorf, M., 'Market-Orientated Ethnography: Interpretation Building and Marketing Strategy Formulation', *Journal of Market Research*, 31 (1994), 484–504.

Aronczyk, M., and Powers, D., *Blowing up the Brand: Critical Perspectives on Promotional Culture* (New York: Peter Lang, 2010).

Art of our Time: The Saatchi Collection (New York: Lund Humphries in association with Rizzoli, 1984).

Art & Music: The Saatchi Gallery Magazine (London: Art & Music Publications, 2008).

ASH: Key Dates in the History of Anti-Tobacco Campaigning (2015), <http://www.ash.org.uk/files/documents/ASH_741.pdf>.

Ash, J., and Wilson, E., *Chic Thrills* (London: Pandora, 1992).

Bagwell, K., 'The Economic Analysis of Advertising', Discussion Paper No. 0506–01, Department of Economics, Columbia University, New York, 2005.

Bailey, R. A., 'An Exploration of the Meanings of Hotel Brand Equity', *Service Industries Journal*, 26/1 (2006), 15–38.

Balchin, P. N., and Rhoden, M., *Housing Policy: An Introduction* (London: Routledge, 2002).

Bangs, L., and Marcus, G., *Psychotic Reactions and Carburetor Dung* (London: Heinemann, 1988).

Barr, A., and York, P. P., *The Official Sloane Ranger Handbook: The First Guide to what Really Matters in Life* (London: Ebury, 1982).

Barrett-Lennard, G. T., 'The Empathy Cycle: Refinement of a Nuclear Concept', *Journal of Counseling Psychology*, 28/2 (1981), 91–100.

Bartels, R., *The History of Marketing Thought* (Columbus, OH: Publishing Horizons, 1988).

Baskin, M., and Pickton, D., 'Account Planning: From Genesis to Revelation', *Marketing Intelligence & Planning*, 21/7 (2003), 416–24.

Baudrillard, J., *Selected Writings*, ed. M. Poster (Cambridge: Polity, 2001).

Bauman, Z., *Intimations of Postmodernity* (London: Routledge, 1992).

Baumol, W. J., Blinder, A. S., and Swan, C., *Economics Principles and Policy* (New York: Harcourt Brace Jovanovich, 1979).

Becker, G., 'A Theory of the Allocation of Time', *Economic Journal*, 75/29 (1965), 493–517.

Beckett, A., *When the Lights Went out: Britain in the Seventies* (London: Faber, 2010).

Beckett, A., *Promised you a Miracle: UK80–82* (London: Allen Lane, 2015).

Bell, D., *The Cultural Contradictions of Capitalism* (New York: Basic Books, 1996).

Bell, T., *Right or Wrong: The Memoirs of Lord Bell* (London: Bloomsbury, 2014).

Benson, J., *Affluence and Authority: A Social History of Twentieth-Century Britain* (London: Hodder Arnold, 2005).

Benson, J. J., *The Rise of Consumer Society in Britain, 1880–1980* (London: Longman, 1994).

Benson, J. J., and Ugolini, L., *A Nation of Shopkeepers: Five Centuries of British Retailing* (London: I. B. Tauris, 2003).

Benson, S., 'The Department Store: A Social History', *Journal of American History*, 84 (1997), 674–5.

Bernays, E. L., *Crystallizing Public Opinion* (New York: Boni & Liveright, 1923).

Bernays, E. L., *Propaganda* (Port Washington and London: Kennikat Press, 1972).

Biel, A., 'Converting Image into Equity', in D. Aaker and A. Biel (eds), *Brand Equity and Advertising* (Hilldale, NJ: L. Erlbaum, 1993).

Binet, L., and Field, P., *Marketing in the Era of Accountability* (Henley on Thames: WARC, 2007).

Bingham, A., 'Monitoring the Popular Press: An Historical Perspective, History and Policy', in M. Temple (ed.), *The British Press* (Maidenhead: Open University Press, 2008).

Bingham, A., *Family Newspapers? Sex, Private Life, and the British Popular Press 1918–1978* (Oxford: Oxford University Press, 2009).

Black, C., *The PR Practitioner's Desktop Guide* (London: Thorogood, 2001).

Black, C., *The PR Professional's Handbook* (London: Kogan, 2014).

Bland, M., Theaker, A., and Wragg, D. W., *Effective Media Relations: How to Get Results* (London: Kogan Page, 2005).

Blasco, W. J., *Appetite for Change: How the Counterculture Took on the Food Industry* (New York: Cornell University Press, 2007).

Blow, L., Leicester, A., and Oldfield, Z., *Consumption Trends in the UK, 1975–99* (London: Institute for Fiscal Studies, 2004).

Blythman, J., *Shopped: The Shocking Power of British Supermarkets* (London: Harper Perennial, 2007).

Bobrow-Strain, A. B., *White Bread: A Social History of the Store-Bought Loaf* (Boston: Beacon Press, 2012).

Bocock, R., *Consumption* (London and New York: Routledge, 1993).

Bodansky, D., *Nuclear Energy: Principles, Practices, and Prospects* (New York and London: Springer, 2004).

Boller, B. O., 'Viewer Empathy in Response to Drama Ads: Development of the VEDA Scale', unpublished working paper number 402–489, Fogleman College of Business and Economics, Memphis State University, Memphis, TN, 1989.

Bonner, P., and Aston, L., *Independent Television in Britain: New Developments in Independent Television, 1981–92: Channel Four, TV–AM, Cable and Satellite* (Basingstoke: Palgrave MacMillan, 2003).

Bor, R., Miller, R., and Goldman, E., *Theory and Practice of HIV Counseling: A Systemic Approach* (London: Cassell, 1992).

Botan, C. H., and Hazleton, V., *Public Relations Theory* (London: L. Erlbaum, 1989).

Botan, C. H., and Hazleton, V., *Public Relations Theory II* (Mahwah, NJ, and London: L. Erlbaum, 2006).

Bourdieu, P., *Distinction: A Social Critique of the Judgement of Taste* (Cambridge, MA: Harvard University Press, 1984).

Bourdieu, P., 'The Forms of Capital', in J. Richardson (ed.), *Handbook of Theory and Research for the Sociology of Education* (New York: Greenwood, 1986), 241–58.

Bovill, D., *Patterns of Pay: Estimates from the Annual Survey of Hours and Earnings, UK, 1997 to 2013* (London: Office of National Statistics, 2014).

Brandis, R., *Economics: Principles and Policy* (Homewood, IL: Richard D. Irwin, 1963).

British Rate and Data Directory 1981 (London: Brad Group, 1980).

British Lifestyles 1996 (London: Mintel International Group, 1996).

Broom, G. M., *Cutlip & Center's Effective Public Relations* (11th edn; Harlow: Pearson Education, 2012).

Broom, G. M., and Dozier, D. M., 'Advancement for Public Relations Role Models', *Public Relations Review*, 12/1 (1986), 37–56.

Broom, G. M., and Dozier, D. M., *Using Research in Public Relations: Applications to Program Management* (London: Prentice-Hall, 1990).

Bruner, J. S., *Acts of Meaning* (Cambridge, MA, and London: Harvard University Press, 1990).

Buckingham, D., and Davies, H., *Children's Television in Britain: History, Discourse and Policy* (London: British Film Institute, 1999).

Burns, G., and Goldman, H., *Wisdom of the 90s* (London: Robson, 1992).

Burrows, P., 'Patronising Paternalism', *Oxford Economic Papers*, 45/4 (1993), 542–72.

Byron, M. S., 'The Marketing Value of Brand Extension', *Marketing Intelligence & Planning*, 9/7 (1991), 9–13.

Calder, N. (ed.), *The World in 1984 . . . The Complete New Scientist Series* (Harmondsworth: Penguin Books, 1965).

Callahan, F., 'Advertising Influences on Consumers', *Journal of Advertising Research*, 14/3 (1974), 45.

Callebaut, J., Hendrickx, H., and Janssens, M., *The Naked Consumer Today: Or an Overview of why Consumers Really Buy Things, and what this Means for Marketing* (Antwerp: Censydiam, 2002).

Campaign's Data Marketing Yearbook 1989/1990 (London: Haymarket, 1989).

Campaign's Data Marketing Yearbook 1990/1991 (London: Haymarket, 1990).

Campbell, C., 'The Romantic Ethic and the Spirit of Modern Consumerism', in D. Miller (ed.), *Acknowledging Consumption: A Review of New Studies* (London: Routledge, 1995), 96–126.

Campbell, J. Y., and Cochrane, J. H., *By Force of Habit: A Consumption-Based Explanation of Aggregate Stock Market Behavior* (1994; Cambridge, MA: National Bureau of Economic Research, 1995).

Cannon, G., *Food and Health: The Experts Agree. An Analysis of One Hundred Authoritative Scientific Reports on Food, Nutrition and Public Health Published throughout the World in Thirty Years, between 1961 and 1991* (London: Consumers' Association, 1992).

Carmichael, C. W., Botan, C. H., and Hawkins, R., *Human Communication and the Aging Process* (Prospect Heights, IL: Waveland Press, 1988).

Carmichael, S. W., *Moon Men Return: USS Hornet and the Recovery of the Apollo 11 Astronauts* (Annapolis, MD: Naval Institute Press, 2010).

Carrell, B., Newsom, D., and Newsom, D. P., *Public Relations Writing, Form and Style* (4th edn; Belmont, CA, and London: Wadsworth, 1995).

Carrera, S., and Beaumont, J., *Income and Wealth* (London: Office of National Statistics, 2010).

Carrington, C., *The British Overseas: Exploits of a Nation of Shopkeepers* (Cambridge: Cambridge University Press, 1950).

Carter J., 'Crisis of Confidence', *pbs.org* (1979), <http://www.pbs.org/wgbh/amer icanexperience/features/primary-resources/carter-crisis/>.

Carter, S., *John Webster: The Earth Person's Adman* (London: adam&eveDDB, 2014).

Casey, T., *The Social Context of Economic Change in Britain: Between Policy and Performance* (Manchester: Manchester University Press, 2008).

Caslin-Bell, S., *The 'Gateway to Adventure': Women, Urban Space and Moral Purity in Liverpool, c.1908–c.1957* (Manchester: University of Manchester Press, 2013).

Castle, A., Harlan, J., and Kubrick, C., *The Stanley Kubrick Archives* (Cologne and London: Taschen, 2005).

Cateforis, T., *Are We not New Wave?: Modern Pop at the Turn of the 1980s* (Ann Arbor: University of Michigan Press, 2011).

Cateforis, T.E., *The Rock History Reader* (New York and London: Routledge, 2013).

A Century of Home Ownership and Renting in England and Wales (London: Office of National Statistics, 2013).

Chamberlin, E. H., *The Theory of Monopolistic Competition: A Re-Orientation of the Theory of Value* (Cambridge, MA: Harvard University Press, 1962).

Chen, K. F., and Lui, C. M., 'Positive Brand Extension Trial and Choice of Parent Brand', *Journal of Product and Brand Management*, 13/1 (2004), 25–36.

Cherfas, J., *Darwin up to Date* (1982; London: IPC Magazines, 1983).

Cheng, T., Brisson, H., and Hay, M., *The Role of Content in the Consumer Decision Making Process* (New York: Neilsen, 2014).

Choi, Y., and Thorson, E., *Memory for Factual, Emotional, and Balanced Ads under Two Instructional Sets: Proceedings of the American Academy of Advertising Annual Conference 1983* (New York: American Academy of Advertising, 1983).

Chomsky, N., *Necessary Illusions: Thought Control in Democratic Societies* (London: Pluto, 1989).

Chomsky, N., *Letters from Lexington: Reflections on Propaganda* (Monroe, ME: Common Courage Press, 1993).

Chomsky, N., *The State–Corporate Complex: A Threat to Freedom and Survival* (Toronto: University of Toronto Press, 2011).

Chomsky, N., *Power and Terror: Conflict, Hegemony, and the Rule of Force* (London: Pluto, 2011).

Chomsky, N., *Hopes and Prospects* (London: Penguin, 2011).

Chomsky, N., Barsamian, D., and Naiman, A., *How the World Works* (London: Hamish Hamilton, 2012).

Chomsky, N., Foucault, M., and Elders, F., *Human Nature: Justice vs Power: The Chomsky–Foucault Debate* (London: Souvenir Press, 2011).

Claire, S., 'Applying Account Planning to Public Relations', *Journal of Communication Management*, 4/1 (1999), 95–105.

Cohen, J., and Easterly, W., *What Works in Development?: Thinking Big and Thinking Small* (Washington: Brookings Institution Press, 2009).

Collect: The International Art Fair for Contemporary Objects (London: Crafts Council, 2010).

Collins, A., *Heaven Knows I'm Miserable Now: My Difficult 80s* (London: Ebury, 2005).

Collins, M., *Modern Love* (2001; London: Atlantic, 2004).

Colour Television in Britain (Bradford: National Media Museum, 2011).

Conekin, B., Mort, F., and Waters, C., *Moments of Modernity: Reconstructing Britain: 1945–1964* (London: Rivers Oram, 1999).

Conservative Manifesto 1979, <http://www.politicsresources.net/area/uk/man.htm>.

Corey-Wright N., *I Love 1986* (London: BBC, 2006).

Cornwall, A., Harrison, E., and Whitehead, A., *Gender Myths and Feminist Fables: The Struggle for Interpretive Power in Gender and Development* (Oxford: Blackwell, 2008).

Costanzo, P., and Goodnight, J., 'Celebrity Endorsements: Matching Celebrity and Endorsed Brand in Magazine Advertisements', *Journal of Promotion Management*, 11/4 (2006), 49–62.

Cox, H., and Mowatt, S., *Revolutions from Grub Street: A History of Magazine Publishing in Britain* (Oxford: Oxford University Press, 2015).

Crafts, N. F. R., Gazeley, I., and Newell, A., *Work and Pay in Twentieth-Century Britain* (Oxford: Oxford University Press, 2007).

Crisford, J. N., *Public Relations Advances* (London: Business Books, 1964).

Cross, G. S., *Time and Money: The Making of Consumer Modernity* (London: Routledge, 1993).

Crossman, R. H. S., *The Crossman Diaries: Selections from the Diaries of a Cabinet Minister, 1964–1970* (London: Mandarin, 1991).

Cutlip, S. M., Center, A. H., and Broom, G. M., *Effective Public Relations* (London: Prentice Hall, 2006).

D'Souza, S., *What is Account Planning?* (London: Royal Society of Account Planning, 1986).

Dalrymple, T., *Spoilt Rotten: The Toxic Cult of Sentimentality* (London: Gibson Square, 2010).

Damasio, A. R., *Descartes' Error: Emotion, Reason, and the Human Brain* (New York: G. P. Putnam, 1994).

Danny, M., Gary, W., and Louise, T., 'Tactical Publicity or Strategic Relationship Management? An Exploratory Investigation of the Role of Public Relations in the UK Retail Sector', *European Journal of Marketing*, 30/12 (1996), 69–84.

Daunton, M. J., Hilton, M., and Daunton, M., *The Politics of Consumption: Material Culture and Citizenship in Europe and America* (Oxford: Berg, 2001).

David, A. A., 'The Value of Brand Equity', *Journal of Business Strategy*, 13/4 (1992), 27–32.

Davies, G., 'Positioning, Image and the Marketing of Multiple Retailers', *International Review of Retail, Distribution and Consumer Research*, 2/1 (1992), 13–34.

Davies, K., Gilligan, C., and Sutton, C., 'Structural Changes in Grocery Retailing: The Implications for Competition', *International Journal of Physical Distribution and Materials Management*, 15/2 (1985), 3.

Davies, N., *Flat Earth News* (Rearsby: W. F. Howes, 2009).

Davis, A., *Promotional Cultures: The Rise and Spread of Advertising, Public Relations, Marketing and Branding* (Cambridge: Polity, 2013).

Davis, H. L., and Silk, A. J., *Behavioral and Management Science in Marketing* (New York: J. Wiley, 1978).

Davis, M. H., 'The Effects of Dispositional Empathy on Emotional Reactions and Helping: A Multidimensional Approach', *Journal of Personality*, 51/2 (1983), 167–84.

Day, J., Reynolds, P., and Lancaster, G., *Understanding the Relationship between the Small and Medium Sized Enterprises (SMEs), Their Advisers and Counsellors: An Application of the Divergent/Convergent Paradox in Respective Thinking Patterns* (London: University of North London, Business School, 2001).

De Certeau, M., *The Practice of Everyday Life* (Berkeley and Los Angeles: University of California Press, 1984).

De Graaf, J., *Affluenza: The All-Consuming Epidemic* (San Francisco: Berrett-Koehler, 2005).

De Groot, J., *Consuming History: Historians and Heritage in Contemporary Popular Culture* (London: Routledge, 2009).

Deem, R., *All Work and No Play? A Study of Women and Leisure* (Milton Keynes: Open University Press, 1986).

Delaney, S., *Get Smashed: The Story of the Men who Made the Adverts that Changed our Lives* (London: Sceptre, 2007).

Delaney, S., *Mad Men & Bad Men: When British Politics Met Advertising* (London: Faber and Faber, 2016).

Delphy, C., and Leonard, D., *Close to Home: A Materialist Analysis of Women's Oppression* (London: Hutchinson, in association with the Explorations in Feminism Collective, 1984).

Demaris, R., 'Positioning: The Battle for your Mind (Book Review)', *Journal of Marketing*, 56/1 (1992), 122–5.

Denman, J., and McDonald, P., *Unemployment Statistics from 1881 to the Present Day* (London: Office of National Statistics, 1996).

Deregulation: Cutting Red Tape (London: Department of Trade and Industry, 1994).

Devlin, M., *Measuring Sponsorship Effectiveness: Examining the Connection between Fan Identification and Physiological Response to Sports Sponsorship Evaluation after Exposure* (Birmingham, AL: University of Alabama Press, 2013).

Dilenschneider, R. L., 'Marketing Communications in the Post-Advertising Era', *Public Relations Review*, 17/3 (1991), 227–36.

A Discussion Paper on Proposals for Nutritional Guidelines for Health Education in Britain (London: National Advisory Committee on Nutritional Education (NACNE), 1983).

Donoghue, T., and Rabin, M., 'Studying Optimal Paternalism, Illustrated by a Model of Sin Taxes', *American Economic Review*, 93/2 (2003), 186–91.

Douglas, M., and Isherwood, B., *The World of Goods: Towards an Anthropology of Consumption* (London: Allen Lane, 1979).

Doyle, P., 'Building Successful Brands: The Strategic Options', *Journal of Consumer Marketing*, 7/2 (1990), 5–20.

Dozier, D. M., Grunig, L. A., and Grunig, J. E., *Manager's Guide to Excellence in Public Relations and Communication Management* (Mahwah, NJ, and Hove: L Erlbaum, 1995).

Eagleton, T., *Ideology* (London: Longman, 1994).

Earle, J. S., and Telegdy, A. I., *Ownership and Wages: Estimating Public–Private and Foreign–Domestic Differentials Using LEED from Hungary, 1986–2003* (London: National Bureau of Economic, Regeneration, 2007).

EC Directive on Working Time, No. 93/104/EC (1993), <http://eur-lex.europa.eu/legal-content/EN/TXT/?uri=CELEX%3A31993L0104>.

Edwards, A., *Early Reagan: The Rise of an American Hero* (London: Hodder & Stoughton, 1987).

Edwards, W., Weiss, J. W., and Weiss, D. J., *A Science of Decision Making: The Legacy of Ward Edwards* (Oxford: Oxford University Press, 2009).

'EEC Council Television without Frontiers Directive', *Official Journal of the European Communities*, 298/23 (1989).

Einhorn, B., Kaldor, M., and Kavan, Z., *Citizenship and Democratic Control in Contemporary Europe* (Cheltenham: E. Elgar, 1996).

Ekant, V., Ilda, B., and Brett, A. S. M., 'If Kate Voted Conservative, Would You? The Role of Celebrity Endorsements in Political Party Advertising', *European Journal of Marketing*, 44/3–4 (2010), 436–50.

Ekman, P., *Emotions Revealed: Understanding Faces and Feelings* (London: Weidenfeld & Nicolson, 2003).

Eldridge, S. A., *Interloper Media: Journalism's Reactions to the Rise of WikiLeaks* (Sheffield: University of Sheffield, 2014).

Elliott, R., Filipovich, H., Harrigan, L., Gaynor, J., Reimschuessel, C., and Zapadka, J. K., 'Measuring Response Empathy: The Development of a Multicomponent Rating Scale', *Journal of Counseling Psychology*, 29/4 (1982), 379–87.

Elms, R., *In Search of the Crack* (London: Viking, 1988).

Elms, R., *The Way we Wore: A Life in Threads* (London: Picador, 2006).

Eltis, W. A., and Sinclair, P. J. N., *Keynes and Economic Policy: The Relevance of the General Theory after Fifty Years: Conference: Papers* (Basingstoke: Macmillan, 1988).

Employment and Training Act 1981, <http://www.legislation.gov.uk/ukpga/1981/57/contents>.

Environment Today: A Collection of Articles from New Scientist (London: Reed International, 1972).

Escalas, Jennifer E., and Stern, B., 'Sympathy and Empathy: Emotional Responses to Advertising Dramas', *Journal of Consumer Research*, 29/4 (2003), 566–78.

Evans, B., *Thatcherism and British Politics, 1975–1997* (Stroud: Sutton, 1999).

Evans, B., and Lawson, A., *A Nation of Shopkeepers* (London: Plexus, 1981).

Evans, E. J., *Thatcher and Thatcherism* (London and New York: Routledge, 2004).

Evans, R. B., *Production and Creativity in Advertising* (London: Pitman, 1988).

Eves, H., and Newsom, C. V., *An Introduction to the Foundations and Fundamental Concepts of Mathematics* (New York: Holt, Rinehart & Winston, 1965).

Ewen, S., *Captains of Consciousness: Advertising and the Social Roots of the Consumer Culture* (1976; London: Basic Books, 2001).

Fallon, I., *The Brothers: The Rise & Rise of Saatchi & Saatchi* (London: Hutchinson, 1988).

Farquhar, P. H., 'Managing Brand Equity', *Journal of Advertising Research*, 30/4 (1989), 7–12.

Featherstone, M., *Consumer Culture and Postmodernism* (London: Sage, 1991).

Fedorov-Davydov, G. A., Dvornichenko, V. V., and Davis-Kimball, J., *The Silk Road and the Cities of the Golden Horde* (Berkeley, CA: Zinat Press, 2001).

Fendley, A., *Commercial Break: The Inside Story of Saatchi & Saatchi* (London: Hamish Hamilton, 1995).

Fernandez-Corugedo, E., and Muellbauer, J., *Consumer Credit Conditions in the United Kingdom* (London: Bank of England, 2006).

Field, I. T., *The Moors Murders: The Media, Cultural Representations of Ian Brady, Myra Hindley, and the English Landscape, c.1965–1967* (Manchester: University of Manchester Press, 2016).

Financial Services Act 1986, <http://www.legislation.gov.uk/ukpga/1986/60/contents>.

Fine, B., 'Addressing the Consumer', in F. Trentmann (ed.), *The Making of the Consumer: Knowledge, Power and Identity in the Modern World* (6th edn; Oxford: Berg, 2006).

Fine, B., Heasman, M., and Wright, J., *Consumption in the Age of Affluence: The World of Food* (New York and London: Routledge, 1996).

Fisher, T., 'The Sixties: A Cultural Revolution in Britain', *Contemporary Record*, 3 (1989), 22–3.

Fiske, J., 'The Cultural Economy of Fandom', in L. A. Lewis (ed.), *The Adoring Audience: Fan Culture and Popular Media* (London: Routledge, 1992).

Fletcher, W., *Creative People* (London: Business Books, 1990).

Fletcher, W., *Powers of Persuasion: The Inside Story of British Advertising 1951–2000* (Oxford: Oxford University Press, 2008).

Fletcher, W., *Advertising: A Very Short Introduction* (Oxford: Oxford University Press, 2010).

Floud, R., and Johnson, P., *The Cambridge Economic History of Modern Britain*, iii. *Structural Change and Growth, 1939–2000* (Cambridge: Cambridge University Press, 2003).

Foreman-Peck, J., and Millward, R., *Public and Private Ownership of British Industry 1820–1990* (Oxford: Clarendon Press, 1994).

Foresight, *The (R)etail (R)evolution: From a Nation of Shopkeepers to a World of Opportunities* (London: UK Technology Foresight Programme, Retail and Consumer Services Panel, 2000).

Fournier, S., 'Consumers and their Brands: Developing Relationship Theory in Consumer Research', *Journal of Consumer Research*, 24/4 (1998), 343–53.

Fowler, C., *A Nation of Shopkeepers?: Retail Developments in Eighteenth Century England* (Portsmouth: University of Portsmouth, Department of Economics, 1997).

Foy, P., and Pommerening, D., 'Brand Marketing: Fresh Thinking Is Needed', *Management Review*, 68/11 (1979), 20.

Francis, M., 'A Crusade to Enfranchise the Many: Thatcherism and the "Property-Owning Democracy"', *Twentieth Century British History*, 23/2 (2012), 275–97.

Frank, T. *The Conquest of Cool: Business Culture, Counterculture, and the Rise of Hip Consumerism* (Chicago: University of Chicago Press, 1997).

Frey, L. R., Botan, C. H., and Kreps, G. L., *Investigating Communication: An Introduction to Research Methods* (Boston and London: Allyn and Bacon, 2000).

Friedan, B., *Feminine Mystique: 10th Anniversary Edition* (New York: Norton, 1973).

Friedan, B., and O'Farrell, B., *Beyond Gender: The New Politics of Work and Family* (Washington: Woodrow Wilson Center Press, 1997).

Fyfe, S., Williams, C., Mason, O. J., and Pickup, G. J., 'Apophenia, Theory of Mind and Schizotype: Perceiving Meaning and Intentionality in Randomness', *Cortex*, 44/10 (2008), 1316–25.

Gabriel, Y., and Lang, T., *The Unmanageable Consumer: Contemporary Consumption and its Fragmentation* (London: Sage, 1995).

Galbraith, J. K., *The Affluent Society* (London: Penguin, 1999).

Galbraith, J. K., *The Economics of Innocent Fraud: Truth for our Time* (Boston: Houghton Mifflin, 2004).

Gamble, A., *The Free Economy and the Strong State: The Politics of Thatcherism* (Basingstoke: Macmillan Education, 1988).

Gamble, A., *Britain in Decline: Economic Policy, Political Strategy and the British State* (Basingstoke: Macmillan, 1994).

Gamble, A., 'The Thatcher Myth', *British Politics*, 10/1 (2015), 3–15.

Gardner, C., and Sheppard, J., *Consuming Passion: The Rise of Retail Culture* (London: Routledge, 1989).

The Gentle Computer (London: Harrison Raison & Co, 1966).

Gershuny, J. I., *Changing Times: Work and Leisure in Postindustrial Society* (Oxford: Oxford University Press, 2000).

Geuens, M., and Pelsmacker, P., 'Feelings Evoked by Warm, Erotic, Humorous or Non-Emotional Print Advertisements for Alcoholic Beverages', *Academy of Marketing Science Review*, 1 (1998).

Glickman, L. B., *Consumer Society in American History: A Reader* (Ithaca, NY, and London: Cornell University Press, 1999).

Golden, L., and Johnson, K. A., 'The Impact of Sensory Preferences and Thinking versus Feelings Appeals on Advertising Effectiveness', in R. P. Bagozzi and A. M. Tybout (eds), *Advances in Consumer Research* (Ann Arbor: Association of Consumer Research, 1983), 203–8.

Goldman, R. L., *Reading Ads Socially* (London: Routledge, 1992).

Goldman, R., and Papson, S., 'Advertising in the Age of Hypersignification', *Theory, Culture and Society*, 11/3 (1994), 23–54.

Goldman, R., and Papson, S., *Nike Culture: The Sign of the Swoosh* (London: Sage, 1998).

The Goldman Sachs Foreign Exchange Handbook (London: Euromoney Publications in association with Goldman Sachs, 1992).

Goodman, D. J., and Cohen, M., *Consumer Culture: A Reference Handbook* (Santa Barbara, CA, and Oxford: ABC-CLIO, 2004).

Goodman, P. P. D., *Growing Up Absurd: Problems of Youth in the Organized System* (London: Victor Gollancz, 1961).

Gore, A., *Earth in the Balance: Forging a New Common Purpose* (London: Earthscan Publications, 1992).

Gorn, G., 'The Effects of Music in Advertising on Choice Behavior: A Classical Conditioning Approach', *Journal of Marketing*, 46/1 (1982), 94.

Grant, B. K., *Shadows of Doubt: Negotiations of Masculinity in American Genre Films* (Detroit, MI: Wayne State University Press, 2011).

Gratz, R. B., *The Living City: How America's Cities Are Being Revitalized by Thinking Small in a Big Way* (Washington: Preservation Press, 1994).

Gray, P. J., 'Desktop Publishing', *Evaluation Practice*, 7/3 (1986), 40–9.

Green, E. H. H., *Thatcher* (London: Hodder Arnold, 2006).

Greer, K. R. C., *Thinking Networks: The Large and Small of It: Autonomic and Reasoning Processes for Information Networks* (Belfast: Kieran Greer, 2009).

Gregory, A., *Planning and Managing Public Relations Campaigns: A Strategic Approach* (London: Kogan Page, 2010).

Grüne-Yanoff, T., 'Paradoxes of Rational Choice Theory', in S. Roeser, R. Hillerbrand, P. Sandin, and M. Peterson (eds), *Handbook of Risk Theory: Epistemology, Decision Theory, Ethics, and Social Implications of Risk* (Dordrecht and London: Springer, 2012).

Grunig, J. E., 'Symmetrical Presuppositions as a Framework for Public Relations Theory', in C. H. Botan and V. J. Hazelton (eds), *Public Relations Theory* (Hillsdale, NJ: L. Erlbaum, 1989), 17–44.

Grunig, J. E., 'Public Relations Research: A Legacy of Scott Cutlip', *Public Relations Review*, 17/4 (1991), 357–76.

Grunig, J. E., *Excellence in Public Relations and Communication Management* (Hilldale, NJ: L. Erlbaum, 1992).

Grunig, J. E., 'Collectivism, Collaboration and Societal Corporatism as Core Professional Values in Public Relations', *Journal of Public Relations Research*, 12/1 (2000), 23–48.

Grunig, J. E., Grunig, L.A., and Toth, E. L., *The Future of Excellence in Public Relations and Communication Management: Challenges for the Next Generation* (Mahwah, NJ: Lawrence Erlbaum; London: Eurospan [distributor], 2007).

Grunig, J. E., and Hunt, T., *Managing Public Relations* (New York and London: Holt, Rinehart and Winston, 1984).

Gurney, P., *Co-Operative Culture and the Politics of Consumption in England, 1870–1930* (Manchester: Manchester University Press, 1996).

Gurney, P., 'The Battle of the Consumer in Post-War Britain', *Journal of Modern History*, 77/4 (2005), 956–87.

Guthrie, S., *Faces in the Clouds: A New Theory of Religion* (Oxford: Oxford University Press, 1993).

Guru: Theodore Levitt, <http://www.economist.com/node/13167376>.

Habberstad, H., *Anatomy of Account Planning* (London: Royal Society of Account Planning, 2000).

Haley, R. I., and Baldinger, A. L., 'The ARF Copy Research Validity Project', *Journal of Advertising Research*, 40/6 (2000), 114–35.

Hall, R. E., *The Rational Consumer: Theory and Evidence* (Cambridge, MA: MIT Press, 1990).

Hallett, G., 'Market Overview in Desktop Publishing', *Data Processing*, 28/9 (1986), 488–92.

Hamilton, J., *Thomas Cook: The Holiday Maker* (Stroud: The History Press, 2005).

Hammond, N., *How to Solve the Cube in 37 Seconds* (Derby: Blackhall, 1981).

Hantula, D. A., and Wells, V. K., *Consumer Behavior Analysis: (A) Rational Approach to Consumer Choice* (London: Routledge, 2013).

Harari, Y. N., *Sapiens: A Brief History of Humankind* (London: Vintage, 2015).

Harrison, S., *Napoleon's Nation of Shopkeepers, or Notes on a Border Family: The Pulestons of Wem, Clive, Wrexham, Rhosymedre, Cockshutt, Rhuabon, Lee Brockhurst and English Frankton* (London: S. Harrison, 1989).

Hatton, R., and Walker, J. A., *Supercollector: A Critique of Charles Saatchi* (Esher: Institute of Artology, 2010).

Haygood, D. M., 'Hard Sell or Soft Sell? The Advertising Philosophies and Professional Relationship of Rosser Reeves and David Ogilvy', *American Journalism*, 33/2 (2016), 169–88.

Haynes, J., and Newsom, D., *Public Relations Writing: Form and Style* (Boston: Wadsworth, 2011).

Heath, R., 'How the Best Advertisements Work', *AdMap*, 27 (2002).

Heath, R., 'Emotional Engagement: How Television Builds Big Brands at Low Attention', *Journal of Advertising Research*, 49/1 (2009), 62–73.

Heath, R., 'Creativity in Television Advertisements does not Increase Attention', *AdMap*, 512 (January 2010), 26–8.

Heath, R., Brandt, D., and Nairn, A., 'Brand Relationships: Strengthened by Emotion, Weakened by Attention', *Journal of Advertising Research*, 46/4 (2006), 410–19.

Heath, R., and Feldwick, P., '50 Years of Using the Wrong Model of Television Advertising', *AdMap*, 481 (March 2007), 36–8.

Heath, R. G., Nairn, A. C., and Bottomley, P. A., 'How Effective Is Creativity? Emotive Content in TV Advertising does not Increase Attention', *Journal of Advertising Research*, 49/4 (2009), 450–63.

Hebdige, D., *Subculture: The Meaning of Style* (1979; London: Routledge, 1988).

Hegarty, J., *Hegarty on Advertising: Turning Intelligence into Magic* (London: Thames & Hudson, 2011).

Heinberg, R., *The End of Growth: Adapting to our New Economic Reality* (Gabriola, BC: New Society, 2011).

Henry, B., *British Television Advertising: The First 30 Years* (London: Century Benham, 1986).

Herman, E. S., *Manufacturing Consent: The Political Economy of the Mass Media* (London: Bodley Head, 2008).

Hewison, R., *The Heritage Industry: Britain in a Climate of Decline* (London: Methuen, 1987).

Hill, J., *'What Shall We Do With Them When They're Not Working?': Leisure and Historians in Britain* (Manchester: Manchester University Press, 2012).

Hilton, M., 'The Fable of the Sheep, or, Private Virtues, Public Vices: The Consumer Revolution of the Twentieth Century', *Past & Present*, 176/1 (2002), 222–56.

Hilton, M., *Consumerism in Twentieth-Century Britain: The Search for a Historical Movement* (Cambridge: Cambridge University Press, 2003).

Hiott, A., *Thinking Small: The Long, Strange Trip of the Volkswagen Beetle* (London: Random House, 2012).

Hirschman, E., 'Humanistic Inquiry in Marketing Research: Philosophy, Method, and Criteria', *Journal of Marketing Research*, 23/3 (1986), 237.

Historical Exchange Rates, <http://www.ukforex.co.uk/forex-tools/historical-rate-tools/historical-exchange-rates>.

'History of Weight Watchers', *dwlz.com* <http://www.dwlz.com/WWinfo/historyofww.html>.

Historical Mean Gross Weekly Earnings (London: Office of National Statistics, 2016).

Hochschild, A. R., *The Time Bind: When Work Becomes Home and Home Becomes Work* (New York: Owl Books, 2000).

Holbrook, M. B., and O' Shaughnessy, J., 'The Role of Emotion', *Advertising Psychology and Marketing*, 2 (1989), 45–54.

Holt, D. B., *How Brands Become Icons: The Principles of Cultural Branding* (Boston: Harvard Business School Press, 2004).

Holt, D., and Thompson, C. J., 'Man-of-Action-Heroes: The Pursuit of Heroic Masculinity in Everyday Consumption', *Journal of Consumer Research*, 31/2 (2004), 425–40.

Hoorens, V., 'Self-Enhancement and Superiority Biases in Social Comparisons', *European Review of Social Psychology*, 4/1 (1993), 113–39.

HOPE (Hackers on Planet Earth) Conference: Report (London: IPC Magazines, 1994).

Hornsby G., *The Secret Life of the National Grid* (London: BBC, 2010).

Horowitz, D., *The Anxieties of Affluence: Critiques of American Consumer Culture, 1939–1979* (Amherst, MA: University of Massachusetts Press, 2005).

Housing Act 1980 <http://www.legislation.gov.uk/ukpga/1980/51/contents>.

Howard, J., *The Evolution of UK PR Consultancies 1970–2010* (London: PRCA, 2011).

Hunt, T., and Grunig, J. E., *Public Relations Techniques* (Fort Worth, TX, and London: Harcourt Brace, 1994).

Huntsworth: Group Board', *huntsworth.com* (2009). <https://web.archive.org/web/20090426121238/http://www.huntsworth.com:80/people/>.

Hutchinson, S., 'Consumer Public Relations', in A. Theaker (ed.), *The Public Relations Handbook* (4th edn; Abingdon: Routledge, 2012).

Jackson, B., Saunders, R., and Jackson, B., *Making Thatcher's Britain* (Cambridge: Cambridge University Press, 2012).

Jackson, S., and Moores, S., *The Politics of Domestic Consumption: Critical Readings* (London: Prentice Hall, 1995).

Jacoby, J., *Brand Loyalty: Measurement and Management* (New York: Wiley, 1978).

Jacques, M., and Hall, S., *New Times: The Changing Face of Politics in the 1990s* (1989; London: Lawrence & Wishart, 1990).

Jameson, F., 'Postmodernism, or the Cultural Logic of Late Capitalism', *New Left Review*, 146 (1984).

Jansson-Boyd, C. V., *Consumer Psychology* (Maidenhead: Open University Press, 2010).

Jaspert, J., Cavanagh, S., Debono, J., Lubbock, V. E., and Collings, R. E., *Thinking of Small Children: Access, Provision and Play* (Camden: Women's Design Service and London Borough of Camden, 1988).

Jenkins, M., *Thinking about Growth: A Cognitive Mapping Approach to Understanding Small Business Development* (London: Cranfield School of Management, 1993).

Joachimsthaler, E., Pfeffer, M., Zinnbauer, M., and Honer, T., *Social Currency Study* (New York: Vivaldi Partners, 2010).

Jobling, P., *Advertising Menswear: Masculinity and Fashion in the British Media since 1945* (London: A & C Black, 2014).

Johar, J. S., and Sirgy, M. J., 'Value-Expressive versus Utilitarian Advertising Appeals: When and Why to Use which Appeal', *Journal of Advertising*, 20/3 (1991), 23–33.

Johnson, A., *2001: The Lost Science* (London: Apogee, 2012).

Johnson, B., *Naked Video* (London: BBC Two, 1986).

Joachimsthaler, E., Pfeffer, M., Zinnbauer, M., and Honer, T., *Social Currency Study* (New York: Vivaldi Partners, 2010).

Jowitt, H., and Lury, G. 'Is it Time to Reposition Positioning?', *Journal of Brand Management*, 20/2 (2012), 96–103.

Junge britische Kunst: Zehn Künstler aus der Sammlung Saatchi (Cologne: Sonderschau Art Cologne, 1993).

Kahneman, D., 'Maps of Bounded Rationality: Psychology for Behavioral Economics', *American Economic Review*, 93/5 (2003), 1449–75.

Kahneman, D., *Thinking, Fast and Slow* (New York: Farrar, Straus and Giroux, 2011).

Kahneman, D., and Miller, D. T., 'Norm Theory: Comparing Reality to its Alternatives', *Psychological Review*, 93/2 (1986), 136–53.

Kahneman, D., and Tversky, A., 'Choices, Values and Frames', *American Psychologist*, 39/4 (1984), 341–50.

Kaldor, N., 'The Economic Aspects of Advertising', *Review of Economic Studies*, 18/1 (1950), 1–27.

Kaldor, M., Smith, D. and Vines, S., *Democratic Socialism and the Cost of Defence: The Report and Papers of the Labour Party Defence Study Group* (London: Croom Helm, 1979).

Kay, W., *Battle for the High Street* (London: Corgi, 1989).

Kazi, T. B., 'Superbrands, Globalization, and Neoliberalism: Exploring Causes and Consequences of the Nike Superbrand', *Inquiries Social Sciences, Arts & Humanities*, 3/12 (2011).

Keat, R., Abercrombie, N., and Whiteley, N., *The Authority of the Consumer* (London: Routledge, 1994).

Keel, A., and Nataraajan, R., 'Celebrity Endorsements and Beyond: New Avenues for Celebrity Branding', *Psychology and Marketing*, 29/9 (2012), 690–703.

Keller, K., 'Conceptualizing, Measuring and Managing Customer-Based Brand Equity', *Journal of Marketing*, 57/1 (1993), 1–22.

Keller, K., *Strategic Brand Management: Building, Measuring and Managing Brand Equity* (Upper Saddle River, NJ: Prentice Hall, 1998).

Keller, K. L., and Aaker, D. A., *Managing the Corporate Brand: The Effects of Corporate Marketing Activity on Consumer Evaluations of Brand Extensions* (Cambridge, MA: Marketing Science Institute, 1997).

The Key Issues of the 1980s (London: Social Futures Group, the Henley Centre for Forecasting, 1982).

Kessler, S., *Chiatt/Day: The First Twenty Years* (New York: Rizzoli International, 1990).

Keynes, J. M., *Essays in Persuasion* (Basingstoke and New York: Palgrave Macmillan, 2010).

Keynes, J. M., 'The Economic Possibilities for our Grandchildren (1929)', in J. M. Keynes, *Essays in Persuasion* (Basingstoke and New York: Palgrave Macmillan, 2010).

Kimber, R., *British Governments and Elections since 1945*, <http://www.politicsresources.net/area/uk/uktable.htm>.

King, S., *What is a Brand?: The Definitive Essay on Brand Building* (London: JWT, 2008).

King, S., *The JWT Planning Guide (1974)* (London: Royal Society of Account Planning, 2009).

King, S., Lannon, J., and Baskin, M., *A Master Class in Brand Planning: The Timeless Works of Stephen King* (Hoboken, NJ: Wiley, 2007).

King, S., and Pitchford, R., 'Private or Public? A Taxonomy of Optimal Ownership and Management Regimes', *Working Papers in Economics and Econometrics*, no. 343 (Canberra: Australian National University, Faculty of Economics and Commerce, 1998).

Kitchen, P. J., *Public Relations: Principles and Practice* (London: Thomson, 1997).

Kitchen, P. J., and Proctor, R. A., *The Development of Marketing in Small Businesses: An Initial Proposal* (Newcastle-under-Lyme: University of Keele Press, 1991).

Kitchen, P. J., and Proctor, R. A., 'The Increasing Importance of Public Relations in Fast Moving Consumer Goods Firms', *Journal of Marketing Management*, 7/4 (1991), 357–70.

Kitchen, P., and White, J., 'Public Relations Developments', *Marketing Intelligence & Planning*, 10/2 (1992), 14–17.

Klein, N., *No Logo* (London: Flamingo, 1999).

Kleinman, P., *The Saatchi & Saatchi Story* (London: Weidenfeld & Nicolson, 1987).

Koff, R. M., *Using Small Computers to Make your Business Strategy Work* (New York and Chichester: Wiley, 1984).

Koshar, R., *Histories of Leisure: Leisure, Consumption, and Culture* (Oxford: Berg, 2002).

Kotler, P., *Marketing Management: Analysis, Planning, and Control* (Englewood Cliffs, NJ: Prentice-Hall, 1967).

Kotler, P., *Principles of Marketing* (Englewood Cliffs, NJ: Prentice Hall, 1980).

Kotler, P., 'Global Standardization: Courting Danger', *Journal of Consumer Marketing*, 3/2 (1986), 13–15.

Kotler, P., *Marketing: An Introduction* (Englewood Cliffs, NJ: Prentice Hall, 1987).

Kotler, P., *Marketing Insights from A to Z: 80 Concepts Every Manager Needs to Know* (New York: Wiley, 2003).

Kotler, P., and Mindak, W., 'Marketing and Public Relations: Should they Be Partners?', *Journal of Marketing*, 42/4 (1978), 13–20.

Kotler, P., and Zaltman, G., 'Social Marketing: An Approach to Planned Social Change', *Journal of Marketing*, 35/3 (1971), 3–12.

Kuang-Jung, C., and Chu-Mei, L., 'Positive Brand Extension Trial and Choice of Parent Brand', *Journal of Product and Brand Management*, 13/1 (2004), 25–36.

Kubrick S., *2001: A Space Odyssey* (Los Angeles: MGM, 1968).

Kumar, V., Aaker, D. A., and Day, G. S., *Essentials of Marketing Research* (New York: Wiley, 1999).

Kuznets, S., 'Economic Growth and Income Inequality', *American Economic Review*, 45 (March 1955), 1–28.

L'Etang, J., 'The Myth of the "Ethical Guardian". An Examination of its Origins, Potency and Illusions', *Journal of Communication Management*, 8/1 (2003), 53–67.

L'Etang, J., *Public Relations in Britain: A History of Professional Practice in the 20th Century* (Mahwah, NJ, and London: L. Erlbaum, 2004).

L'Etang, J., *Public Relations: Concepts, Practice and Critique* (London: Sage, 2008).

L'Etang, J., and Pieczka, M., *Critical Perspectives in Public Relations* (London: International Thomson Business Press, 1996).

L'Etang, J., and Pieczka, M., *Public Relations: Critical Debates and Contemporary Practice* (Mahwah, NJ, and London: L. Erlbaum, 2006).

Labour Party Research Department., *Campaign Notes: General Election, 1950* (London: Labour Party, 1950).

Lancaster, K., and Dulaney, R.A., *Modern Economics: Principles and Policy* (Chicago: Rand McNally, 1979).

Lansley, S., *After the Gold Rush: The Trouble with Affluence: 'Consumer Capitalism' and the Way Forward* (London: Century, 1994).

Larson, E., *The Naked Consumer: How Our Private Lives Become Public Commodities* (New York: H. Holt, 1992).

Lash, S., and Urry, J., *Economies of Signs and Space* (London: Sage, 1994).

Lasher, W. R., *Strategic Thinking for Small Business and Divisions* (Oxford: Blackwell, 1999).

Lauterborn, R., 'New Marketing Litany: Four Ps Pass 7Cs Words Take Over', *Advertising Age*, 61/41 (1990), 26.

Law, A., *Creative Company: How St Luke's Became 'The Ad Agency to End All Ad Agencies'* (New York: Wiley, 1999).

Lawson, N., *Speech on Energy Policy, Given by the Rt Hon. Nigel Lawson MP Secretary of State for Energy to the International Association of Energy Economists on 28 June 1982* (London: Department of Energy, 1982).

Lawson, N., *Memoirs of a Tory Radical* (London: Biteback, 2010).

Lee, M. J., *Consumer Culture Reborn: The Cultural Politics of Consumption* (London: Routledge, 1993).

Leiss, A. C., *Apartheid and United Nations Collective Measures, an Analysis* (New York: Carnegie Endowment for International Peace, 1965).

Leiss, W., Kline, S., and Jhally, S., *Social Communication In Advertising: Persons, Products and Images of Wellbeing: William Leiss, Stephen Kline, Sut Jhally* (Toronto: Methuen, 1986).

Leiss, W. E., *Prospects and Problems in Risk Communication: Symposium: Papers* (Waterloo: University of Waterloo Press, 1989).

Leisure outside the Home: Market Review (Hampton: Key Note, 2010).

Lelis, S., *An Exploration of the Rational-Basis for how People Search Online Consumer Reviews* (Manchester: University of Manchester Press, 2009).

Levi-Strauss, C., *Myth and Meaning* (Toronto: Toronto University Press, 1978).

Levitt, T., 'The Globalization of Markets', *Harvard Business Review*, 61/3 (1983), 92–102.

Levitt, T., *The Marketing Imagination* (New York: Macmillan, 1983).

Lewis, D., *Information Overload: Practical Strategies for Coping in Today's Workplace* (London: Penguin, 1999).

Lewis, L. A., *The Adoring Audience: Fan Culture and Popular Media* (London: Routledge, 1992).

Linder, S. B., *The Harried Leisure Class* (New York: Columbia University Press, 1970).

Lippmann, W., *Public Opinion* (New York and London: Free Press, 1997).

Liquidators Report: Newsfield Limited Trading History (Manchester: Messrs Kidsons, Impey & Partners, 1991).

Liu, C., 'Politics between Public and Private: Land Ownership Transfer in Socialist Beijing (1950s–1970s)', unpublished paper, University of Durham, 2015).

Liu, J., Li, J., Feng, L., Li, L., Tian, J., and Lee, K., 'Seeing Jesus in Toast: Neural and Behavioral Correlates of Face Pareidolia', *Cortex*, 53 (2014), 60–77.

'LM magazine—The Proto Lads [*sic*] Lifestyle Magazine (1986–1987)', thoseweleftbehind. co.uk, <https://thoseweleftbehind.co.uk/2008/06/22/lm-magazine-the-proto-lads-lifestyle-magazine-1986-1987/>.

Lodziak, C., *Manipulating Needs: Capitalism and Culture* (London: Pluto Press, 1995).

Long Term Futures Revisited: Into the 21st Century (London: Henley Centre, 1982).

Lowe, F., *Dear Lord Leverhulme, I Think We may have Solved your Problem* (Oxted: Hurtwood, 2002).

Lucas, C., *A Bill to Promote Public Ownership of Public Services, to Introduce a Presumption in Favour of Service Provision by Public Sector and Not-for-Profit Entities, and to Put in Place Mechanisms to Increase the Accountability, Transparency and Public Control of Public Services, Including those Operated by Private Companies* (London: UK Parliament, House of Commons, 2014).

Lunt, P. K., and Livingstone, S. M., *Mass Consumption and Personal Identity: Everyday Economic Experience* (Buckingham: Open University Press, 1992).

Lury, C., *Consumer Culture* (Cambridge: Polity, 1996).

Lyon, D., *Postmodernity* (Buckingham: Open University Press, 1999).

McAllister, M. P., and West, E., *The Routledge Companion to Advertising and Promotional Culture* (London: Routledge, 2014).

MacCallum, J., *'Rational' versus 'Sensible' Consumer Behavior* (Montreal: McGill University, Department of Economics, 1990).

McCracken, G. D., *Culture and Consumption: New Approaches to the Symbolic Character of Consumer Goods and Activities* (Bloomington IN: Indiana University Press, 1988).

McCracken, G. D., *Culture and Consumption II: Markets, Meaning, and Brand Management* (Bloomington, IN: Indiana University Press, 2005).

McDonald's, *McDonald's Annual Review* (London: Communications Department, McDonald's UK, 1993).

McDonald's, *Nutrition: A Question of Balance* (London: Communications Department, McDonalds UK, 1993).

McDonald's, *McDonald's Annual Review* (London: Communications Department, McDonald's UK, 1994).

McDonald's, *Environment—Facing the Challenges: 14 Things that McDonald's is Doing* (London: Communications Department, McDonald's UK, 1994).

McDonald's, *McDonald's Fact File: Policy Statement* (London: Communications Department, McDonald's UK, 1995).

McDowell, L., *Redundant Masculinities?: Employment Change and White Working Class Youth* (Oxford: Blackwell, 2003).

McGrath, M., and Heitmeyer, J., *The 'New' Male Consumer: Appearance Management Product Advertising and the Male Physical Ideal in Men's Interest Magazines from 1965–2005* (Tallahassee: Florida State University, ProQuest Dissertations Publishing, 2006).

McGuire, J. W., 'An Information Processing Model of Advertising Effectiveness', in H. L. Davis and A. J. Silk (eds), *Behavioral and Management Science in Marketing* (New York and Chichester: Wiley, 1978), 156–80.

McGuire, J. W., *Inequality: The Poor and the Rich in America* (New York: Wadsworth, 1969).

McKendrick, N., Brewer, J., and Plumb, J. H., *The Birth of a Consumer Society: The Commercialization of Eighteenth-Century England* (1982; London: Hutchinson, 1983).

McKeon, R., McKeon, Z.K. and Swenson, W.G., *Selected Writings of Richard McKeon* (Chicago; London: University of Chicago Press, 1998).

McKevitt, S., *Why the World is Full of Useless Things* (London: Cyan, 2006).

McKevitt, S., *City Slackers: Workers of the World . . . You are Wasting Your Time!* (London: Cyan, 2006).

McKevitt, S., *Everything Now: Communication, Persuasion and Control: How the Instant Society is Shaping what We Think* (London: Route, 2012).

McKevitt, S., and Ryan, T., *Project Sunshine* (London: Icon, 2013).

McKevitt, S., and Ryan, T., *The Solar Revolution: One Planet, One Solution: How to Fuel and Feed 10 Billion People* (London: Icon, 2014).

Maconie, S., *Cider with Roadies* (London: Ebury, 2003).

Maggard, J. P., 'Positioning Revisited', *Journal of Marketing*, 40/1 (1976), 63–6.

Majima, S., 'Affluence and the Dynamics of Spending in Britain, 1961–2004', *Contemporary British History*, 22/4 (2008), 573–97.

Mailley, J., 'The Prevention of Mobile Phone Theft: A Case Study of Crime as Pollution: Rational Choices and Consumer Demand', unpublished paper, Loughborough University, 2011.

Mann, J., and Goldman, R., *A Casebook in Time-Limited Psychotherapy* (London: Jason Aronson, 1994).

Marchand, R., *Advertising the American Dream: Making Way for Modernity, 1920–1940* (Berkeley and Los Angeles: University of California Press, 2003).

Marron, D., 'Producing Over-Indebtedness: Risk, Prudence and Consumer Vulnerability', *Journal of Cultural Economy*, 5/4 (2012), 407–21.

Marshall, A., and Guillebaud, C. W., *Principles of Economics* (9th Variorum Edition; London: Macmillan for the Royal Economic Society, 1961).

Martin, B., *Difficult Men: Behind the Scenes of a Creative Revolution: From the Sopranos and the Wire to Mad Men and Breaking Bad* (London: Penguin, 2013).

Martinez-Vazquez, J., and Winer, S. L., *Coercion and Social Welfare in Public Finance: Economic and Political Perspectives* (Cambridge: Cambridge University Press, 2014).

Marwick, A., *The Sixties: Cultural Revolution in Britain, France, Italy, and the United States, c.1958–c.1974* (London: Bloomsbury, 2012).

Marx, K., and Engels, F., *Capital* (1867; Chicago and London: Encyclopaedia Britannica, 1990).

The Media and the PR Industry: A Partnership or a Marriage of Convenience? Gallup Survey for Two-Ten Communications (London: Gallup Social Surveys, 1991).

Michie, D., *The Invisible Persuaders* (London: Bantam, 1998).

Michie, J. E., *The Economics of Restructuring and Intervention* (New York: Edward Elgar, 1991).

Miles, I., 'Time, Goods and Wellbeing', in F. T. Juster and F. P. Stafford (eds), *Time, Goods and Wellbeing* (Ann Arbor: University of Michigan Press, 1985), 119–22.

Miles, S., *Consumerism: As a Way of Life* (1998; London and Thousand Oaks, CA: Sage, 2006).

Miles, S., Anderson, A., and Meethan, K., *The Changing Consumer: Markets and Meanings* (London and New York: Routledge, 2002).

Miller, D., *Material Culture and Mass Consumption* (1987; Oxford: Basil Blackwell, 1991).

Miller, D., *Acknowledging Consumption: A Review of New Studies* (London: Routledge, 1995).

Miller, D., *Theory and Issues in the Study of Consumption* (London: Routledge, 2001).

Miller, D., *Consumption and its Consequences* (Cambridge: Polity, 2012).

Miller, D., and Dinan, W., 'The Rise of the PR Industry in Britain, 1979–98', *European Journal of Communication*, 15/1 (2000), 5–35.

Mishara, A. L., 'Klaus Conrad (1905–1961): Delusional Mood, Psychosis, and Beginning Schizophrenia', *Schizophrenia Bulletin*, 36/1 (2009), 9–13.

Mitchell, A., and Olson, J., 'Are Product Attribute Beliefs the Only Mediator of Advertising Effects on Brand Attitude?', *Journal of Marketing Research*, 18/3 (1981), 318.

Michie, D., *The Invisible Persuaders* (London: Bantam, 1998).

Mitka, M., 'Celebrity Endorsements', *Journal of the American Medical Association*, 299/6 (2008), 625.

Moffitt, M. A., 'Public Relations from the Margins', *Journal of Public Relations Research*, 17/1 (2005), 3–4.

Monkman G., *Life Lessons from Charles Saatchi* (2013), <http://www.adnews.com.au/news/life-lessons-from-charles-saatchi>.

Moore, H. F., and Kalupa, F. B., *Public Relations: Principles, Cases, and Problems* (Homewood, IL: Irwin, 1985).

Moore, J., 'British Privatization: Taking Capitalism to the People', *Harvard Business Review*, 70/1 (1992), 115–24.

Mort, F., *Cultures of Consumption: Masculinities and Social Space in Late Twentieth-Century Britain* (London: Routledge, 1996).

Mort, F., 'The Commercial Domain: Advertising and the Cultural Management of Demand', in P. Jackson, M. Lowe, D. Miller, and F. Mort (eds), *Commercial Cultures, Economics, Practices, Economies* (Oxford: Berg, 2000).

Mort, F., *Capital Affairs: London and the Making of the Permissive Society* (London: Yale University Press, 2010).

Moss, D., Warnaby, G., and Thame, L., 'Tactical Publicity or Strategic Relationship Management? An Exploratory Investigation of the Role of Public Relations in the UK Retail Sector', *European Journal of Marketing*, 30/12 (1990), 69–84.

Murray, R., 'Fordism and Post-Fordism', in M. Jacques and S. Hall (eds), *New Times: The Changing Face of Politics in the 1990s* (1989; London: Lawrence & Wishart, 1990).

National Food Survey 1940–2000 (London: Office for National Statistics, 2004).

A Nation of Shopkeepers: Trade Ephemera from 1654 to the 1860s in the John Johnson Collection: An Exhibition in the Bodleian Library, Autumn 2001 (Oxford: Bodleian Library, 2001).

Neil, A., *Full Disclosure* (London: Macmillan, 1996).

Neville, R., *Play Power* (London: Paladin, 1971).

Newman, K., *Financial Marketing and Communications* (London: Holt, 1984).

Newman, M., *Creative Leaps: 10 Lessons in Effective Advertising Inspired at Saatchi & Saatchi* (Singapore and Chichester: Wiley, 2003).

Newsom and Boys' Clubs: A Report of the NABC Working Party on Boys' Clubs and the Newsom Report (London: National Association of Boys' Clubs, 1968).

Newsom, C. V., *A Television Policy for Education* (Washington: Library of Congress, 1952).

Newsom, D., *Bridging the Gaps in Global Communication* (Malden, MA, and Oxford: Blackwell, 2007).

Newsom, D., and Carrell, B., *Silent Voices* (Lanham, MD, and London: University Press of America, 1995).

Newsom, D., and Carrell, B., *Public Relations Writing: Form and Style* (Belmont, CA, and London: Wadsworth, 1995).

Newsom, D., Turk, J. V., and Kruckeberg, D., *This Is PR: The Realities of Public Relations* (Boston: Wadsworth, 2010).

Newsom, J., *Four Years Old in an Urban Community* (London: Penguin, 1970).

'Next: Company History', *nextplc.co.uk*, <http://www.nextplc.co.uk/about-next/our-history>.

'Nike: The Internationalization Startegy of Adidas', in D. Holtbrügge and H. Haussmann (eds), *The Internationalization of Firms: Case Studies from the Nürnberg Metropolitan Region* (Augsburg: Rainer Hampp Verlag, 2017).

Nixon, S., *Hard Looks: Masculinities, Spectatorship and Contemporary Consumption* (London: University College London Press, 1996).

Nixon, S., *Advertising Cultures: Gender, Commerce, Creativity* (London: Sage, 2003).

Nixon, S., ' "Salesmen of the Will to Want": Advertising and its Critics in Britain 1951–1967', *Contemporary British History*, 24/2 (2010), 213–33.

Nixon, S., *Hard Sell: Advertising, Affluence and Transatlantic Relations, c.1951–69* (Manchester: Manchester University Press, 2013).

Novosti, R., 'The Soviet Economy in the Era of Leonid Brezhnev', *ria.ru* (2010), <http://ria.ru/history_spravki/20101108/293796130.html>.

Nowak, K., 'Magazine Advertising in Sweden and the United States: Stable Patterns of Change, Variable Levels of Stability', *European Journal of Communication*, 5/4 (1990), 393–422.

O'Hare, M., *The Last Word: New Scientist* (Oxford: Oxford University Press, 1998).

O'Hear, A., 'Diana, Queen of Hearts: Sentimentality Personified and Canonised', in D. C. Anderson and P. Mullen (eds), *Faking it: The Sentimentalisation of Modern Society* (London: Penguin, 1998).

Obelkevich, J., and Catterall, P., *Understanding Post-War British Society* (London: Routledge, 1994).

Offer, A., *The Challenge of Affluence: Self-Control and Wellbeing in the United States and Britain since 1950* (Oxford: Oxford University Press, 2007).

Officer, L. H., and Williamson, S. H., *What Was the UK GDP Then?*, <http://www.measuringworth.com/ukgdp/>.

Ogilvy, D., *Confessions of an Advertising Man* (London: Southbank, 2004).

Otnes, P., *The Sociology of Consumption: An Anthology* (Atlantic Highlands, NJ: Humanities Press, 1988).

Oxley, C., *The Real Saatchis: Masters of Illusion* (London: Channel 4, 1999).

Packard, V., *The Hidden Persuaders* (New York: David McKay, 1957).

Padgett, D., and Allen, D., 'Communicating Experiences: A Narrative Approach to Creating Service Brand Image', *Journal of Advertising*, 26/4 (1997), 49–62.

Panwar, J. S., and Bapt, D., 'New Product Launch Strategies: Insights from Distributors Survey', *South Asian Journal of Management*, 14/2 (2007), 82.

Parfitt, B., 'Retrospective PC Zone', *mcvuk.com* (2006), <http://www.mcvuk.com/news/read/retrospective-pc-zone/01797>.

Parsons, T., *Worth the Detour* (Stroud: The History Press, 2008).

Pelsmacker, P. De, and Maggie Geunes, 'The Communication Effects of Warmth, Eroticism and Humour in Alcohol Advertisements', *Journal of Marketing Communications*, 2/4 (December 1996), 247–62.

Periodicals and the Alternative Press (London: Royal Commission on the Press, 1977).

Philip, K., and Murali, K. M., 'Flawed Products: Consumer Responses and Marketer Strategies', *Journal of Consumer Marketing*, 2/3 (1985), 27–36.

Pieczka, M., 'The Disappearing Act: Public Relations Consultancy in Theory and Research', unpublished paper, ICA Annual Conference Montreal, Canada, 2008.

Pimlott, B., *Harold Wilson* (London: HarperCollins, 1992).

Piore, M. J., and Sabel, C. F., *The Second Industrial Divide: Possibilities for Prosperity* (New York: Basic Books, 1984).

Planning for Social Change 1986: Full Colour Future from the Henley Centre (London: Henley Centre for Forecasting, 1986).

Plummer, J., 'How Personality Makes a Difference', *Journal of Advertising Research*, 40/6 (2000), 79–83.

Pollitt, S., and Feldwick, P., *Pollitt on Planning: Three Papers on Account Planning* (Henley-on-Thames: Admap, 2000).

'Political Monitor: Satisfaction Ratings 1997–Present', *ipsos-mori.com* (2016), <https://www.ipsos-mori.com/researchpublications/researcharchive/88/Political-Monitor-Satisfaction-Ratings-1997Present.aspx>.

Post-Family Leisure Trends—UK (London: Mintel International Group, 2000).

Powell, H., *Promotional Culture and Convergence: Markets, Methods, Media* (Abingdon: Routledge, 2013).

Praag, B. M. S. van, *Individual Welfare Functions and Consumer Behavior: A Theory of Rational Irrationality* (Amsterdam: North-Holland Publishing, 1968).

Preston, I. L., *The Great American Blowup: Puffery in Advertising and Selling* (Madison: Wisconsin University Press, 1996).

Princen, T., Maniates, M., and Conca, K., *Confronting Consumption* (Cambridge, MA, and London: MIT Press, 2002).

Professional Academy, *Marketing Theories: The Marketing Mix—from 4 Ps to 7 Ps*, <http://www.professionalacademy.com/blogs-and-advice/marketing-theories—the-marketing-mix—from-4-p-s-to-7-p-s>.

Public Ownership and Private Industry: Speakers' Notes (London: Labour Party, 1964).

The Public Relations Yearbook 1990 (London: PRCA, 1989).

Randall, C. C., Block, J., and Funder, D. C., 'Overly Positive Self-Evaluations and Personality: Negative Implications for Mental Health', *Journal of Personality and Social Psychology*, 68/6 (1995), 1152–62.

Randall, Q., 'A Historical Overview of the Effects of New Mass Media: Introductions in Magazine Publishing during the Twentieth Century', *First Monday* (September 2001).

Rawsthorn, A., 'Split Personality which Made JWT Vulnerable: How did this Prestigious Worldwide Agency Fall Victim to WPP's Audacious Bid?', *Campaign*, 3 July 1987.

Resale Prices Act 1964, <http://www.legislation.gov.uk/ukpga/1976/53>.

'Resale Price Maintenance', *OECD, Policy Roundtable* (1997), <http://www.oecd.org/competition/abuse/1920261.pdf>.

Rees, D., and Crampton, L., *Q Rock Stars Encyclopaedia* (London: Dorling Kindersley, 1999).

Reeves, R., *Reality in Advertising* (London: Macgibbon & Kee, 1961).

Rein, I. J., Kotler, P., and Shields, B., *The Elusive Fan: Reinventing Sports in a Crowded Marketplace* (New York: McGraw-Hill, 2006).

Reiner C., *Dead Men Don't Wear Plaid* (New York: Universal Pictures, 1982).

Ries, A., and Trout, J., *The Positioning Era Commeth: Reprint of a Three-Part Series in Advertising Age* (Chicago: Crain Publications, 1972).

Ries, A., and Trout, J., *Marketing Warfare* (New York and London: McGraw-Hill, 1986).

Ries, A., and Trout, J., *Bottom-up Marketing* (New York and London: McGraw-Hill, 1989).

Ries, A., and Trout, J., *Horse Sense: The Key to Success is Finding a Horse to Ride* (New York and London: McGraw-Hill, 1991).

Ries, A., and Trout, J., *The 22 Immutable Laws of Marketing* (London: HarperCollins, 1994).

Ries, A., and Trout, J., *Marketing Warfare* (London: McGraw-Hill, 1997).

Ries, A., and Trout, J., *Positioning: The Battle for your Mind* (New York and London: McGraw-Hill, 2001).

Ricardo, D., *On the Principles of Political Economy and Taxation* (1817; London: Dover, 2004).

Rich, L., 'Omnicom Grows Organically', *Adweek, Eastern Edition*, 10 February 1997.

Rogers, D., *Campaigns that Shook the World: The Evolution of Public Relations* (London: Kogan, 2015).

Rogers, E. M., *Diffusion of Innovations* (New York and London: Free Press, 1995).

Rosen, B., Boddewyn, J., and Louis, E., 'US Brands Abroad: An Empirical Study of Global Branding', *International Marketing Review*, 6/1 (1989).

Rothwell, T. S., *A Nation of Shopkeepers* (London: Herbert Joseph, 1947).

Russell Hochschild, A., *The Time Bind: When Work Becomes Home and Home Becomes Work* (New York: Owl Books, 2000).

The Saatchi Gift to the Arts Council Collection (London: Hayward Gallery, 2000).

Salmon, J., and Ritchie, J., *Inside Collett Dickenson Pearce* (London: Batsford, 2000).

Salmond, A., 'Parliamentary Debates, Commons 1987-8' vol.129.col. 1008 (1988).

Salzman, M., *Lost in Place: Growing up Absurd in Suburbia* (London: Bloomsbury, 1996).

Sampson, P., Samuel, V. K., and Sugden, C., *Faith and Modernity* (Oxford: Regnum Lynx, 1994).

Saunders, P., 'Beyond Housing Classes: The Sociological Significance of Private Property Rights in Means of Consumption', *International Journal of Urban and Regional Research*, 8 (1984), 202–25.

Schank, R. C., *Scripts, Plans, Goals and Understanding: An Inquiry into Human Knowledge Structures* (Hillsdale, NJ: Erlbaum, 1977).

Schor, J. B., *The Overworked American: The Unexpected Decline of Leisure* (New York: Basic Books, 1993).

Schor, J. B., *The Overspent American: Why We Want What We Don't Need* (New York: Harper Perennial, 1999).

Segal, L., *Slow Motion: Changing Masculinities, Changing Men* (London: Virago, 1990).

Share Ownership—Register Survey Report—2012 (London: Office of National Statistics, 2013).

Shavvitt, S., 'The Role of Attitude Objects in Attitudinal Functions', *Journal of Experimental Social Psychology*, 26 (1990), 124–68.

Shavvitt, S., 'Value-Expressive versus Utilitarian Advertising Appeals: When and Why to Use which Appeal', *Journal of Advertising*, 20/3 (1992), 23–33.

Sheldon, A. E., *Land Systems and Land Policies in Nebraska* (Lincoln, NB: Nebraska State Historical Society, 1936).

Shenk, D., *Data Smog: Surviving the Information Glut* (San Francisco: HarperEdge, 1997).

Shimizu, A., *Advertising Theories and Strategies* (Tokyo: Souseisha, 1989).

Shimizu, A., *Kōkoku jiten = Advertising Handbook* (Tokyo: Dōbunkan, 1956).

'A Short History of British Television Advertising', *nationalmediamuseum.org.uk*, <www.nationalmediamuseum.org.uk>.

Shute, V. E., *Public Ownership and Control in the Private Sector* (Birmingham: University of Aston in Birmingham, 1979).

Shyle, I., and Hysi, V., 'The Study of Brand Equity as a Relationship between Brand Personality and Consumer Personality', unpublished paper, Economic & Social Challenges Dedicated to Economy & Business Doctoral Students Conference, Tirana, Albania, 2012.

Silberberg, E., and Suen, W. C., *The Structure of Economics: A Mathematical Analysis* (Boston: Irwin/McGraw-Hill, 2000).

Simms, A., *The Naked Consumer: Why Shoppers Deserve Honest Product Labelling* (London: New Economics Foundation, 2001).

Simon, Á. O., *Balogh, Kaldor and the Economic Policy of the Labour Party 1940–1970* (Cambridge: University of Cambridge Press, 2009).

Skidelsky, R., and Skidelsky, E., *How Much Is Enough? The Love of Money, and the Case for the Good Life* (London: Penguin, 2013).

Slater, D., *Consumer Culture and Modernity* (Cambridge: Polity, 1997).

Smil, V., and Knowland, W. E., *Energy in the Developing World: The Real Energy Crisis* (Oxford: Oxford University Press, 1980).

Smith, D., 'Consultancy and Client: A Problem Shared Is a Problem Solved', *Public Relations Year Book 1985* (London: FT Business Information, 1984).

Smoking and Health (London: Royal College of Physicians, 1962).

Snow, C. P., *The Two Cultures and the Scientific Revolution* (Cambridge: Cambridge University Press, 1960).

Snow, C. P., *Science and Government* (London: Oxford University Press, 1960).

Snow, C. P., *A Postscript to Science and Government* (Cambridge, MA: Harvard University Press, 1962).

Snow, C. P., *Homecomings* (Harmondsworth: Penguin, 1962).

Southwell, T., *Getting away with it: The Inside Story of* Loaded (London: Ebury, 1998).

Spencer, C., 'Applying Account Planning to Public Relations', *Journal of Communication Management*, 4/1 (1999), 95–105.

Spin-off: A Selection of Cartoons from New Scientist, etc. (London: George G. Harrap & Co, 1965).

St Clair, J., 'Nike's bad air', *counterpunch.org* (2008), <http://www.counterpunch.org/2008/06/28/nike-s-bad-air/>.

Stacks, D. W., *Primer of Public Relations Research* (New York: Guildford Press, 2011).

Stearns, P. N., *Consumerism in World History: The Global Transformation of Desire* (New York and London: Routledge, 2006).

Steinberg, D. L., and Kear, A., *Mourning Diana: Nation, Culture and the Performance of Grief* (London: Routledge, 2002).

Stewart, G., *Bang!: A History of Britain in the 1980s* (London: Atlantic, 2013).

Stigler, G. J., *The Theory of Price* (New York: Macmillan, 1977).

Stigler, G. J., and Becker, G. S., 'De Gustibus Non Est Disputandum', *American Economic Review*, 67/2 (1977), 76–90.

Stout, P., and Leckenby, J., 'Measuring Emotional Response to Advertising', *Journal of Advertising*, 15/4 (1986), 35–42.

Strong, M. C., *The Great Indie Discography* (Edinburgh: Canongate, 2003).

Stubbs, P. (ed.), *New Science in the Solar System: A New Scientist Special Review* (London: New Science Publications, 1975).

The Surgeon General's Report on Nutrition and Health (Washington: Public Health Service, National Library of Medicine, 1988).

Swenson, R. A., *Margin: Restoring Emotional, Physical, Financial, and Time Reserves to Overloaded Lives* (Colorado Springs, CO: NavPress, 2004).

Tauber, A. M., 'Brand Leverage: Strategies for Growth in a Cost Controlled World', *Journal of Advertising, Research* (August–September 1988), 26–31.

Telecommunications Act 1984, <http://www.legislation.gov.uk/ukpga/1984/12/contents>.

Television Act 1964, <http://www.screenonline.org.uk/tv/id/1107497/>.

Temple, M., *The British Press* (Maidenhead: Open University Press, 2008).

Tench, R., Sun, W., and Jones, B. J., *Corporate Social Irresponsibility: A Challenging Concept* (Bingley: Emerald, 2012).

Tench, R., and Yeomans, L., *Exploring Public Relations* (Harlow: Pearson, 2013).

Thaler, R., 'Toward a Positive Theory of Consumer Choice', *Journal of Economic Behavior and Organization*, 1/1 (1980), 39–60.

Thaler, R. H., and Sunstein, C. R., 'Libertarian Paternalism', *American Economic Review*, 93/2 (2003), 175–9.

Theaker, A., *PR Director: Practical Guide to Media Relations* (London: PR Director, 2000).

Theaker, A., *The Public Relations Handbook* (London: Routledge, 2004).

Theaker, A., and Yaxley, H., *The Public Relations Strategic Toolkit: An Essential Guide to Successful Public Relations Practice* (New York: Routledge, 2012).

Thirlwall, A. P., and Kaldor, N., *Essays on Keynesian and Kaldorian Economics* (New York: Palgrave Macmillan, 2015).

Thomas Cook Packaged and Sold, <http://news.bbc.co.uk/onthisday/hi/dates/stories/may/26/newsid_3003000/3003665.stm>.

Thompson, H. S., and Steadman, R., *Fear and Loathing in Las Vegas* (London: Paladin, 1972).

Tobin, N., 'Can the Professionalisation of the UK Public Relations Industry Make it More Trustworthy?', *Journal of Communication Management*, 9/1 (2005), 56–64.

Traci, H. F., and Lukas, P. F., 'An Examination of Brand Personality through Methodological Triangulation', *Journal of Brand Management*, 13/2 (2005), 148.

Threadgould, M., *Bread: A Loaf Affair* (London: BBC, 2010).

Trentmann, F. (ed.), *The Making of the Consumer: Knowledge, Power and Identity in the Modern World* (6th edn; Oxford: Berg, 2006).

Trentmann, F., *Empire of Things: How We Became a World of Consumers, from the Fifteenth Century to the Twenty-First* (London: Penguin, 2016).

Trott, D., *Predatory Thinking* (London: Pan, 2014).

Trout, J., *Big Brands, Big Trouble: Lessons Learned the Hard Way* (Chichester: Wiley, 2001).

Trout, J., and Rivkin, S., *The Power of Simplicity: A Management Guide to Cutting through the Nonsense and Doing Things Right* (New York and London: McGraw-Hill, 1999).

Trout, J., and Rivkin, S., *Differentiate or Die: Survival in our Era of Killer Competition* (New York: Wiley, 2000).

Trout, J., Rivkin, S., and Ries, A. P., *The New Positioning: The Latest on the World's Business Strategy* (New York and London: McGraw-Hill, 1996).

Tungate, M., *Adland: A Global History of Advertising* (London: Kogan Page, 2007).

Tungate, M., *Branded Male: Marketing to Men* (London: Kogan Page, 2008).

Tungate, M., *Luxury World: The Past, Present and Future of Luxury Brands* (London: Kogan Page, 2009).

Tungate, M., *Branded Beauty: How Marketing Changed the Way We Look* (London: Kogan Page, 2011).

Tunstall, J., *The Media in Britain* (London: Constable, 1983).

Turner, A. W., *Rejoice! Rejoice!: Britain in the 1980s* (London: Aurum Press, 2013).

Tversky, A., and Kahneman, D., 'The Framing of Decisions and the Psychology of Choice', *Science*, 211/4481 (1981), 453–8.

Van Leuvan, J., 'Public Relations and Marketing: An Overview', *Public Relations Review*, 17/3 (1991), 215–17.

Vaughn, R., 'How Advertising Works: A Planning Model', *Journal of Advertising Research*, 20/5 (1980), 27–33.

Veblen, T., *What Veblen Taught: Selected Writings of Thorsten Veblen* (New York: Augustus M. Kelley, 1964).

Veblen, T., *The Theory of the Leisure Class* (1899; Fairfield, NJ: A. M. Kelley, 1991).

Verhoef, E. T., and Small, K. A., *Product Differentiation on Roads: Second-Best Congestion Pricing with Heterogeneity under Public and Private Ownership*, Environment Discussion Paper, 99-066/3 (Tinbergen, Netherlands: Tinbergen Institute, 1999).

'Video Game Magazine Preservation', *retroactionmagazine.com* (2016), <http://ret roactionmagazine.com/retrolinks/videogaming-magazine-preservation/>.

Vinen, R., *Thatcher's Britain: The Politics and Social Upheaval of the Thatcher Era* (London: Pocket, 2010).

Viorst, J., *Necessary Losses: The Loves, Illusions, Dependencies and Impossible Expectations that All of Us Have to Give up in Order to Grow* (London: Simon & Schuster, 1989).

Wakeham, L., Monck, N., Clemeti, D., Carsberg, B., Grimstone, G., and Gamble, A., 'The Privatisation of British Telecom (1984)', in *The 'S' Factors—Lessons from IFG's Policy Success Reunions* (London: Institute for Government UK, 2012).

Walters, A. A., *Britain's Economic Renaissance: Margaret Thatcher's Reforms, 1979–1984* (Oxford: Oxford University Press, 1986).

Ward, D. J., and Niendorf, R. M., *Consumer Finance* (London: Richard D. Irwin, 1978).

Ward, W. J., *Ulysses-to-Date, or Elgie Soothing Syrup's Great Odyssey* (London: Ward, 1923).

Weick, K. E., *Sensemaking in Organizations* (Thousand Oaks, CA, and London: Sage, 1995).

Weiner, I. B., *Principles of Rorschach Interpretation* (2nd edn; Mahwah, NJ, and London: L. Erlbaum, 2003).

Weitz, B., and Wensley, R., *Handbook of Marketing* (New York: Sage, 2006).

Werber, N., Baker, T., Carr, D., and Millers, M., *John Webster: The Human Ad Man* (London: London School of Communication Arts, 2013).

Wernick, A., *Promotional Culture: Advertising, Ideology and Symbolic Expression* (London: Sage, 1991).

Wertime, K., *Building Brands & Believers: How to Connect with Consumers* (Singapore: Wiley, 2002).

West S., *Playing at Work: Organizational Play as a Facilitator of Creativity*, <http://www.thecreativeindustries.co.uk/uk-creative-overview/facts-and-figures/employment-figures>.

Wheen, F., *How Mumbo Jumbo Conquered the World* (New York: Public Affairs, 2004).

White, P. G., *A Nation of Shopkeepers?: A Users' Guide to the 1971 Census of Retail Distribution and Other Services* (Reading: Centre for Advanced Land Use Studies, 1976).

Whiteley, N., *Design for Society* (London: Reaktion, 1993).

Williams, C., *Consumer Behavior: Fundamental and Strategies* (New York: West Publishing, 1982).

Williams, H., *Great Speeches of our Time: Speeches that Shaped the Modern World* (London: Quercus, 2013).

Williams, K., *The Kenneth Williams Diaries*, ed. R. Davies (London: HarperCollins, 1993).

Williams, R., 'Advertising: The Magic System', *Advertising & Society Review*, 1/1 (2000).

Willis, P., *Common Culture: Symbolic Work at Play in the Everyday Cultures of the Young* (Milton Keynes: Open University Press, 1990).

Willis, P., 'Public Relations and the Consumer', in R. Tench and L. Yeomans (eds), *Exploring Public Relations* (2nd edn; London: Financial Times/Prentice Hall, 2009), 409–24.

Willner, J., and Parker, D., '*The Relative Performance of Public and Private Enterprise under Conditions of Active and Passive Ownership*', Working Paper Series/Centre on Regulation and Competition, no. 22, University of Manchester, 2002.

Wilson B., 'Football and Fries: Why McDonald's Sponsors Sports', *BBC News*, <http://www.bbc.co.uk/news/business-11332724>.

Wilson, C., *Mad, Sad, or Bad?: Newspaper and Judicial Representations of Men who Killed Children in Victorian England, 1860–1900* (Colchester: University of Essex, 2012).

Wilson, G., *Money in the Family: Financial Organisation and Women's Responsibility* (Aldershot: Avebury, 1987).

Wilson, H., *The Future of British Transport: A Reprint of the Speech Made by the Rt Hon. Harold Wilson, during the Debate in the House of Commons on the Beeching Railway Report, 30 April 1963* (London: Labour Party, 1963).

Wilson, H., *Labour's Plan for Science* (London: Labour Party, 1963).

Wilson, H., '*A Time for Choice': A Speech by Harold Wilson to Delegates at the Trades Union Congress on 7 September 1964* (London: Trades Union Congress, 1964).

Wilson, H., *Speech Delivered in London on 10th March 1969 by the Prime Minister Rt Hon. Harold Wilson, M.P. at the Twentieth Anniversary Dinner of Jewish Vanguard* (London: Poale Zion, 1969).

Winer, R., and Neslin, S. (eds), *The History of Marketing Science* (Singapore: World Scientific Publishing, 2014).

Winer, R., and Neslin, S., *The History of Marketing Science* (Singapore: World Scientific NOW, 2014).

Winship, J., *Inside Women's Magazines* (London: Pandora, 1987).

Wolfe, T., *The Pump House Gang* (1968; London: Black Swan, 1989).

Wong, S., *On the Consistency and Completeness of Paul Samuelson's Programme in the Theory of Consumer's Behaviour: A Study by the Method of Rational Reconstruction* (Cambridge: University of Cambridge Press, 1974).

Wood, O., 'Using Faces: Measuring Emotional Engagement for Early Stage Creative', ESOMAR, Best Methodology, Annual Congress, Berlin, 2007.

Wood, O., 'Using an Emotional Model to Improve the Measurement of Advertising Effectiveness', unpublished paper, Market Research Society Annual Conference, London, 2010.

Wood, O., 'How Emotional Tugs Trump Rational Pushes: The Time has Come to Abandon a 100-Year-Old Advertising Model', *Journal of Advertising Research*, 52/1 (2012), 31–9.

The X Certificate, <www.screenonline.org.uk/film/id/591679/index.html>.

Yoo, D.-J., *Consuming Modernity: Women, Food and Promotional Culture in Contemporary Korea* (Loughborough: Loughborough University of Technology, 1986).

Young British Art: The Saatchi Decade (London: Booth-Clibborn, 1999).

Zambardino, A., and Goodfellow, J., 'Account Planning in the New Marketing and Communications Environment (has the Stephen King Challenge Been Met?)', *Marketing Intelligence & Planning*, 21/7 (2003), 425–34.

Zamir, Eyal, and Teichman, Doron (eds), *The Oxford Handbook of Behavioral Economics and the Law* (Oxford: Oxford University Press, 2014).

Zeitlin, J., 'Victoria de Grazia, Irresistible Empire: America's Advance through Twentieth-Century Europe', *Journal of Cold War Studies*, 10/3 (2008), 189–91.

Zukier, H., 'The Paradigmatic and Narrative Modes in Goal-Guided Inference', in R. M. Sorrentino and E. T. Higgins (eds), *Handbook of Motivation and Cognition* (New York: Guildford Press, 1986).

Index